Deadly Medicine

A trading card of Edward Temmit, who "Distills and Prepares the Greatest Variety of all Cordiall Drams of any Person in EUROPE." This seventeenth-century emblem of the Distillers Company of London reveals the early association between native Americans and English producers of alcohol. From *Lyson's Collectanea*, vol. 1, © copyright British Museum.

Deadly Medicine

Indians and Alcohol in Early America

Peter C. Mancall

CORNELL UNIVERSITY PRESS

Ithaca and London

Copyright © 1995 by Cornell University

First published 1995 by Cornell University Press.

Printed in the United States of America

⊗ The paper in this book meets the minumum requirements
of the American National Standard for Information Sciences—
Permanence of Paper for Printed Library Materials, ANSI Z39.48-1984.

Library of Congress Cataloging-in-Publication Data

Mancall, Peter C.
    Deadly medicine : Indians and alcohol in early America / Peter C. Mancall.
        p. cm.
    Includes bibliographical references (p.   ) and index.
    ISBN 0-8014-2762-2 (cloth : alk. paper)
    1. Indians of North America—Alcohol use—History.   I. Title.
E98.L7M28 1995
362.29'2'08997—dc20
                                                            95-1445
                                                            CIP

For E. L. M., who practices only good medicine

Coll. Putnam told a Story of an Indian upon Connecticutt River who called at a Tavern in the fall of the Year for a Dram. The Landlord asked him two Coppers for it. The next Spring, happening at the same House, he called for another and had 3 Coppers to pay for it.—How is this, Landlord, says he, last fall you asked but two Coppers for a Glass of Rum, now you ask three?—Oh! says the Landlord, it costs me a good deal to keep Rum over the Winter. It is as expensive to keep an Hogshead of Rum over Winter as a Horse.—Ay says the Indian, I cant see thro that, He wont eat so much Hay—*may be He drink as much water.*—This was *sheer Wit, pur Satyre,* and *True Humour.* Humour, Wit, and Satyr, in one very short Repartee.

—Diary and Autobiography of John Adams, November 10, 1771

Everyone is sane until he is drunk.
—Medieval Irish proverb

Contents

CONTENTS

Illustrations

Preface

Alcohol killed and impoverished Indians in colonial America. Although not all Indians drank, and many who did may not have suffered as a result, the historical record bears vivid witness to the costs of drinking to Indians. Probably not enough alcohol reached Indian villages to cause the degenerative diseases associated with heavy drinking, but there was more than enough liquor to cause tensions within families and within communities. Despite the violence, accidents, and poverty that typically accompanied the liquor trade, Indians were not passive victims of malevolent purveyors of alcohol. Many eagerly sought liquor. This book explores the relationship between Indians and alcohol in early America, with a particular focus on the liquor trade and its consequences for residents of the eastern woodlands. Here lie the origins of a problem that still afflicts Indian communities: abusive drinking.

Historians are in general agreement about the impact of liquor on Indians in British America. Indians, so the accepted logic goes, came to enjoy the sensations brought by drinking, so they traded their furs and skins to get rum or brandy. Some nefarious traders, knowing the desire of some Indians for alcohol, set out to get Indians drunk in order to defraud them in trade or in land deals. Once inebriated, Indians erupted in violence, often harming themselves as well as their neighbors. Coming in the wake of epidemic diseases and interracial hostilities, the alcohol trade contributed to the decline of Indians in eastern North America. Historians have demonstrated time and again that abusive drinking crossed tribal barriers throughout British Amer-

PREFACE

ica as liquor sellers hauled their wares into virtually every Indian village from the Atlantic to the Mississippi.

Yet though historians have recognized the destructive force of alcohol for American Indians, few have treated Indian drinking as a subject in its own right. They have seen liquor's costs as one part of another story. Given the pervasive spread of the liquor trade in British America (and in New France as well) and the fact that Indians of widely divergent backgrounds participated in it, stories told by Indians and colonists involved in the production, sale, and consumption of liquor can tell us much about the way North American Indians—particularly in the eastern woodlands—coped with the European colonization of their continent.

Despite the extensive documentation, Indian drinking is not easy to describe because most Indians who drank left little evidence of why they did so. Missionaries' records and travelers' accounts, though no doubt influenced by the observers' own perspectives, provide some clues to life in Indian villages. Minutes of treaty meetings, part of the standard arsenal of documents kept by every colony, suggest what Indians and colonial officials thought about the trade at the moments when they met. If we look at these records and pay particular attention to their context, we can find patterns amid the mass of data. In essence, we need to inventory the thousands of references to Indian drinking. By doing so, we can get beyond the stereotypes of the drunken Indian and the duplicitous trader and thus understand how this particular commerce shaped relationships between the peoples of early America. We can also find striking similarities in the experiences of vastly different groups of Indians; Indians who lived surrounded by colonists, such as those at Stockbridge, often had the same response to alcohol as Indians who lived beyond the boundaries of colonial settlements.

Still, these records do not allow us easy access to what Indians thought, or suggest that this story can be told from the Indians' perspective. And that perspective is vital, as historians of early America have noted, because Indians were not mere witnesses to the colonization of North America. In addition to being the most obvious losers in the battle for control of territory between the Atlantic and the Mississippi, they were innovative survivors who adjusted to the presence of colonists by migrating and creating new communities. Many Indians in British America also stayed to live among the colonists; they went to colonial churches, appeared in colonial courts, negotiated with colonial officials, traded and even lived with colonists. And whether they lived in their own villages or among colonists, Indians bought alcohol from colonists, and at times drank with them as well. Though the surviving documents may not tell the Indians' side of the story as fully as they reveal colonists' views, the extant records still demonstrate that we need to understand the Indian side of the history of Indian–colonist relations if we are ever to make sense of the early American past.

In the pages that follow I attempt to explain the involvement of Indians and colonists in the sale and use of liquor. The primary focus here is on the experiences of Indians living in what I, along with other historians, call "Indian country," territory that was not yet settled by colonists. Though we know of many cases of Indians who drank in areas dominated by colonists, most of the evidence for Indians' participation in the alcohol trade comes from regions where the economic lives of Indians and colonists were dominated by the exchange of furs and deerskins for goods the colonists could supply. For this reason, I have drawn most of the evidence from areas where that trade was carried on from approximately 1650, when the rum trade began in earnest, to the early 1770s, when the American Revolution disrupted the colonial economy. Most of the documentation I have used has come from the hinterland of Pennsylvania and New York, the Great Lakes region and the Ohio Valley, the Mississippi Valley, and the interior of the southeast, particularly North and South Carolina.

Indians in these regions participated actively in trade with colonists, and by doing so became involved in a transatlantic commercial world. They did so for their own reasons. When epidemic disease spread through the interior of the continent, Indians had to reorient their daily lives. They sought the most successful strategies for survival and material gain in a world that was unstable and ever changing. In the process, as historians have demonstrated, they had to alter many of their communities, especially because many Indian villages had to absorb refugees from the east. These newly emergent communities often lacked a single tribal identity. Though Indians in these communities often made alliances with members of other communities for specific purposes, especially to go to war or to negotiate with colonists, village polities often became more important than ancestral identities. Indians, with the notable exception of converts to Christianity, typically retained their particular cultural and religious beliefs, but their day-to-day behavior was often determined less by these inherited values than by local circumstance. This state of affairs helps explain why no entire tribe or nation escaped the ravages of the liquor trade.

The chapters that follow trace the rise of that trade in Indian country and the efforts to limit its destructive consequences. In the Prologue I venture to speculate on Indians' motivations for drinking and to link them to historical processes. I proceed then to place the stereotype of the drunken Indian in its larger historical context (in chapter 1) and chart the course of the liquor trade (in chapter 2). Chapter 3 examines the reasons Indians may have had for drinking to the point of complete intoxication; chapter 4 describes the social costs of the trade to Indian villages; chapter 5 deals with colonists' and Indians' efforts to battle the commerce. Chapter 6 describes the impact of alcohol on Indians living in Mexico and Florida (New Spain) and in Canada (New France); Dutch attitudes are treated along with British in appropriate places elsewhere. I do not deal with the Russian fur trade in the northwest because it developed in earnest after the American Revolution and thus is beyond the chronological focus of this work. Chapter 7 analyzes the place of the liquor trade in the first British Empire. The Epilogue deals with the legacy of Indian drinking in early America.

Punctuation and spelling have been silently corrected in places to make quotations more readily understandable. Whenever it has been possible to do so I have left quotations in their original form. All dates are rendered in New Style (Gregorian calendar), with the beginning of the year on January 1 instead of March 1 (the beginning of the year under the Julian calendar).

Assistance I have received from individuals and institutions has enabled me to complete this book, and I am happy to thank them for their efforts. I received financial support for this project from a New Faculty Research Grant and two grants from the General Research Fund of the University of Kansas. A National Endowment for the Humanities Travel to Collections grant and a Phillips Fund grant from the American Philosophical Society provided funds for archival research, as did a travel grant from the Hall Center for the Humanities at the University of Kansas, which supported a necessary trip to Paris to find a crucial document. A summer research fellowship at the Library Company of Philadelphia and the Historical Society of Pennsylvania provided me with an opportunity to gather many of the materials for the book; a Summer Stipend from the National Endowment for the Humanities provided support for research and writing; and a Mellon Resident Research Fellowship at the Library of the American Philosophical Society allowed me to fill some of the gaps in my research.

I drafted most of the book while I was a fellow at the Charles Warren Center for the Study of American History at Harvard University, and I take this opportunity to thank the Center, then under the direction of Bernard Bailyn, for its support. Like other American historians, I found the Warren Center an ideal place to pursue my work; I can think of few places that can offer the type of stimulating collegiality necessary to hone historical arguments, in addition to the virtually unparalleled collections of Harvard's libraries. An Arts Faculty Fellowship at University College Galway provided time to refine my argument and complete the writing; I thank Nicholas Canny and Thomas Boylan for their help in arranging that support.

I thank the librarians and archivists at the following institutions: Widener, Houghton, and Tozzer libraries at Harvard; Watson Libary at the University of Kansas (particularly Mary Rosenbloom); Van Pelt Libary at the University of Pennsylvania; the Library Company of Philadelphia, particularly Mary Ann Hines and Philip Lapsansky; the Historical Society of Pennsylvania (particularly Linda Stanley); the Library of the American Philosophical Society (particularly Roy Goodman); the Archives Nationale (Paris); the library of the Royal Irish Academy (Dublin); the library of the College of Physicians (Philadelphia); and the manuscript room of the Library of Congress. I received assistance as well from Arlene Shy and Robert Cox of the William L. Clements Library at the University of Michigan and from Georgia Barnhill at the American Antiquarian Society.

Such institutional debts are easier to acknowledge than the personal debts I accrued while writing this book and presenting parts of the argument at conferences. For their suggestions at scholarly conferences I especially thank Karen Ordahl Kupperman, William Rorabaugh, James Kirby Martin, and Joe White Eyes. I also thank historians who called my attention to particular documents or provided suggestions: James Axtell, Fred Anderson, Richard Brown, Lee Davison, Barbara DeWolfe, Philip Ethington, Robert Frankel, Ives Goddard, Robert Grumet, Eric Hinderaker, Ray Hiner, Fred Hoxie, Susan Hunt, Karen Kupperman, Ron Roizen, Amy Schwartz, Thomas Siegel, Russell Snapp, John Sweet, Lisa Wilson, Peter Wood, and Don Worster. I received remarkable aid from research assistants while I was at the Warren Center: Dominique Padurano, Jonathan Rosenberg, and particularly Sarah Dressler, whose translation skills and enthusiasm greatly helped. Lisa Steffen provided further assistance in Kansas and London. I am also grateful for the contributions of people who read parts of the book or papers that became the basis for chapters, particularly Mark Kishlansky, Steven Pincus, Mary Odem, Nancy Green, Lou Ferleger, Debra Coon, Dan Wildcat, Elizabeth Kuzensof, Joshua Rosenbloom, Ann Schofield, and Tony Rosenthal. Stephen Kunitz read and improved the prologue; Stephen Aron provided great assistance with chapter 2. Two anonymous readers for Cornell University Press provided excellent suggestions for improving the manuscript. I also thank Beth LaDow and Joshua Alper for their hospitality while I was doing re-

PREFACE

search, and Bud Saxberg for providing the only reasonable rent in Cambridge while I was at the Warren Center. Morwena Canny took time from her busy schedule to translate a crucial document. Keith Shaw drew the map under the direction of Barbara Shortridge in the cartography laboratory at the University of Kansas. Barbara Salazar edited the manuscript with remarkable skill. These people, as well as the audiences for presentations at the American Historical Association, the Organization of American Historians, Ethnohistory, the Warren Center, the Boston Area Early American History Seminar (at the Massachusetts Historical Society), the British History Seminar at Harvard, and the Social and Economic History Seminar in Kansas, all improved the book. An early version of chapter 4 appeared as " 'The Bewitching Tyranny of Custom': The Social Costs of Indian Drinking in Colonial America," in *American Indian Culture and Research Journal* 17:2 (1993), 15–42.

I am particularly delighted to single out several friends and colleagues who did far more than was necessary. I thank Bernard Bailyn for his consistent support of the project, and especially the critical feedback I received from him during my year at the Warren Center. Peter Agree of Cornell University Press took an early interest in the project and provided sound advice throughout the years it took to bring it to fruition. Alan Taylor, who set up the seminar at the MHS, provided his shrewd insights on various important matters. Beth LaDow, Eric Hinderaker, and James Merrell read early versions of the manuscript and pointed out ways to improve the book. Lou Masur read the manuscript with care and I have profited immeasurably from his advice. I thank Jacqueline C. Mancall for her many suggestions about archival research, and especially Elliott L. Mancall, who has had an abiding interest in this project and who helped me understand the medical aspects of alcohol use. And, of course, Lisa Bitel read every draft of every chapter, thus living up to her marital vow to love, honor, and edit. This book is a testament to her wise counsel and unflagging support.

PETER C. MANCALL

Lawrence, Kansas

Abbreviations

The following abbreviations are used for sources frequently cited:

AC: Archives de Colonies, Archives Nationales, Paris.

APS: American Philosophical Society Library, Philadelphia.

BWM: Papers of Baynton, Wharton & Morgan (microfilm), 10 reels. Van Pelt Library, University of Pennsylvania, and Watson Library, University of Kansas.

Clem. Lib.: William L. Clements Library, University of Michigan.

Conn. Pub. Recs.: J. H. Trumbull and C. J. Hoadly, eds. *Public Records of the Colony of Connecticut.* 15 vols. Hartford, 1850–1890.

CRSC Indian Affairs, 1750–1754: William L. McDowell Jr., ed. *Colonial Records of South Carolina: Documents Relating to Indian Affairs, May 21, 1750–August 7, 1754.* Columbia, 1958.

CRSC Indian Affairs, 1754–1765: William L. McDowell Jr., ed. *Colonial Records of South Carolina: Documents Relating to Indian Affairs, 1754–1765.* Columbia, 1970.

CRSC Journals: William L. McDowell Jr., ed. *Colonial Records of South Carolina: Journals of the Commissioners of the Indian Trade, September 20, 1710–August 29, 1718.* Columbia, 1955.

Doc. Hist. N.Y.: E. B. O'Callaghan, ed. *The Documentary History of the State of New York.* 4 vols. Albany, 1849–1851.

Docs. Am. Rev.: K. G. Davies, ed. *Documents of the American Revolution, 1770–1783.* 21 vols. Shannon, Ireland, 1972–1981.

ABBREVIATIONS

EWT: Reuben G. Thwaites, ed. *Early Western Travels, 1748–1846*. 32 vols. Cleveland, 1904–1907.

Force, *Tracts*: Peter Force, ed. *Tracts and Other Papers, Relating Principally to the Origin, Settlement, and Progress of the Colonies in North America, from the Discovery of the Country to the Year 1776*. 4 vols. Washington, D.C., 1836–1846.

Franklin, *Treaties*: *Indian Treaties Printed by Benjamin Franklin, 1736–1762*, with an Introduction by Carl Van Doren and Historical and Bibliographical Notes by Julian P. Boyd. Philadelphia, 1938.

Ga. Col. Recs.: A. D. Chandler, ed. *Colonial Records of the State of Georgia*. 26 vols. Atlanta, 1904–1916.

HSP: Historical Society of Pennsylvania.

HSP Colls.: *Collections of the Historical Society of Pennsylvania*.

JAH: *Journal of American History*.

JAMA: *Journal of the American Medical Association*.

Ill. Colls.: *Collections of the Illinois State Historical Library*.

Jes. Rel.: Reuben G. Thwaites, ed. *The Jesuit Relations and Allied Documents*. 73 vols. Cleveland, 1896–1901.

Johnson Papers: James Sullivan et al., eds., *The Papers of Sir William Johnson*. 14 vols. Albany, 1921–1965.

JSA: *Journal of Studies on Alcohol*.

LC: Library of Congress.

Md. Arch.: W. H. Browne et al., eds. *Archives of Maryland*. 72 vols. Baltimore, 1883–1972.

MHS Colls.: *Collections of the Massachusetts Historical Society*.

N.C. Col. Recs.: William L. Saunders, ed. *Colonial Records of North Carolina*. 10 vols. Raleigh, 1885–1890.

NEJM: *New England Journal of Medicine*.

N.H. Prov. P.: Nathaniel Bouton et al., eds. *Documents Relating to the Province of New Hampshire*. 40 vols. Portsmouth, 1862–1943.

N.J. Col. Recs.: W. A. Whitehead et al., eds. *Documents Relating to the Colonial History of the State of New Jersey*. 31 vols. Newark, 1880–1923.

N.Y. Col. Docs.: E. B. O'Callaghan and Berthold Fernow, eds. *Documents Relative to the Colonial History of the State of New York*. 15 vols. Albany, 1856–1887.

Pa. Arch.: Samuel Hazard et al., eds. *Pennsylvania Archives*. 9 ser., 138 vols. Philadelphia and Harrisburg, 1852–1949.

Pa. Col. Recs.: *Pennsylvania Colonial Records*. 16 vols. Harrisburg, 1838–1853.

PMHB: *Pennsylvania Magazine of History and Biography*.

ABBREVIATIONS

PRO Trans.: Records of the British Colonial Office, Class 5 (transcripts, on microfilm), Watson Library, University of Kansas.

QJSA: Quarterly Journal of Studies on Alcohol.

R.I. Col. Recs.: J. R. Bartlett, ed. *Records of the Colony of Rhode Island and Providence Plantations in New England.* 10 vols. Providence, 1856–1865.

RMM: Records of the Moravian Mission among the Indians of North America, from the Archives of the Moravian Church, Bethlehem, Pennsylvania (microfilm), Harvard College Library and American Philosophical Society Library.

Va. Exec. J.: H. R. McIlwaine et al., eds., *Executive Journals of the Council of Colonial Virginia, 1680–1754.* 6 vols. Richmond, 1925–1967.

VMHB: Virginia Magazine of History and Biography.

Wis. Colls.: Collections of the State Historical Society of Wisconsin.

WMQ: William and Mary Quarterly.

PROLOGUE
History and Physiology

He called it *urine of the chief of hell.*
—Jean Bossu, *Travels* (1771)

Jean Bossu, a French traveler in the Mississippi Valley in the mid–eighteenth century, thought he had found a cure for Indian drunkenness. While visiting a group of Illinois, he recorded in his journal how he turned one man away from his drinking. The story reveals the arrogance with which many colonists viewed Indian drinkers and provides us with a case study of an Indian who could not control his thirst for alcohol, a person who today would be called an alcoholic.

Bossu wrote about the man, whom he never named, in his *Travels*, published in 1771, noting that he had hired him to be "my hunter during the winter" and that he came from Mitchigamias, an Illinois village. The hunter angered Bossu when he "one day having got a very great quantity of game, instead of bringing it to me, he went to treat with some Frenchmen, who gave him brandy in exchange, of which he drank so much as to lose the use of his reason." Bossu would not put up with such behavior. "As he entered my lodgings in this condition, I received him very ill," he wrote; "I took away the musket which I had given him, and turned him off by pushing him out of doors: he came, however, into my kitchen against my will, lay down in it, and would not go out of it." Once the man had recovered from his stupor, he "well conceived what a great fault he had committed; and, being willing to atone for it, he took a gun, powder, and shot, and went out." He came back the next day,

very haughtily, loaded with game: he had round his naked body a gir-
dle, between which all the heads of the wild fowls were put; he loosened
it, and threw them into the middle of my room; he then sat down near
my fire, without speaking; he lighted his calumet, and giving it to me
to smoke out of it, he said, "I own I had lost my senses yesterday, but
I have found them again: I acknowledge my fault; and I beg thee to
excuse it. I agree that I had deserved the treatment I received, being
turned out of thy hut; thou hast done well to let me come in again. . . .

The hunter was especially thankful because other Indians would have re-
proached him for being cast out of Bossu's house.

Bossu, like virtually all Europeans of the age, knew well the problems that
intoxication could bring, noting that "drunkenness debases men to the rank
of brutes, and that this vice is corrected with difficulty even amongst the
French. The Indians imitate them easily in it, and say the white people have
taught them to drink the *fiery water* [brandy]." But though the Indian had
been contrite, "one day [he] found the door of the King's magazine open,"
and "he sneaked in like a serpent, got to a barrel of brandy, and shed half
of it, by endeavouring to fill a bottle with it." This time Bossu fired him. But
Bossu was not, at least in his own estimation, a heartless soul, and he recognized that the man was useful. He "had only one fault," surely not enough
to remove him permanently from his employ. Further, the hunter's wife
"begged me to give him physic, to prevent his drinking," and Bossu "willingly undertook the cure, with the assistance of his wife and relations."

It was at this point that Bossu hatched his scheme for curing the hunter's
drinking problem.

Once this hunter was drunk, but desired still more brandy, I got the
people to tell him I had some, but that I was very tenacious of it. He
came immediately, and asked me for some: I said, I had brandy, but I
would not give it for nothing. He said he was poor; however, if I would
take his wife, he would hire her to me for a month. I answered, that the
chiefs of the white warriors did not come to the red men to enjoy their
wives; that if he would sell me his son, I would willingly take him as a
slave, and give him in return a barrel of brandy.

The hunter agreed, and Bossu added that "we made the bargain in the presence of several witnesses, and he delivered his son to me."

To Bossu the situation had become comical. "I was ready to laugh at this farce, from the very beginning of it," he declared. He then provided the hunter with a special potion.

I made him drink upon the bargain some brandy, into which I had put long pepper. When he had drunk it, he was bound, and brought to sleep. When he was recovered of his drunkenness, the Cacique of the village and his relations, who were in the secret, came to him into his hut, where he lay upon a mat; they displayed to him all the horror of the unnatural action he had committed by selling his own offspring. The poor Indian came crying to me, and said, *Indagé wai panis*, *i.e.* I am unworthy of living; I do no longer deserve to bear the name of father.

The hunter was particularly angry about the brandy Bossu had provided, "which had fired all his stomach; he called it *urine of the chief of hell*, that is, of the evil spirit that caused it."
Bossu was quick to point out that he had had help in his efforts.

His wife, who is naturally humorous, and who was diverting herself at his expence, asked him very coolly where his son was. He still excused himself, saying, that, knowing me to be very kind, he expected I would return him his son; that he knew the grand chief of the French, and the father of the red men, had no slaves in his empire. I told him he was in the right, but that I had adopted his son, and would take him in that quality with me to France, in order to make him a Christian, and that all the furs of his nation would not be sufficient to redeem him.

The hunter's relatives "seemed to be grieved" at this news, and they "advised the drunkard Indian to go to the *chief of the prayer*, or the man that speaks with the great Spirit; for thus they call the priests," to see what could be done. Bossu informed him that if the abbé Gagnon, the Sulpician missionary who was the chaplain at Fort Chartres, asked him to do so, he would return the son "on condition that he should be baptised, and that I should be his godfather," and only if he received "an abjuration of drunkenness, which had proved so fatal to him." The Indian, Bossu reported, "said my words were strong, and he should remember them while he lived," and he even asked Bossu to adopt him as a brother. He then promised to take an oath that he would not drink again. "Since that time he has never drank wine, or any spirituous liquors." Even when Bossu sent "people to offer them to him," the hunter refused, claiming that he had taken an oath and would not anger God ("the Lord of life") by violating it. Since Bossu had earlier convinced the hunter that he could keep track of his drinking, the hunter apparently had more than enough reason to keep his promise.[1]

What did Bossu make of the incident? Midway through the story he paused to put the hunter's behavior in a context presumably understandable to his audience. "Many Europeans make no difference between the Indians and brutes, imagining that they have neither reason nor common sense," he wrote. "However, the circumstance which I have now related, and a great many more, sufficiently shew, that these people are susceptible of sentiments of honour; they know how to do themselves justice when they do ill." Lest any of his readers believe they were dealing with uncivilized savages, Bossu pointed out that "there are nations among the Europeans of whom one may remark as ridiculous and barbarous customs as among the American Indians."[2]

Bossu's scheme to cure the Indian hunter of his drinking problem made an important point about Indian drinking in general. Though he did not know why the Indian drank, he believed that some coercion from his family and community, mixed with some Catholicism and a touch of homemade medicine, could effect a solution to the problem. The Indian drinker was shown the error of his ways and he reformed. In that act, the hunter demonstrated that he was the master of his drinking, and not a simple victim of liquor-toting traders or some ingrained vulnerability to alcohol.

Bossu's account invites us to look for the connections between the past and the present, at least on the question of Indian drinking. And the need for such a pursuit could not be more pressing. Within the past generation, clinical researchers, at times drawing on historical accounts, have redefined our understanding of drinking; social scientists have joined in, often applying their theories to Indian drinking practices. The published findings of these investigators, detailed in specialized scholarly journals, often reappear in newspaper reports recounting the most startling and disheartening discoveries: the existence of a gene that purportedly causes alcoholism; the correlation between maternal drinking and fetal alcohol syndrome; the link between liquor and degenerative diseases; the close association of drinking with other forms of social pathologies. The findings of such reports suggest that any person who conformed to certain socioeconomic, genetic, or behavioral characteristics would, given the opportunity to consume sufficient amounts of distilled or brewed beverages, suffer catastrophic consequences.

Studies such as these attract attention because of the public's concern for what we too easily call "alcoholism." Yet however serious the consequences of abusive drinking, we are still struggling to understand why people drink in the ways they do. After all, alcoholism is not a disease in the normal sense of the word. Its characteristics differ from those of the epidemic diseases caused by microorganisms that invaded the Western Hemisphere after the end of the fifteenth century. No mosquitoes, fleas, rats, or infected humans are necessary to transmit it through thousands of miles of territory. At the present time most physicians have moved away from what has been termed the "disease concept of alcoholism."[3] Clinicians now generally hold that alcoholism is a behavioral disorder rather than an illness in a biological sense. Still, many remain convinced that there is a genetic trigger to the process of becoming an alcoholic, thus suggesting physiological as well as psychological roots to abusive drinking.[4]

Although the precise nature of alcoholism remains elusive,[5] and though the debate about its genetic component seems sure to rage for years, there is no real doubt about the maladies that are associated with or result from heavy drinking. People who consume large quantities of alcohol, whether they are diagnosed as "substance abusers" or not, suffer from a variety of somatic derangements. Modern clinical studies amply support the long-recognized connection between alcohol and liver disease (cirrhosis). Prolonged abuse and its attendant chronic nutritional neglect lead to numerous other disorders that involve virtually all body systems and not infrequently result in death. Abusive drinking and the malnutrition that often accompanies it can adversely affect the hematologic system, with resultant anemia, and drinking can cause serious pancreatic disease; alcoholic pancreatitis can in turn lead to intestinal malabsorption and diabetes. Alcohol may also have a debilitating and potentially fatal impact on muscle, including the heart; alcoholic cardiomyopathy, a clinically distinct illness involving the cardiac musculature, causes severe and at times fatal heart failure, even among people with no coronary artery disease. Widespread somatic muscle necrosis, so-called acute alcoholic myopathy, causes an outpouring of myoglobin, which may secondarily lead to renal failure.[6] Alcohol abuse and nutritional neglect commonly lead to devastating disorders of both the central and peripheral nervous systems: acute inebriation; abstinence syndromes such as alcoholic hallicinosis and delirium tremens; and nutritionally dependent disorders such as alcoholic neuritis (polyneuropathy), Wernicke-Korsakoff syndrome, nutritional (alcoholic) amblyopia, pellagra, and cerebellar degeneration, among others, are widely recognized and well defined in the alcoholic population.[7] The link that some colonial observers noted between excessive consumption of alcohol and disease is amply supported by contemporary clinical experience.

It is of course impossible to know if residents of Indian country suffered from any of these maladies in the seventeenth and eighteenth centuries. Much of the surviving evidence is vague. Further, since alcohol-related diseases leave no trace on bone, they are impossible to recover through paleopathological analysis.[8] But recent experience amply documents the catastrophic toll that alcohol has taken on Indian communities in the twentieth century. Deaths related to alcoholism are four times higher for Indians than for the general population; 70 percent of all treatments provided by physicians at Indian Health Service clinics are for alcohol-related disease or trauma.[9] Alcohol abuse is the most persistent predisposing condition among White Mountain Apache men and women who suffer from invasive pneumococcal disease.[10] Maternal drinking has contributed to the growing incidence of fetal alcohol syndrome (FAS), a congenital defect with long-term implications, and has also led to an increased rate of other neonatal problems.[11] Other health-related consequences are also widespread. Alcohol plays a role in perhaps 90 percent of all homicides involving Indians and in most suicides and accidental-injury deaths.[12] Psychiatrists have reported that in one Indian community problems related to alcohol abuse remain widespread for years, with three-fourths of the men and over a third of the women having been diagnosed at some point as abusers of alcohol or dependent on it.[13] Inebriated Indians in New Mexico are too often killed along the roads, either hit by cars as they walk or succumbing to hypothermia after they have passed out.[14] The children of parents who abuse alcohol have an increased risk of injury from abuse and neglect as well.[15] Alcohol abuse has been found among Indian children as young as thirteen, at least some of whom seek complete intoxication; at least one case of delirium tremens in a nine-year-old boy, the son of an alcoholic father, has been reported in northern New Mexico.[16]

But these problems and even the desire to drink are not spread evenly across Indian America today; many Indians do not drink and not all who do so suffer as a result. Many researchers have demonstrated that there is no single response of Indians to alcohol. As in the colonial period, some Indians resist drinking altogether and others drink to varying degrees. Even within particular groups, such as the Navajos, wide discrepancies in drinking styles are found, as measured by the incidences of social pathologies and alcoholic cirrhosis rates. According to some studies, culture and physiology at times seem to matter less than proximity to a large supply of liquor. Accounts of Navajo drinking patterns, for example, reveal that Indians who live close to cities drink more than those who live on reservations where liquor sales are forbidden. Further, the degree to which individual Indians have become acculturated to non-Indian society has a direct bearing on drinking styles.[17] Particular groups' ability to work together to prevent alcohol-related problems also accounts for measurable differences in the degree of abusive drinking in specific communities.[18]

The variation in individual responses to alcohol provides further evidence that genetics alone does not determine how or why individual Indians choose to drink. Clinical studies have found no identifiable genetic trait that leads American Indians to abusive drinking.[19] No measurable differences of any significant degree have been found to indicate that Indians metabolize alcohol more slowly than non-Indians.[20] Further, Indians in North America have enough aldehyde dehydrogenase isozyme (ALDHI) to prevent the so-called flushing mechanism that occurs in individuals, notably Asians, whose livers normally contain less ALDHI; thus American Indians' sensitivity to alcohol resembles that of the general American population, and cannot be explained on the basis of a simple inborn enzyme deficiency.[21]

Despite this clinical evidence, many Indians today claim there are innate differences in the ways Indians and non-Indians respond to alcohol. When anthropologists surveyed Navajos in the 1980s, two-thirds of the women and over half of the men contended that Indians had a "physical weakness" for alcohol that non-Indians lacked. Indians forty and over held to such beliefs in greater numbers than younger Indians (72 percent to 59 percent). Hence at least these Indians' understanding of the place of alcohol in their lives contradicts available medical evidence.[22]

There are no easy ways to apply modern clinical knowledge or contemporary beliefs to drinking in Indian country during the seventeenth and eighteenth centuries. Perhaps Indians then drank as they did because they, like most colonists, enjoyed the sensations created by alcohol. Perhaps Indians drank then because the world they knew was crashing down around them. Repeated epidemics swept Indian country. Land-hungry colonists wanted the land Indians occupied. Missionaries sought to change their spiritual beliefs. The fur and deerskin trade reduced the population of game animals and made economic survival more precarious. And many Indians had to move, often against their wishes, to new communities of refugees. In such circumstances, according to at least one psychological theory, the conditions were ripe for Indians to drink as a way to escape, however temporarily, from their problems.[23]

If Indians chose to seek escape from their troubles in liquor, they were certainly not alone. Throughout Western history, at least since the early modern period, widespread social change has been accompanied by increases in drinking rates. When the Industrial Revolution forced people to reorient their daily lives, workers sought solace in alcohol, much to the chagrin of public officials and clerics.[24] Their recourse to drinking did not represent a new development in human affairs; Tanakh and the New Testament, as well as writings of the Greeks and Romans, all indicate that some people drank to excess in ancient times.[25] The rise of ever more efficient ways of distilling alcohol, and the proliferation of cheap gin in particular, provided Europeans from 1500 or so onward with ample means to cope with the horrors of their world. London, the metropolis that had the greatest influence on the development of North America, was awash in liquor.[26] In the middle of the eighteenth century Paris had 3,000 public drinking places—approximately one for every 200 residents of the city—and purveyors of alcohol outnumbered members of any other occupation.[27] Europeans have long been attached to the bottle, and rates of abusive drinking have increased in direct response to widely perceived crises.[28]

Certainly, then, there is nothing unique or necessarily genetic about drinking, even destructive drinking, in the wake of destabilizing social and economic change. Indians drank at least in part because the world they knew was eroding around them. Whether liquor was supposed to bring power, as many believed, or to make them forget their problems, its effects were welcomed at the time. The tragic dimension of the story is not that Indians drank but that their drinking only exacerbated the crises that were besetting their communities.

Jean Bossu would never have understood Indian drinking in those terms, nor would any explanations that pivoted on genetics have made any sense in his pre-Mendelian world. But Bossu still knew something important that modern observers have too often missed. Though contemporary clinical and social science research has convinced most of us that drinking is dangerous, it has also unfortunately missed the point that historians have been trying to make since the time of Herodotus and Plutarch: people do not always respond to stimuli in logical or predetermined ways. Indians in colonial America made choices when they drank. Those decisions might seem irrational and self-destructive. But they were made in response to the opportunities available; they were not the outward manifestation of some genetic predisposition.

Bossu recognized the crucial role that an individual and his or her community played in the decision to drink or to stop drinking. If we are to understand Indian drinking in early America, we need to eschew abstract explanations and search, as far as possible, for the actual motivations that led Indian men and women to drink. Clinical, psychological, and anthropological literature all provide guidance. But we need to go further and analyze the abundant documentary sources. By exploring the origins of Indian drinking, we can find the human contexts and contingent forces that led these early Americans to destructive behavior.

CHAPTER ONE
Stereotypes

I almost despair of success in any attempts to stop the
traders from carrying rum to them. . . .
—William Nelson to the Earl of Hillsborough, February 5, 1771

When Benjamin Franklin wrote his *Autobiography* he included one of American literature's most enduring descriptions of intoxicated Indians. Indians, he believed, "are exteamly apt to get drunk, and when so are very quarrelsome and disorderly." As a result, he and his fellow negotiators of a treaty at Carlisle, Pennsylvania, in 1753 informed the Indians present that "if they would continue sober during the Treaty, we would give them Plenty of Rum when Business was over." The Indians abided by their promise, no doubt inspired by the knowledge that the only people in the town who had rum were Franklin and the other negotiators. Once their business was concluded, the colonists, true to their word and to custom, offered liquor. Franklin recorded what happened.

The hundred or so Indians got rum in the afternoon, Franklin wrote. By nightfall they had apparently consumed the entire available supply, and the commissioners walked into their camp after "hearing a great Noise." "We found," Franklin recalled years later, "they had all made a great Bonfire in the Middle of the Square. They were all drunk Men and Women, quarrelling and fighting. Their dark-colour'd Bodies, half naked, seen only by the gloomy Light of the Bonfire, running after and beating one another with Firebrands, accompanied by their horrid Yellings, form'd a Scene the most resembling our Ideas of Hell that could well be imagin'd." Realizing there was little they could do to calm the Indians, Franklin and the other commissioners returned to their camp. When several Indians came asking for more rum at midnight, the colonists this time declined to provide it.

The next day the Indians were "sensible they had misbehav'd in giving us that Disturbance," and sent three of their "old Consellors to make their Apology." Though acknowledging their behavior, the Indians' spokesman laid the blame on the rum itself, "and then endeavour'd to excuse the Rum, by saying, *The Great Spirit who made all things made every thing for some Use, and whatever Use he design'd any thing for, that Use it should always be put to; Now, when he made Rum, he said,* LET THIS BE FOR INDIANS TO GET DRUNK WITH. *And it must be so.'* " Such logic no doubt fitted Franklin's understanding of Indian drinking behavior.[1]

Franklin's appraisal of Indians' drinking practices did not reflect some desire to condemn all consumption of alcohol. Though he believed temperance a necessary condition in a search for what he termed "moral Perfection," and though his *Autobiography* also contained cautionary tales relating to excess drinking by other colonists (such as his putative business partner Hugh Meredith),[2] Franklin was certainly not abstemious and did not expect others to be so. His admonition in his scheme for moral perfection—"Eat not to Dulness. / Drink not to Elevation"—reveals an acceptance of the place of alcohol in the average American diet of the eighteenth century. And long before he had sat down to write the *Autobiography*, Franklin was already an ardent observer of colonists' drinking ways, particularly the excessive consumption characteristic of Philadelphia's working people.[3] As early as 1737 he printed what he termed "The Drinkers Dictionary" in the *Pennsylvania Gazette*, listing 228 terms for drunkenness then in use, presumably in Philadelphia taverns. The terms included "He's been at Geneva," "He's been among the Phillippians," "He's contending with Pharoah," and "He's eat a Toad & half for Breakfast."[4] Franklin was certainly no stranger to the taverns in colonial America's largest metropolis.

Yet by writing about Indians' drinking in the way he did, Franklin suggested, and countless other early Americans would have agreed, that the consequences of drinking almost always seemed more dangerous among Indians than among colonists. It would be a relatively simple matter to dismiss Franklin's description as exaggerated, especially the suggestion that the spectacle at Carlisle so closely resembled eighteenth-century conceptions of Hell. But Franklin was expressing complicated ideas that were widespread among colonists.

Franklin was writing from a particularly good vantage point. By the time he wrote his *Autobiography* he had long believed that drinking could create social turmoil in Indian communities. His *Pennsylvania Gazette* periodically ran articles describing the actions of intoxicated Indians, often dwelling on the tragic or near-tragic consequences of their sprees.[5] Franklin also believed that alcohol made Indians foolish or incompetent, at times to the advantage of colonists.[6] And by 1763 he had printed and sold the minutes of treaties which included Indians' or colonists' complaints about the devastations that alcohol created in Indian communities.[7] As one of the commissioners at Carlisle in 1753, Franklin joined Richard Peters and Isaac Norris in a public statement noting that liquor destroyed Indian communities. "[T]he Quantities of strong Liquors sold to these *Indians* in the Places of their Residence, and during their Hunting Seasons, from all Parts of the Counties over *Sasquehannah*, have encreased of late to an inconceivable Degree," they wrote, "so as to keep these poor *Indians* continually under the Force of Liquor, that they are hereby become dissolute, enfeebled and indolent when sober, and untractable and mischievous in their Liquor, always quarrelling, and often murdering one another. . . ." If the trade continued, the consequences would be disastrous. Liquor traders "by their own Intemperance, unfair Dealings, and Irregularities, will, it is to be feared, entirely estrange the Affections of the *Indians* from the *English*. . . ."[8]

But it was his *Autobiography* that best captured the stereotype of the drunken Indian. However closely it resembled any actual occurrence, Franklin's image of wild Indians fighting or seducing one another in the half-light of a campfire drew inspiration from two other, related phenomena: colonists' trepidations about the dangers of excessive drinking and anxiety about the nature of American Indians and their proper place in British American society. Accounts of Indians who drank to intoxication and acted disorderly thus represented the fusion of these disparate fears. The mere prospect terrified countless numbers of colonists, and they proved more than willing to accept lurid descriptions of drunken Indians. Colonial officials, who presumed they could control the liquor trade, acted on their fears by making it illegal in most instances to provide alcohol to Indians.

But despite fears about drunken Indians carousing through the countryside inflicting mayhem, alcohol continued to reach Indian communities. In fact, some traders, and even some influential colonial officials, believed that the trade was necessary to support British interests in North America. Though greed undoubtedly motivated many traders to haul their wares into the thinly peopled periphery of colonial settlements, their actions, though condemned, reflected a perfectly logical extension of the dominant colonial attitude toward most Indians. Colonists, after all, had wanted to trade with

Indians since the late sixteenth century, and liquor was a commodity that always found buyers in Indian country. If Indians needed to trade to become civilized, as promoters of colonization had often insisted, then the alcohol trade could not be dismissed merely because it precipitated problems. And therein lay the most confusing aspect of the liquor trade: how should colonists manage a trade that brought temporary (and even long-term) social trauma and yet seemingly provided an ideal avenue for achieving the goal, initially generated in the early colonial period, of integrating Indians into the market and thus the society of the colonists?

The colonists' solutions to that problem allow us to move beyond the stereotype of the drunken Indian toward a better understanding of a phenomenon that baffled colonial observers. To grasp the origins of the stereotype, we need to recognize the central role that alcohol played in colonial society. Since most colonists drank constantly and suffered little from it, they could not understand why Indians could not control their drinking. But Indians' demand for alcohol and the colonists' demand for pelts and deerskins forced the issue, and so did the prevailing economic wisdom that commerce would be good for Indians.

"The Art of Getting Drunk"

Colonists drank heavily, at least by the standards of the late twentieth century. Inns, taverns, and ordinaries were central features of virtually every colonial settlement; colonists built them next to public institutions, such as courts, and along roads for travelers (figure 1). Alcoholic beverages such as beer, ale, and hard cider were available in countless households throughout the colonies. Most colonists drank every day. Drinking apparently did not raise the hackles of most colonists, though the constant appearance of inebriates in the pages of travelers' journals and personal diaries suggests that there were many in this world who could not easily control themselves when they drank.[9] Given the amount of liquor being consumed, periodic disorder was predictable. By 1770, according to one modern estimate, colonists consumed an average of three pints of distilled beverages every week, or approximately seven shots a day.[10] Rum was the most popular liquor, both straight and mixed with a variety of other substances; according to one 1759 account, colonists consumed forty-four kinds of drinks containing some form of alcohol, and rum was an ingredient of eighteen of them.[11]

Indians never drank that much. Even if they had wanted to, there was not enough liquor available in Indian country, that ever-receding territory

1. The central position of alcohol in colonial society was evident in the location of taverns or ordinaries near the center of their communities' public areas. In this map from seventeenth-century Maryland, the ordinary is next to the courthouse. Courtesy, Maryland State Archives, Special Collections (Charles County Court Collection), MSA SC 1497.

to the west of the line of colonial settlements, for even the most determined drinker to consume liquor at that rate. It was not the amount Indians drank that concerned colonists, it was the way they behaved when they drank. Indians were not versed in what James Boswell termed "the art of getting drunk";[12] to colonists, Indians were given to ranting and raving and quarreling. Since Indians in the territory that became British America had no alcohol before Europeans brought it, it is not surprising that they were unskilled in the art of intoxication. But their inexperience was also potentially fatal, and led Franklin and others (including many Indians, who made their thoughts known on the subject) to believe that Indians would ultimately drown in a sea of distilled spirits.

A history of enthusiastic drinking did not make colonists immune to the dangers of liquor. Though alcohol had long held a privileged position in the diets of Europeans, and in popular culture as well (figure 2),[13] colonists had always known that excessive consumption of liquor could cause physiological degeneration, moral turpitude, and social turmoil (figure 3). Heavy drinking, combined with a poor diet and a hot climate, felled colonists in Carolina and in the Caribbean, a fact that English observers related to their readers.[14] But other elements of drink-related decay elicited the sternest warnings in the colonial period. The authors of the Bible, who recognized the important and joyous role that alcohol played in Jewish and Christian ceremonies,[15] provided evidence of the troubles caused by drunkenness: Noah ashamed at being found naked and inebriated by his children (Gen. 9:20–29) and tables "full of vomit and filthiness" after a surfeit of wine (Isa. 28:7–8). "Wine measurably drunk and in season bringeth gladness of the heart, and cheerfulness of the mind," reads another passage, "but wine drunken with excess maketh bitterness of the mind, with brawling and quarrelling" (Ecclus. 34:25–31). No wonder that the ancient Israelites believed, if Tanakh can be taken as a reflection of social practice, that kings and princes should avoid alcohol "lest they drink, and forget the law, and pervert the judgement of any of the afflicted"; wine was suitable only for those "ready to perish," those "that be of heavy hearts," and those who could find in inebriation an escape from the misery of poverty (Prov. 31:4–7).

Early Americans did not have to indulge in biblical exegesis on their own because moralists (especially Puritan clerics) frequently denounced excessive drinking. As early as 1673 Increase Mather had drawn a distinction between alcohol, which was "in itself a good creature of God," and its excessive consumption: "the wine is from God," he intoned, "but the Drunkard is from the Devil." He saw drunkenness as "a great *Waste of a man's Estate*." To

The Royalist Club

2. Dr. Alexander Hamilton, "The Royalist Club." Alcohol—that "good creature of God," according to Cotton Mather—lubricated social gatherings throughout colonial America. This image, from Hamilton's *History of the Honorable Tuesday Club*, reveals a scene in a typical eighteenth-century tavern, where alcohol flowed freely. Courtesy, Maryland Historical Society, Baltimore.

prove his point, Mather drew on unquestionable authorities: lessons from Scripture, particularly Paul's efforts to make the drunkards at Corinth turn from their wicked ways.[16] Other clerics joined in with declarations that became ever more shrill. By the early eighteenth century the pleas from the

Mr. Neilson's battle, with the Royalist Club

3. Dr. Alexander Hamilton, "Mr. Neilson's battle with the Royalist Club." In an illustration to accompany his *History of the Honorable Tuesday Club*, Hamilton, whose diary reveals that he was no stranger to alcohol-induced revels, captures the chaos that ensued when drinking sessions turned raucous. Courtesy, Maryland Historical Society, Baltimore.

STEREOTYPES

pulpit would have convinced even casual observers that the colonists were themselves unable to control the liquor available in their society.[17] And although New England colonists no doubt heard these sermons most frequently, ministers elsewhere exhorted their audiences in virtually the same ways. Josiah Smith added to the moralists' standard arsenal when he warned the congregation at Cainbay, South Carolina, in March 1729 that inebriates ran a great risk of falling from their horses on their way home from the tavern.[18]

The lessons of moralists were not lost on colonial legislators. In efforts to regulate domestic life throughout British America, lawmakers designed statutes to punish anyone who drank too much. These laws were intended not to stop the consumption or trading of liquor but to punish people who violated commonly held beliefs about the proper way to drink it. Fears of drunkenness appeared early in the colonial period.[19] In every colony people who wanted to sell alcohol had to abide by certain laws, and tavern licenses typically went only to those deemed to be upright citizens. When drinking problems became more apparent to colonial officials, doubtless in direct response to the ever greater availability of distilled spirits, statutes specifically sought to stop abusive drinkers from continuing their destructive ways. In some places, those who had established reputations as drunkards were prohibited from consuming alcohol and their names were publicly posted; any tavernkeeper who ignored the list and served one of these drinkers risked a fine. And in virtually every colony tavern legislation became stricter over time. People accused of violating the law found themselves in court, and conviction brought a fine. But despite the clerics' warnings and the courts' fines, colonists continued to drink, and to do so publicly and often to excess.[20] Any colonist who lacked firsthand knowledge of the dangers of alcohol could read newspaper accounts of the horrors caused by excessive drinking, such as the death of a five-year-old Boston child who consumed a bottle of rum in his parents' absence.[21]

But while colonial officials feared the disorder that attended drunkenness, colonists could draw on longstanding traditions that tolerated or actually promoted drinking. Alcohol had been a staple of life in England for generations, and though it had been linked to violence since at least the fourteenth century,[22] efforts to restrict consumption focused on drunkenness and disorderly conduct, not on the elimination of drinking. By the time promoters of colonization were creating plans for North America, there were at least 17,000 alehouses, taverns, and inns in England, or so a government survey of 1577 reported; and women sold ale in rural villages to augment the family

[19]

income, as they had been doing since the Middle Ages.[23] Further, alcohol remained a popular topic for humor in the sometimes scurrilous cheap publications that circulated in the country.[24]

Though county officials increased their efforts to limit what they believed were drink-related excesses in the early seventeenth century, especially in areas where Puritanism was particularly popular, such efforts were never intended to turn the English into a nation of teetotalers. Alehouses served vital functions for the poorer members of many rural communities, not least among them the provision of nutrition, comradeship, and a place for the creation of the web of relations that held village life together.[25] Even when James I attacked illegal alehouses in 1616, he appealed for assistance to curtail only the wildest excesses of drinkers who acquired their alcohol illegally; he made no serious attempt to quash the sale of ale in the realm.[26] The only real efforts to limit consumption of alcohol in early modern England were made much later, during the eighteenth century, and were related specifically to the rise in gin consumption among the urban poor, a development that terrified the wealthier residents of London and elsewhere and that brought out the able propaganda efforts of William Hogarth, among others. Hogarth's images present clear evidence of British views of alcohol in the mid–eighteenth century. In *Beer Street* (figure 4) the populace appears healthy and happy, and civic order reigns. *Gin Lane* (figure 5) suggests a society where hard liquor has brought depravity, despair, and death; a coffin swinging from a gallows is only the most obvious representation of doom associated with the availability of cheap gin. The battle against the so-called gin craze did not eliminate gin, but it did succeed in reducing its consumption by the poor and thus lessened the apparent risk to the social order.[27]

Given the wide acceptance of alcohol in English culture, it is not surprising that Americans made no serious efforts to control liquor consumption until after the Revolution, and then only because leading physicians, notably Benjamin Rush, began to identify what they believed were cases of actual addiction to alcohol.[28] No wonder, then, that colonists drank heavily, concerned not about drinking per se but only about the dangers of drunken excess. Most colonists seemingly believed that alcohol posed no serious problems for a drinker who knew the arts described by Boswell. But when liquor reached people who could not be expected to follow the rules for its consumption, most colonists saw a threat to their social order.

4. William Hogarth, *Beer Street*. As Hogarth makes clear in this image from 1751, a society in which beer is the primary beverage is free of social ills; peace and contentment rule the day. Courtesy, Spencer Museum of Art, The University of Kansas (Gift of Mr. and Mrs. Dolph Simons, Jr.).

Cultural Conversion

Indians, most colonists believed, should not drink because they could not control themselves when they did. But colonists' fears could not, in them-

5. William Hogarth, *Gin Lane*. "What must become an infant who is conceived in *Gin*? with the poisonous Distillations of which it is nourished, both in the Womb and at the Breast?" asked the novelist and temperance reformer Henry Fielding in 1751. Hogarth agreed, writing at the bottom of the image: "Gin cursed Fiend with Fury fraught, / Makes human Race a Prey; / It enters by a deadly Draught, / And steals our Life away." Courtesy, Spencer Museum of Art, The University of Kansas (Gift of Mr. and Mrs. Dolph Simons, Jr.).

selves, stop Indians from procuring liquor. In fact, when Indians traded furs or skins for alcohol, they were doing what the promoters of colonization had always wanted them to do: trade the commodities of the Western Hemisphere for goods produced within the empire. Though colonial officials repeatedly claimed that they would prefer Indians to receive less dangerous substances, and though many Indians acquiesced when they accepted seemingly trivial goods such as mirrors, glass beads, and "Jew's harps," colonial traders recognized that demand for alcohol provided a sure way to maintain trade. Greed, to be sure, motivated the traders, but the alcohol trade cannot be attributed to avarice alone. For traders who provided liquor to Indians could have argued that they were in fact encouraging the Indians to participate in a transatlantic commercial economy, and thus were helping them continue the process of cultural conversion.[29]

From the Elizabethan period onward, as historians have demonstrated, promoters of English colonization wanted to integrate Indians into the English world. To be sure, the Indians needed to change their ancestral ways. Missionaries led the charge in many communities, especially when they took up residence in Indian country. These clerics and other colonists wanted to spread Protestant Christianity to Indians, at first through the teachings of English colonists and later through converted Indians; such religious teachings would benefit the souls of Indians while simultaneously limiting the spread of Catholicism by French Jesuits. But the conversion of Indians went beyond religion. The English wanted America's natives to take on English cultural trappings. They wanted Indians to live in English-style settlements, speak English, wear English clothing, and replace the serial polygamy of the eastern woodlands with monogamous marriage. They wanted to invert Indian gender roles as well by getting Indian men to perform agricultural labor, which had traditionally been women's work in the eastern woodlands.

The colonizers' goals were grandiose; they sought nothing less than to overhaul the Indians' world. To do so, they needed to control the wild excesses of Indian life; they had to "reduce" Indians and make them more tractable. They believed they would succeed because Indians already possessed so many of the attributes necessary for civilization: agriculture, trade, language, organized society, and a belief in a supreme being. These were the logical possession of all peoples, even Indians, whose origins lay in Genesis.[30]

Within this scheme for cultural conversion two central features emerged: Indians needed to convert to Christianity, and they needed to engage in trade. The religious aspect was in no way peculiar to the British; the French

6. "Qua Ratione Indi Sue Commercia" (How Indians conduct their commerce). In this sixteenth-century image, Indians have gathered together to exchange goods. Such familiar scenes of markets and fairs taught Europeans that America's natives were capable of commerce. From H. Benzoni, *Americae Pars Quinta* (Frankfurt, 1595). Courtesy, The Library Company of Philadelphia.

and the Spanish were busily converting Indians to Christianity as well. But the emphasis on trade, though shared by other Europeans, was more important than religion to the promoters and the colonists who actually tried to settle British America.

The English believed that Indians had always participated in some crude form of trade. Unaware that eastern woodlands Indians at times possessed goods produced hundreds of miles away, as we know from modern archaeological investigations, Elizabethans tended to believe that the exchange that took place in the mainland colonies was primitive. An etching published in 1595 shows Indians at an event resembling a country fair (figure 6); though no currency appears to change hands, the Indians, only partially clad and savage-looking to early modern eyes, are clearly engaging in forms of exchange familiar to any English man or woman who saw the picture.[31] Reports of early English travelers in the Western Hemisphere mention trade between Indians and Europeans even before either could understand the other's language, though surviving records suggest that such behavior might have been more in the way of gift exchange than trade.[32] Even without converting to English ways, Indians along the east coast of North America traded extensively with colonists who profferred desirable goods. And the colonists, in turn, looked upon such exchange as vital to their interests; the Virginia Company, for example, was so concerned with maintaining the trade and good relations with Indians that early laws of the settlement promised the death penalty to any colonist who traded with Indians without authorization or for any colonist who stole from Indians.[33]

Whatever might be said about the ultimate profitability of the fur and skin trades,[34] by the mid–seventeenth century some Indians had begun to organize their economies around commerce with colonists. By doing so, they integrated themselves, with ample encouragement from colonists, into the trade empire. Over time countless numbers of Indians followed their lead. Trade did not prevent all conflicts between colonists and Indians, as various early American conflagrations made clear. But early conflicts did not escalate to the level of hostility so frequently evident in Ireland, where British military leaders at times carried out campaigns of terror against the native Catholic population.[35] Firmly established within the system of commerce, many Indians were perfectly positioned to enrich the empire in their twin roles as purchasers of English goods and suppliers of American furs for the European market.

But the scheme, though perhaps beautiful on paper and worked out in precise detail by promoters, contained a flaw: what happened if Indians traded for goods that caused trouble? When early promoters of colonization, such as the two Richard Hakluyts, were writing during Elizabethan times, they could not have imagined such problems, in large measure because the commodities they thought Indians would purchase were largely innocuous.[36] But once the rum trade began after the mid–seventeenth century, colonists had to recognize that precise limits had to be placed on Indian purchases lest these new trading partners pose threats to colonial settlements. After all, though Indians could adopt civilized ways, the vast majority never became integrated into colonial society; even the so-called praying Indians whom John Eliot had converted to Christianity in Massachusetts lived primarily in their own towns and not in colonial settlements, and even they could, under the influence of alcohol, cause problems, or so colonists believed.[37] Colonists traded with Indians; colonists entered into elaborate treaties with Indians; colonists at times even lived with Indians. But most colonists never stopped seeing Indians as Indians. Unlike Elizabethan promoters who never crossed the Atlantic, few English colonists believed that Indians were their equals in any sense. The prospect of intoxicated Indians rampaging through colonial villages thus terrified most colonists, and their terror ensured that the stereotype of the drunken Indian survived for decades.

"The Passion for Strong Drink"

Once the rum trade began, colonists had to determine how they were to maintain trade with Indians but exclude from that commerce a commodity Indians apparently desperately wanted. For many colonists who did not engage in trade with Indians, the decision was straightforward: the trade should be forbidden. For those involved in the commerce, the answer was the opposite: rum had to be made available if the fur and skin trades were to be profitable. Colonial officials could be found on both sides of the divide, perhaps recognizing, as Franklin had done, the importance of alcohol for Indians and the need to reduce the trade if they could not eliminate it.

The fear of intoxicated Indians causing trouble in colonial settlements led legislators in virtually every colony to outlaw the trade, though statutes varied from province to province.[38] But as the statutes, especially their preambles, make clear, the liquor trade continued in spite of the acts intended to ban it. As will become clear, the commerce developed a momentum of its own, and found defenders as well as detractors. Its survival led some observant colonists to speculate about the seemingly permanent link between savagery and drinking. After all, if even civilized Britons and colonists could not always control their desire to become intoxicated, some colonial officials came to believe by the 1770s, why should anyone expect Indians to be moderate? "I almost despair of success in any attempts to stop the traders from carrying rum to them [Indians]," William Nelson, then governor of Virginia, wrote to Hillsborough, the secretary of state for colonies, in 1771, "when I consider how bewitching the passion for strong drink is among the lower and unthinking part of mankind, in so much that it is one of the greatest evils, I am told, in England which cannot be suppressed by all the wisdom of the wisest legislature in the world. . . ." Under such circumstances, he asked rhetorically, "can it be expected that any law, made by the Assemblies to stop the progress of such an abuse that is committed at the distance of perhaps an hundred miles from any magistrate who hath a power to punish, can do it?"[39] Peter Chester, governor of West Florida, made the point more directly. "It is often bad enough with white people when they are [drunk]," he wrote to Dartmouth, the colonial secretary, in 1774. "[T]herefore what can be expected from Indians who are void of sense and reason, born in savage ignorance and brought up in the same way, but the most barbarous and inhuman murders and cruelties?"[40]

The image of the drunken Indian that emerges from such accounts leaves an indelible impression on the mind, even two hundred years after the event. But not all Indians conformed to the stereotype of the murderous drunk, as is clear from the experience of Andrew Montour, the son of a French woman (a captive raised by the Iroquois) and an Oneida, who served as an interpreter for the province of Pennsylvania during treaty negotiations.

Andrew Montour had a drinking problem, or so his close associate Conrad Weiser claimed in a remarkable letter to the lieutenant governor of Pennsylvania in 1754. "I must say something to you about Andrew M. not to ridicule him but to inform you how to act with him," Weiser wrote to Richard Peters. "[I]n the first place, when we met at John Harris he called for so much punch that himself the half King & other Indians got Drunk, the same at Tobias Hendricks. . . ." Weiser had firsthand knowledge of Montour's drinking. "I bought 2 quarts of Rum there to use on our Journey but he Drunk most all the first day," Weiser recalled, noting that Montour subsequently "abused me very much" and "*Corsed* & Swore" at him. But when the liquor wore off, Montour "asked pardon," a practice he repeated after other drinking binges. Such behavior was too much at times, even for Weiser. "I left him Drunk at Hehwick, on one legg he had a stocking and no shoe on the other, a shoe and no stocking. . . ." But after painting a picture of Montour as a drunken fool who kept getting intoxicated, Weiser told Peters that Montour remained a valuable ally. "[N]otwithstanding what I said here I dont take him to be in himself an Ill natured fellow," he concluded, "but it is rather a habbit he took from the Indians and Indian traders, he is always extremely good natured to me when he is sober, and always will act according to my advice. . . ."[41]

Montour was not a threat to Weiser, nor did his drinking consistently interfere with his work for the province. In this sense he resembled the Delaware leader Teedyuscung, who drank at treaties, sometimes to the consternation of colonial observers, but who remained a powerful force in intercultural negotiations.[42] But not even the sober Montour could counter the stereotype of the drunken Indian, because that stereotype was not based on observations of Indians alone. It also evolved from colonists' views of the unalterable inferiority of Indians, a view that shaped the liquor trade in Indian country until the end of the colonial period.

When Franklin wrote about the drunken Indians at Carlisle, he told his readers something they already knew: in a world where alcohol was abundant, some people could not control their thirst, and chaos resulted. Indians suffered particularly from liquor, colonial officials such as Nelson and Chester came to argue, because they were not yet civilized. It would have been impossible for a savage to control his or her appetite without first accepting the twin precepts of British culture: Christianity and commerce. For Indians in territory under constant attack from epidemic diseases and land-hungry settlers, rum-toting traders became a particularly disturbing threat. But colonial officials never succeeded in stopping the traders from carrying their wares to Indian clients; to do so would have demanded extraordinary and unthinkable efforts to intervene in a specific sector of the economy. Further, some colonists believed that such actions would violate the traders' right to participate in the market economy and, by extension, would limit Indians' ability to participate in commerce as well. Instead, colonists who did not directly profit from the liquor trade witnessed one of the great spectacles of early modern America: the wasting away of Indian communities. In the peculiar commercial and racial logic of British America, alcohol had found an empire.

CHAPTER TWO
Trade

Two Keggs of prime [rum] will make three dash'd.
—Raymond Demere to Governor William Henry
Lyttleton, January 31, 1757

By the late sixteenth century, English empire builders had created a place for Indians in their vision of empire, but they had not yet worked out exactly how the indigenous peoples of America would become fully integrated into the crown's colonies. They knew that this process of cultural "reduction" would be difficult, especially since they had to compete with the French for the hearts and minds of America's native peoples. But even though events in North America were often beyond the control of Europeans, many Britons and colonists believed that Indian men and women needed to become English men and women, and that that transformation could not take place until Indians and colonists found some common meeting ground. Since it was unlikely that both natives and newcomers would be pleased about the competition for land and souls, the integration of Indians into the British Empire depended ultimately on the creation of ties that had historically bound Europeans together: trade relations. Indians, that is, had to become participants in the Atlantic market if they were ever to become civilized. They also needed to be kept away from the influence of the Catholic Church, and thus from French and Spanish colonizers.

But once the English empire builders determined, in ideological terms, that Indians needed to become their exclusive trade partners, they still had to work out exactly how native Americans would become consumers of trade goods. It was at this crucial juncture, at the meeting place of ideology and everyday life, that economic development in the Atlantic basin came to serve the interests of the crown. Soon after the creation of permanent colonies on the American mainland, colonists began to establish trade links with Indians. The colonists' material desires in their trade with Indians were clear: they wanted furs, slaves, and skins. But trade networks could function only if Indians were willing to become consumers as well as producers. This inescapable point soon convinced colonists that they needed to import goods Indians wanted and could not, or chose not to, produce for themselves. By the late seventeenth century at the latest, colonists throughout eastern North America, from northern New England to the Carolinas, decided that one commodity sure to draw the trade of Indians was liquor, particularly rum distilled from West Indies sugar.

We cannot grasp the commerce in liquor without assessing the chain of events that linked producers of sugar to consumers of rum. From the rise of plantations in the West Indies, particularly in the latter half of the seventeenth century, to the shipment of slave-produced sugar and rum to Europe and the mainland colonies of North America and the distribution of rum to Indians, producers of sugar sought to enmesh themselves in the commerce that sustained the British Empire. They succeeded because other colonists, many of them only marginally involved in commerce, decided to increase their earnings by distributing alcohol to Indians, often illegally, during the latter decades of the seventeenth century and the early decades of the eighteenth century. Over time, by 1770 or so, fur and skin traders came to dominate the commerce, though they never chased nontraders from the field.[1] By the middle of the eighteenth century, some Indians themselves participated in the trade, transporting liquor to eager consumers in Indian country. By the end of the colonial period, liquor had reached Indians far from the Atlantic.

The trade developed along with colonization. It thus began early in the Chesapeake and New England, though neither market proved enduring. The commerce gained momentum when colonists transported alcohol into the middle colonies and the southeast, from the end of the seventeenth century to the end of the colonial period; and it received an enormous boost when English traders began to vie with French traders in the Great Lakes region and in the Ohio and Mississippi valleys by the middle of the eighteenth century. These areas, in which Indian populations controlled more territory than colonists did, proved fertile ground indeed for liquor sellers.[2] Traders responded to opportunity by trying to haul wares wherever they could find clients. Indians who lived in or near colonial settlements had greater access to alcohol than Indians who resided farther away and who had less frequent contact with colonists. By the end of the colonial period, Indian and colonial traders led horses and paddled canoes loaded with kegs of rum deep into Indian country.

In this economic event lies a story with far-reaching consequences for the many peoples struggling, in their own ways, to survive in Indian country and in British America. It reveals in the clearest possible terms how sugar and rum became ideal commodities to further the goals of empire builders and how the alcohol trade encouraged Indians to expand their participation in the transatlantic market economy. The story emerges when we trace rum from the people who produced it to those who distributed it, and ultimately to those who consumed it.

Producers

Sometime around the year 1000 Europeans got their first taste of sugar, and the history of the continent and of other regions with which Europeans came into contact was never the same again. Without knowing it, the travelers who brought sugar to Europe, along with explorers traveling to the east, set in motion a chain of events that would change the relations between Europeans and peoples elsewhere in the world, particularly in Africa and the Americas. Sugar, to Europeans, was seemingly a gift from God, "an unsuspected and inestimable present from Heaven," in the words of one medieval chronicler. In the early modern period it found its way into foods, medicines, and liquor.[3] People perched to take advantage of the commerce in sugar found themselves, like later tobacco and rice growers in the mainland colonies, enhancing the commercial prospects of the British Empire at the same time that they profited themselves. By the eighteenth century, sugar had become one of the most important commodities in the expanding marketplace of the Atlantic commercial world, and the English took a central role in its production and consumption.

Sugar first appeared in Europe during the Crusades when some European would-be empire builders brought it back from what today is known as the Middle East. To them sugar was "a most precious product," one opined, "very necessary for the use and health of mankind." Over the next few centuries demand for the product increased immensely, and its production grew apace. By the mid–fifteenth century the Portuguese were busy transforming Madeira into the world's first sugar plantation. Forty years before Columbus ventured westward the Portuguese sanctioned the creation of a sugar mill on Madeira; by 1546 Portuguese sugar producers were shipping their product to Bristol, anticipating a tremendous growth in demand for it in England. Within decades sugar exports reached the heart of Christian Europe—Rome, Venice, Genoa, France, Constantinople, Flanders. The demand for sugar spurred the rapid growth of Madeira's population, which increased from 800 at the middle of the fifteenth century to perhaps 20,000 by 1500. This earliest production of sugar also brought slaves into the labor force; by the time news of Columbus's journeys circulated in Europe, perhaps 2,000 slaves were at work producing sugar on Madeira.[4]

Once the potential profits of sugar became apparent, would-be sugar barons moved ever westward in their search for suitable lands for the crop. By the early sixteenth century Portuguese and Italian merchants had created sugar plantations in the Canary Islands—at the time, the farthest boundary of the European world. Explorers then carried the crop even farther: Columbus, who stopped over at the Canary Islands before proceeding westward in 1493, took sugar to Hispaniola. By 1527 Europeans had established an *ingenio de azúcar*, a sugar plantation, on Jamaica, and though the industry remained relatively small during the rest of the century, it exploded in the early seventeenth century. By 1628 the Portuguese had established over 230 sugar plantations in Brazil, and they produced sugar continually, even when the price dropped, because economic success became inextricably linked to keeping their plantations active. Eventually the English and French too became active participants, developing the industry in the Caribbean basin after 1650.[5] Though some Europeans remained suspicious about its eventual success,[6] English planters, among others, committed themselves to sugar by the middle of the seventeenth century, and thereafter their pursuit of the business came to define their economic existence.[7]

Sugar production began in earnest in the West Indies in the 1640s, though planters did not begin to get high-quality yields until after 1650. Still, within a few years of experimenting with growing techniques and the apparatuses for producing sugar and rum, planters began to realize great profits. Richard Ligon, the first historian of Barbados, wrote at some length in the 1670s about the costs associated with establishing a sugar works; in spite of what he termed the "fallings back" that a planter might encounter—such as continual losses in human and animal labor and the loss of imports or exports at sea—a planter might expect to clear a profit of £7,516 19s each year once the plantation was established, a sizable profit indeed from an investment that Ligon estimated at about £14,000. Though there were drawbacks to becoming a sugar magnate in the Caribbean, including the possibility of never seeing family and friends in England again and living in a colony where one's health was always at risk from the climate and inadequate medical attention, Ligon thought the venture worthwhile. The planter, Ligon wrote, "can by his own Industry, and activity, (having youth and strength to friends,) raise his fortune, from a small beginning to a very great one, and in his passage to that, do good to the publique, and be charitable to the poor, and this to be accomplished in a few years, deserves much more commendation and applause. And shall find his bread, gotten by his painful and honest labour and industry, eat sweeter by much, than his that only minds his ease, and his belly."[8]

Planters succeeded because the English came to love sugar. By the early 1720s, in fact, the English so adored the product that they imported over 60 million pounds of it. With reexports totaling less than one-sixth of imports, some contemporary essayists, such as Joshua Gee, worried about the adverse impact of the sugar trade on the empire's finances.[9] Though Gee perhaps overestimated the deleterious effects of the trade, his description of the growth in domestic consumption of sugar proved largely accurate. From 1663 to 1775 consumption of sugar grew by a factor of 20 in England and Wales.[10]

In the West Indies successful sugar planters, or at least those able to manage the complicated transactions needed to sustain a sugar plantation,[11] lived opulently. Unable to achieve the status and wealth they sought in England, they strove to create an English society in the Caribbean. On some of the islands—particularly Barbados, which by the late 1660s became known as the "jewel in the British crown," they imported not only the language and legal customs of the mother country but, more revealing of their economic attitudes, also aspects of English culture which they thought would properly show off their wealth. Thus Britons in Barbados established newspapers, theaters, and even a bowling green. Planters who accumulated sufficient property to live grandly in England tended to return there; those who could achieve the good life only in the islands were determined at least to live like the English, even though clothing suitable to the English climate, houses with thick walls and glazed windows, and the customary English diet were not conducive to health or longevity in the Caribbean.[12]

Those who succeeded in creating profitable plantations drew the admiration of many travelers. The English in Barbados, a British historian wrote in the early eighteenth century, "live as plentifully, and some of them as luxuriously as any in the world. They have every thing that is requisite for Pomp or Luxury; they are absolute Lords of all things, Life and Limb of their Servants excepted, within their own Territories; and some of them have no less than 7 or 800 Negroes, who were themselves, and their Posterity, their Slaves for ever."[13] Ligon too praised individuals who succeeded, and looked forward to the day when owners of small plots of land would realize they could not compete with the wealthy sugar planters and sold their holdings.[14]

Yet succeeding in the sugar and rum business was not easy. In order to profit in the trade, a planter had to manage a large estate, often with several hundred slaves. In addition to land and slaves, he had to buy livestock and the equipment to transform cane into sugar and rum;[15] and he had to keep the entire plantation running all year round in an environment that bore no similarity to England and that was always potentially lethal.

Planters were ever ready to complain about the commercial problems they encountered, particularly when they felt aggrieved by the economic policies of the crown. "Most of Us Planters are behind hand, and in debt," the absentee planter Edward Littleton wrote in the late 1680s in response to a planned rise in the tax on sugar, "and so we were, before the Impositions gave us their helping hand. For there is no place in the World, where it is so easy to run into debt, and so hard to get out of it." Though the burden of paying the tax would ruin them, and thus cost the empire revenue, the planters remained loyal. "We renounce the Doctrine of *Grotius*, That Colonies owe an Observance to their Mother Country, but not an Obedience," Littleton declared. "It is Obedience as well as Observance, that we owe eternally to *England*; and though our dear Mother prove never so unkind, we cannot throw off our Affection and Duty to her." Never one to shirk excessive rhetoric in his efforts to make his point—he even compared a country that taxed its colonies' sugar plantations with a mother who knowingly poisoned her child with arsenic—Littleton made clear the great costs associated with the establishment of a profitable sugar plantation. The equipment needed to process cane, the human and animal labor, the English-produced textiles to clothe the plantation's inhabitants, the maintenance of a militia—all these costs and more, he argued, were burden enough for the planter.[16]

Despite the self-serving cant planters offered in their attempts to reduce any tax they felt singled them out unfairly, Littleton and other sugar producers were correct in believing that they were vital for the economic health of the empire. Sugar brought profits to the English as soon as planters figured out how to make it of high enough quality to compete with other sugar making its way into Europe. Further, as Littleton pointed out, the people who ran plantations in the islands purchased various goods from the home territories, particularly cloth from England and beef from English-owned estates in Ireland. In addition, the rising demand for sugar in North America and Europe led to a rise in the number of ships needed for the business—as many as 800 by the 1680s, according to Littleton—and thus stimulated the shipbuilding industry and kept thousands of otherwise unemployed English people at work. Rather than threaten the English economy by depopulating Britain and Ireland, as some feared at the time, the colonies provided a necessary boost at a time of growing unemployment and social disorder. In the end the empire profited the most from the venture. "And therefore the Plantations ought in reason to be valued, since they give *profitable* Employments to so many thousands of People," Littleton argued, "whereas the Fishing Trade and the Linnen Trade will not turn to profit."[17]

Consumed with self-indulgent dreams about their crucial role in supporting commerce in an empire based on mercantile policies, planters devoted themselves to their enterprise with little regard for the hundreds of thousands of people, virtually all of them forced migrants from West Africa, who died producing sugar and rum. Planters, to be sure, cared about mortality on their estates, mostly because a dead slave had to be replaced. But the human costs of plantation agriculture in the Caribbean were great indeed for the Africans transported to produce sugar.

To those Europeans who never ventured to the Caribbean, sugar production probably seemed no worse than most other occupations. Beginning in the seventeenth century and continuing well into the eighteenth century, travelers to the islands sent back reports describing, often in great detail, how planters built and ran their sugar works. The physician Hans Sloane left a particularly concise account, which traced the processes needed to transform sugar into rum. "I have seen Sugar made at several Plantations," he wrote in the early eighteenth century.

[T]hey make it by bruising Canes between Iron Rollers, in a Mill drawn by Oxen. The juice is conveyed into the Boiling house, where in a Cistern is mixt about two handfuls of Lime, with One hundred and fifty Gallons of juice, and then both are let into six Coppers one after another, where it is boiled and scumm'd. The Scum is conveyed to the Still-house, only that of the fifth Copper is put into a Jar, that it may be again boiled, in the first Copper, because it is purer than the rest, and so will yield Sugar. In the sixth, with a little Oil or Grease, to lay its huffing and boiling over, it is boil'd up to Sugar, and so cool'd in Troughs, and carried into Pots, where, by a stick run through it, a hole is made, whereby the Molossus is drained from it, and leaves the Sugar white. This Molusses

[35]

is mix'd with Water, as well as scum or juice from bad Canes, is carried into the Distilling-house; where, after Fermentation, when it begins to subside, they in the night time distil it till thrown into the Fire it burns not: this in the day time is Re-distilled, and from Low-Wines is call'd high Wines or Rum.[18]

The images that accompanied many such reports emphasized the mechanical wonders of sugar making and the benign conditions for workers. Those that portrayed planters at all tended to show colonists acting benevolently toward workers (figures 7 and 8).[19] Other illustrators went even further and depicted no colonists at all; the workers, all African, performed their tasks in an orderly and presumably peaceful and productive fashion.[20]

But despite such images, which circulated throughout Europe in works written in French, Italian, German, and Latin as well as English, sugar production did involve risk. Slaves who worked in sugar mills always feared having their fingers or hands caught in the works; those who worked in distilleries faced added risks. Even "season'd" slaves could be quickly killed. "If a Stiller slip into a Rum-Cistern, it is sudden death," Littleton wrote, "for it stifles in a moment. If a Mill-feeder be catch't by the finger, his whole body is drawn in, and he is squeez'd to pieces. If a Boyler get any part into the scalding Sugar, it sticks like Glew, or Birdlime, and 'tis hard to save either Limb or Life."[21] Noxious fumes in cisterns could also prove fatal to anyone sent down to clean one.[22]

Inadequate conditions on the slaving vessels weakened and killed many Africans before they arrived, and mistreatment and work-related accidents made for appallingly high mortality rates in the islands. According to Littleton, one-third of all the slaves a planter purchased died "before they ever come to do him service."[23] Such a mortality rate would not have surprised Richard Blome, a more sympathetic observer than Littleton. "The *Negro slaves* are never out of their *Bondage*, and the *Children* they get, are likewise perpetual *slaves*," Blome wrote in a description of Barbados published in London in 1678. "They have but mean allowance of *Dyet, Cloaths*, and *Lodging*. . . ." Included in what Blome termed the "very inconsiderable" diet of slaves was meat that did not meet the standards of the planters: "when any of the *Cattle* dye of any distemper, or by accident, it is given to the *Negroes*, who feed like Princes on it." Planters clothed their slaves inadequately and housed them miserably. "The *Lodging* of these poor wretches is worst of all," Blome wrote, "for having laboured all the day in so hot a *Countrey*, without any nourishing *Dyet*, at night they must be contented to

7. An Italian engraving of a West Indian sugar plantation during the eighteenth century. From *Il Gazzietiere Americano*, 3 vols. (Livorno, 1763). Courtesy, Library Company of Philadelphia.

8. Slaves producing sugar in the West Indies in the late seventeenth century. From [Charles de Rochefort], *Histoire naturelle et morale des îles Antilles de l'Amérique*, dernière ed. (Rotterdam, 1681). Courtesy, American Philosophical Society Library.

lye hard, on nothing but a *board*, without any *Coverled*, in their *Hutts*, or rather *Hogsties*; but Christian *servants* are something better Treated, being allowed *Hammocks*."[24]

Poor diet, inadequate clothing, harsh work regimes, housing even worse than the kind supplied in the mainland colonies, and often brutal punishment led to staggering mortality among slaves in the West Indies.[25] Forty-three percent of all slaves imported to work on the Codrington plantation on Barbados in the early 1740s died within three years. Mortality rates for recent migrants were high elsewhere as well, and even near the end of the eighteenth century perhaps one-fourth of all migrants died within one and a half years of their arrival.[26] The availability of slaves seemingly encouraged planters to work their laborers to death rather than provide for their basic needs. Edward Littleton estimated that he had to purchase six new slaves each year in order to keep his supply constant, and he was not alone. Planters imported approximately 264,000 slaves from 1640 to 1700, yet the slave population in the Caribbean was only 100,000 at the end of the seventeenth century. Eighteenth-century mortality rates were no better. Planters on Barbados purchased 85,000 slaves from 1708 to 1735, but the actual population of slaves there increased by only 4,000 during those years, from 42,000 to 46,000.[27] The birth rate generally lagged far behind the death rate on many plantations, and child mortality, estimated at perhaps 50 percent for one Jamaican plantation with particularly good eighteenth-century records, made the survival of the slave population even more difficult.[28]

West Indian producers of sugar and rum thus became the proprietors of a system of production based on murderous exploitation of laborers in the name of profits for themselves and for the empire. As would become evident at each stage of the liquor trade in North America, a similar spirit of opportunism and search for revenue led colonists far removed from the killing fields of Barbados to engage in commerce that supported the West Indian planters. They did so by catering to a seemingly insatiable demand for rum.

Colonial Distributors

Planters became eager participants in an evolving commercial system that tied together the economies of Europe, Africa, and the Americas. At the heart of the system lay the idea, deeply embedded in English imperial thought since the Elizabethan period, that the purpose of colonies was to produce goods valued in the empire. The Elizabethans could never have imagined how the production of goods in the tropics and other parts of the empire would change hands over thousands of miles; yet by the late seventeenth century, long-distance trade was becoming routine. Hundreds, perhaps thousands of colonists became involved in the distribution of goods throughout the empire, from the palisaded and finely stuccoed homes of the gentry to the longhouses and winter camps of the Indians who traded furs and skins. For much of the first half-century of the trade, the primary suppliers of Indian drinkers were not deeply involved in trade. By the beginning of the eighteenth century the situation had changed, and the alcohol trade was increasingly dominated by more or less full-time fur traders. Still, these traders were not the only colonists to provide liquor to Indians; as Franklin recorded in his *Autobiography*, colonial officials included rum in the gifts customarily presented before or after negotiations.

To be sure, when planters began to realize that they could make substantial profits from sugar, long-distance trade in the British world had evolved little since the founding of what became permanent colonies on the mainland

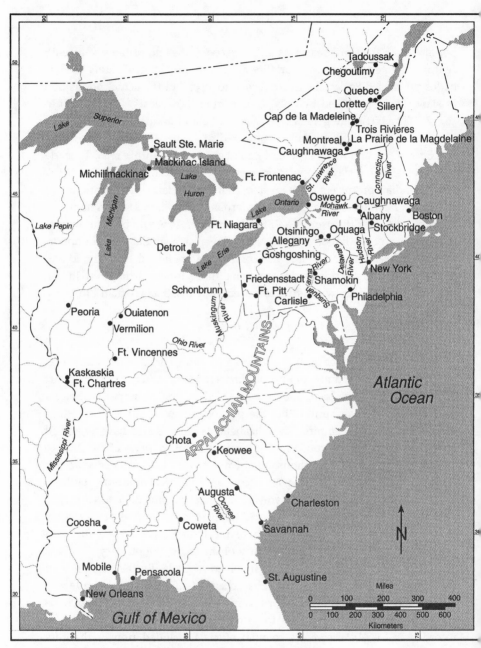

Colonial settlements and Indian towns, eighteenth century

and the islands. The early seventeenth century, from an economic perspective, was an age of experimentation and expansion; the discovery of profitable staple crops and the creation of the commercial conditions necessary for large-scale trade dominated economic planning. Between 1650 and 1700, however, British colonists interested in commerce settled into the production of staple crops valued in the empire. Planters in the Chesapeake colonies devoted much of their land to tobacco, despite fluctuations in its price brought on by overproduction. Planters in South Carolina, eagerly seeking staple crops since their arrival on the mainland—many of them had lived earlier in the Caribbean—settled on rice and indigo, and found an enormous market for their crops in Europe. The creation of British colonies in New York in the mid-1660s and in Pennsylvania in the early 1680s expanded the production of cereal crops within the empire; almost half of the grain products exported from the middle colonies at the end of the colonial period went to the West Indies. And colonists in New England, particularly those in the ports of Boston and Salem, became involved in the organization of long-distance trade and the development of processing centers. These separate developments, each propelled by the internal economic demands of colonists coping with a discrete environmental and commercial landscape, proved vital to the continued prosperity of the plantation economy in the islands.[29]

The timing of commercial development in the British Atlantic world could hardly have been more auspicious for planters in the West Indies. As the demand for sugar grew, planters had transformed the islands from cornucopias of nature's bounty to deserts. By the 1650s only continued imports of food from Ireland, the mainland colonies, and England kept them and their laborers alive.[30] Planters chose to become dependent on food imports because they discovered that sugar products could be traded virtually anywhere. They did not even have to distill rum in order to profit from the liquor trade; if they chose, they could simply trade sugar in the form of molasses to distillers in England and the mainland colonies, particularly in New England, who took the risks and bore the expense of distilling it into rum.

Almost as soon as colonists in the islands began to produce sugar in large quantities, would-be distillers in New England and elsewhere began to import molasses. Like the sugar trade, the mainland distilling industry grew from the mid–seventeenth century to the end of the colonial period. By the time of the American Revolution there were approximately 140 distilleries in the mainland colonies, most of them in northern ports—Boston, Newport, Portsmouth, New York City, Philadelphia. In 1770 the combined output of these distilleries totaled almost 5 million gallons of rum (3.5 million gallons shy of the amount consumed each year in North America). Mainland colonists also established sugar refineries, particularly in Boston, New York, and Philadelphia, though the number of these works—there were twenty-six of them in 1770—lagged substantially behind that of distilleries.[31] These distillers provided nearly all of the rum drunk in Canada after the British claimed it following their victory in the Seven Years' War.[32]

In the latter half of the seventeenth century, some of the rum made its way to Indians. Though good records relating to sales of liquor to Indians are difficult to find because the trade was often illegal, surviving documents suggest that at first the distribution of liquor to Indians was not monopolized by backwoods traders. Liquor was traded wherever Indians and colonists met: in cities, in small colonial towns, in Indian villages, along trade routes, in casual encounters between individuals and in large trading and treating sessions. Most obviously, the alcohol trade took firm root in trading centers throughout British America, New France, and, while it existed, New Netherland, where traders even worked regularly out of Fort Albany.[33] Archaeological evidence testifies to this trade: pieces of rum bottles have turned up at Mohawk village sites from the 1640s, in territory claimed by the Dutch.[34]

Virtually every major settlement had liquor purveyors. Colonial observers noted the existence of the liquor trade in Montreal, Boston, New York City, Albany, Philadelphia, Pittsburgh, Charleston, Augusta, and Savannah, to name only the most notable centers. By the end of the seventeenth century liquor had become a staple of the fur trade in New York City.[35] And, much to the consternation of proprietary officials, residents of Philadelphia often sold alcohol to Indians who traveled to the city for meetings; the practice caused so much trouble that officials issued proclamations forbidding these transactions at crucial times.[36] Drunken Indians apparently could be found in and around the city just the same; the missionary Christian Frederick Post complained bitterly in his journal in July 1758 that when he reached Germantown on his journey westward, he "found all the *Indians* drunk," and the Indian who was supposed to guide him to the Ohio country was so intoxicated that Post left him behind.[37]

Post had observed only a minor part of what by then had become an extensive branch of the liquor commerce. The trade spread everywhere because it was profitable. By the eighteenth century, traders in furs and skins, along with their associates in mainland ports, knew that liquor, particularly rum, was an ideal trade good, and they pursued it vigorously.

The logic of the trade was obvious. The Indians' demand for durable commodities such as guns and blankets declined over time as they acquired as many of them as they could reasonably use. Their demand for alcohol, by contrast, seemed to be constant. Since Indians could not or would not produce alcohol for themselves,[38] and since no alcoholic drink lasted long, Indian drinkers had to return to traders to get more. Thus, alcohol became a highly valued object of trade. When English and French traders competed for pelts, they used liquor and other so-called luxury goods to woo Indian hunters into profitable alliances. Many colonists, even farmers who traded with Indians to supplement their income, found the alcohol trade extremely profitable. While profits on most trade goods averaged around 100 percent, rum could bring profits of 400 percent or more, at least in part because virtually all traders watered it first. Most of the rum that traders sold to Indians was one-third water; as an agent in South Carolina wrote in 1757, "two Keggs of prime [rum] will make three dash'd."[39] Southern traders certainly knew how to stretch their supplies of rum; in the 1760s some sailors who stopped at Mobile added salt water to rum so that, as one colonist noted, it was "good for nothing but the Indians"; even the commissary of John Stuart, the southern superintendent of Indian affairs, purportedly added 87 gallons of water to 33 gallons of rum that he sold to the Choctaws.[40] Though some traders excessively diluted their wares—Indians complained in New York in the 1760s when they discovered that some traders had sold them only water when they thought they had purchased rum[41]—such instances of outright fraud were rare. But as long as the bottle contained some rum, many colonists saw little problem with selling diluted liquor to Indians. The practice was so common that one colonist found in possession of diluted rum in New Amsterdam was threatened with deportation because local officials presumed that it was intended for Indians; certainly no colonist would drink it.[42]

During the early colonial period, surviving records suggest, colonists gave Indians alcohol in much the same way that they would have offered it to other colonists. During the 1580s English explorers in territory that became Carolina greeted local Algonquian leaders with wine, meat, and bread, and claimed the Indians "liked exceedingly thereof." A generation later Henry Hudson provided alcohol to unnamed Indians to find out "whether they had any treacherie in them"; one of the Indians became intoxicated, "and that was strange to them," the chronicler of the voyage reported, "for they could not tell how to take it."[43] A decade or so later Edward Winslow took Quadequina, the brother of Massasoit, some strong water, and the two of them drank together.[44] David de Vries, traveling along the Delaware River

DEADLY MEDICINE

in 1643, noted that the captain of the ship "exchanged here some of his wines for beaver-skins."[45] Captain John Smith gave an Indian "aqua vitae" to restore him when he apparently suffocated in captivity. "[I]t pleased God to restore him againe to life," Smith later recalled, "but so drunke and affrighted, that he seemed Lunaticke," a condition that "tormented and grieved" his brother.[46]

By the mid–seventeenth century, increasing numbers of colonists engaged in such transactions, despite the laws that by then outlawed them. Cases arose in New Netherland, where the trade had been illegal since 1643, as early as the late 1640s, when members of the court of Rensselaerswyck heard complaints about drunken Indians and tried to determine who had sold them the liquor.[47] The Dutch and the English prosecuted any colonists caught selling liquor to Indians; those convicted had to pay a fine and some were banished from the colony where the offense was committed.[48] The stakes in such cases could be high, especially when exoneration of the accused could lead to the filing of charges against those who had brought the complaint.[49]

Court records reveal more than the punishment of lawbreakers; they also show the myriad ways in which Indians acquired alcohol. At times tavern-keepers or brewers, women as well as men, illicitly sold alcohol to Indians; in other instances farmers with surplus beer or townspeople with other intoxicating beverages (especially rum) poured alcohol into containers Indians brought with them in exchange for skins. A Charleston woman sought a pardon from the county court in 1684 for her sale of alcohol to an Indian woman, claiming she needed the money to support her family while her husband was away at sea.[50] Colonists also gave Indians rum in lieu of wages in payment for labor.[51] Sometimes Indians and colonists drank together in taverns and elsewhere.[52] Such drinking, as John André's drawing of a tavern in Montreal (figure 9) suggests, did not represent an effort to defraud the Indians. On the contrary, their presence in taverns, where they may very well have been as welcome as any other paying patron, reveals that Indians could enjoy the public consumption of liquor without suffering any horrific consequences. Even servants on occasion sold liquor to Indians.[53] The fears of such sales led Connecticut legislators in 1687 to pass an act specifically prohibiting the sale of alcohol to Indians by any "servant or slave, male or female"; anyone who violated the act faced corporal punishment or a fine.[54]

In view of the abundance of statutes prohibiting drinking by Indians,[55] court records serve as stark testimony to the fact that illicit trade was taking place. Dutch and English colonists may have had sharply different ideas about how to live in the area that became New York, but both groups un-

9. A tavern scene near Montreal, 1775. Although most of the alcohol sold to Indians changed hands at trading posts, Indians also drank with colonists in taverns, as this pencil sketch by John André suggests. Courtesy, William L. Clements Library, University of Michigan.

derstood the importance of the Indian trade even when it violated prevailing laws. Everywhere, or so it seemed to some observers, the logic of the market overcame the force of law, as well as any fears of drunken Indians. English and Dutch colonists defended their right to sell alcohol to Indians even when the trade was illegal. In the late 1730s, some colonists informed the Housatonic Indians that a ban on the liquor trade "was an unreasonable Incroachment upon their Liberty; that those who abridg'd them of the Liberty of using Drink, would by and by incroach upon their other Liberties; that they were us'd worse than *Slaves*; that they were treated as if they were *Dogs*, and the like." The argument apparently worked: the Indians who heard it soon demanded alcohol.[56] The trade did not always go smoothly, it should be added. In the mid-1680s Indians attacked one Pennsylvania colonist who, having earlier sold them alcohol, refused to sell them any more; contrary to rumors that the Indians killed him, the colonist survived the assault, though the Indians did steal his rum.[57] But in spite of the risk, settlers far from established towns became involved in the trade because Indians had goods they wanted. "The people inhabiting the Frontiers of the Province carry on a trade with the Indians by bartering rum for Horses," John Stuart complained to the Earl of Hillsborough in January 1769. "[T]he Chiefs complained of this as the source of many disorders their young men being

[45]

thereby encouraged to steal horses from the neighbouring Provinces besides the danger of committing outrages when intoxicated which may involve their Nation in trouble."[58]

Settlers not otherwise involved in commerce sold liquor to Indians because they wanted a share of the profits, especially if they were going to suffer the consequences of Indians' drinking binges. The entire situation disgusted Jaspar Danckaerts when he traveled through New York in 1679 and 1680. At Gouanes in the Hudson Valley he witnessed a terrifying drinking bout, replete with Indians who "were all lustily drunk, raving, striking, shouting, jumping, fighting each other, and foaming at the mouth like raging wild beasts." Those who did not participate had to seek cover elsewhere. "And this was caused by Christians," Danckaerts wrote. "Such are the fruits of the cursed cupidity of those who call themselves Christians for the very little that these poor naked people have." But why, in view of the violence of these sessions, did the settlers provide liquor to the Indians?

They brought forward this excuse, that if they did not do it, others would, and then they would have the trouble and others the profit; but if they must have the trouble, they ought to have the profit, and so they all said, and for the most part falsely, for they all solicit the Indians as much as they can, and after begging their money from them, compel them to leave their blankets, leggings, and coverings of their bodies in pawn, yes, their guns and hatchets, the very instruments by which they obtain their subsistence.

Danckaerts found the subject "so painful and so abominable, that I will forbear saying any thing more for the present."[59] Similar transactions in late-seventeenth-century Pennsylvania so angered Francis Daniel Pastorius that he called such settlers "nominal Christians" who provided alcohol to Indians "for their accursed self-interest."[60]

As we have seen, some tavernkeepers, too, sold liquor to Indians. William Beeckman complained to Peter Stuyvesant in 1660 that he saw "many drunken savages daily and I am told, that they sit drinking publicly in some taverns." Such practices at times annoyed some members of the community, but the sales continued.[61] Widespread fears of the drunken excesses of Indians may have limited the sale of liquor to them in some taverns. The spread of what one Pennsylvania official referred to as "low Tippling Houses" in Philadelphia led the president of the Provincial Council, James Logan, to order that proprietors of establishments "without any Regard to the Laws & good Government of the Place, but solely intent on their own private Lucre," stop all such sales.[62] Legislators in Georgia forbade tavern-keepers to sell alcohol to Indians or blacks unless they "first produc[ed] their Owner or Overseers leave in writing for doing so."[63]

If some colonists complained about their neighbors' selling of alcohol to Indians,[64] others presumed that such transactions legitimated their own, smaller-scale sales of alcohol. Thus Jan Juriansen Becker, indicted in New Netherland in 1660 for selling liquor to Indians, claimed that he did so because he believed that such transactions were widely acceptable in that society. Having taken up the position as commissary, Becker claimed that local Indians had "considered him as a chief" and brought him presents, notably fowl and deer, and in return he "never hesitated to give or present them a drink of brandy, but that only to Sachems, . . . whom neither Dutchmen nor Swedes disdain openly to provide with liquor to drink with at the tavern, which is done so free, frank and open, as anything, that is allowed, can be done. . . ." As a result, Becker never thought that "he made himself liable to punishment thereby, the more so as such bartering, even the sale of brandy, was there a common and necessary custom. . . ." Becker's claims may have been self-serving, but the testimony of other members of the community supported his assertion that the presentation of alcohol to Indians was customary and even necessary. Those who testified claimed "that if the poor inhabitants of the Colony of New-Amstel and others did not sell or barter liquor to the savages for Indian corn, meat or other things, they would perish from hunger and distress." Two others claimed that the director of South-Colony had earlier sent them "with several ankers of brandy and Spanish wine" to trade for the Indians' corn, wampum, and furs. Under the circumstances, it was perhaps predictable that Becker would protest any punishment imposed on him. When the court fined Becker 500 guilders and ordered him and his wife to leave the colony, he claimed that he had been misled by the actions of others, including "high and low officers of the State" who had sold liquor publicly to Indians. But Becker lost and had to be "punished as an example to others."[65]

Becker's defeat did not signal any great shift on the part of colonial officials in either New Netherland or British America, many of whom provided liquor to Indians, usually in the parcels of gifts they offered at the beginning or conclusion of treaty negotiations. The exception was not casual or hidden. In a proclamation banning the sale of alcohol to Indians in the city and county of Albany in September 1689, Robert Livingston noted that the prohibition was complete, "always Provided that it shall and may be in the

Power of the Mayor aldermen & Commonality of the said Citty if they see cause to give any smal quality of Rom to any Sachims who come here about Publick Businesse. . . ."[66] New York officials did not want to alienate any Indians, particularly Iroquois, on whom they depended, and who could turn to the French if the English did not provide what they wanted. A generation later, in response to Iroquois protests that the rum trade at Oswego had caused great problems in their communities, two governors in the 1720s provided rum to Indian sachems in their parting gifts, though each also made sure the Indians would not get the liquor until they reached Schenectady.[67]

Gift-giving rituals were well known to any colonist who wanted to get business done in Indian country; the often extensive customs permeated treaty meetings in eastern North America. The inclusion of alcohol in these rituals made sense to the participants, who were accustomed to providing gifts to Indians not only at diplomatic sessions but on other occasions as well.[68] Most gift exchange took place in public, where the givers and receivers could recognize the function of the gift in solidifying alliances. Thus in Pennsylvania in 1732 several Delaware sachems were pleased to receive the governor's gift of a cask of rum, "for which wee Return your heart Thanks and are Glad that the Govern[men]t has us In Remembrance tho att Such a far Distance."[69] Indians who traveled to subsequent treaties in the province received similar gifts.[70] In 1749 the president of Georgia provided Indian headmen with a keg of rum or wine, much to the consternation of the Indians' host. By providing that much, he had exceeded standards widely adhered to, as Harmon Verelst had made clear in 1737 when he ordered Thomas Carston to provide to the Indians he summoned for meetings in Savannah, "while they Stay, such Wine and Beer as shall be absolutely necessary but not exceeding a Pint of Wine or a Quart of Beer a day to each Person."[71] Still, not all colonial officials held to such standards of moderation, as Governor Arthur Dobbs of North Carolina made clear in 1754. Colonial officials present at a trading session treated 1,100 Indians "with meat and liquor for several days," Dobbs reported, and "by repeated presents and liquor" persuaded the Cherokees to agree to cede their claims "to the lands they claimed towards the Mississippi to the Crown of Britain."[72]

In such instances, the politics of giving gifts outweighed the possible consequences of a drunken binge and even the not inconsiderable expense. "I am obligd to Make presents of Rum," George Croghan reported from Fort Pitt in May 1760, because earlier officials had "Made itt a Custom I have nott been able to Reeche throw itt as yett tho itt is very Expenciffe."[73] But even though he complained, Croghan understood the importance of providing alcohol to Indians; as early as 1749 a commercial firm in which he was a partner had obtained 200 gallons of rum for its fur trade operations, and in 1765 he obtained over two gallons of beer "by order for Indians," though he did not note if he was going to give or sell the beer to them.[74]

British officials believed that gifts of liquor to Indians were necessary to stave off French influence. "The Officers at all Posts, where the Savages frequent, should be enabled to treat particulars, such as Chiefs and well affected, with a little Rum, Pipes & Tobacco, with provisions in cases of necessity," one observer realized in the mid-1760s, "they having been accustomed to much more from the French, & expect it from us; the expence is a trifle, but the want of that Civility may be severely felt."[75] Indians' demand for liquor could be so great that even officials who sought to maintain Sir Jeffrey Amherst's ban on the trade during the Seven Years' War at times felt compelled to provide rum to them, as William Walters reported to Sir William Johnson from Niagara in April 1762.[76] Georgia officials similarly acceded to the Indians' desires. When a group of Oconee River Indians approached them in September 1767 with a request for "a Cagg of Rum for each of the Indian Houses Burnt" by settlers on the river, council members advised the governor to give them what they asked.[77] And the trader James Stanley Goddard told Johnson that he would have to give Indians presents of liquor if he was to persuade them to trade at Michilimackinac.[78] Whatever the precise logic at work in specific circumstances, British officials either gave alcohol to Indians or condoned such gifts by their subordinates.[79]

The Traders' Liquor Business

The ritual presentation of liquor at meetings and the sale of alcohol by individual colonists from their homes became but a small part of the liquor trade by the early eighteenth century. By then fur and skin traders, who had long realized the potential profits to be made from peddling rum or brandy, made liquor a standard part of the goods they transported to Indian communities. Colonial traders had, of course, been using liquor in their transactions for decades. Traders working in Pemaquid, now part of Maine, sold alcohol to Indians during the mid–seventeenth century.[80] The importance of the trade was sufficiently clear by the mid-1670s, when Thomas Glover noted that Indians near the Chesapeake sold deerskins and a limited quantity of beaver pelts for goods they could not produce themselves, notably "Guns, Gunpowder, Shot and Brandy."[81] John Lederer went further, informing the readers of his pamphlet that "sometimes you may with Brandy or Strong liquor dispose them to an humour of giving you ten times the value of your commodity," though he admitted that Indians were sometimes "so hidebound, that they will not offer half the Market-price, especially if they be aware that you have a designe to circumvent them with drink, or that they think you have a desire to their goods, which you must seem to slight and disparage."[82] Where the fur and skin trades were more important—in the western reaches of New York and Pennsylvania, in the Ohio Valley and Great Lakes region, in the Illinois country, and in the southeast—colonists engaged in the commerce took such lessons to heart.

To be sure, the early eighteenth century represented a transitional stage in the liquor trade. Thus at a meeting in Albany in August 1722 a group of Mahicans told Governor William Burnet that "Traders & People" in colonial settlements offered rum instead of the goods the Indians requested.[83] The phrase suggests that these Indians drew a distinction between more or less full-time fur traders and other colonists, presumably farmers or artisans, who traded with Indians as a secondary pursuit.

By the 1720s the transitional phase was drawing to a close; by that time traders had in all likelihood taken over most of the liquor business. The shifting population of Indians probably determined the change in suppliers. Fur and skin traders were more willing than settlers and soldiers to go to great lengths to meet the Indians' demand for liquor, especially in the eighteenth century, when the decline of the Indian population and westward migration reduced most colonists' opportunities to sell liquor to Indians. Since fur and skin traders required Indian clients and could sustain or finance treks into the interior, they became the most logical liquor vendors. Long supply lines did not deter traders from transporting large quantities of liquor into the rural hinterland. In Canada, Hudson's Bay Company traders made brandy a staple of their fur trade at the four posts they operated in the late 1750s.[84] Even soldiers who had to cope with what they saw as the riotous and violent excesses of drunken Indians at times sold liquor to them; Louisiana officials knew about the trade but, as one reported in 1751, "Everybody has seen it and no order brought to it."[85]

Some traders in British America took advantage of officials' gift-giving custom to advance their trade. Or at least that is what Shemekenwhoa, a Shawnee leader, told proprietary officials in Pennsylvania in 1701 when he informed them that "Sylvester Garland had brought to the settlement of Indians of their nation several Anchors of Rum, to the quantity of about 140 Gallons, & that to induce them to receive it & trade with him, he pretended he was sent by ye Gov[erno]r, and gave one Cask as a present from him, upon whc, being entreated to drink, they were afterwards much abused."[86] John Long, working the Great Lakes region at the end of the colonial period, often gave Indians liquor—once to newlyweds, who became so "merry" that the woman burst into song—apparently to promote his trade; if his Indian clients ever wanted more rum than he had on hand, he simply watered it further.[87] Traders were often more than mere suppliers of alcohol; many eagerly joined in the festivities with their drinking clients, a feature of hinterland life that occasionally annoyed provincial officials. Conrad Weiser, who recognized the importance of gifts to Indians, frowned upon the practice of some traders, such as Henry Nolling, who got drunk with them. At one point he and George Croghan even staved one of Nolling's eight-gallon casks of whiskey in order to prevent further disturbances at an impending treaty session.[88]

Whether traders offered rum for presents or for sale, they succeeded in spreading liquor throughout Indian country. In 1704 a group of Conestogas informed Pennsylvania officials that traders had brought "great Quantities of Rum" to their town, thereby reducing many to poverty and exposing them to danger. Pennsylvania officials heard such complaints later as well, from groups of Shawnees and Mingos in 1741 and from the Iroquois sachem Shickellamy in 1745.[89] Traders succeeded in spreading news of their supply to local Indians, or became renowned for having liquor available at their homes or stores. When a group of Tutelos traveled to Shamokin in 1748, the sons and daughters-in-law of Shickellamy took them down the Susquehanna to a trader who had a barrel of brandy waiting for them, as well as some flour; "we hear his intention," the Moravian missionary Joseph Powell wrote in his diary, "is by this opportunity to Deale with them."[90] Well into the 1750s colonial agents working in western Pennsylvania complained about the actions of illegal rum sellers.[91] In the Ohio Valley the missionary David Jones, visiting a Delaware and Shawnee town in the early 1770s, noted that a Maryland-born colonist kept "a sort of tavern" there, though he did not describe any drinking on the premises.[92] John Lawson on several occasions described Indians who were on their way to English settlements to get alcohol (one of them even stole rum, along with other goods, from a trade post); and Indians in the southeast flocked to Pensacola in the mid-1770s to get rum.[93] The lesson of such observations was clear: many Indians knew where to go to get liquor and did not have to wait for a trader to bring it to them. As Pontiac explained to Croghan, his community had moved from the Detroit region to the Miami River to escape frequent problems with drunkenness. Still, he noted, "we live so nigh this place, that when we want to drink, we can easily come for it."[94] News about the availability of alcohol circulated throughout Indian country, much to the chagrin of traders at Niagara, who complained to Johnson in the early 1760s that since Lord Amherst had banned the commerce, Indians had by-passed them and taken their furs to Toronto, where liquor was available.[95] Traders who traveled through Indian villages with rum ran the risk of being robbed if for some reason they chose not to sell it—yet another sign that many Indians had come to expect liquor whenever it was available.[96] Indians throughout the interior would have agreed with the Iroquois Hendrick, who noted in 1720 that traders brought rum "so plentifully as if it ware water out of a fountain."[97]

By the late colonial period, from which the most extensive records have survived, the trade network functioned with ever greater efficiency. Not all traders sold large quantities of rum, or at least not all recorded such sales in their accounts. Inventories of the stores supplied by the commissioners of Indian affairs at Philadelphia and at Fort Augusta (at Shamokin) listed no alcohol on those premises, at least on the days when resident agents took inventories in 1763.[98] But the commissioners' records for their store at Pittsburgh revealed that their agents did sell rum to groups of Delawares, Minggos, Shawnees, and Ottawas on at least six occasions between November 20, 1760, and March 15, 1761, in amounts ranging from three quarts to twenty gallons.[99] Other evidence suggests the commissioners' ongoing participation in the trade: an undated invoice notes the need for twenty ten-gallon kegs of rum for the trade at Pittsburgh; an invoice from November 1763 notes that agents at the trading house included five gallons of rum among the presents offered "at sundry times" to Shawnees who went there; and a schedule of prices to be charged for trade goods dated April 1763 lists the price for rum as 8s per gallon. None of these transactions was particularly large, but their very presence in the accounts of a quasi-public group that aimed to preserve peaceful ties with Pennsylvania's Indians suggests that even well-connected members of that provincial society saw fit to ignore the colony's statute prohibiting the sale of liquor to Indians, or at least to violate its spirit.[100]

The amounts of alcohol mentioned in the commissioners' accounts are insignificant in comparison with the liquor transported to Indian communities by the prominent Philadelphia trading house of Baynton, Wharton & Morgan. Agents for this firm hauled substantial quantities of rum to English posts in the Ohio and Illinois country, despite the problems associated with overland and water carriage of liquor across the Appalachian Mountains.

The firm's accounts, which are quite possibly the most detailed records left by any trading house in the British mainland colonies, repeatedly list rum and other forms of alcohol. Though some of the sales were intended for the use of British soldiers stationed in the region,[101] most were intended for Indians, and many were paid for by the crown (through the Indian Department's funds) to maintain or create alliances in the westernmost reaches of the empire. George Croghan received 91 gallons of rum from the firm, along with other trade goods, on July 7, 1766, "on Acct. of the Crown for Presents to the Indians." In succeeding weeks he received other shipments for the same purpose totaling 581 gallons and two quarts, including a single shipment of 135 gallons on July 24.[102] Edward Cole, the commissary for Indian affairs in the Illinois country and another agent of Baynton, Wharton & Morgan, received 59 gallons in August and September 1766, and noted in his account that he had to pay the former commandant at Kaskaskia 257 livres in September 1766 because he had "supplied Sundy Indians with Liquor &c."[103] The firm recognized the importance of supplying their post at Fort Chartres with liquor for Indian clients; an inventory of goods on hand on November 12, 1766, listed a total of 1,236 gallons of rum there at the time.[104] George Morgan himself, one of the partners in the firm, had almost 8,000 gallons of alcohol, most of it distilled spirits from the West Indies, at his trading post at Kaskaskia, in the Illinois country, in December 1767; he intended to sell most of it to Indians, but an unexpected decline in the number of Indians who actually came to Kaskaskia that year made his supply last longer than he anticipated.[105] At the end of the decade Morgan continued to charge the crown for Indian Department expenses related to rum for Indians; between July 13, 1769, and April 30, 1770, his shipments totaled 356 gallons and one quart. Though the amount of liquor may not have been enormous, it accounted for approximately 80 percent of the value of goods charged to the Indian Department for the use of the crown in these accounts (£503 6s out of £621 7s 9d).[106]

Baynton, Wharton & Morgan were not the only distributors of liquor to trading centers in the west. Other traders carried equally large amounts of liquor to backcountry posts. Traders brought at least 6,500 gallons of rum to Fort Pitt in 1767, and Alexander McKee, the commissary of Indian Affairs at the post, believed that "double that Quantity is brought here by them exclusive of large Quantities brought up by Sutlers and others." The quantities of rum used in the trade elsewhere far surpassed the amounts reported from Kaskaskia and Fort Pitt. According to Jehu Hay, the Detroit commissary of Indian affairs, traders brought over 24,000 gallons of rum to that post in

1767. As both McKee and Hay informed Sir William Johnson, the fur trade thrived at both posts; traders had received more than 300,000 skins that year.[107] Johnson was already well aware of the extent of the rum trade; in 1764 he estimated that traders sold 50,000 gallons of rum to Indians in the territory under the auspices of the northern department of the superintendent of Indian affairs, and the trade was probably more extensive to the south. John Stuart, the southern superintendent, estimated that southeastern Indians consumed 30,000 gallons of rum in three months in 1776, suggesting a monthly consumption of 10,000 gallons (or yearly consumption of 120,000 gallons).[108]

The liquor trade grew in the far north as well, in territory controlled by the British Hudson's Bay Company (HBC). From rather modest sales of 70 gallons in 1700 from their post at Fort Albany–Eastmain, the HBC eventually sold brandy at its major stores at Moose Factory, York Factory, and Fort Churchill; in 1753 total sales topped 2,300 gallons, and they remained close to 2,000 gallons each year until 1763.[109] Looked at from another angle, the growth in sales of brandy reflected an increase in the number of skins Indians spent on liquor. In 1730, Indians traveling to the post at Eastmain used just over 11 percent of their skins to purchase brandy and tobacco; by the time the English controlled Canada in the mid-1760s, Indians, presumably of the next generation, were using over 20 percent of their skins on these goods.[110]

Correspondence from traders and colonial officials near Hudson's Bay revealed that the business flourished in the eighteenth century. Indians eagerly sought brandy, Governor Anthony Beale wrote from Fort Albany in August 1714; it was "the only commodity that encourages your trade of small furs."[111] Thomas McCliesh, the chief at Fort Albany, similarly recognized the importance of brandy in the north. "Brandy is a rare commodity," he wrote in July 1716, "for I can have more done towards the promoting the trade in small furs for two gallon of brandy than for forty beaver in any other sort of goods in the factory, it is become so bewitching a liquor amongst all the Indians especially amongst those that trade with the French."[112] Alcohol remained an important means to obtain pelts from Indians for decades, and Indians were sophisticated enough to reject brandy they considered inferior.[113] Many Indians did anything they could to get liquor, despite its manifest costs. One observer noted that some drank themselves to death after a ship carrying brandy had run aground near their encampment. Another, traveling among Indians allied with the French during the Seven Years' War, noted that Indians who came to Fort Duquesne wanted brandy but became "raging mad as soon as they have drunk it" and then "they fight each other and kill each other."[114]

There is little doubt that colonial traders succeeded in transporting substantial quantities of alcohol to Indian drinkers. But were Indians, as some provincial officials suggested during the late colonial period, selling their furs for liquor alone? A series of exchanges recorded by Baynton, Wharton & Morgan in the late 1760s suggests the actual standing of alcohol in the fur trade and the role of traders in the distribution of liquor to Indians. Rather than devote their entire stock of pelts to alcohol, Indians continued to want other trade goods as well. Some of these goods were, like alcohol, fungible. Indians who used guns on their hunts or in war always returned to traders for powder and shot, and many desired tobacco and paint as well. Other goods wore out with use, notably various types of shirts, either produced by colonists or imported from Europe. And other goods got lost or were so desirable that Indians wanted more of them: mirrors, combs, kettles, wampum. But the demand for alcohol seemed insatiable, or so most traders seem to have believed.

Alcohol, which reached the Illinois country (with devastating effect)[115] only in the early eighteenth century, figured in all of the twenty-five transactions enumerated by the firm's agents there in the mid-1760s between colonists and Indians who had no skins to trade. Those Indians, in other words, chose to go into debt for the traders' wares, or expected crown officials to give them what they wanted to maintain good relations. And colonists shared those expectations. Their dealings thus represented a particular economic sensibility in which liquor played a vital role. On nine occasions rum was the costliest commodity the Indians purchased; on eight visits rum added up to the second costliest commodity; and in none of the transactions did it rank below fourth in value (see Appendix I).

These exchanges of various goods took place from autumn to spring. The Indians involved appealed to Edward Cole, a commissary of Indian affairs in the Illinois country—who presumably received his supplies from Baynton, Wharton & Morgan—to advance them goods in anticipation of the pelts they would harvest later. Thus a group of thirteen Arkansas Indians informed Cole that they intended "to pass their winter Hunt contiguous to this place" and they wanted to know "upon what terms [the English] wou'd grant them a free & open Trade, as they promised to come in the spring with all their peltries to this post." Other Indians sought goods to maintain amicable ties with the English, always a concern to provincial officials even after the end of the Seven Years' War, or because they needed the goods.

Thus a group of sixty Indians who lived near Fort Vincent asked for goods "to renew & brighten the Chain of friendship before they went to their Winter's Hunt & beg'd to be pittied."[116]

The amount of rum distributed reveals distinct differences in purchasing patterns among the groups, at least at this point in their economic calendar. Still, though the differences in potential consumption are sizable—a group of Arkansas Indians received half a gallon of rum apiece, or approximately thirty times as much liquor as a group of Peorias—the size of the group had relatively little impact on the allotment of liquor received. That is, Cole or those working for him granted rum in roughly equal amounts to groups that varied widely in size. In all likelihood, the liquor that went to large groups was not equitably distributed. Virtually every other account of Indian drinking notes that some individuals drank while others abstained. Since these Indians were on their way to the hunt, and were purchasing powder and shot along with the alcohol, the risk of violence may have seemed especially great to those who abstained, and thus may have limited the numbers who actually drank the rum.

The surviving accounts reveal more than the total amount of liquor distributed to Indians in the hinterland; they also provide some details about the patterns of these transactions and, on occasion, the specific reasons traders provided alcohol to Indians. Baynton, Wharton & Morgan's accounts for Kaskaskia during 1769 and 1770 again provide perhaps the best evidence. Sometime before July 8, 1769, two Kickapoo chiefs received half a gallon of rum at the post, along with five pounds of tobacco and one tomahawk. On July 8 a group of Kaskaskia chiefs received one three-gallon keg of rum. On the nineteenth the agent provided one-half gallon of wine, along with two blankets, to "a Cabbin of sick Indians." That same day a group of Vermilions received two gallons of rum along with one pound of vermilion and thirteen pounds of tobacco. The purchases continued through May 15, 1770, when this particular account ended. Every Indian or group of Indians who appeared in these records received some form of alcohol, typically rum. By the end of the ten-month period, Baynton, Wharton & Morgan had provided alcohol to Kickapoos, Kaskaskias, Vermilions, Chickasaws, Arkansas, Shawnees, and Mohawks—to Indians, that is, whose traditional territories reached from eastern New York to the northern plains. Further, some transactions had a specific purpose. Baynton, Wharton & Morgan provided one keg of rum to "the Kaskaskia nation" for "two of their Young Men being kill'd supposed by the Chickasaws," and three gallons to "the Shawnese Indians who conducted the Troops down the Ohio." Another account from the same period notes the provision of two and one-half gallons of rum to "a Party of Indians" for "taking two deserters."[117]

The records from the 1760s, fragmentary though they are, suggest that crown officials continued to believe that allotments of liquor were necessary to retain the allegiance of Indians even after the French threat receded. They also demonstrate that the distribution network had become fairly elaborate, and that the liquor commerce was fully integrated into the commercial world of fur and skin traders. These accounts are not the only evidence for the spread of the business. The journals of travelers who ventured between New Orleans and the Illinois country in the 1750s, laws intended to halt distribution of liquor to Indians in West Florida, continued prosecutions for illegal sales of liquor in New England, complaints by southern officials that the commerce in rum dominated the deerskin trade, and reports of government commissaries indicating alcohol sales throughout a far-flung network of posts—all reveal the ubiquity of liquor in the lives of Indians in British America. Further, this evidence demonstrates beyond any doubt that alcohol remained a staple in intercultural encounters and exchanges for over two hundred years after its probable introduction. However deleterious its impact on Indians—which colonists and Indians alike reported at great length, as we shall see—the alcohol trade became an indelible fixture of Indian–colonist relations until the American Revolution.

The Indian Liquor Trade

Colonial liquor vendors transported most of the alcohol into Indian communities, so it is not surprising that their actions provoked the concern of provincial officials and Indian leaders. But they were never the only purveyors of rum in the interior, and by the mid–eighteenth century a fair number of Indians, many of them women, also became distributors of liquor. Though they received the alcohol from colonists, these Indian liquor vendors operated what might best be termed an internal trade network. However limited it may have been, especially in comparison with the transactions of a firm such as Baynton, Wharton & Morgan, the Indians who worked in this trade system created the last important channel for the liquor trade in the interior. And their transactions offer the best testimony that not all Indians, contrary to the view of many colonial officials, immediately consumed all the alcohol they laid their hands on.

Although their numbers were small, some Indians by the early eighteenth century were transporting liquor from colonial fur traders to Indian consumers, not all of them members of their own nation. A group of Iroquois, for example, purchased a large quantity of rum in Albany in 1730 and transported it to a Delaware community at Allegheny, prompting Delaware drinkers to sell their pelts to local traders (and even robbing them to get more goods for the Iroquois) so they could buy the rum. The very fact of this trade led a group of Shawnees in Pennsylvania to send wampum belts in 1738 to other Indians, including Iroquois, Delawares, and Shawnees living elsewhere, with the message that the rum trade would not be permitted at their community at Allegheny. Indians in the Ohio Valley in the late colonial period also used wampum to warn other Indians not to transport alcohol to their communities, including a group of Senecas who had arrived with rum.[118]

John Lawson left a particularly vivid desciption of this type of commerce, which he witnessed during his travels through Carolina in the early eighteenth century. The "Westward *Indians*" had no rum until the Tuscaroras and their neighbors took it to them, Lawson noted, but once the trade began, the Tuscaroras in particular carried "it in Rundlets several hundred Miles, amongst other *Indians*." Sometimes the people who hauled the alcohol succumbed to temptation and drank at least part of their supply, though some enterprising Indian merchants had learned a valuable lesson from colonial traders and simply added water to the remaining alcohol to bring it up to the proper volume (if not quite the same taste). But enough remained for sale to make liquor an integrated part of intertribal exchange. "Those that buy Rum of them," Lawson reported, "have so many Mouthfuls for a Buck-Skin, they never using any other Measure; and for this purpose, the Buyer always makes Choice of his Man, which is one that has the greatest Mouth, whom he brings to the Market with a Bowl to put it in." The seller measured the capacity of the bowl, closely observed the man as he took the liquor in his mouth, and made sure he did not swallow any of it. "[I]f he happens to swallow any down, either through Wilfulness or otherwise, the Merchant or some of his Party, does not scruple to knock the Fellow down, exclaiming against him for false Measure." In that case, the buyer had to find another man to replace him, and the operation commenced again, much to the evident delight of other Indians. "[T]his Trading is very agreeable to the Spectators," Lawson concluded, "to see such a deal of Quarrelling and Controversy, as often happens, about it, and is very diverting."[119]

Few other colonists left so detailed a record of the internal trade, but many, particularly travelers, took note of its existence; together their writings demonstrate that this particular commerce must have been carried out throughout the colonial hinterland and become more developed over time. An agent at Coweta Town, South Carolina, in 1752 reported the arrival of a group of Savannah Indians with "three or four Caggs of Rum," which they quickly distributed to the Indians and colonists in the village. Five years later another agent informed Governor Lyttleton that an Indian who transported six kegs into another town caused a drinking melee "which occasioned a great Deal of Noise and Trouble."[120] James Kenny, who was in charge of a provincial store at Pittsburgh, noted that the Beaver King from Tuscarora's Town was an active agent in the liquor trade, carting alcohol from Pittsburgh back to his community, leading them to long binges—one lasted six days—as well as violence and poverty.[121] Indian leaders often took alcohol back to their communities with them after meetings with colonial officials; such practices were particularly common in the south during the mid–eighteenth century, presumably because colonial officials were eager to maintain their ties to the numerous Indians of the region.[122] Traveling through the southeast in 1772, David Taitt wrote in his journal that "the Coosa Kings brother" had "brought five Keggs of Rum from Pensacola, to buy horses and Corn etca. to Carry to his people at Chactahatchie River"; he later encountered "two Indians with four horses Loaded with Rum etca. from Augusta."[123] At the same time David Jones encountered Indians in the Ohio Valley suffering from frostbite, apparently incurred while they were hiding the liquor they were transporting to prevent other Indians from stealing it.[124] At almost the same time, a missionary in the region noted that a group of "about twenty strange Indians" arrived in a mission community on the Muskingum River on their way to the Shawnees with six kegs of rum.[125] Conrad Weiser, meeting with Indians at Logstown in 1748, complained to Pennsylvania officials that their efforts to stop the liquor trade failed at least in part because "you send down your own skins by the traders to buy rum for you; you go yourselves down and fetch horse loads of strong liquor." The recent return of a Logstown resident from Maryland, who brought with him "three horse loads of liquor," convinced Weiser that these Indians "love [liquor] so well" that they "cannot be without it."[126] A decade later the commissary at Fort Augusta, at the juncture of the two branches of the Susquehanna River, reported that the Delaware leader Teedyuscung had obtained "cags of rum" from local colonists, and was on his way upriver to sell the alcohol at Tioga.[127]

Indians knew where to go to get alcohol from other Indians. Goshgoshing, in northwest Pennsylvania, "was the rum-market for the Senecas," according to the missionary David Zeisberger, who noted that the Senecas had "secured the rum in Niagara and brought it thither for sale."[128] Some of the

Indian purveyors, like those Zeisberger observed in the Ohio country near the end of the colonial period, actually moved away from their towns to keep the trade going when their communities had turned against them. "Many engage in rum traffic," he reported, "especially women, who fetch it from the white people and sell at a considerable profit to the Indians, often taking from the latter everything they have, sometimes even their rifles on which they depend for subsistence."[129]

Indian women often played pivotal roles in this Indian rum trade. One Indian woman purchased liquor in Charleston in the 1680s, though the surviving record does not reveal whether she transported the alcohol to other Indians or drank it herself.[130] Women's participation in the liquor trade was clearer in other instances. Mohican women profited when they bought liquor from nearby colonists, one of them a tavernkeeper, and sold it to their neighbors in Stockbridge in the 1730s.[131] At times women traveled the countryside with alcohol, as Joseph Powell, the Moravian missionary at Shamokin, discovered in 1748 when he encountered a young Delaware woman carrying a keg of brandy to the town. She asked him if she could hide it in his house so that it would not be stolen. Not one to support Indian drinking, he advised her to pour it into the Susquehanna. His diary contains no evidence about what ultimately happened to the liquor.[132] Women pursued the profits of alcohol despite the occasional opposition of men in their communities. "Brother once more, we dont like a great deale of rum," Squadook, a Penobscot sagamore, wrote to the governor of Massachusetts in September 1751. Though he took responsibility for the actions of his community, Squadook requested provincial assistance, particularly noting that "the women must have none. This we ask of you the Governour and Council. The women buy and sell to the men and are debauched thereby. I believe you will think I speak well, rum is the cause of quarrels amongst us."[133] According to Charles Beatty, a Presbyterian minister who traveled through the Ohio country in 1766, some women carried on the trade openly, receiving rum in exchange for sex from colonial traders and then selling the liquor to members of their villages. Intercultural sexual liaisons were not rare in the area, but these transactions troubled community leaders.[134]

Colonial leaders did not readily accept the existence of this Indian liquor network. In some circumstances the enlistment of Indians as sellers of intoxicating beverages to other Indians genuinely rankled them. Thus Willem Hoffmeyr, a Brazilian-born colonist in New Netherland in the mid-1650s, found himself fined and banished from the colony for three years for having beer "sold and peddled for him by one savage to other savages," among other offenses.[135] But though some colonists might be exiled for such offenses, there was little even the most conscientious colonial official could do to stop the trade. After all, they had jurisdiction only over other colonists; the movements of Indians with alcohol were simply beyond their control.

Once any Indians participated in the liquor trade, it took on a new dimension: now some Indians became accomplices in their villages' destruction. In some ways, the Indians who dealt in alcohol became indistinguishable from others who did the same—tavernkeepers and farmers, skin and fur traders. All made sure that alcohol found its way to Indians who wanted to drink. The dominion of the sugar planters, many of whom probably never laid eyes on an Indian, thus came to include the peoples in the marchlands at the far western reaches of the empire as well as the forced African migrants working on their plantations. By the mid–eighteenth century, sugar and rum had joined tobacco, rice, and wheat in the holds of ships traveling between far-flung English colonies. It remained for consumers of liquor, particularly Indians, to decide how best to incorporate this commodity into their lives.

CHAPTER THREE
Consumption

The Keowee Indians dreamed last Night that they must have a
Cagg of Rum before they go to War or they shall have no Success. I am pretty well acquainted with their way of dreaming,
for they have dreamed me out of a good many Pounds of Beef
and Salt since I came here, and I am afraid they'l dream for
some of this fresh Pork ere they go to War.
  —Lachlan Mackintosh to Governor William Henry Lyttleton,
     February 17, 1758

At a congress of 2,000 Choctaws and Chickasaws in Mobile in 1765 the Reverend Samuel Harte delivered a sermon, addressing his remarks to one Indian leader in particular. "The Indian Chief was very attentive and after
Dinner ask'd Mr. Harte, where this Great Warriour God Almighty, which he
talk'd so much off, liv'd? and if He was a Friend of His Brother George over
the Great Water? Mr. Harte then expatiated on the Being of God, and his
Attributes—But could not instil any Sentiment into the Indian, or bring Him
to any the least Comprehension of Matters—" According to the Anglican
itinerant Charles Woodmason, who was present, Harte "dwelt so long on
his Subject as to tire the Patience of the Savage, who at length, took Mr.
Harte by the Hand, with one of his, and filling out a Glass of Rum with the
other, concluded with saying 'Beloved Man, I will alway think Well of this
Friend of ours God Almighty whom You tell me so much of, and so let us
drink his Health'—and then drank off his Glass of Rum."[1]
   The idea of an Indian raising a glass of rum in a toast to the God of the
English does not easily fit our ideas of Indians' drinking practices. It especially goes against the information colonists reported so often about Indians'
lack of control in their drinking. More common perhaps were William Bradford's lament that Indians' drinking represented "the beastly practices of the
mad Bacchanalians" and the Reverend John Clayton's observation in 1687
that "there are not greater beasts in the world" than drunken Indians.[2] Travelers, traders, and government officials all believed that Indians drank only

to get drunk, and that when they were drunk they became licentious and violent. Few other aspects of Indian life seemed so barbaric to Europeans and colonizers, and their writings emphasized what they saw as the excessive indulgences of Indians gone, like the followers of Bacchus, seemingly mad under the influence of alcohol.

But not all Indians who drank were mad. Many drank as they did for specific purposes. As the French natualist Nicholas Denys realized, even Indians who wanted liquor were not always fooled by traders. "[T]here is this much certain," he wrote, "that as long as they are able to visit the ships, they never get drunk; for they would not then be able to preserve the judgment which is necessary for making dupes of the sailors and captains, and for securing their bread." To understand why the Indian who toasted God did so, we need to get beyond the stereotype of the drunken Indian. Although virtually all of the surviving evidence comes from colonial observers, we can, if we are sensitive to the clues, recapture at least some Indians' views on drinking.[3]

Surviving reports, however deeply mired in long-held cultural fears of alcoholic excess, provide sufficient evidence for us to place Indian drinking in a more specific historical context. That is, we can use the documents to adduce patterns of behavior among Indian drinkers. The meaning of an isolated incident that may have seemed aberrant or bizarre to a colonist can make more sense when we see it in combination with other incidents. Since observers' reports contain vital clues as to why Indians drank as they did,[4] we need to move beyond the authors' moralizing to arrive at a conclusion that would have shocked many colonists: Indians did not necessarily believe that to use alcohol as they did was to abuse it. The introduction of new words referring to drinking and alcohol in numerous Indian languages suggests that Indians needed terminology to explain the novel sensations that alcohol produced.[5] Those words presumably helped Indians understand liquor's effect, or at least facilitated discussion of liquor in Indian communities. Such discussions were necessary when many Indians devised what they believed to be sensible ways to drink. Even drinking to the point of unconsciousness made sense on occasion; it depended on the purpose of drinking. Rather than accept the judgment that Indians drank as they did because they lacked rules for drinking, we need to attend to the specific circumstances in which they drank.[6]

When Indians created rules for drinking liquor, they were in some sense not doing anything particularly novel. Many groups had long developed rituals to accompany the drinking of specific beverages (figures 10 and 11).

XV.
QVOMODO IMPERATOR
REGNI GVIANÆ, NOBILES SVOS OR-
nare & præparare soleat, si quando ad prandium vel
cœnam eos inuitare velit.

10. "The people in the kingdom of Guiana . . . are completely given over to
drunkenness, and surpass all nations in drinking," noted the caption to this image
in the late sixteenth century. "150 recline at once, drinking continuously for seven
or eight days, until they can no more." From Nino de Sylvia et al., *Americae Pars
VIII* (Frankfurt, 1599). Courtesy, The Historical Society of Pennsylvania.

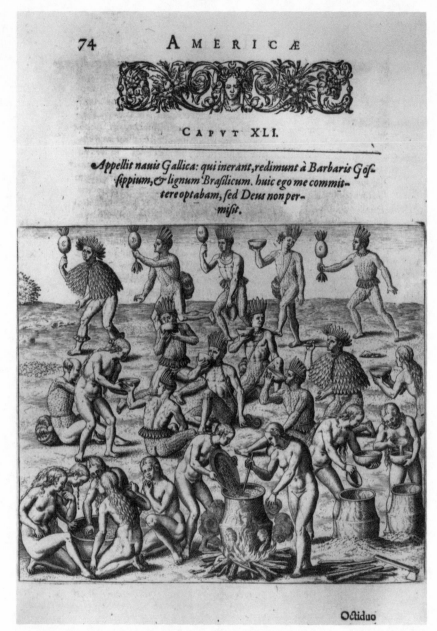

11. Although eastern woodlands Indians had no alcohol before Europeans provided it, they did have beverages reserved for rituals, notably the emetic "black drink" that was consumed in much of the southeast. From Johan von Staden, *Americae Pars Tertia* (Frankfurt, 1592). Courtesy, Library Company of Philadelphia.

CONSUMPTION

Compounds derived from various plants, notably the "black drink" made from the leaves of yaupan holly (*Ilex vomitoria*) consumed by Indians throughout the southeast, played a vital role in ceremonies. Creek men swallowed black drink in public rituals to establish or maintain political and social ties, both within the village and with visitors; those who drank also often smoked tobacco, another product used for ritual purposes. Since black drink contained caffeine, it acted as a stimulant, and on many occasions as an emetic; with either use, the drinker apparently sought a state of ritual purity.[7] The Guale Indians of the Georgia coast created an elaborate ritual for the consumption of cassina, also involving vomiting.[8] Such rituals could have a devastating impact on participants, as John Smith recognized in the early seventeenth century. "Every spring" Indians near Chesapeake Bay "make themselves sicke with drinking the juyce of a root they call *Wighsacan*, and water," he wrote in the 1620s, "whereof they powre so great a quantitie, that it purgeth them in a very violent manner; so that in three or foure days after, they scarce recover their former health."[9]

Indian cultures in the eastern woodlands were diverse and developed no single style of using mood-altering substances. Some Indians chose to integrate liquor into religious rituals; for others, alcohol had more political or social utility. In either case, drinking had functions other than inebriation for its own sake. Many Indians drank for three reasons: first, they valued the sense of power drunkenness apparently conferred; second, they employed alcohol in hospitality rituals; and third, they relied on liquor for mourning ceremonies. Further, Indians' assumption that a man who turned violent under the influence of alcohol could not be held accountable for his actions strongly suggests that they saw liquor as a powerful force that could not always be controlled.

Most of the records that reveal Indians' drinking practices focus on men. Indian women drank too, and some participated in rituals involving alcohol, but observers took less notice of women. Since many women avoided drinking sessions and even hid from drunken men, witnesses may have believed that women rarely drank. But women's absence from the documentary record does not mean that they abstained. Like Indian men, women also conformed to certain rules when they drank, even if we cannot recapture their practices.[10]

DEADLY MEDICINE

"The Water That Takes Away One's Wits"

Indians' ideas about drinking seem not to have changed much over the decades. Everywhere, observers claimed, Indians drank for the purpose of getting drunk. Complete drunkenness apparently conferred power on the drinker and, by extension, on the people who controlled the supply of alcohol. But inebriation was in itself a desirable state.

For many Indians in the eastern woodlands, liquor was not at first the destabilizing force it would eventually become. To be sure, from the start Indians knew about liquor's ability to alter one's perceptions, and many quickly discovered that drinking a great deal at any given time could lead to unconsciousness. Recognizing the power of alcohol yet apparently believing that it could bring benefits to the drinker, these Indians soon developed rules for drinking. In particular, as anthropologists have made clear for other societies,[11] many Indians tried to integrate alcohol into existing ceremonies. Though alcohol never took on the exact role it had taken in societies where liquor existed before colonization, Indians in eastern North America did integrate rum and brandy into hospitality and mourning rituals; some also wanted liquor to be available for marriages and ceremonial dances, though the desire for alcohol on these occasions has left only brief traces in the documentary record. Some Indians also recognized the anaesthetizing effects that alcohol could have for people in pain.[12] Still others absorbed alcohol into spiritual and psychological quests, using the disorientation associated with it to achieve a greater sense of personal power.

The most noteworthy aspect of Indian drinking styles, and the feature that most often caught the attention of colonial observers, was Indians' insistence on drinking to the point of intoxication. "The Savages have always been gluttons," the Jesuit missionary Paul Le Jeune, who lived among Indians in the St. Lawrence Valley, wrote in the 1630s, "but since the coming of the Europeans they have become such drunkards, that,—although they see clearly that these new drinks, the wine and brandy, which are brought to them, are depopulating their country, of which they themselves complain,— they cannot abstain from drinking, taking pride in getting drunk and in making others drunk."[13] Le Jeune described a people who seemingly drank with no reason or actual understanding of what they were doing, but his account also demonstrates that by the 1630s many Indians in Canada had already developed specific ideas about alcohol. "[G]ive two Savages two or three bottles of brandy," Le Jeune wrote, "they will sit down and, without eating, will drink, one after the other, until they have emptied them." Two years later he noted the same phenomenon. Indians, he wrote then, "are only too eager for our drinks,—both men and women experiencing a singular pleasure, not in drinking, but in becoming drunk, glorying in this and in making others so."[14] For these Indians liquor had only one use: intoxication. Drinking all the alcohol available at once reflected a conscious choice, not behavior learned from colonists.[15]

This aspect of Indian drinking remained constant for decades. A Jesuit missionary among the Cayugas (Oiogouens) wrote that though liquor had "wrought great havoc among them," and had thus "hindered the progress of the Gospel," the Indians in that community knew what they were doing. The missionary noted that "some drink only to intoxicate themselves; that they say so openly, and sing their intention to do so, before executing it, and that they are heard to shout: 'I am going to lose my head; I am going to drink of the water that takes away one's wits.' "[16]

François Vachon de Belmont, who became a Sulpician missionary in the early 1680s and traveled from France to northeastern Canada to convert Indians to Christianity, wrote the most extensive critique of Indian drinking patterns that has survived. Liquor, he argued, caused three basic changes in Indians. First, it "enlivens their natural sluggishness, dispels their timidity, their sense of shame and inferiority, which their dull nature gives them." Second, liquor prompted them "to undertake with vigor and bravado almost any evil action such as anger, vengeance, or impurity." Third, drunkenness provided Indians with "a valid excuse for any evil which they might commit in such a condition." These changes were unique to Indians, or so he thought when he wrote that "this is a peculiar kind of insobriety."[17]

Indians' determination to get drunk was most evident when the alcohol available to a group was limited. Rather than share the liquor equally, as Europeans presumably would do in such circumstances, the Indians chose one of their number to drink all of it and become inebriated, while the others remained sober. There was "only one degree of drunkenness worthwhile," Belmont wrote, "the sort which they call 'Gannontiouaratonseri,' complete insobriety. And when they begin to feel the effects of the brandy they rejoice shouting, 'Good, good, my head is reeling.' " Most of those who drank in this fashion were young men "who are professedly given to bravado, whose pride urges them to seek notoriety whereby they may receive attention for some deed or other."[18] The Reverend John Clayton, rector of the parish at James City, Virginia, during the mid-1680s, offered a similar view: "[T]hey will allways drink to excess if they can possibly get [spirits], but do not much care for them unless they can have enough to make them drunk.

[69]

I have heard it said that they wonder much of the English for purchasing wine at so dear a rate when Rum is much cheaper & will make them sooner drunk."[19]

Indians treated alcohol as if it were some sort of medicine that had to be taken in great quantity if the drinker were to derive any benefit from it. "They are great lovers of strong drink," Daniel Denton wrote in 1670, "yet do not care for drinking, unless they have enough to make themselves drunk; and if there be so many in their Company, that there is not sufficient to make them all drunk, they usually select so many out of their Company, proportionable to the quantity of drink, and the rest must be spectators." But the spectators were not passive witnesses to the process, according to Denton. "And if any one chance to be drunk before he hath finisht his proportion, (which is ordinarily a quart of Brandy, Rum, or Strong-waters) the rest will pour the rest of his part down his throat."[20] James Adair noted that liquor transformed Indians "into the likeness of mad foaming bears," and that "Indians in general do not chuse to drink any spirits, unless they can quite intoxicate themselves."[21] Or, as Francis Daniel Pastorius put it in 1700, Indians "love drunkenness." Cadwallader Colden agreed; in 1727 he wrote that Indians loved rum "more than their life."[22]

Whatever their particular motivation for getting drunk, at least some Indians who did so apparently felt liberated from their inhibitions. Many purportedly boasted about their powers. When they drank, one British official reported, "it is Usual for the Indians to utter Many Absurdities, they will tell the persons they most Esteem *that they are Cowards, that they will put them to death, that they are the Lords of the Ground they live upon &ca. . . .*"[23]

At times the release manifested itself in open sexual relations, both within the community and with colonial outsiders. The naturalist Nicholas Denys, who traveled through Acadia in the mid–seventeenth century, described in some detail the lascivious actions of intoxicated Indians, especially at a "drunken orgie" that he claimed could last up to three days; French sailors willingly took part in such affairs, apparently causing little ill will among Indians as a result.[24] Bernard Romans, another naturalist, left a more revealing description of the impact of alcohol on relations between men and women in a Choctaw community near the end of the colonial period. When the men began drinking, the women went to hide their weapons and returned "with a callebash under their wrappers." The men offered the women the bottles, and the women took "a draught and when not observed they empty it into the callebash, which when full they empty into bottles brought for that purpose, and thus they will accumulate two or three bottles full, and with the help of a little water, still make them more." After the men ran out of rum, the women informed them that they had still more, and the men then had to bargain with the women in order to get more to drink. "[I]n this way of trade," Romans concluded, the women "will often get all the effects the men can command for such a delicate nectar."[25] Though Romans avoided any hint that the drinking session then led to sexual liaisons, the women's deliberate manipulation of the liquor supply for their own ends suggests that alcohol eroded inhibitions that traditionally limited women's power in this community.

The sense of power that came to Choctaw women in drinking sessions reflects a wide range of alterations in village mores precipitated by alcohol. Their actions confirm that though drunkenness was the goal of drinking sessions, Indians sometimes tried to control the possible dangers of widespread intoxication by channeling the release of energies toward socially acceptable purposes. That is, drunkenness was not random but often integrated into a web of social relations associated with other aspects of public life. By the late colonial period, the Ojibway had a series of rituals and rules that regulated their use of alcohol. One group near Lake Superior created a system that encouraged drunkenness but made sure that the community did not suffer as a result: while the men drank, the women, who remained sober, exchanged rice for trade goods.[26]

John Lawson was particularly sensitive to the uses of alcohol and drunkenness by southeastern Indians, and he too noted the crucial role liquor could play in sexual relations. On his travels through South Carolina he observed the negotiations between colonial traders and local Indian women. Some women, he reported, were known as "Trading Girls, which are those design'd to get Money by their Natural Parts." They wore their hair in a distinctive way so that they would readily be identified as available. When a trader wanted to have sex with one of these women, according to Lawson, his supply of alcohol became crucial to the negotiations with the local "king" who governed such liaisons. If the trader had "got Rum to sell, be sure," Lawson wrote, "the King must have a large Dram for a fee, to confirm the Match."[27]

Other situations suggested an even closer link between liquor and sex. Lawson believed that Indian men plied Indian women with rum, and that this practice revealed both the high acceptance liquor enjoyed in their communities and its ability to undermine civility in them. In an attack on the morals of some Indian men, Lawson described the tactics they employed to find a sex partner. "When they have a Design to lie with a Woman, which they cannot obtain any otherwise than by a larger Reward than they are able to give, they then strive to make her drunk," he wrote, "which a great many of them will be; then they take the Advantage, to do with them what they please, and sometimes in their Drunkenness, cut off their Hair and sell it to the *English*, which is the greatest Affront can be offer'd them."[28] Alcohol did more than encourage sexual relations; used for such a purpose, apparently with no fear of punishment, it also became a threat to harmony between men and women.

In these varied sexual acts, the use of alcohol was typically public, as most drinking was. The public and communal function of drinking emerged clearly in gift-giving ceremonies. As we have seen, Indians were usually the repicients in gift exchanges involving liquor, but some Indians also gave liquor to their neighbors or to their visitors. In the early seventeenth century, according to an English colonist in the Chesapeake, Powhatan "caused to be fetched a great glasse of sacke, some three quarts or better, which Captain *Newport* had given him five or seaven yeeres since, carefully preserved by him, not much above a pint in all this time spent, and gave each of us in a great oister shell some three spoonefuls" before he directed other Indians to provide adequate lodgings for their visitors. Powhatan's sharing of his carefully preserved liquor stock with his guests reveals that alcohol was already seen as a means to retain good relations with the newcomers to the Chesapeake. Though evidence of such sharing is rare even for the eighteenth century, the practice was not unknown; one prosperous Connecticut Indian, known as King George, lived "after the English mode," and treated his guests "with a glass of good wine."[29]

The demands of hospitality and the desire to share one's supply of alcohol with one's neighbors emerged throughout the East, and so did the belief that drinking together could solidify relations between the drinkers. Indians who treated with colonial leaders often requested a supply of liquor to take back to their villages. In the mid–eighteenth century, one Wea leader eagerly sought a barrel of brandy at a Miami trading post so that he could return to his village with the proper gift for the community, and thereby avoid shame.[30] Exactly the same logic prompted a group of St. Joseph Indians to seek alcohol from George Croghan when he was traveling in the Ohio country in 1765. Well versed in the intricacies of hinterland political and economic dealings, Croghan gave them two kegs of rum, along with other goods, "for your young People," as he told them, "that you may return home without shame as you desired."[31] In doing so, he was following established practice:

officials had been including alcohol among their gifts to Indians since at least the 1730s.[32]

Provincial officials reinforced the customary uses of drinking by getting Indians to share in a ubiquitous colonial drinking custom: toasting. The Indian chief who lifted a glass to the Christians' God in response to the Reverend Harte's sermon was hardly unique. The minutes for a treaty between Iroquois leaders and Pennsylvania officials in Philadelphia in 1742 noted that when George Thomas, the lieutenant governor of the province, ended the first day's meeting, he called for "Wine and other Liquors, according to the *Indian* Custom. . . ."[33] On the contrary, the Indians' had adopted the colonists' custom as a means to extend their drinking sessions. Conrad Weiser told of a group of Iroquois who were greeted with "a Dram round" when they came to the post at Oswego in June 1745 to meet colonial officials. Their thirsts not yet quenched, they wanted more. "The Black Prince asked for another to drink the King's health," Weiser recalled, "which they had, & afterwards the said Indian, at a 2d. visit asked for a 3d. to drink the Governor of N. York's health, which they had also." The next day the Indians came back, and after Weiser "treated them with a Dram," he gave them two gallons of rum to take away with them, "to drink the King of Great Britain's health in Montreal after their Arrival."[34] Knowing the importance of toasts, Weiser later treated Indians in the Ohio country with rum, and "the King's health was drunk by Indians and white men."[35] The missionary Christian Frederick Post, traveling in 1758 with a message from Governor William Denny of Pennsylvania to the Indians in the Ohio valley, watched one colonial official make a series of toasts during a meeting with a group of Cherokees and Catawbas. After drinking to the king's health, Post wrote, he "drank King *Beaver's,* Shingas; and all the Warriors' healths." Though Post did not record any reciprocal toasts on the part of the Indians, he did note that they "parted in love, and well satisfied."[36] George Croghan, the intrepid colonial negotiator, kept a list of toasts, presumably for use in such venues; James Kenny thought that a colonial official who refused to toast the king "was not very fit to be Trusted as an Indian Agent for ye Crown of England."[37] Though these occasions all suggest the seriousness with which colonists and Indians adopted toasting rituals when they treated with colonial officials, some Indians also mocked the convention, as one colonist noted in the late seventeenth century when he passed by a group of Indians in the midst of a drunken revel. According to his account, "one cried to another swear swear, you be Englishman swear, w[i]th that he made a horrid yelling, imperfectly vomited up oaths, whereupon the other cryd, oh! now your [sic] be Englishman."[38]

When Indians mocked colonial rituals in such ways, colonists apparently did not always get the joke. The Iroquois sachem Canasatego, in Lancaster to negotiate a treaty with officials of Virginia, Maryland, and Pennsylvania in 1744, used the British-French rivalry and the importance of toasting to get some rum. "You tell us you beat the *French*," he declared on July 3, "if so, you must have taken a great deal of Rum from them, and can the better spare us some of that Liquor to make us rejoice with you in the Victory." In response, Pennsylvania's lieutenant governor, George Thomas, and the other commissioners "ordered a Dram of Rum to be given to each in a small Glass, calling it, *A French Glass*." Canasatego saw his opening. The next day he told the colonists, "We mentioned to you Yesterday the Booty you had taken from the *French*, and asked you for some of the Rum which we supposed to be Part of it, and you gave us some; but it turned out unfortunately that you gave us it in *French* Glasses, we now desire you will give us some in *English* Glasses." Thomas took them at their word, hoping that Canasatego's speech demonstrated the Iroquois's commitment to the English. "We are glad to hear you have such a Dislike for what is *French*," he declared. "They cheat you in your Glasses, as well as in every thing else." But the colonists were far from "*Williamsburg, Annapolis*, and *Philadelphia*, where our Rum Stores are," and the Indians had already consumed most of the rum that the commissioners had brought with them. "[B]ut, notwithstanding this, we have enough left to fill our *English* Glasses, and will shew the Difference between the Narrowness of the *French*, and the Generosity of your Brethren the *English* towards you." The Indians were delighted and "gave, in their Order, five *Yo-hahs*." The commissioners ordered the rum "and some middle sized Wine Glasses," and then "drank Health to the *Great King of* ENGLAND and the *Six Nations*, and put an End to the Treaty by three loud Huzza's, in which all the Company joined."[39]

Mastery of the protocols of treaties enabled Indians to get alcohol when they participated in colonial drinking rituals, but other drinking rituals are more difficult to interpret. Some documents suggest that Indians also drank alcohol in an attempt to gain an altered spiritual state, perhaps an actual possession of their souls by spirits. Some scholars have connected this desire for a state of altered consciousness to the importance of dreams in the cultures of the eastern woodlands; such a link is tempting, for the importance of dreams and visions in early America is amply documented.[40]

But residents of Indian country did not make explicit links between drinking and dreaming, and the medical literature on drinking casts doubt on such an interpretation. Since drunkenness does not cause hallucinations—alcoholic hallucinosis is a withdrawal symptom experienced by habitual drinkers when they stop drinking—it is perhaps unwise to presume that Indians drank to induce visions.[41]

The documents suggest a different sort of quest. Some Indians believed themselves to become more powerful when they were drunk. "The Savages have told me many a time that they did not buy our liquors on account of any pleasant taste they found in them, or because they had any need of them," a missionary recalled in the early 1640s, "but simply to become intoxicated,—imagining, in their drunkenness, that they become persons of importance, taking pleasure in seeing themselves dreaded by those who do not taste the poison."[42] A century later the colonial agent Lachlan Mackintosh informed Governor William Lyttleton of South Carolina that a group of Keowee Indians needed rum because in a dream they learned that their upcoming battle would go badly unless they had rum before it.[43] Louis Antoine de Bougainville perhaps expressed prevailing thoughts most clearly when he wrote in 1757 that "their paradise is drinking." Though he exaggerated when he said that Indians could think of no better way to die than by drinking themselves to death, he sensed that some Indians drank in order to transport themselves psychologically to an altered state.[44]

Liquor's ability to alter perception led many Indians to consider it a sacred substance. Such beliefs crossed various cultural boundaries in Indian America. Montagnais in the St. Lawrence Valley believed that liquor had magical powers.[45] Similarly, some Plains Indians, who first received alcohol from traders in the seventeenth century, valued liquor because they appreciated its seemingly supernatural powers. The Teton Sioux termed it *mni wakon,* translated as "sacred water." Drinking liquor proved an ideal way of communicating with the spirit world; it emboldened warriors, some of whom then turned their newfound powers on other members of their communities.[46] The seventeenth-century French historian Pierre François Xavier de Charlevoix also wrote that Indians believed alcohol had supernatural power. When the Count de Frontenac asked one Ottawa Indian—"who was a bad christian and a great drunkard," in Charlevoix's opinion—"what he thought the brandy he was so fond of was made of, he said, of tongues and hearts; for, added he, after I have drank of it I fear nothing and I talk like an angel."[47] Indians elsewhere, perceiving supernatural qualities in alcohol, tried to harness liquor to their needs. By the early nineteenth century, if not earlier, Ojibways had integrated alcohol into healing rituals. To this day some Indians believe that supernatural forces control the supply of alcohol; the Passamaquoddys, who apparently received alcohol in the early colonial period, have long thought that the positive and negative spirits that control the world fight over, among other things, the provision of liquor to their communities.[48]

Perhaps the most significant sign of the religious importance of intoxication was the role that drinking came to play in mourning rituals. Eastern woodlands Indians had long practiced elaborate burial rites, as even early observers noted in detail, and when they included alcohol in such rituals they were using drunkenness to serve an already well-established custom.[49] The earliest sign of the use of alcohol in mourning rituals appeared in the writing of David Peterson de Vries, who traveled along the east coast of North America in the 1630s and 1640s. After asserting that these Indians "have no religion, as far as I could learn, except that they pay some respect to the sun and moon," he acknowledged that they "make no offerings, except they observe certain superstitions, in their drunken festivals." This was particularly evident in ceremonies marking the death of a community leader. "They hold a solemn feast upon the death of their cassique chiefs, or other great friends," de Vries wrote in 1655, "making the best provision of their strongest liquor, which they call *Perrouw*, for three or four days, or as long as their liquor lasts; and spending the time in dancing, singing, and drinking,—in which they exceed all other heathen nations that I have ever seen,—esteeming him the bravest fellow who first gets drunk. While they are drinking, the wives of the next friends of the deceased stand crying and howling." Though de Vries dismissed the significance of the ritual, and noted that the Indians' "priests and soothsayers" at times communicated with the Devil, his account of the ritual suggests early incorporation of alcohol into longstanding custom.[50]

By the mid–eighteenth century, though the documentary record does not offer many examples, other Indians also drank at funerals or at feasts commemorating fallen community members. One missionary reported that the Housatonic Indians had previously gotten drunk at dances and in mourning ceremonies but had abandoned the practice. The Protestant missionary Gideon Hawley, who repeatedly ran into alcohol-associated problems during a 1753 trip to Oquaga, a community of Indians of various tribes on the Susquehanna River, inadvertently initiated such a ritual. Discovering too late that one of his traveling companions was peddling liquor during the journey, Hawley soon witnessed the use of liquor in a mourning ritual. "We soon saw the ill effects" of the trader's rum, he wrote in his journal in 1753.

"The Indians begin to drink, and some of our party were the worse for it. We perceived what was coming." That night the missionary awoke to "the howling of the Indians over their dead," and calm did not soon return. "We arose very early the next morning," he wrote. "We soon saw the Indian women and their children skulking in the adjacent bushes, for fear of the intoxicated Indians, who were drinking deeper. The women were secreting guns, hatchets, and every deadly or dangerous weapon, that murder or harm might not be the consequence. Poor unhappy mortals! without law, religion or government; and therefore without restraint." Hawley was not the ideal enthnographer to come upon such a scene, for he became angered by the inebriated Indians (one of whom nearly shot his head off, apparently by accident) during his journey.[51] But drunken Indians singing over the deaths of their friends and relatives provide at least a hint that some drunkenness was intended either to facilitate contact with the spirit world or to help the drinkers mourn a loved one's departure to that world.

Later, near the end of the colonial period, better evidence suggests that Indians who lived farther west, beyond the limits of colonial settlements, actively sought liquor for funerals and memorial rites. The descriptions of such ceremonies in the Great Lakes region and the Ohio Valley, territory at the far margins of British trade interests, suggest the ties between inebriation and contact with the spirit world. When the trader Peter Pond traveled through the Great Lakes region in the early 1770s he witnessed the ritual use of alcohol by a group of Fox Indians who had traveled to a particular area

to Pay thare Respect to thare Departed frend. They Had a small Cag of Rum and sat around the grave. Thay fild thar Callemeat [Calumet] and Began thar saremony By Pinting the Stem of the Pipe upward—then giveing it a turn in thare and then toward ye head of the Grav—then East & West, North & South after which thay smoaked it out and fild it agane & Lade [it] By—then thay took Sum Rum out of the Cag in a Small Bark Vessel and Pourd it on the Head of the Grave By way of giving it to thar Departed Brother—then thay all Drank themselves. . . .

They continued to drink and reminisce about their lost friend, who was himself a drinker of some repute. "They Amused themselves in this manner til thay all fell a Crying and a woful Nois thay Mad for a While til thay thought Wisely that thay Could Not Bring him Back and it would Not Due to Greeve two much—that an application to the Cag was the Best Way to

Dround Sorrow & Wash away Greefe for the Moshun was Put in Execution and all Began to be Marey as a Party Could Bea. Thay Continued til Near Nite." Later, still apparently inebriated, the men "apeared Very amaras" toward the women in the area, most of whom apparently did not drink; when the men urged Pond to join in, he decided it was time to leave.[52] The trader John Long, too, realized the link between mourning rituals and drinking when several Chippewas approached him to ask for "a small keg of the strong water, to drink to the health of our brother and sister, whom we have sent to the far country. . . ."[53]

The drinking observed by these travelers conformed to general patterns of consumption in Indian communities. The drinking that took place at mourning rituals followed typical drinking practices and was thus dominated by men. But perhaps the most significant evidence of the spiritual significance of drink came in a ceremony observed by the missionary David Zeisberger in the Ohio Valley in the late colonial period. After describing the often troublesome behavior that alcohol caused in Indian villages—people who drank at Zoneschio, the town where he stayed, did not want to live there because of the drunken excesses that took place there—Zeisberger noted a particularly unusual disturbance. "Our hostess with other women became very drunk and disturbed us the whole night," he wrote in his journal. But then they came to apologize and explain their actions. "They excused themselves," he noted, "asking us not to remember it against them, because they were obliged to drink for the dead. For this reason, they were not able to offer us any of their liquor, a cause for thankfulness on our part."[54]

The women's explanation, brief though it was, offers a rare glimpse into the ways at least one group of Indians used liquor to advance a particular social goal. The women apologized because they had violated commonly accepted norms in two distinct ways: by disturbing visitors and by failing to share with them. But the demands of the dead had to be attended to, and these women placed that obligation above whatever they might have owed to Zeisberger and his party. In an age when offering hospitality was universal in Indian country, the women's steadfast determination to become drunk because they owed it to the memory of the dead, or to maintain necessary alliances with the spirit world, suggests that religious principles dictated many of the contours of these Indians' lives. The intoxication needed to perform this particular ceremony suggests that alcohol had already become an integral part of this community's way of maintaining its religious identity. And with death from disease or war so often stalking Indian communities, many villages had ample opportunity to practice such rites.

The inclusion of liquor in hospitality customs and mourning rituals reveals that alcohol did not necessarily disrupt community life. Like Indians in Central America and the Southwest, who had long possessed liquor,[55] Indians in eastern North America tried to harness the power of alcohol and to make drunkenness serve traditional or other socially approved ends. European observers rarely appreciated the careful patterns evident in many drinking festivals, so fearful were they of the violence that they quickly came to associate with drinking. And though most of that violence was vented on other Indians, these observers always feared that they themselves would become the ultimate victims. Still, their descriptions reveal that most Indians got drunk not to satisfy some craving but for reasons that made sense at the time. And perhaps the greatest proof of liquor's power among eastern woodlands Indians emerged in an unexpected place: the ways in which villages treated members who committed violence when they were drunk.

"The Liquor Is Criminal and Not the Man"

According to abundant documentary sources, a variety of Indian groups, at least partly in response to the threats posed to their communities by epidemic diseases and land-hungry colonists, worked assiduously to reduce any tensions within their villages and strictly punished people who exacerbated them by violent behavior. Anyone who committed an act of aggression generally received swift retribution from the victim or the victim's kin group.[56] But many Indians forgave perpetrators who had been drinking when they committed their crimes, because they had been drunk. The practice amazed missionaries, perhaps because they were witnessing Jesus' injunction to turn the other cheek being transformed into a justification for distinctly unchristian behavior.

Throughout Indian country, common ways of seeking vengeance did not apply to Indians who committed indiscretions when they were drunk. Time and again the Jesuit fathers recorded Indians' conversations on the subject. The missionary Jacques Bruyas, who believed that drunkenness was (along with "dreams, And Impurity") one of the chief impediments to Indians' conversion to Christianity, noted in the late 1660s that though Onneiouts (Oneidas) "often became Intoxicated with the intention of killing those to whom they bear ill will, yet all is then forgiven, and you have no other

Satisfaction than this: 'What wouldst thou have me do? I had no sense; I was drunk.' " Later he elaborated on the prevailing logic of such situations. "When our Savages have received an injury from any one," Bruyas reported, "they get half drunk and do with impunity all that Passion suggests for them. All the satisfaction one receives from them is embraced in two words: 'He was drunk; he had lost his reason.' "[57] Indians in Pennsylvania in the late seventeenth century apparently shared this belief. Gabriel Thomas noted that the Indians he encountered in the province rarely quarreled if they were sober, only when they were "Boozy"; under such circumstances, other community members "readily pardon it, alledging the Liquor is Criminal and not the Man."[58] Indians in New France shared the same notion in the early eighteenth century.[59] Near the end of the colonial period Lieutenant Henry Timberlake noted that among the Indians he knew best, the Cherokees, "no one will revenge any injury (murder excepted) received from one who is no more himself."[60]

Perhaps Indian communities exonerated the perpetrators of drink-related crimes because drunkenness had seemingly magical effects. Whatever beliefs Indians had about alcohol's links to the spirit world, some took advantage of prevailing customs to release their aggressions against others. Such actions could be personal, as one French observer argued in January 1690 when he noted that Indians "get drunk very often on purpose to have the priviledge of satisfying their old grudges," because punishment "cannot be inflicted on them" in such circumstances.[61] Sometimes such actions were carried out with the sanction of the larger community; in 1679 the family of a woman whose former husband had beaten her, reportedly in a drunken rage, made "themselves drunk" and then "avenged the cruel treatment inflicted on their relative."[62] Some colonial observers agreed that Indians took advantage of such attitudes to attack their enemies without fear of retribution. A Sulpician missionary certainly thought so. "It is a somewhat common custom amongst them when they have enemies," he reported, "to get drunk and afterwards go and break their heads or stab them to death, so as to be able to say afterward that they committed the wicked act when they were not in their senses." He even believed that it was the Indians' "custom not to mourn for those who have died in this manner, for fear of causing pain to the living by reminding him of his crime."[63]

The ability of attackers to escape punishment in this way suggests that communities accepted the idea that liquor was responsible for their actions; it made no sense to punish the person who committed the crime when the true offender was alcohol. "They never call any Man to account for what he did, when he was drunk," the explorer John Lawson recorded in the early eighteenth century, "but say, it was the Drink that caused his Misbehaviour, therefore he ought to be forgiven." For the Saponis, the prohibition was so strict that when colonists executed one of them for a crime he committed while intoxicated in the 1720s, tension grew between them and officials in Williamsburg.[64]

The practice was so deeply entrenched among Indians in Carolina in the 1730s that a Lower Creek leader, Tomochichi, was able to persuade the Indian victim of an assault by a drunken colonist to forgive the perpetrator. The act was remarkable because James Oglethorpe was on the verge of punishing the colonist for his actions. At first the victim, Fanseen, did not want the perpetrator to go unpunished, but he yielded to Tomochichi's logic: the " 'Englishman being drunk, he beat you; if he is whipt for so doing, the Englishmen will expect that if an Indian should insult them when drunk, the Indian should be whipt for it.' " Reminding Fanseen that he too tended to become argumentative when he drank, Tomochichi persuaded him to petition Oglethorpe for the man's release. "As soon as I granted [the pardon]," Oglethorpe reported, "Tomo chi-chi and Fanseen ran and untied him; which I perceived was done to shew that he owed his Safety to their Intercession."[65] Self-interest perhaps explained part of the Indians' actions; but more important was the idea that any action committed by a drunken person, even a drunken colonist, should be forgiven.

Exonerating someone accused of a crime while drunk made sense if the status of being drunk carried specific meaning in Indian villages. "They pardon murder committed by drunkards," the traveler Louis Antoine de Bougainville wrote in 1758, when he was in Montreal. "A drunken man is a sacred person. According to them it is a state so delicious that it is permitted, even desirable to arrive at; it is their paradise. Then one is not responsible for his acts." Such a posture differed dramatically from the normal procedures followed after an assault. "[O]rdinarily, they themselves calmly punish cold-blooded murderers with a speedy death," Bougainville noted, "neither proceeded nor followed by any formalities."[66] Members of some communities even fashioned a punitive judicial system by identifying miscreants who needed to be eliminated and then getting their putative executioner drunk so that he (all of the known cases involved men) would then be free of revenge from the family of the deceased. Conrad Weiser, one of the most astute observers of Indian behavior in the middle colonies, recorded a variant of such practices. "The criminal is made drunk," he wrote in 1746, "and perhaps a quarrel is begun with him by the one who is appointed to do it, who then charges him with his offence, and at the same time informs him of the cause of his *death*. And in the ensuing quarrel he is *killed*, and the *rum* bears the blame, so that the *avenger of blood* has no power over the doer of the deed."[67]

The functions served by drinking varied with the group of Indians: to enhance hospitality, to appease deities, to bring temporary respite from quotidian troubles, to create or solidify alliances, to facilitate bouts of spirit possession, to lower inhibitions and allow freer communication.[68] But the transformation of alcohol from an agent with seemingly beneficial uses to a substance that contributed to violence posed problems for many Indian communities. Whether Indians turned violent when they drank because they learned to do so from traders or because liquor allowed them to overcome customary restraints, the very fact of the violence—most of it directed against other Indians, contrary to the fears of colonists—indicates the adoption of a particular cultural use of alcohol. Without a long tradition of knowing how to respond to the effects of alcohol, Indians who drank did so, at least at first, without fully understanding its threat to their communities. Even when the dangers of alcohol had become widely known, many Indians continued to use it in socially acceptable ways.

Colonists' search for profit explains their motivations for maintaining the trade, but it does not tell us why Indians kept on drinking once they knew that alcohol devastated their communities. To solve that puzzle, we need to keep in mind the events that were reshaping the lives of eastern woodlands Indians. The death that daily surrounded and threatened them then is almost incomprehensible to us now. We know that the population of American Indians declined by at least 90 percent by the end of the colonial period, mostly because of the spread of epidemic diseases. But it is difficult to grasp what it must have been like for Indians in a village when smallpox or measles swept through, killing half or more of the community, and then to have to migrate to a new area to create a new community, only to have the new village assaulted by more pathogens. Add to the recurring epidemics the periodic participation of many Indians in wars, and the threats posed to communities by an expanding, land-hungry colonial population, and it seems obvious that these Indians constantly battled tragedy and disaster. Death was everywhere, and it ripped families apart, upset the social order, interfered with vital economic pursuits, and eroded the social ties needed to hold communities together.

If Indians drank because they were depressed by the ubiquitous presence of death, they would not be alone. Throughout the world groups that have experienced profound and unsettling change have tended to drink heavily when liquor was available.[69] Perhaps young Indian men felt these pressures more intensely than other members of their community and so they drank more often. After all, young men had special responsibilities in the hunt, and they were less successful in that area of their lives than they had been before colonization because the game was being depleted. Perhaps they simply had greater access to alcohol because they were the ones most likely to meet liquor-toting traders. But since we know that drinking crossed gender and generational boundaries, it seems likely that the urge to drink could be felt by anyone.[70]

Mourning rituals represented some Indians' most obvious efforts to use alcohol to come into contact with the spirit world and to incorporate alcohol into their traditional cultural activities. Though ritual uses of alcohol were relatively rare, according to the documentary record, they suggest the positive potential some Indians saw in liquor.[71] That is, some Indians drank—maybe even drank destructively—voluntarily and for positive results. And it is at this point that we gain some understanding as to why Indians drank generally.

Drinking represented an effort to redefine the contours of one's daily life. Drinking to the point of intoxication could have been an attempt to escape the world, and if Indians drank for that reason, we could certainly understand why. Yet Indians drank for more specific reasons as well. Drinking provided many Indians with an avenue to a more desired state of mind, one in which they seemed to have temporarily gained power and control over their lives once again. Many Indian drinkers probably enjoyed the sensation of drunkenness, though they were quick to point out that they did not particularly like the taste of the alcohol the colonists sold to them.[72] That many Indians used this enhanced sense of power to act violently toward others signifies not some sort of cultural inferiority, as colonists would have us believe, but the enormous frustrations and angers that understandably built up among peoples who witnessed their world always on the defensive, always under assault by a colonizing power. Indians did not succumb meekly to colonizers; some fought back with guns and other weapons, and many learned how to negotiate with their uninvited British and French visitors, using refined diplomatic skills to advance the concerns of their communities and thereby shape their part of the postcontact world.[73] But many others sought accommodation and tried to better their position by getting what they could from colonists. A direct link between drinking and heightened powers

DEADLY MEDICINE

may not have been recognized by all eastern woodlands Indians, but Indians quite possibly learned about the power of alcohol from one another, perhaps along trade routes that at least occasionally bore the weight of Indians carrying rum to other Indians who wanted the release alcohol brought.

In the long run, of course, the magic that Indians tried to harness through drinking became overpowering. Most Indians in early America drank to get drunk, often with horrendous consequences. But they also drank because they believed, as other peoples have done, that liquor could restore them to positions of authority in a world that had spun out of their control. In such a context, the Indian who toasted the English God was neither fool nor dupe; he was merely trying to harness the power of a sacred substance and put it to the task of appeasing a seemingly powerful deity. Like Indians who adopted other European wares in an effort to improve their lives, the toasting Indian leader believed he could better his life by drinking. To us, such a view seems irrational, especially since we know that drinking was the social and economic ruin of countless Indian villages. But to him, and to many other Indians, such a perspective probably made as much sense as any other effort to regain a psychological stronghold in a world gone seemingly astray.

CHAPTER FOUR
Costs

... the fruits whereof are murther & other outrages. ...
—Massachusetts General Court, May 6, 1657, outlawing the sale
of liquor to Indians in the province

Whatever path liquor purveyors took to haul their wares to Indian drinkers, the binges that typically followed revealed a remarkable similarity of drinking practices among the diverse inhabitants of Indian country. By failing to rein in inebriates, Indian communities throughout the eastern woodlands found themselves forced to cope with often daunting challenges. In alcohol's empire, Indians suffered.

The documentary record of the social costs of alcohol is vast. Evidence of Indian drinking and of the problems it created appears in colonial statutes, travelers' accounts, traders' ledgers, missionaries' diaries, and treaty negotiations, to name only the most prominent locations. Yet the abundant accounts are not necessarily the surest evidence of abusive drinking among Indians. Colonists' descriptions become formulaic, often resembling Franklin's depiction of inebriated Indians at Carlisle. Further, colonial sources emphasize the consumption of alcohol by hunters; they pay far less attention to the drinking practices of older men, women, and children.[1] Finally, colonists often ignored the many Indians who abstained, thus giving the mistaken impression that all Indians drank. Still, the surviving evidence, however flawed, points unambiguously toward one conclusion: Indians paid dearly to quench their thirst for rum.

Indians agreed with colonists that liquor brought problems, though they drew their own conclusions about how alcohol changed their lives and who was responsible for liquor-related troubles. There are, to be sure, problems in interpreting Indian testimony too. It has survived in documents written primarily by colonists and was thus no doubt constructed through certain culturally defined parameters. Further, colonists were not always aware of the benefits that many Indians believed they derived from alcohol, especially of the value they placed on the disorientation of inebriation.

Although Indians throughout eastern North America often organized their drinking in culturally approved ways, many nonetheless came to believe that liquor created tension and animosity in their villages, dangerously reoriented the economies of their communities, led to domestic violence, and facilitated the further conquest of eastern North America by colonists. Though some Indians blamed other Indians for the ill effects of drinking, many placed the responsibility for their problems on colonists, who either participated in the trade directly or allowed it to continue in spite of mounting evidence of its enormous costs. Colonists, not Indians, had initiated what an anonymous author, purported to be a Creek Indian, had termed "the bewitching Tyranny of Custom."[2] As many Indians discovered, the alcohol trade became perhaps the most insidious aspect of European colonialism in North America.

Alcohol undermined Indian villages by eroding the civility necessary to maintain community. It contributed to the demographic catastrophe that reduced Indian populations. The pursuit of rum and brandy led Indians into poverty. And drinking spawned a culture of violence. Corpses did not always litter the ground after a rum shipment arrived in an Indian community, but sometimes they did, and those bodies were only the most visible reminder of the toll the liquor trade took in Indian country.

Alcohol and Civility

To Indians and colonists alike, most Indian communities were orderly. It might have seemed to migrants from Europe that Indian villages bore no resemblance to Old World communities, and many certainly objected to the transhument practices of eastern woodlands Indians. But from the time that John White portrayed the orderly settlement of Indians in coastal Carolina, visual depictions of Indian villages suggested stability and a type of model, if primitive, form of economy.[3] The residents' views on their communities obviously would have varied from place to place, but the documentary evidence suggests that most believed they inhabited an orderly universe. At treaty negotiations Indians often requested retention of the territory around particular towns, suggesting a sense of continuity even among peoples suffering population loss. And one of the things Indians hoped to preserve in their communities was goodwill among the residents. Indian leaders and their colonial counterparts alike recognized that social harmony in Indian villages would promote peaceful relations between Indians and colonists.

Alcohol threatened the preservation of order in Indian villages, as countless observers maintained. Even in treaty negotiations, the solemn decorum that characterized the formal sessions broke down entirely when Indians received parcels of liquor. Where the alcohol trade was greatest, the problem was most evident. Indian agents in South Carolina and the hinterland of the middle colonies complained that they could not conduct business once the Indians began to drink. As one reported in 1760, Indians along the Susquehanna River were "Like as Maney Raiging Divels" who wanted to roast visiting colonists. Drinking did not have to lead to accidents and deaths to disrupt the peace. The problem of disorder became magnified when Indian communities drank for several days at a time.[4] "From the 16th to the 26th we *cold* do nothing," a frustrated George Croghan reported from western Pennsylvania in January 1754, "the Indians being Constantly drunk."[5]

To missionaries the disorder that alcohol caused went beyond mere annoyance. One Moravian flatly stated in the 1740s that "when [an Indian] is drunk, he looks like a Devil."[6] The rum trade, by encouraging Indians in licentiousness and disorder, interfered with the missionaries' efforts to convert them to English ways. Inebriated Indians could not, they believed, make the rational choice to convert; made senseless by liquor, they could not grasp the full import of the missionaries' teachings, or, worse still, they turned against God in their drunken raving.[7] Such views were common among Catholics in Canada—one observer noted that whenever French colonists and Indians got together with brandy "there is an open hell"[8]—and British colonists had similar thoughts. David Brainerd, working at Shamokin in 1745, wrote that Indians there "are accounted the most drunken, mischievous, and ruffianlike fellows, of any of these parts . . . satan seems to have his seat in this town in an eminent manner." Soon after, he noted that Indians there "live so near the white people that they are always in the way of strong liquor, as well as of the ill examples of *nominal* Christians; which renders it so unspeakably difficult to treat with them about Christianity."[9] At times missionaries themselves came under fire for allegedly taking liquor to Indians and thus compromising the effort to spread Christianity. In a sermon published in Boston in 1704 Cotton Mather attacked an "Indian-Preacher" who armed himself with both Scripture and liquor, "but he minded his Bottel more than his *Bible*."[10] Zeal to stop the trade was also evident among Indian converts, notably Samson Occom, who railed against the "sin" of intemperance and associated drinking with a wide range of problems.[11]

Some of the disorder the liquor trade precipitated mattered more to colonial observers than Indian participants. The role of alcohol in the sex lives of Indians, for example, fascinated some colonists. They believed, no doubt drawing insight from their own cultures, that liquor released Indians from their sexual inhibitions. Drunken Indian men and women ran naked through the streets of Quebec and "in full view and to the great horror of all, they engaged openly, like wild beasts, in shameful and unspeakable acts with one another," according to a French observer in the late seventeenth century.[12] Natural historians, always keen to describe Indian practices, paid close attention to the relationship between liquor and sex. Nicholas Denys, during his travels in Acadia, and Bernard Romans, during his sojourn in East and West Florida, noted that consumption of alcohol had an immediate impact on Indians' sexual behavior.[13] So did William Bartram, who, while touring the southeast in the early 1770s, found a rapid change in a group of Creeks drinking near Mount Royal, in Georgia, after they had returned from St. Augustine with "a very liberal supply of spirituous liquors, about twenty kegs, each containing five gallons." Once they began to drink, they continued for ten days. "In a few days this festival exhibited one of the most ludicrous bacchanalian scenes that is possible to be conceived," Bartram wrote. "White and red men and women without distinction, passed the day merrily with these jovial, amorous topers, and the nights in convivial songs, dances, and sacrifices to Venus, as long as they could stand or move; for in these frolics both sexes take such liberties with each other, and act, without constraint or shame, such scenes as they would abhor when sober or in their senses; and would endanger their ears and even their lives. . . ." At last, however, the liquor ran out. Most of the Creeks were "sick through intoxication," and when they sobered up, "the dejected lifeless sots would pawn every thing they were in possession of, for a mouthful of spirits to settle their stomachs, as they termed it."[14]

While some colonists lamented the sexual license that liquor led to, others focused on the disorder that they knew must accompany drinking. On the eve of settlement the governor and deputy of the New England Company forbade colonists bound for Massachusetts Bay to sell liquor to Indians. "Wee pray you endeavor," they wrote, "though there be much strong waters sent for sale, yett so to order it as that the savages may not for [our] lucre sake bee induced to the excessive use, or rather abuse of it, and of any hand take care [our] people give noe ill example. . . ."[15] William Bradford, ever wary of any threat to Plymouth's order, acted swiftly to limit what he believed were the dangerous excesses of Thomas Morton's antics at Merrymount. Among Morton's sins, along with providing the Indians with firearms and scrawling salacious verse on a Maypole, was his apparent provision of liquor to Indians.[16]

Indians too were concerned about turmoil during drinking bouts. A group of Chickasaws informed a colonial official in 1725 that they were unable to keep members of their village under control because "if the Young Men were drunk and Mad," they "could not help it," but they would do their best to minimize the problems.[17] Several Nanticokes were more desperate when they appealed to Maryland authorities in November 1713. "[T]hough we are all good Friends," their spokesman declared when he protested the sale of liquor by two colonists, "yet Rum & Cyder will make Indians quarrel & Storys will be made & Indian Women with child will be frighted."[18] Were these Nanticokes alluding to some miscarriages brought on by the fears pregnant women experienced during drinking melees? Here, as in so many cases, the surviving evidence provides only tantalizing clues to some of the most wrenching costs of the liquor trade.

Alcohol also disrupted Indian families, often with disastrous consequences. A French observer reported horrifying news: "A husband will kill his wife, and those women who get as drunk as the men knife their husbands and their children and strangle them without knowing what they are doing."[19] Such horrors, if they took place, presumably occurred infrequently, though stories of such assaults appeared in early histories of particular groups.[20] Other family tensions were more common. A group of Delaware Indians told Charles Beatty, who was traveling through the Ohio country in 1766 on an exploratory venture for the Presbyterian Church, that they wanted to complain about the participation of Indian women in the trade. "[T]here are some that do at times hire some of our Squaws to goe to Bed with them & give them rum for it," they declared; "this thing is very Bad, & the Squaws again selling the Rum to our People make them Drunk. . . ." Though intercultural sexual relations were not new in the region, these Indians found the inclusion of rum in the relationship wholly inappropriate. "[W]e Beseech you," they concluded, "to advise our Brothers against this thing & do what you can to have it stopped. . . ."[21] Other colonists feared that traders who took advantage of Indian women by plying them with alcohol would weaken necessary alliances, especially during wartime. James Sterling, the commissary of the British post at Fort Detroit, filled his letters with condemnations of his counterpart at Niagara, John Collbeck, who was constantly drunk himself, allowed his employees to drink whenever they wanted, and kept "a Seraglio of Indian Squahs in the Same Condition."[22]

By the mid–eighteenth century, faced with a growing body of evidence that drunken Indians threatened colonists as well as Indians, some observers blamed the traders. "While the present ill adapted measures are continued," James Adair wrote in a plea for better organization of the Indian trade, "nothing less than the miraculous power of deity can possibly effect the Indians reformation; many of the present traders are abandoned, reprobate white savages. Instead of showing good examples of moral conduct, besides their other part of life, they instruct the unknowing and imitating savages in many diabolical lessons of obscenity and blasphemy."[23] It would have been impossible to imagine a worse group of people to be in constant contact with Indians.

Yet many colonists held that Indians were ultimately accountable for their own behavior, and excoriated them for their drinking. Their efforts to stop Indians from drinking often seem little more than criticisms of particular Indians' ways of life, especially their inability to control their appetites. Governor George Johnstone of West Florida, addressing a group of Chickasaws and Choctaws in Mobile in March 1765, urged them not to drink, stressing the economic and social hardships that drinking brought. The governor cast blame on the traders—those "Guilty of carrying that Liquor amongst you ought to be Considered as your real Enemies much more than if they lifted the Hatchet against you"—but he also tried to shame Indians into avoiding liquor. "He who dies in War, his Time shall be remembered," he declared, "but he who is destroyed by Drunkenness shall be forgott like the Hog who has perished in the swamp."[24]

Few expressed the critique of Indian life as effectively as Sir William Johnson, perhaps the best informed colonial official in regard to the rum trade because for many years he had lived in the New York hinterland, first as a trader and then as superintendent of Indian affairs for the northern colonies. Though he, too, blamed traders for carrying rum into the backcountry, he ultimately believed it was Indians' inability to resist liquor that caused their problems. "The Indians in general are so devoted to & so debauched by Rum," he wrote in 1758, "that all Business with them is thrown into confusion by it & my transactions with them unspeakably impeeded. The Mohock Castles in particular are become scenes of perpetual riot, and the Indians selling the necessaries they receive from the Crown thro me for Rum, to the infinite detriment of His Majestys service & the increase of Indian

Expences." But what, he wondered, could he do about the problem? "Provincial penal Laws have been made, but to no purpose. I have done all in my power against this universal Enemy, to indeed His Majestys service in general, but it is too subtle & too powerful a one for me to reduce within proper bounds as to the Indians. . . ."[25]

Nine years later Johnson told a group of Indians who professed to be struggling against their desire for liquor that "the best Medicine I can think of to prevent your falling into your former Vice of drinking is to embrace Christianity" and follow the example of other sober Indians.[26] Earlier that year, it should be noted, Johnson had defended the economic utility of the liquor trade in a report to the Lords of Trade, and he was regularly sending agents into the woods with little but rum to trade with Indians.[27]

Alcohol, Health, and Death

Although most Indians did not, in all likelihood, drink enough to suffer from afflictions common to alcoholics today, the liquor trade can still be linked to health problems. The association between drinking and accidents, some of them fatal, is undeniable, as Indians and colonists recognized.

Once again John Lawson's description of early Carolina provides ample evidence. Indians "will part with the dearest Thing they have" to buy rum, he wrote, "and when they have got a little in their Heads, are the impatients Creatures living, 'till they have enough to make 'em quite drunk; and the most miserable Spectacles when they are so, some falling into the Fires, burn their Legs or Arms, contracting the Sinews, and become Cripples all their Life-time; others from Precipices break their Bones and Joints, with abundance of Instances, yet none are so great to deter them from that accurs'd Practice of Drunkenness, though sensible how many of them (are by it) hurry'd into the other World before their Time, as themselves oftentimes confess." Lawson noted that "most of the Savages are much addicted to Drunkenness," and that it contributed directly to the decline of southern Indians; combined with smallpox, rum "made such a Destruction amongst them, that, on good grounds, I do believe, there is not the sixth Savage living within two hundred Miles of all our Settlements, as there were fifty Years ago."[28]

The accidents and deaths that followed drinking sessions troubled perceptive observers throughout British America. "Drunkenness hath occasioned some *Indians* to be burnt to Death in their little Houses," Samuel Danforth declared in 1709 at the execution of two Indians who had committed murder while intoxicated, "other *Indians* by their being drowned first in Drink, have been exposed to a second drowning in Water. Nor are these the first (who now stand in the midst of this great Assembly) who have committed Murder, when overcome with Drink, and have been Executed for it."[29] The trader and historian James Adair, writing on the eve of the Revolution, also noted decidedly self-destructive behavior. "By some fatality," he wrote, the Catawbas "are much addicted to excessive drinking, and spirituous liquors distract them so exceedingly, that they will even eat live coals of fire."[30] William Byrd joined the chorus. "The trade [the Indians] have had the misfortune to drive with the English," he wrote, "has furnished them constantly with rum, which they have used so immoderately that, what with the distempers and what with the quarrels it begat amongst them, it has proved a double destruction."[31]

Violent drink-related deaths and an apparent decline in the health of drinkers led some observers to see direct links between the trade and mortality among Indians. Drinking, familiar to the Powhatan Indians of the Chesapeake region by the 1680s, prompted the governor of Maryland to speculate that "the Indians of these parts decrease very much, partly owing to smallpox, but the great cause of all is their being so devilishly given to drink."[32] A minister who traveled through Carolina in the early 1730s noted that rum had "occasioned the Death of great Numbers" of Indians there.[33] The Reverend Andrew Burnaby, traveling through Virginia during the mid–eighteenth century, had the same thought when he passed by a remnant Pamunkey population, "the rest having dwindled away through intemperance and disease."[34] A generation later Guy Johnson, who briefly served as superintendent of Indian affairs in the northern colonies after the death of his uncle, Sir William Johnson, also believed that alcohol contributed to the decline in the Indian population. "The State of Population is greatest where there is the least Intercourse with the Europeans," in part because alcohol was "peculiarly fatal to their Constitutions, & to their Increase," especially when it was combined with smallpox.[35] An official report on the state of the trade in the north in the late 1760s made the point explicitly: "[F]rom their more Immediate connections with us and the French, they [the Iroquois] were a good deal reduced by Liquor and diseases, as were the *Shawanese* and *Delawares*, and some of the 8 Nations of Canada...."[36] Drink-related mortality was so widespread among the Choctaws by the mid-1770s that one chief reported "that he had lost above a thousand of his people by Excessive drinking in little more than 18 months, and that a totall Extirpation of their Nation must be the consequence of this destructive Traffick if it cannot be stopped."[37]

Links between drinking and death appeared with increasing frequency in the last decades of the colonial period, the time when the trade was most extensive. Benjamin Franklin, despite his stereotypical description of drunken Indians, recognized the horrors created by the trade. "[I]f it be the Design of Providence to extirpate these Savages in order to make room for Cultivators of the Earth," he wrote, "it seems not improbable that Rum may be the appointed Means. It has already annihilated all the Tribes who formerly inhabited the Sea-Coast."[38] The Swedish naturalist Peter Kalm went further, believing that brandy killed more Indians than epidemic diseases. "A man can hardly have a greater desire of a thing than the Indians have for brandy," he wrote. "I have heard them say that to die by drinking brandy was a desirable and an honourable death; and indeed it was a very common thing to kill themselves by drinking this liquor to excess."[39]

Overly rhetorical and misguided though they may have been, the views Franklin and Kalm expressed reflected an actual social problem. Drinking did cause Indians to die, some from acute alcohol poisoning and some perhaps from tainted liquor; other Indians apparently committed suicide when they were drunk.[40] Many Indians suffered burns when they fell or were pushed into fires during drinking sessions; an occasional corpse lying beside a path bore the signs of alcohol-related death, such as the "Indian Man" recorded in the Bostonian Samuel Sewall's diary in 1685, who was "found dead on the Neck with a Bottle of Rumm between his legs."[41]

Liquor and Violence

The surviving evidence is not sufficiently precise to allow us to make clinical diagnoses of cases of alcohol poisoning, but such deaths apparently were not common. Drunken violence, though, was almost ubiquitous whenever traders, contrary to any existing laws, brought alcohol into Indian communities.[42] These outbursts of violence led to punishments for survivors who had provided liquor to the Indians,[43] and on occasion to death to the Indians involved.

At times colonists caused the trouble.[44] Colonists mistreated Indians when they were drunk, so a group of Maine Indians declared in 1677. "[W]e love yo," their petition declared, "but when we are dronk you will take away our cot & throw us out of dore." Further, mean-spirited colonists sometimes gave Indians liquor "& wen we were drunk killed us."[45] In such circumstances, colonial officials often apologized to Indians for their loss and promised to punish the culprits. John Penn, lieutenant governor of Pennsylvania in the late 1760s, forthrightly took responsibility for the murderous assault of two colonists, Frederick Stump and John Ironcutter, on some Indians who had gotten drunk with them at Stump's house on Middle Creek, near the Susquehanna River. Penn, through his agents at a meeting with Indian delegates, noted that "there are bad and foolish people of all Nations, whom at times the evil Spirit gets the better of and tempts to Murder their most intimate Friends, and even Relations in order to disturb the Peace & Tranquility of their Neighbours." He promised the Indians that he would punish the perpetrators, who had already been apprehended and were then in jail. The Indians accepted Penn's word. The resolution of the meeting was clear: everyone acknowledged the fault of the two colonists, and everyone wanted to prevent reprisals.[46] On another occasion Pennsylvania officials promised a group of Iroquois leaders that a colonist who had killed an Indian in a drunken brawl would be hanged when he was found.[47]

But more frequent, at least according to colonial observers, was violence perpetrated by inebriated Indians. At times the violence was accidental, the victims colonists.[48] More often the lives lost were Indians'. Charles Stuart, brother of the southern superintendent of Indian affairs John Stuart and an agent to the Choctaws, believed that liquor accounted for four-fifths of the trade goods purchased by those Indians in 1770. Traveling among their settlements a few years later, he wrote that he "saw nothing but Rum Drinking and Women Crying over the Dead bodies of their relations who have died by Rum." Liquor was "the cause of their killing each other daily," and the "Cause of every disturbance in the nation."[49] Stuart was not the only one in the southern Indian administration concerned about the violence committed by drunken Indians; his emissary to the Creeks in 1771, David Taitt, often encountered intoxicated Indians seemingly on the verge of attacking him or someone nearby.[50]

Some colonists speculated that Indians feigned drunkenness in order to attack other Indians and avoid the consequences.[51] Others described less deliberate assaults. The sale of rum by unlicensed traders threatened "the general Peace and Tranquility" of southern Indians, the agent Thomas Bosworth wrote in 1752; a "general Peace and Quietness reigns among them," another agent wrote to Governor Glen of South Carolina in 1754, "excepting what Disturbance is occasioned by immoderate Quantities of Rum brought among them, which if a Stop put to, would very much contribute towards a good Harmoney among the Indians."[52]

Most observers noted that fighting typically broke out in the course of drinking binges. Indians in Maine, purportedly inebriated, traveled to a colonial settlement and threatened to attack colonists and their livestock; other colonists apprehended them before they had done much damage, and the colonist who provided them with rum subsequently found himself facing a magistrate in Boston on charges that he had violated laws prohibiting the sale of liquor to Indians.[53] John Toby, a Nanticoke in Pennsylvania, purportedly sexually assaulted an eight-year-old colonial girl. According to the complaint of the girl's father, recorded in a deposition, Toby responded to the allegation by saying "that he had been drunk and did not Remember what he did with the girl." Three colonists then took him off to jail to await a trial.[54] Readers of the first edition of *The American Magazine, or a Monthly View of The Political State of the British Colonies*, published in Philadelphia in January 1741, could read about a murder committed by a drunken Indian. "The *Indians* who live nearer the *English*, and, by Reason of that Vicinity, have more frequent Opportunities of intoxicating themselves with strong Liquors," the magazine reported, "are indeed more dangerous: so that it happen'd once in about fifty Years, that one of them, in a drunken Fit slew an *Englishman*." The murderer was, the readers were reassured, subsequently hanged, and "His Country-men, instead of murmuring at, highly approved of that Act of Justice."[55] Colonists who paid attention to proceedings at court sessions might have gotten the impression that every Indian who become drunk could become a murderer. This must have been the case in New Jersey in the mid-1720s when Weequehela, a prominent Delaware who had long been involved in diplomatic relations between Indians and colonists, was convicted of murdering a colonist named John Leonard when he was drunk. Though he turned himself in to colonial officials and was later hanged, his act only confirmed longstanding beliefs about the effects of alcohol on Indians.[56] For missionaries who lived among Indians, the risks must have seemed so immediate as to justify their efforts to ban the trade in mission communities.[57]

Over time, it became clear to Indians and colonists alike that a culture of violence appeared like a malignancy wherever traders took rum or brandy. Certainly the problem can be traced in part to the effects of alcohol on the body. Liquor disorients perception and dissolves inhibitions. It can bring people together and can also create deep rifts between them. Though Indians at times vented their hostility through slander, as colonists did, and their binges were not always accompanied by violence, drinking bouts became the most notable occasions for hostilities.[58]

Some Indians, perhaps following the lead of colonial leaders, blamed themselves for the ill effects of drinking. "[W]hen we drink it, it makes us mad," declared several leaders of Delaware Valley Indians in the late seventeenth century, "we do not know what we do, we then abuse one another; we throw each other into the Fire, Seven Score of our People have been killed, by reason of the drinking of it, since the time it was first sold us. . . ."[59]

But not everyone was ready to impute total responsibility to the Indians. Some observers believed that violence associated with drinking bouts stemmed ultimately from the lessons Indians had learned from liquor purveyors.[60] Traveling up the Mississippi from New Orleans in the mid-eighteenth century, the French traveler Jean Bossu found Indians who claimed that traders had in fact taught them how to drink at the same time that they introduced alcohol among them.[61] The Dutch traveler Jaspar Danckaerts, journeying through New York near the end of the seventeenth century, encountered an Indian who complained that drinking weakened Indian communities, and laid the blame squarely on the people who sold alcohol to the Indians. Divine spirits governed life on earth and punished those " 'who do evil and drink themselves drunk,' " yet he himself drank to excess and had no fear of retribution. When colonists asked him why he drank, he replied, " 'I had rather not, but my heart is so inclined that it causes me to do it, although I know it is wrong. The Christians taught it to us, and give us or sell us the drink, and drink themselves drunk.' " Apparently annoyed by his answer, the colonists responded that if they lived near the Indians, the Indians would never see them inebriated, nor would they provide liquor to the Indians. " 'That,' " he replied, " 'would be good.' "[62]

Rum, Debt and Poverty

Violence was only the most obvious risk of Indian drinking; to numerous observers the long-term economic consequences of the liquor trade seemed just as devastating to Indians and ultimately to colonists as well. The forms of economic hardship varied with the traders who frequented the community and the nature of its economy. Where traders were willing to extend credit to Indians, many become burdened with debts they could not pay. Where traders demanded immediate payment, Indians traded their most valuable skins and furs for rum or brandy and then could not buy the tools and clothing their families needed. The documentary record is replete with cases of Indians who sank into poverty in just these ways.

Colonial officials at times enacted statutes specifically prohibiting the sale of alcohol on credit, but the laws seldom worked. A 1711 law prohibited the sale of rum by unlicensed traders in South Carolina, but Indians there continued to fall into debt to liquor purveyors. The problem so exasperated officials that they periodically forgave Indians' debts.[63] Yet the problems remained. Thomas Bosomworth, an agent to the Creeks, "could not help remarking the extream Poverty and Nakedness of those Indians that are contiguous to the French Fort [where] they are supplied with Liquor for those Goods they purchase from our Traders. The fatal Effects of which the Indians themselves are sencible off."[64]

Wherever the liquor trade flourished, poverty seemingly followed in its wake. New England Indians "will part with all they have to their bare skins" to purchase rum, the naturalist John Josselyn wrote in the mid-1670s, "being perpetually drunk with it, as long as it is to be had, it hath killed many of them, especially old women who have dyed when dead drunk."[65] Mohicans recognized the link between the rum trade and economic distress by the 1720s, yet problems persisted for decades; missionaries at Stockbridge in the late colonial period claimed that the Mohicans there led dissolute lives amidst near-famine conditions brought by their inattention to their economy.[66] The Charleston merchant Edmund Atkin, who became the southern superintendent of Indian affairs in 1755, went even further in his critique of the economic consequences of the trade, recognizing the potentially disastrous consequences for the English. Rum traders working out of Augusta placed "themselves near the Towns, in the way of the Hunters returning home with their deer Skins," he wrote. "The poor Indians in a manner fascinated, are unable to resist the Bait; and when Drunk are easily cheated. After parting with the fruit of three or four Months Toil, they find themselves at home, without the means of buying the necessary Clothing for themselves or their Families." In such a state, they were "dispose[d] for Mischief"; a "licentiousness hath crept in among [the young] men, beyond the Power of the Head Men to Remedy." Even the quality of the deerskins declined in such circumstances, because the rum peddlers needed to deal and be gone quickly, and Indians accustomed to trading lower-quality skins for liquor proved to be less cooperative commercial partners: "the Indians require the other Traders in their Towns to take [deerskins] in the same Condition." Drunken Indians, Atkin warned, became embittered when liquor was used to acquire their land, as he claimed it was among the Chickasaws on the Savannah River, and any colonist who took it into his head to kill an Indian or two found drunken ones easy targets.[67]

Colonial observers realized that Indians who wanted liquor undermined their customary economic practices, with potentially devastating implications. A French writer argued in the early 1690s that drinking made Indians lazy and reduced the efficiency of hunting expeditions because the Indians "usually suffer sickness, disability and eventually death from the excesses of eau-de-vie."[68] Thirty years later another French observer made the same link: "The Savages no longer Think of hunting in order to clothe Themselves but only to get drink. Brandy is making them poor and miserable; sickness is killing them off."[69] Moravian missionaries in the upper Susquehanna Valley recorded Nanticokes' complaints that drinking upset agricultural rhythms and contributed to famines there, and two decades later a British official in the southeast claimed that Indians there were "neglecting their hunting and planting."[70] Traveling through the upper Mississippi Valley, Jonathan Carver (who on occasion gave rum to Indians) recognized that the liquor trade had the power to threaten otherwise stable village economies. Winnebago settlements were a case in point. "This people," he wrote in 1766, "was it not for their excessive fondness for spirituous liquors, which they purchase of traders at a most extravagant price with their provisions, would live with that ease and plenty which would be almost enjoyed by many white people among us."[71] Some colonial officials recognized the real danger such trade could bring: liquor purveyors threatened the entire system of intercultural trade when they deceived Indians with alcohol.[72] That was the point that Scarooyady, representing a group of Ohio Indians at a treaty in 1753, made to colonial officials. "Your Traders now bring scarce any Thing but Rum and Flour," he declared. "They bring little Powder and Lead, or other Valuable Goods." Now the Indians wanted the sale of alcohol in Indian villages banned; if the commerce persisted, the entire fur trade could be threatened. "When these Whiskey Traders come, they bring thirty or forty Cags, and put them down before us, and make us drink; and get all the Skins that should go to pay the Debts we have contracted for Goods brought of the Fair Traders, and by this Means, we not only ruin ourselves, but them too."[73]

On occasion economic distress encouraged religious interpretations of

alcohol-induced poverty. When Conrad Weiser paid a return visit to Otsiningo in 1737, he found the Onondagas and Shawnees there going through
hard times. They were "short of provisions" and "their children looked like
dead persons and suffered much from hunger." They were having difficulty
finding game, and they knew why: "the Lord and Creator of the world was
resolved to destroy the Indians." One of their seers had "seen a vision of
God," who declared that Indians killed game "for the sake of the skins,
which you give for strong liquor and drown your senses, and kill one another, and carry on a dreadful debauchery. Therefore have I driven the wild
animals out of the country, for they are mine. If you will do good and cease
from your sins, I will bring them back; if not, I will destroy you from off the
earth." The villagers, according to Weiser, had no trouble believing the seer's
story. "Time will show, said they, what is to happen to us," he wrote, "*rum*
will kill us and leave the land clear for the Europeans without strife or
purchase."[74] The vision conveyed an unambiguous message: If Indians
halted the fur trade, they would no longer suffer from the liquor trade; the
hunters' sins could be erased and the community purged of its debauchery.

Knowledge of the costs of the liquor trade was not limited to Indian country. Pamphlets and government publications spread news of the difficulties
Indians were experiencing with alcohol and the problems they could cause
for colonists.[75] Such documents suggest widespread knowledge of Indian
drinking problems among the colonial population. Along with evidence in
various travel narratives and correspondence—many of these reports came
to be entered into the official records of British provinces—these accounts
contribute to a profile of the social costs of the liquor trade. By the mid–
eighteenth century many colonists would probably have agreed with a
French writer who declared that "hell can be no better represented than by
the sight of drunk male and female Savages who are then capable of all
kinds of brutalities, violent acts and murders."[76]

What then were the precise costs of the trade? We know that young men
drank more often than other members of most communities, no doubt because they had the most frequent interactions with traders, especially liquor
purveyors who worked beyond the bounds of legal trading posts. As the
governor of Pennsylvania informed a group of Indians on the Allegheny in
1730, "the Old men whose advice you should take, have complained of the
Abuse and great injury you receive by it [the liquor trade]. They complain
that for drink you give away all the fruits of your Labours, and are left naked
and poor as if you had never hunted at all. . . ."[77] Some young Indian men

in the Ohio Valley were open about their desire for rum in the late 1760s: they refused to join the chiefs and older men of their villages in signing a petition seeking an end to the liquor trade in western Pennsylvania.[78] Governor Peter Chester noted that a similar generational split was apparent among the Creeks in 1774; older men complained that they could not stop younger men from drinking.[79]

These observers could, if they were inclined, have sketched out the rest of the profile. They might have suggested that, in all likelihood, the costs of drinking, whether borne by the young hunters or by the entire community, varied with the seasons; deaths due to accidents were probably more numerous in winter, when inebriated Indians risked death by exposure in northern climates. Regardless of the gender or age of the person who died as a result of an alcohol-related accident, Indian families suffered; the loss of a family member disrupted the domestic economy and had a shattering impact on those who coped with the aftermath of tragedy.[80]

Given the social chaos that attended drinking bouts, it is tempting to attribute Indians' continued desire for drink to the collapse of their traditional values and the breakdown of community authority, and to attribute the collapse to the overwhelming psychological toll that demographic catastrophe must have caused among survivors. But that assessment would not necessarily explain why depressed Indians turned to liquor to soothe their battered consciences. Rather than see the social decline attributable to alcohol as proof of the Indians' retreat in the face of relentless waves of colonists and Old World pathogens, we need to recognize that those Indians who chose to drink did so for their own reasons. And those reasons were intricately bound up with the way Indians understood the world around them and the forces that controlled that world.

Of course, many Indians despised what they saw during and after drinking sprees. Rather than accept the consequences of drunken binges, many decided that they needed to battle the liquor trade. In doing so, they became pioneers of temperance in America.

CHAPTER FIVE
Temperance

It is You that make the liquor, and to you we must look
to Stop it. . . .
            —A Shawnee spokesman to Alexander McKee,
                                              July 1771

The social pathologies wrought by the liquor trade did not go unchallenged. By the early eighteenth century, reform-minded Indians issued appeals for temperance, and their declarations became more frequent from 1750 to 1775. Their protests crossed tribal boundaries: Iroquois, Shawnees, Delawares, Miamis, Choctaws, Catawbas—all sought an end to the liquor trade. Testimony appears in the familiar records of formal meetings between Indians and colonial officials, especially in the middle colonies and the south, where the trade was most prolific. Missionaries spread the message as well, often providing seemingly firsthand information about the struggles against the liquor trade by individual Indians and entire communities. And travelers bore witness to the commitment of many community members, especially women and older men, to stop the violence and poverty that so often accompanied the liquor trade.

Surviving temperance appeals do not, taken together, constitute an ideal body of sources. Virtually all survive in the writings of colonists, most of them officials who believed the liquor trade threatened peaceful ties between the peoples of early America; these colonists may have exaggerated Indians' complaints in an effort to promote their own views. In addition, although many Indians allied themselves with the missionaries who campaigned against the alcohol trade, many others resisted the missionaries' entire conversion program, and their views may well have differed from those of the clerics who chronicled the Indians' temperance efforts. Further, since the appeals did not emanate from any particular group, it is tempting to see them as local reactions to specific events. Finally, though scores of Indian appeals against the liquor trade have survived, they still add up to a small fraction of the documentary record relating to relations between Indians and colonists; and many of them seem less compelling when they are appended to other requests—for a smith, say, or for lower prices on certain trade goods. But even when we take these problems of interpretation into account, the documentary evidence of an Indian temperance campaign cannot be brushed aside.[1]

The temperance appeals of these Indians and their colonial allies reveal a shared perception of the dangers of the alcohol trade. They are not, like the more systematic appeals of later American temperance reformers, from the Washingtonians to Alcoholics Anonymous, the products of an organized movement.[2] They represent widespread but divergent responses to a common problem. These appeals demonstrate that Indians of different nations agreed that their survival depended on the assistance of colonists in their efforts to stop the liquor trade. Further, temperance was not always tied to Christian teachings on sobriety; the movement developed among Indians trying to regain traditional controls over their world as well as among converts. And conversion to Christianity did not in itself guarantee sobriety, as some converts realized when they took note of Indians who fell back to drinking once again.[3]

Despite the power of their appeals against liquor, Indians' temperance efforts did not, in general, prove effective. Traders continued to haul distilled spirits into Indian country, and officials continued to sanction the trade. Many officials, notably the superintendents for Indian affairs and their deputies, proved either unwilling or unable to provide the aid that temperance reformers required. Appeals against liquor gained force in the years from 1750 to 1775, when the trade was most extensive, but many officials were not swayed. When colonial traders claimed that the liquor trade had to remain open so that Indians, like others in the empire, could engage in their own pursuit of happiness, some officials agreed. Further, the reformers failed to engineer a consensus among Indians about the dangers of liquor. Some Indians went on trading for alcohol while their neighbors sought to ban it. Still others took a middle course, seeking to limit the trade but not to stop it altogether.

The vehemence with which temperance-minded Indians pursued their quest, despite the opposition they encountered, demonstrates their commitment to the cause. By opposing the commerce they sought to protect their cultural identities in the wake of conquest and colonization.[4] Their persistence also signals their belief that they were fighting for the very lives of their communities.

"To Keep the Indians Temperate and Sober"

Not all colonists supported the liquor trade; many, especially legislators, actively sought to stop it. Their reasons for doing so varied over time and from place to place, to be sure, but by the mid–eighteenth century (and usually much earlier) lawmakers in virtually every colony came to believe that the trade created too many problems for colonists and Indians alike.

The liquor trade became a logical target for regulation in any attempt to preserve order, for many colonists viewed drinking by Indians (and by slaves) as potentially more threatening to society than drinking by colonists. Few were suggesting, then, that liquor needed to be outlawed. Though some colonists recognized its dangers—rum was "a cursed bane of health and of society," according to the naturalist Bernard Romans[5]—legislators routinely tried to harness only its excess consumption. But in their moral calculus, Indian drinkers posed a constant threat to any colonists they encountered, and anyone who sold liquor to Indians was endangering others. Their drinking had to be stopped to preserve peaceful relations and to prevent sporadic attacks on colonists.

The earliest prohibitions against Indian drinking explicitly aimed to prevent such problems. New Netherland in 1643 prohibited "all Tapsters and other Inhabitants" from selling "directly or indirectly any liquors to Indians." When the problem persisted—a 1654 act noted that "many Indians are daily seen and found intoxicated, and being drunk and fuddled, commit many and grave acts of violence"—further acts raised the fine assessed for any violation, and called for "arbitrary corporal punishment" for recidivists. An act of 1656 prescribed a more severe punishment, banishment from the colony, as the only way to promote "public peace and quiet, between the good Inhabitants of this province and the Barbarians." In 1654 Dutch officials authorized detention of any Indian found drunk until the inebriate revealed who had sold the alcohol; nine years later a new act, one of the last issued in the province, stipulated a fine (in Flemish pounds) to be paid by Indians found inebriated on the Sabbath.[6]

Laws to prevent the trade varied from colony to colony in British America. In seventeenth-century New England, not surprisingly, much of the legislation designed to prevent the traffic reflected Puritan beliefs, particularly a great concern for public order and the impact of drunkenness on the religious conversion of the region's Indians. Massachusetts officials outlawed sales to Indians in the early 1630s, practically at the beginning of their effort to establish a "Bible commonwealth." But that ban proved less than durable when providing alcohol to Indians served the purposes of colonists eager to trade with them. A 1641 ordinance repealed the ban for some colonists engaged in trade with Indians, and a 1644 bounty offered to reduce the wolf population provided three bushels of corn or three quarts of wine to any Indian who brought in the head of a wolf to a town constable. By the late 1640s, problems caused by Indian drunkenness led Massachusetts officials to forbid the trade to all but a few particular colonists, who could sell wine to Indians in their own communities only.[7]

But in the late 1650s, when the first generation of provincial leaders were coping with the problems of passing their authority and mission on to the next generation (many of whom did not share their parents' religious enthusiasm),[8] Massachusetts officials returned to their earlier position. In 1657, sensing that colonists' trading activities were still causing the "fruits of drunkeness murther and other outrages," they again instituted a total ban. In a single moment all exemptions were quashed; only small amounts of liquor, for medicinal purposes, could be legally provided in the future. Six years later, recognizing that illegal sales continued, officials tried to eliminate the "sinn of drunkeness" among Indians by passing an act that authorized incarceration, a fine, or the whip for any Indian who was found intoxicated.[9]

By the end of the seventeenth century, statutes in Massachusetts and Maine prohibited the trade almost in its entirety. No individuals acting on their own could sell liquor to any Indians; only government-appointed agents in charge of government-supplied trading houses could provide any alcohol to Indians, and they were supposed to do so only with great caution. And though criminal procedures against Indians for drunkenness were not common—only twenty such cases were heard between 1675 and 1750 in one Massachusetts county court—the records of surviving cases suggest that Indians in the colony continued to get liquor, at times from other Indians.[10] In the 1730s Governor Jonathan Belcher informed the General Assembly he had received complaints about traders who sold alcohol to Indians "in the Eastern Parts"; without further suppression, the commerce would have "fatal Consequences to the Government."[11]

Other New England colonists shared the Puritans' beliefs about the dangers of the trade. New Hampshire authorities outlawed the sale of alcohol to Indians in 1640, and in 1686 they banned any sales except by people specifically licensed to engage in them.[12] Plymouth officials imposed a severe fine of £20 on a colonist whom a jury found guilty of selling alcohol to Indians.[13] Rhode Island officials in 1654 passed a law that fined any colonist who sold liquor to Indians and noted that it would be lawful for colonists to seize any alcohol they found in an Indian's possession. But the very next year an act allowed certain ordinary keepers to provide alcohol to Indians, though with the provision that no customer receive more than a quarter of a pint of liquor or wine per day. Any colonist who sold more than that amount, and by doing so allowed an Indian to become intoxicated, would be fined; any Indian found inebriated would also have to pay a fine or be whipped or "laide neck and heels." Shortly thereafter, provincial officials again banned any sales of alcohol to Indians, though colonists who had Indian servants could provide them with a dram for their refreshment.[14] Connecticut officials, "sensible of sad effects and consequences of grievous sinn to the great dishonor of God" as well as the hazard that drunken Indians posed to their lives, in 1659 sought to reduce the traffic by allowing colonists to seize West Indian rum and Kill Devil brought into the province; only those who possessed a license from the General Court could legally sell any alcohol to Indians, though they were careful to note that all alcohol had to be consumed on the premises, under the watchful eye of the seller.[15]

But in Connecticut and Rhode Island, as in Massachusetts, officials eventually adopted total prohibitions on the sale of alcohol to Indians. In 1669 the Connecticut General Assembly ordered that any colonist identified by an intoxicated Indian as the person who had sold the alcohol had to "purg himselfe by an oath" or pay a fine; drunken Indians, according to an act of 1681, would be whipped or face a similar punishment, a penalty greater than the 10s fine or one- to three-hour confinement in the stocks that colonists had to suffer after the passage of a 1706 act.[16] In 1673 Rhode Island legislators similarly sought to strengthen their acts against the liquor trade.[17]

In some sense, the shift toward prohibition in seventeenth-century New England reflected the perceived threat that intoxicated Indians posed to colonial settlements. In some places the fear of drunken Indians had no basis in any violence actually committed against colonists; only two cases involving drunken Indians were recorded in Middlesex County, Massachusetts, from the late seventeenth century to the mid–eighteenth century, and in each case the person attacked was another Indian.[18]

The movement toward a total ban drew strength from the initial religious purpose of these colonies. Rhode Island legislators in 1673 referred to the "abominable filthynes" caused by the trade, terminology that suggested the corruption of Indian morals that colonists believed occurred during drinking bouts. By the early eighteenth century, when the liquor trade in New England had become fairly inconsequential, at least in comparison with the trade then being carried on elsewhere in British America, its very survival became stark testimony to the failure of colonial officials to bring civilization to America's natives. Indians in Rhode Island who drank at public dances annoyed their colonial neighbors, and officials responded by levying a 40s fine on anyone who sold them alcohol.[19] The spectacle of carousing Indians seemingly signaled the failure of the campaign, first generated during the Elizabethan era, to convert Indians into English men and women.

Connecticut officials were particularly blunt in their assessment of the role played by alcohol in the cultural conversion effort. In an act of 1717, legislators there wrote that "drunkeness and idleness may well be looked upon as among the strongest chains that hold them fast, in their ignorance of and prejudices against the religion of the gospel"; after sixteen more years of flourishing trade, the Mohegans had become impoverished, their "manners debauched, and themselves rendered more untractable to receive the Christian faith."[20] The desire to maintain peaceful relations with the region's Indians was still important, but the very fact that intoxication was still rampant among them, at least on occasion, was perhaps the cruelest reminder that the Puritans' effort to convert them to English ways had become bankrupt.

Colonists who battled the liquor trade in the middle colonies shared the New Englanders' concern for public order but seldom referred to a desire to convert Indians to English customs. Legislation in New York and Pennsylvania was inconsistent and officials sanctioned efforts to work around the laws on occasion; they also gave Indians presents of rum when they met to discuss political or economic matters. As early as 1689 colonial officials banned the trade around Albany, though the ban did not prevent the giving of rum to Indian sachems who came into the city on "Publick Businesse." Such a ban would have interfered with negotiations with the province's Indians, and would also have violated prevailing notions that small amounts of alcohol were not so dangerous. As one official had noted in 1686, "to keep the Indians temperate and sober is a very good and Christian performance but to prohibit them all strong liquors seemes a little hard and very turkish."[21]

Still, in May 1709 New York legislators passed a law preventing the "Selling or giveing of Rumm or other Strong liquors" to Indians in Albany County, and they renewed it periodically until June 1713. But then they let it expire, and no similar statute was passed until July 1755, in response to complaints from Iroquois sachems about the troubles alcohol was causing. That law had an important provision: the trading house at Oswego, still the most important in the province, was exempted from its restrictions. That law remained in force only until July 1757.[22]

Pennsylvania authorities, following the lead of William Penn and the first generation of legislators who had passed laws against the selling of alcohol to the Indians in the early 1680s, revived their efforts in 1701, much to the appreciation of Indian sachems from the "Susquehannah and Shawanah." Orettyagh, one of the sachems, "Exprest a great Satisfaction" with the law, "and Desired that that Law might Effectually be put in Execucon and not only discoursed of as formerly it has been," for the Indians "had long Suffered by the Practice" and hoped it would now end.[23] But provincial officials eventually backed away from their strict prohibitionist stance in 1722; traders could not sell liquor to the Indians, but colonial officials negotiating treaties were allowed to give them "any reasonable quantity of rum." Later laws designed to prevent "abuses in the Indian trade" similarly exempted colonial officials from their provisions, but occasional official proclamations made the government's prohibitionist sentiments known throughout the province (figure 12), as James Kenny noted when he wrote in 1762 that "its been Advertis'd here again Neither to sell or give Strong Liquor to ye Indians."[24] In New Jersey, where the fur and skin trades had become relatively insignificant by the early eighteenth century, efforts to stop the trade, such as they were, were concentrated at the local level; the colony never enacted specific legislation to outlaw the commerce.[25] Further, officials throughout the middle colonies actively repudiated any land deal if the Indians involved could convince them that the prospective purchasers had made them intoxicated in order to get a better deal.[26]

To the south, from Maryland to West Florida, the colonies enacted laws banning the trade, but these statutes, like those of the middle colonies, tended to be short-lived, inconsistent, and ineffective. Maryland's council outlawed the trade in 1687, and periodically prohibited the sale of liquor to specific Indian communities in response to requests by their leaders. The province's general assembly passed a series of temporary and limited bills against the trade in the late seventeenth century, but no permanent legislation followed. Legislators made their reasons for banning the trade clear in a proclamation issued by the council in December 1683: liquor sellers caused Indians to become "drunk and mad" and thereby risked precipitating "a chargeable and expensive Warr." Even that prospect, though, did not lead them to ban the trade outright.[27]

By the HONOURABLE

JAMES HAMILTON, Efq;

Lieutenant-Governor, and Commander in Chief, of the Province of *Pennfylvania*, and Counties of *Newcaftle*, *Kent*, and *Suffex*, on *Delaware*,

A PROCLAMATION.

WHEREAS upon the Settlement of this Province it was early difcover'd, and conftant Experience fince fhews, that the Selling, or giving of ftrong Liquor to the *Indians*, is attended with great Mifchiefs and Inconveniencies, by reafon of its pernicious Effects, in prompting them, when under the Influence of it, to commit many Outrages and Irregularities; and notwithftanding the wife and good Laws provided againft it, we ftill find, upon every *Indian* Treaty, or other Occafion of large Companies of *Indians* coming to *Philadelphia*, that many Perfons there do prefume, in Contempt of fuch Laws, to fell, or indifcreetly give Rum, and other ftrong Liquors, to the *Indians*, to the great Danger, Difturbance and Offence, of the Inhabitants: Wherefore, for the preventing thefe Mifchiefs and Diforders, I have thought fit, with the Advice of the Council, to iffue this Proclamation, hereby, in his Majefty's Name, ftrictly forbidding all Perfons (thofe only excepted, to whom the Care of the *Indians*, at their Treaties with us, is committed) upon any Pretence whatfoever, to fell, or give any Rum, or other fpirituous or ftrong Liquors, to the *Indians*, on pain of being profecuted with the utmoft Rigour of the Law: And I do hereby earneftly recommend it to all and every the Juftices of the Peace within the faid Province, and efpecially thofe within the City of *Philadelphia*, that they take all proper Meafures to detect, and bring to condign Punifhment, all Offenders herein, and give all due Encouragement to Perfons to difcover, and give Information againft fuch Offenders; and to take Care that the Moiety of the Penalty of *Twenty Pounds* Forfeiture (by the faid Laws) for each Offence, be recover'd and paid to fuch Informers; and in cafe of the Inability of any Offender to pay the fame upon their Conviction, that then the Juftices do give the Informer or Profecutor a Certificate or Order upon the Provincial Treafurer for the *Five Pounds*, which, upon Sight of fuch Certificate, he is by the faid Laws required to pay. And hereof all Perfons concern'd are to take Notice, and not to fail in their Obedience, as they will anfwer the contrary at their Peril.

> *Given under my Hand, and the Great Seal of the Province of* Pennfylvania, *at Philadelphia, this* 11th *Day of* Auguft, *in the Twenty-third Year of the Reign of our Sovereign Lord* George II. *King of* Great-Britain, France, *and* Ireland, *&c. and in the Year of our Lord, One Thoufand Seven Hundred and Forty-nine.*

By His HONOUR's Command,
RICHARD PETERS, Secretary.   JAMES HAMILTON.

GOD Save the KING.

PHILADELPHIA: Printed by B. FRANKLIN, Printer to the Province.

12. One weapon in the legal assault on the liquor trade was a ban on the sale of alcohol to Indians. This proclamation was issued by Lt. Gov. James Hamilton of Pennsylvania, August 11, 1749. Courtesy, The Historical Society of Pennsylvania.

Inconsistency and limited statutes were the order of the day elsewhere in the Chesapeake and the south. Virginia legislators passed no acts relating to the trade for almost a century after the founding of Jamestown, but in 1705 an act prohibited the sale of rum and brandy on any land still belonging to Indians; the next year, in response to a complaint from a group of Pamunkey Indians, the council passed a ban on sales of alcohol "in any Indian Town within this Government," and in 1712 the Council issued a proclamation prohibiting the sale of rum "within the precincts allotted to the Tributary Indians." An act of 1744, which noted that Nottoways and Nansemonds were drinking to excess and being taken advantage of by traders who extended credit to them, prohibited all sales of alcohol to these Indians except for cash; any trader who sold liquor on credit would be fined. The colony's officials finally did recognize the need for a ban; acts of 1757 and 1765, intended to establish and maintain trade relations with Virginia's Indians, forbade the sale of liquor to them.[28] South Carolina officials in 1691 passed an act preventing the sale of liquor to Indians on their own lands, and in 1707 included a prohibition of rum in an "Act for Regulating the Indian Trade and Making it Safe to the Publick."[29] But traders there routinely evaded the law, and when Indians demanded liquor from colonial officials, as they regularly did, even the governor felt compelled to give it to them.[30] Legislators in Georgia and West Florida enacted legislation as well near the end of the colonial period, and North Carolina officials expressed an interest in a ban on the trade, though they never actually passed one.[31] Still, southern colonial officials did at times live up to their word; as James Adair reported, one governor ordered the arrest of a trader "on Mobille River" who had sold the liquor that was responsible for a fatal attack on two Choctaws.[32]

From New England to West Florida, the statutes devised by colonial legislators stressed the three most common consequences of the liquor trade: it interfered with the cultural conversion of Indians; it threatened the safety of colonists; and it endangered peaceful relations between colonists and Indians, especially in the western borderlands. Governor George Thomas of Pennsylvania summarized widely held official opinion in 1744. "I cannot but be apprehensive that the Indian Trade, as it is now carry'd on, will involve us in some fatal Quarrel with the Indians," he informed the provincial assembly. "Our Traders in defiance of the law carry Spirituous Liquors amongst them, and take the Advantage of their inadequate Appetite for it to Cheat them of their Skins, and their Wampum, which is their Money, and often to Debauch their Wives into the Bargain. Is it to be wonder'd at then, if, when they recover from their drunken Fit, they should take severe Revenge?"[33]

Colonial laws reflected the serious problems the trade presented for colonists, though the fact that many of the laws were temporary, or applied only to specific areas, or exempted some traders endangered whatever efficacy a more complete ban might have achieved. Though some colonists claimed that their temperance work succeeded,[34] any efforts to end the trade faced a more intransigent problem: the woods were dark, as colonists and Indians often claimed, and what went on out in Indian country was often quite beyond the control of even the most zealous colonial official. Provincial officials could not even control sales to Indians who lived near colonial settlements. If the liquor trade was to be reduced, it would be up to Indians themselves to find the solution.

"Rum Is the Thing That Makes Us Poor & Foolish"

Indians could do little to battle smallpox or measles, and efforts to resist the expansion of colonial settlements into their lands tended to be ineffective. But the battle against the alcohol trade was a contest whose outcome seemed, to the Indians at least, far from inevitable. The nature of this battle reveals much about interracial relations in eastern North America. The Indians knew that they fought for more than the redemption of individual drunkards or isolated incidents of alcohol abuse. They realized that they were waging a war that would have a long-lasting impact on all their lives and their relations with the uninvited colonists who continually intruded farther into what the historian James Merrell has aptly termed the "Indians' New World."[35] The only way to stop alcohol from destroying their world, these reformers believed, was to ban it entirely.

Some Indians succeeded in limiting the consumption of liquor in their own villages. Groups of converts sporadically banned alcohol in their towns, though missionaries, especially Jesuits in New France, complained that in this, as in other aspects of their lives, the Indians were often apostates; the continued pressures of alcohol purveyors managed to wrest many of these new Christians from their abstemious ways.[36] Still, these clerics boasted in the latter decades of the seventeenth century of mission communities in the St. Lawrence Valley such as Lorette and La Prairie de la Magdelaine, each of which attracted Indians who sought to flee the liquor trade, and some Mohawks flocked to Caughnawaga in an ill-fated attempt to escape alcohol vendors.[37]

Elsewhere success seemed more possible, even by the missionaries' standards. A group of Abenakis living near the Kennebec River in the 1640s promised a Jesuit missionary that they would "give up the liquors of Europe," a claim he apparently believed.[38] In Maryland in 1679 Tequassino and Hatsawap, two Nanticoke leaders, appproached colonial officials to seek their help in prohibiting the sale of alcohol to Indians, and the council immediately agreed. Thirteen years later the council issued a similar proclamation in response to the appeal of a group of Piscataways.[39] By then William Penn had already encountered Indians, young and old, who refused to drink, and he joined other seventeenth-century officials in an effort to ban the trade.[40] Other Indians, too, absolutely refused to drink alcohol, including some Naudowessie (Sioux) Indians whom Jonathan Carver met along the Mississippi River in 1767. "Some of these chiefs could not be prevailed upon to tast any spiritious liquours on any account as they look upon it as a bad medison," he wrote in his journal. "The Naudowessee of the plains have scearsly any knowledge of spiriteous liquor and are not at all inclind to it."[41] Still others who did drink refused to do so at certain times; some Choctaws of Bernard Romans' acquaintance would not drink on one occasion because "rum is by them avoided like poison" during their preparations for war.[42] Even Indians in towns where the trade was once rampant ended it.[43]

Some Indians who had converted to Christianity, not surprisingly, embraced the temperance cause that missionaries so eagerly promoted. The missionary David Brainerd, who worked among Indians at Crossweeksung in New Jersey in 1745, believed that "the power of God seemed to descend" among Indians there, allowing his message to get through even to "old men and women, who had been drunken wretches for many years." Some members of the community became obsessed with concern for their souls, among them "a man advanced in years, who had been a murderer, a *pawaw* or conjurer, and a notorious drunkard"; under Brainerd's power, he was "brought now to cry for mercy with many tears."[44] The missionary John Sergeant claimed that many converts among the Housatonic Indians also embraced abstinence, though there were still, according to one minister, some "who were too free with strong Drink."[45] Christian Indians who lived in two Moravian communities in the Ohio Valley, Languntoutenunk (Friedensstadt) and Welhik Tuppek (Schonbrunn), pledged in 1772 that they would not allow rum into their villages, nor would they associate with "drunkards."[46] Others in the region seized casks of rum and spilled the liquor onto the ground.[47] Samson Occom, a Mohegan who became a missionary and who himself purportedly had problems with liquor, exhorted his "Indian Brethren" to stop drinking in what became the most famous printed assault of any Indian on the liquor trade. Occom's attack on Indian intemperance clearly shows the influence of his Christian teachings. Writing in response to the execution of Moses Paul, a Christian Indian who had murdered Moses Cook "in a drunken fray," Occom wrote a broadside in 1772 warning of the dangers of alcohol (figure 13):

> My kindred Indians, pray attend and hear,
> With great attention and with godly fear;
> This day I warn you of that cursed sin,
> That poor, despised Indians wallow in.

The sin was drunkenness, and it led to a host of social problems in addition to this particular murder.

> Mean are our houses, and we are kept low,
> And almost naked, shivering we go;
> Pinch'd for food and almost starv'd we are,
> And many times put up with stinking fare.

> Our little children hovering round us weep,
> Most starv'd to death we've nought for them to eat;
> All this distress is justly on us come,
> For the accursed use we make of rum.

Occom continued his attack on liquor in sixteen verses, most often noting the social costs of drinking: drunken Indians were unable to "go, stand, speak, or sit"; they risked being defrauded and scorned; children and women also became drunkards; Indians who drank descended to a lower order of existence, "on level with the beasts and far below." Occom appealed to Indians to "embrace an offer'd Christ" and thus presumably to shed the barbarous traits that led them to drunkenness.[48] His sermon on the subject covered these points in greater depth, often echoing the tone of Puritan assaults on excessive drinking; it proved so popular that it was published in a ninth edition by 1774.[49] As Occom no doubt knew well, even Indians who converted to Christianity occasionally stumbled into intemperance.[50]

Many Indian women also battled the trade, though their sentiment was not shared by all women in the eastern woodlands. Rather than seek to end the trade, women tended to try to limit its worst consequences. Colonial

Mr. Occom's Addreſs

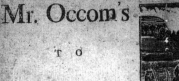

TO HIS

INDIAN BRETHREN.

On the Day that MOSES PAUL, an Indian, was executed at NEW-HAVEN, on the 2d of SEPTEMBER, 1772,
for the Murder of MOSES COOK.

I.
MY kindred Indians, pray attend and hear,
With great attention and with godly fear;
This day I warn you of that curſed ſin,
That poor, deſpiſed Indians wallow in.

II.
'Tis drunkenneſs, this is the ſin you know,
Has been and is poor Indians overthrow;
'Twas drunkenneſs that was the leading cauſe,
That made poor Moſes break God's righteous Laws.

III.
When drunk he other evil courſes took,
Thus hurried on, he murdered Moſes Cook;
Poor Moſes Paul muſt now be hang'd this day,
For wilful murder in a drunken fray.

IV.
A dreadful wo pronounc'd by God on high,
To all that in this ſin do lie;
O devilish beaſtly luſt, accurſed ſin,
Has almoſt ſtript us all of every thing.

V.
We've nothing valuable or to our praiſe,
And well may other nations on us gaze;
We have no money, credit or a name,
But what this ſin does turn to our great ſhame.

VI.
Mean are our houſes, and we are kept low,
And almoſt naked, ſhivering we go;
Pinch'd for food and almoſt ſtarv'd we are,
And many times put up with ſtinking fare.

VII.
Our little children hovering round us weep,
Moſt ſtarv'd to death we've nought for them to eat;
All this diſtreſs is juſtly on us come,
For the accurſed uſe we make of rum.

VIII.
A ſhocking, dreadful ſight we often ſee,
Our children young and tender, drunkards be;
More ſhocking yet and awful to behold,
Our women will get drunk both young and old.

IX.
Behold a drunkard in a drunken fit,
Incapable to go, ſtand, ſpeak, or ſit;
Deform'd in ſoul and every other part,
Affecting ſight! enough to melt one's heart.

X.
Sometimes he laughs, and then a hideous yell,
That almoſt equals the poor damn'd in hell;
When drown'd in drink we know not what we do,
We are deſpiſed and ſcorn'd and cheated too.

XI.
On level with the beaſts and far below
Are we when with ſtrong drink we reeling go;
Below the devils when in this ſin we run,
A drunken devil I never heard of one.

XII.
My kindred Indians, I intreat you all,
In this vile ſin never again to fall;
Fly to the blood of CHRIST, for that alone
Can for this ſin and all your ſins atone.

XIII.
Though Moſes Paul is here alive and well,
This night his ſoul muſt be in heaven or hell;
O! do take warning by this awful ſight,
And to a JESUS make a ſpeedy flight!

XIV.
You have no leaſe of your ſhort time you know,
To hell this night you may be forc'd to go;
Oh! do embrace an offer'd CHRIST to-day,
And get a ſealed pardon while you may.

XV.
Behold a loving JESUS, ſee him cry,
With earneſtneſs of ſoul, "Why will ye die?"
My kindred Indians, come juſt as you be,
Then Chriſt and his ſalvation you ſhall ſee.

If you go on and ſtill reject Chriſt's call,
'Twill be too late, his curſe will on you fall;
The Judge will doom you to that dreadful place,
In hell, where you ſhall never ſee his face.

13. Samson Occom, perhaps the most famous Indian convert who battled the liquor trade, issued this strong condemnation of the commerce in 1772. After enumerating the social chaos that liquor caused, Occom warned of the eternal damnation that awaited those who continued to abuse alcohol. "If you go on and still reject Christ's call, / 'Twill be too late, his curse will on you fall; / The Judge will doom you to that dreadful place, / In hell, where you shall never see his face." Courtesy, American Antiquarian Society.

commentators noted with approval the important role women played in restricting potential violence during drinking sessions. "[T]hese people take care seldom or never to drink all at once," Jean Bossu reported from the Illinois country in the early 1750s, "those who are sober keep in bounds the rest, and the women hide both offensive and defensive weapons."[51]

The efforts of women to make known the horrific consequences of drunken violence perhaps contributed to the growing clamor against liquor sellers in the early decades of the eighteenth century. Some reformers claimed at least partial victory. In 1738 one hundred Shawnees informed Pennsylvania officials that they would destroy any alcohol that came into their towns near Allegheny, and to get their message across they sent wampum belts with the same message to the French, Iroquois, Delawares, and Shawnees along the Susquehanna; they also poured forty gallons of rum into the street.[52] By 1748 Indians at Otsiningo, a tribally diverse town along the Susquehanna River in south-central New York, warned liquor purveyors to stay away. They had stopped drinking, and as a result, so they believed, their harvest had been more successful; they even claimed that their town would be a better place for the regional blacksmith than Shamokin, at the confluence of the two branches of the Susquehanna, where he would have to protect himself from the many drunken Indians who frequented that town.[53] Several years later a group of Iroquois sachems told colonial officials that they would not allow sales of rum in their villages, and Mohawk leaders not only banned liquor at their two castles but asked colonial leaders to stop local settlers from selling rum to them.[54] A group of Delawares in the Ohio Valley asked a missionary in the early 1770s to "write to governor Penn for them, desiring that he would inform his people, that if any brought rum [to] their side of Allegini river or Ohio, they had appointed six men, on pain of death, to stave every keg."[55] The missionary David Zeisberger, also traveling through the Ohio Valley near the end of the colonial period, encountered Indians warning colonists and other Indians not to bring rum into their communities. He noted that "rarely will a family move far away from all society, though they frequently live apart from the towns in order to avoid being annoyed by drunkards."[56] Feelings ran high; in 1747 Saciody told George Croghan that rum sellers were such threats to Indian villages that they ought to be executed.[57]

Individual Indians also successfully battled the liquor trade. Extant documents suggest a close relationship between these Indians and missionaries. The missionary John Heckewelder told of an Indian named Thomas who ventured with his sons from their home on the Susquehanna to Bethlehem in 1769 to sell his pelts. A colonist there accused him of having become a Moravian because " 'you used to come to us to sell your skins and peltry, and now you trade them away to the Moravians.' " Not appreciating the colonist's sarcasm, Thomas proceeded to explain why he had changed his trade partners.

"See! my friend!, when I come to this place with my skins and peltry to trade, the people are kind, they give me plenty of good victuals to eat, and pay me in money or whatever I want, and no one says a word to me about drinking rum—neither do I ask for it! When I come to your place with my peltry, all call to me: 'Come, Thomas! here's rum, drink heartily, drink! it will not hurt you.' All this is done for the purpose of cheating me. When you have obtained from me all you want, you call me a drunken dog, and kick me out of the room. See! this is the manner in which you cheat the Indians when they come to trade with you. So now you know when you see me coming to your town again, you may say to one another: 'Ah! there is Thomas coming again! he is no longer a Moravian, for he is coming to us to be made drunk—to be cheated—to be kicked out of the house, and be called a *drunken dog.*' "[58]

Indians did not need to embrace Christianity to find a religious motivation for abstaining from alcohol. David Brainerd, for one, described an unnamed Indian man at Shamokin "who was a devout and zealous Reformer, or rather, restorer of what he supposed was the ancient religion of the Indians." Brainerd described the Indian's appearance at some length, noting "his *pontifical garb*, which was a coat of *boar skins*, dressed with the hair on, and hanging down to his toes; a pair of bear skin stockings; and a great *wooden* face painted, the one half black, the other half tawny, about the colour of an Indian's skin, with an extravagant mouth, cut very much awry; the face fastened to a bear skin cap, which was drawn over his head." As the Indian approached Brainerd, he shook "a dry *tortoise shell* with some corn in it"— an instrument, the missionary believed, for "his idolatrous worship." To Brainerd, the man's "appearance and gestures were so prodigiously frightful" that he did not seem human. "No one would have imagined from his appearance or actions, that he could have been a human creature, if they had not some intimation of it otherwise." Yet this otherworldly apparition, who claimed that "God had taught him his religion," preached a message of temperance similar to that of Christian missionaries. "I was told by the Indians, that he opposed their drinking strong liquor with all his power,"

Brainerd wrote, "and that, if at any time he could not dissuade them from it by all he could say, he would leave them, and go crying into the woods."[59]

Other Indians too articulated native religious reasons for urging an end to the liquor traffic. Some proved willing to stop the fur trade altogether if that was the only way to end the liquor trade, as Weiser discovered when he encountered the seer at Otsiningo in 1737. On rare occasions Indians blurred the line between the alcohol trade and all aspects of European colonialism. Two revivalists, the Delaware Prophet (Neolin) and the Munsee Wangomend, sought an end to ties between Indians and colonists. " 'You are to make sacrifices,' " the Delaware Prophet declared, " 'in the manner that I shall direct; to put off entirely from yourselves the customs which you have adopted since the white people came among us; you are to return to that former happy state, in which we lived in peace and plenty, before these strangers came to disturb us, and above all, you must abstain from drinking their deadly *beson* [medicine], which they have forced upon us, for the sake of increasing their gains and diminishing our numbers.' " If the Indians succeeded in casting off European ways, " 'the great Spirit [will] give success to our arms; then he will give us strength to conquer our enemies, to drive them from hence, and recover the passage to the heavenly regions which they have taken from us.' " According to the Delaware James Mokesin, adherents to the new religion would also consume "a Sort of Bitter Drink made of Roots & Plants & Water." The drink, which allegedly would kill any non-Delaware who consumed it, "is sd to be Physick to purge out all that they got of ye White peoples ways & Nature." Wangomend, too, sought to persuade other Indians to abandon "the *poison* brought to them by the white people," though he soon turned his attentions to "a more popular and interesting subject, and began to preach against witchcraft and those who dealt in the black art."[60]

For the most part, however, Indians' appeals to halt the alcohol trade were not part of an effort to insulate Indian communities from the larger market, especially because many trade goods had become integrated into their economies.[61] The Mohican Aupaumut made this point clear when he met with the governor of New York in 1722. "When our people come from Hunting to the Town or Plantations and acquaint the Traders & People that we want Powder and Shot & Clothing," he explained, "they first give us a large cup of Rum, and after we get the taste of it crave for more so that in fine all the Beaver & Peltry we have hunted goes for drink, and we are left destitute either of Clothing or Ammuniation." The solution was simple, Aupaumut told the governor: "[W]e desire our father to order the Tap or Crane to be shut & to prohibit ye selling of Rum, for as long as the Christians will sell Rum, our People will drink it."[62] A group of sachems at Oquaga informed Sir William Johnson that they wanted exchange with colonists to continue, but not for liquor. "Brother, we lately Saw a Canoe coming down the River," they told him in January 1770, "which at first Sight much comforted our Hearts; but when we came to look into it we Saw nothing but a heap of Caggs and Barrels filled with Rhum, which at once made us tremble." They reminded Johnson of their troubles with liquor: "there are Some among us So disorderly by reason of Rhum that we are unable to keep them in any Regulation." Alcohol was a "troublesome thing, tis master of us, and in every respect bad." Still, these Indians did not want colonial traders to stop coming to their town; indeed, they preferred "White Traters" to Indian traders, believing the colonists would treat them more fairly. They only wanted to stop the alcohol trade.[63]

It seemed reasonable to the Indians that officials should halt the flow of alcohol. After all, officials throughout the colonies had long believed that liquor made Indians violent and thus threatened the ever-fragile peace in the backcountry, not only in the established provinces but to the west as well. Conochquieson, an Oneida sachem, applied to Johnson in 1758 "for having a stop put to the selling of any Strong Liquors to our People, for it not only disturbs us in our Meetings & Consultations where the drunken People come in quarrelling & very often have Weapons in their hands but it likewise carrys off many of our People both old & young." All the Oneidas, Onondagas, and Cayugas wanted from traders, he concluded, were clothes and ammunition. A group of Miamis in May 1767 also petitioned the commander of Fort Detroit to prevent the sale of brandy in their villages. A group of Shawnees, Delawares, and Mingoes from the Ohio Country sought a similar prohibition in November 1768. "Rum is the thing that makes us Indians poor & foolish," the Shawnee chief Benewisco told Johnson, "and some of our Nations have thought a good deal about that matter, and if all the other Nations will agree to it we intend to desire you to prevent its being sent into our Country...."[64] Colonists who listened to Indians could have benefited as well, as Choctaw chiefs made clear when they informed John Stuart that if he could stop the rum trade, "you will well deserve to be for ever look'd upon as our Father and Benefactor."[65]

The Catawba headman Hagler leveled a devastating attack on the trade and its consequences. "Brothers," he told representatives of North Carolina's government at a treaty session in August 1754, "here is One thing You Yourselves are to Blame very much in, That is You Rot Your grain in Tubs, out of which you take and make Strong Spirits You sell it to our young men and give it them, many times," leading them to commit violent acts and suffer illness and death. Hagler's response resembled that of other Indian appeals. "I heartily wish You would do something to prevent Your People from Dareing to Sell or give them any of that Strong Drink, upon any Consideration whatever for that will be a great means of our being free from being accused of those Crimes that is Committed by our young men and will prevent many of the abuses that is done by them thro' the Effects of that Strong Drink. . . ." Two years later Hagler brought up the subject again in a meeting with the chief justice of the province. "I desire a stop be put to the selling strong Liquors by the White people to my people especially near the Indian Nation," he declared. "If the White people make strong drink let them sell it to one another or drink it in their own Families. This will avoid a great deal of mischief which otherwise will happen from my people getting drunk and quarrelling with the White people." Hagler emphasized the source of the liquor, presuming that the government could control the colonists who sold alcohol to the Catawbas and other Indians. Perhaps the governor thought so, too, for he invoked the headman's wishes in proposing a ban on sales of alcohol to Indians in the colony.[66]

Few expressed the Indians' belief in the necessity of officials' intervention as forcefully as a group of Shawnees who petitioned Alexander McKee in 1771 to stop the liquor trade at Fort Pitt. The Shawnees had had problems there the year before, their spokesman declared, because "your Traders brought too great Quantities of Rum amongst us, which has been the Cause of the Death of many of our dearest Friends, and Relations, as well as the Reason of our foolish Young Men Abusing your Traders." Though the traders bore responsibility for these events, the incidents gave the Indians "great Uneasiness" and so they wanted a complete stop to the alcohol trade. The colonists could stop the trade, the Indians believed, because they controlled the production of alcohol. "[I]t is You that make the liquor," the Shawnee spokeman declared, "and to you we must look to Stop it. . . ." If McKee could not solve the problem, the Indians would appeal to Johnson and other colonial leaders "in whose power it must be to remove this Grievance." With the trading season about to start, the Indians wanted a quick resolution to the problem. "[I]f no Method can be fallen upon to prevent their bringing Rum into the Country," the spokesman declared, "the Consequences must be dreadful; All the Western Nations fear it as well as us, and we all know well that it is in your great Men's Power to Stop it, and make us happy, if they thought it worth their Trouble."[67]

Indian leaders sought assistance because they could not stop members of their tribe from drinking. In the wake of demographic catastrophe, the social order of many communities had become so strained that established lines of authority fractured and generational tensions increased. Many communities had never regulated every aspect of an individual's behavior; only matters that had a direct bearing on the community, such as decisions about going to war or what to do with captives, had elicited public concern. Alcohol challenged such traditional ideas when drinkers created problems for their villages. Community leaders, whether sachems, warriors, or matriarchs, wanted to intervene but felt powerless to do so. Their appeals revealed an inability to cope with this particular social problem, which some attributed to forces beyond their control. The language they used suggests a sense of addiction to alcohol, and is similar to modern observations that some Indians who abuse alcohol believe that their desire to drink is beyond their control.[68] When liquor was available, so Indian informants told colonists, at least some Indians would do anything to get it. Rum was "like a Woman," the Choctaw small medal chief Captain Houma said: "when a man wanted her—and saw her—He must have her." Under such circumstances, it made sense for Indians who lived near colonial settlements, such as the Mohicans of Stockbridge, to request colonists' assistance to limit sales of rum and to regulate the actions of nearby tavern keepers.[69]

The predictable evaporation of social mores that followed drinking binges proved to Indian leaders that the effects as well as the flow of alcohol were beyond their control. When a binge got under way, any hope for maintaining civility or preserving moral authority evaporated. A group of Mohawks could not have been clearer in their resolve on this point when they petitioned Johnson to stop the trade near their settlements. The commerce in the area, they declared, kept "them all poor, makes them Idle and Wicked, and if they have any Money or Goods they lay it all out on Rum, it destroys Virtue and the progress of Religion amongst us." The solution seemed obvious to them: end the rum trade, and help the Indians build a church and equip it with a bell, developments that "will tend to make us Religious and lead better lives than we do now."[70]

Indians did not need to become Christians to sense a threat to their community's established order. One Huron chief fully recognized the debilitating impact of liquor on some Indians' ability to act properly. "You are all sensible that the Complaints of all Nations this way have been frequent against Spirituous Liquors being carried amongst them," he told traders and residents of the Pittsburgh area in October 1773. "This, Brethren, is the Scource of many Evils, and Cause of a great deal of our Unhappyness, by it our Young Men [are] not only reduced to the Necessity of stealing to recover what they loose by Drunkenness, but deprived of their Reason and render'd incapable of listening to or taking the Advice of their Wise People."[71]

The sense of helplessness that arose from the failure of temperance-minded Indians to stop the excesses of the drinkers was perhaps best illustrated by Aucus al Kanigut, a Tuscarora chief who went to Johnson Hall in February 1767. "We return you many thanks in bringing our People from Carolina," he said, "where they lived but wretchedly being Surrounded by white People, and up to their Lips in Rum, so that they cou'd not turn their heads anyway but it ran into their mouths. [T]his made them stupid, so that they neglected Hunting, Planting &c." Since their arrival at Oquaga, he told Johnson, they recognized their earlier mistakes. But they believed their victory over alcohol abuse was precarious, so the Tuscaroras asked Johnson for help. The Indians "beg of you," he continued, "to prevail upon the Six Nations to allow us to remain where we now are, fearing that if we return we may fall into the same Error again, as we understand they have Liquor in plenty among them. We also request," he concluded, "you wou'd give us some medicine to cure us of our fondness for that destructive liquor."

Aucus al Kanigut here expressed a sentiment that underlay many other Indians' requests for help. Colonists, it appeared to the Indians, could control their own drinking and the Indians could not. These Indians sought medicine to control their appetites because they had no reliable traditional methods for combating alcohol abuse. But as the Indians learned, some colonists only periodically chose to help them; provincial officials in general sought to limit the trade only when it suited them to do so. More often, they condemned Indians for intemperateness. "The best Medicine I can think of to prevent your falling into your former Vice of drinking," Johnson responded, "is to embrace Christianity, and follow the example of your friends the Chiefs of Onooghquago [Oquaga], who assured me of their desire and readiness to instruct you in the Principles of Morality, if you do that it will tend not only to your present, but future Happiness which shou'd be consulted above all things."[72]

Johnson's moralizing did little to help any Indians; what they lacked was not a set of religious principles but something more important: a long history of solving the problems of drunkenness. Borrowing from English models, colonists had used the twin forces of religion and law to stigmatize and punish people who violated commonly held views on the proper consumption of liquor.[73] By the mid–eighteenth century many Indian groups had long experience with liquor, but few were able to develop effective means for limiting alcohol-related problems. Only a few religious leaders battled drinking, and colonization had brought so many other problems for community leaders to cope with that the formulation of adequate rules to govern drinking had to be set aside. The practice, common in many Indian communities, of exonerating anyone who committed even the worst crimes under the influence of alcohol only hampered reformers' efforts. Under the circumstances, it made perfect sense for them to look to colonists for help. Who better to provide assistance in this cause, these temperance-minded Indians must have believed, than those who produced and distributed liquor and apparently did not suffer as much from its consumption?

The failure of Indians to put a complete stop to the trade was not due to an inability to get their message across. Reports from numerous observers were published on both sides of the Atlantic, and colonial officials kept imperial policy makers well abreast of the troubles liquor caused in Indian communities and of the complaints Indian leaders made about the trade.[74] Time and again Indians claimed that colonists had repudiated earlier agreements to stop the flow of alcohol into the hinterland. Charles Thomson recounted numerous Indian complaints about the alcohol trade in 1759. At a treaty between leaders of the Mingoes, Shawnees, and Conoys at Conestoga in 1722 the Indians, according to Thomson, urged Governor William Keith of Pennsylvania to stop the trade. "At this Treaty the *Indians* complain of the Damage they receive by strong Liquor being brought among them," he wrote. "They say, 'The *Indians* could live contentedly and grow rich, if it were not for the Quantities of Rum that is suffered to come amongst them, contrary to what *William Penn* promised.' " At other sessions Indians protested that traders brought little but rum with them to trading sessions, instead of the goods Indians needed, such as shot and powder. Many Indians sold their clothing for liquor, the Conestoga chief Tawenna noted at a meeting in Philadelphia in 1729, " 'and are much impoverished thereby.' "[75] Time and again Pennsylvania officials heard such laments, even though they often issued proclamations declaring the illegality of the trade and the punishments awaiting any colonist convicted of pursuing it.[76] And a brief work titled *The Speech of a Creek-Indian, against the Immoderate Use of Spirituous Liquors*, published in London in 1754—purportedly based on an edition (now apparently lost) printed earlier in New York—provided sensational evidence about the destructive impact of alcohol on Indian communities (the text is reproduced in Appendix II). Its rhetoric suggests that it was probably the work of a Briton or a colonist engaged in the battle against distilled spirits then raging in England. Whatever its authorship, the very fact of the pamphlet's existence demonstrates the public nature of the assault on the liquor trade carried out by Indians.

To be sure, Indian appeals for temperance often found a receptive audience among colonial officials with responsibility for Indian affairs, many of whom agreed that a total ban on the alcohol trade would greatly improve Indian-colonist relations. "It cannot be imagined the Benefit the Want of Rum is both to the Indians and Traders," Ludovick Grant informed Governor James Glen of South Carolina in March 1752,

> how glad the Indians, both Men and Women, are that it is not suffered anymore to be sold in the [Cherokee] Nation. It was prohibitted in a good Time for had it been continued the Northward Indians would certainly have done Mischief which at last would have fallen upon these People whether Acessary to the same or not, it being done in their Nation. I doubt not but there are some who are so inconsiderate and careless of the Peace of the Province who still advises the Indians to petition for Rum to be brought amongst them, but it is to be hoped your Excellency with the honourable Council will reject such Proposals, they being of a most pernicious Intent only to gratify the Avarice of some self-interested Men without any Regard to the publick Wellfare.[77]

Others stressed the political benefits that would follow an end to the trade. One agent in the southeast noted that persistence of the illegal alcohol trade would "endanger the general Peace and Tranquility" of one group of Indians; Lachlan McGillivray, also involved in the Indian trade, wrote that stopping the sales of liquor "would very much contribute towards a good Harmoney" among the upper Creeks.[78]

But even officials who wanted to stop the trade completely felt powerless to do so. Traders usually avoided punishment, colonists involved in Indian affairs often lamented, and they provided such strong temptations to Indians that few could avoid their entreaties. Pennsylvania officials constantly lamented that they could not control matters "in the woods." Sasoonan could complain about the trade, as he did in Philadelphia in 1715, but the proprietary government could do little in spite of laws banning the commerce, "since it was," so the colonial spokesman recorded at their meeting, "impossible for us to know who came thither into the woods amongst them without their information."[79] James Logan claimed in 1719 that "unless there be some general provision to prohibit or regulate the Sale of strong Liquors to them, this may prove extremely inconvenient, for it will be in vain for any Gov[ernment] to endeavour to regulate that Affair among their own Indians, if all their Neighbours shall have it in their power to break thro' the prescribed Rule with impunity."[80] Proprietary officials simply could not stop the trade in the interior because, as the governor informed a group of Indians in 1722, "the Woods are so thick & dark we cannot see what is done in them."[81] Logan later elaborated on the theme when he presided over negotiations between provincial officials and Iroquois leaders in Philadelphia in 1736. "The Traders of all Nations find the *Indians* are so universally fond of Rum, that they will not deal without it," he declared. "We have made many Laws against carrying it; we have ordered the *Indians* to stave the Caggs of all that is brought amongst them; but the Woods have not Streets like *Philadelphia*, the Paths in them are endless, and they cannot be stopt. . . ."[82]

Prowling those woods were the people who would frustrate any efforts to stop the entire business: colonial fur and skin traders. Long vilified in the annals of western American history, traders were even blamed for teaching Indians improper ways of behaving under the influence of liquor.[83] Robert Hunter Morris was blunt in his report on the Indian trade in 1756. "The English trade with the Indians is carryd on by a set of Low immorals people who carry goods into the Indian country where being beyond the reach of the Law & taking advantage of the Ignorance of the savages and their fondness for strong drink they practice very fraud to render their trade profitable," he lamented. "And tho the Indians in their Conferences with the government frequently complain of their treatment yet such are the Difficulties of a conviction that I never heard of any mans being punished for his fraudulent conduct toward the Indians."[84] A decade later a report on the trade in the northern department noted that such traders were actively undermining any efforts to halt the flow of alcohol into Indian communities.[85] By the 1770s, colonial officials doubted their ability to halt the trade. Many no doubt shared the view of William Nelson, then governor of Virginia, who wrote in 1771 that "it is our duty to try too do something effectual."[86]

Colonial cupidity was thus met in many instances by genuine concern among imperial officials. The reason the trade continued is more complex than greed for skins. Those Indians who tried to halt the alcohol trade also encountered resistance at home.

"One Kegg and One Bottle Is Enough for One Man"

Although many Indians in British America were most adamant in their desire to end the liquor trade, others refused to support a total ban on alcohol. Some, acknowledging the problems associated with unrestrained trade, sought to limit it, but argued that alcohol should be available in certain places or at specified times. Others continued to desire liquor for ritual purposes, and many expected colonial officials to provide them with rum along with other presents at the opening or closing of treaties. Still others hoped to profit by acting as go-betweens for traders. However diverse their views and motives, those who wanted alcohol gave colonial traders more than enough reason to keep the supply of rum constant in Indian country, even when the trade was illegal.

Individual Indians at times suggested that limited amounts of alcohol would not cause great damage if the liquor were sold away from the villages. This suggestion was particularly popular in New York in the 1720s. A delegation of Iroquois sachems went to Albany in September 1726 to complain about various matters, particularly their fears of French encroachments on their lands. Since the English had, in the words of their spokesman, Kanakarighton, a Seneca sachem, "renewed our old covenant and strengthen'd it," the Indians expected the crown's officials to address their concerns. But the alcohol trade was a problem in their communities. "You have two Years ago desired the six Nations to [set] some Beaver Traps on the Onnondages River, which we have consented to, and granted," Kanakarighton said, "but we find our selves deceived by these Beaver Traps, instead of Rum the people who lay there sell us water which they take out of this Trap, and make us pay excessive dear for it, therefore we desire that no Rum may be sent up, for it produces all Evil and Contention between man & wife, between the Young Indians & the Sachims." The Indians did not seek a complete halt to the trade; they wanted the trade limited and would "communicate to the far Indians, that they must fetch strong liquor at Albany."

But Governor William Burnet spurned the proposition. The solution seemed simple enough to him: if "you complain that Rum makes you Disordered," stop buying it. The trade had to continue, he reasoned, because "the far Nations have a great way to come to that trading place [at Oswego] and if they want Rum there they must have it, and if they have a mind to fetch it at Albany they may come hither to fetch it." Still, the governor did promise that he would send a "fit person" to live "at the Trading place and take care that there shall be no disorder or cheating practised by the Traders, and if you shall have any Complaints he will be ready to hear and do You justice." When it came time for the Indians to leave, the governor arranged for provisions for their return journey, including rum—which was to be given to them only after they had gone past Schenectady.[87]

TEMPERANCE

Such a solution did not satisfy the Iroquois and other Indians who in the 1720s wanted a complete prohibition of the sale of liquor at Oswego, the most important trading post in western New York. This trade created turmoil in their villages, presumably because Indian hunters did not drink all of their liquor at the trading post but took at least some of it home with them. "It is true as You say that the Six Nations when they are Sober and not in Drink will not molest or Injure any body," their spokesman declared at a meeting at Albany in October 1728, "but there is one thing in the way that is Strong Liquors which your people bring up to our Country therefore Brother we desire you very Strongly to prohibit the sending or Carrying up Any Strong Liquors which your people bring up to Your Country [as they may beget] A Quarrel betwixt Your people and our Young Indians." Trying to prevent such altercations, but realistic about the demand for liquor and the traders' desire to sell it, the Indians wanted once again to have alcohol available only at Albany. To persuade colonial officials about the need for such a limit, these Indians noted that they had "Already lost many men through Liquor which has been brought up and Occasions our people killing one Another."

Governor John Montgomery refused to ban the sale of liquor at the post. It was, he declared, "absolutely necessary to send rum to oswego for the refreshment of the men in the Garrison there And those that carry up provisions to them." But the governor did promise to "give strict order that none of my people do Send or Carry up Any Strong Liquors to yours," and he expected the Indians to make a formal complaint if anyone violated this order. He proposed no specific punishment or course of action in the event of the expected violations; he simply presumed, as other provincial officials had done earlier, that the problem necessitated no significant action.[88] Further, at a subsequent private meeting with two sachems from each of the Six Nations, the Indians akcnowledged the importance of selling rum at Oswego, and even requested "that the Traders do not mix it with water." The governor promised that they would "not be abused" in the liquor trade, and he too included rum in the presents for their return journey, but again made sure they would not get it until they had passed Schenectady, "for you know," he told them, "the Inconveniency of Your Young mens getting drunk with it here."[89]

Over time, many Indians, including community leaders, still wanted alcohol available for sale somewhere, although preferably not in their neighborhoods. Even Indians well aware of its dangers argued for limited sales. In August 1731 two Indian leaders, the Delaware sachem Sassoonan and the Iroquois Shickellamy, pleaded with Pennsylvania officials to stop rum sellers from traveling to Indian villages because, as Sassoonan declared, " 'tis to be feared by means of Rum Quarrels may happen between them & Murther ensue, which may tend to dissolve that Union & loosen the Tye" between British colonists and Indians; to prevent problems these Indians wanted rum available for sale only in colonial settlements.[90] Two decades later, a group of Cayugas made an identical request, and so did a group of Ohio Valley Indians.[91] In the 1750s some southern Indians, though they agreed that the distribution of rum could create problems, asked for liquor for themselves. An anonymous writer relayed a message from the Mankiller of Tellico to the agent Raymond Demere in January 1757: "he remembers the Talk you gave him when he was there last, and his Thoughts stands good and for ever it will remain, but he desires you may send himself, and not to the Town, a Kegg of Rum, not that it should be given to him for Nothing, but he will see it paid for."[92] Even some Indians who well understood the benefits of temperance wanted liquor. As the Beaver King told James Kenny, though colonists had "stopped ye bung in our Rum kegs, so as to keep it from them, they were now for haveing ye kegs open to their people, as well as ours, when they came, that they might have it to buy as well as others for they loved it."[93] And Pontiac, meeting with George Croghan in Detroit in 1765, noted that "you stoped up the Rum Barrel when we came here, 'till the Business of this Meeting was over," but since the session was "now finished, we request you may open the barrel that your Children may drink & be merry."[94]

Colonial officials, for their part, often supported efforts to limit the trade. Believing that liquor destabilized Indian communities, some officials actually tried to destroy any illegal shipments of rum found in Indian communities. Thus the South Carolina commissioners of Indian affairs in August 1713 ordered their employees "to make a diligent and strict Search for all Rum or other Spirritts brought into or nigh any of the Yamasse or Palachocola Townes and having found the same, you shall cause itt to be destroyed by breaking the Casks or Bottles which contains the same." They did not seek to eliminate the liquor trade. Indeed, they sought mostly to make sure that the available liquor was sufficiently diluted—traders were ordered "(according to the Custom) to mix what Rum is disposed of to Indians, one third Part Water"—and spent some of their appropriation from the colonial assembly on alcohol for Indian leaders.[95]

The provision of gifts of rum to Indians became, over time, a substantial traffic in itself, even among officials who recognized the dangers of alcohol in Indian communities. The commissioners for Indian affairs in South Carolina at times gave alcohol to Indians during their meetings as early as the 1710s.[96] By the 1750s and 1760s, Indians were frequently demanding rum, and the commissioners felt compelled to provide it. As George Cadagan informed Governor James Glen in March 1751, "presents and entertainments" were the only means he could use to attract Indians to negotiations, and it was "impossible for me or any other without Rum to be very useful on such occasions."[97] Apparently it sometimes took quite a bit of rum to be effective: one agent provided forty kegs to the Lower Creeks in January 1753; in February 1756 another agent ordered fifty gallons for the headmen of various towns, a request that cost the province £100.[98] Such quantities were relatively rare, but South Carolina officials gave the Indians what they wanted; Governor Glen even asked Canachaute, a Cherokee headman, to drink a toast to the king's health with the liquor he sent to him in October 1755.[99] Even a 1751 scheme for regulating the trade in South Carolina included a provision that Indians in each district should receive "two Keggs in the Year, and that it be given to them gratis, at two different Times, to wit, one Kegg at the green Corn Dance, and one Kegg when they return from their Winter Hunt."[100]

Apparently so many colonists derived great profits from the business, particularly from 1750 to 1775, that any real effort to stop it was doomed to failure. No colonial law or proclamation could stop liquor purveyors from carting often large quantities of alcohol to Indian consumers, and other colonists, too, proved eager to keep the trade open. Raymond Demere, one of the southern agents, wrote about his difficulties with a trader who had promised liquor to Indians if they would carry corn in their canoes to one of the forts. "He said that the Rum was his and that he had no other Way of paying the Indians," Demere wrote in March 1757, "and that if I would not suffer him to bring his Rum from Keowee he would send to Savannah Town for some." Demere tried to persuade the trader to abandon liquor, blaming it for the death of one Indian; but the trader had already "sent six Horses to Savannah Town to be loaded with that pernicious Liquor." Exasperated, Demere attacked the character of the trader. "I take that little Fellow to be cracked-brain, for he does not know or care what he does. It seems when he was last in Charles Town he took some Advice from a Lawyer about Rum; they told him that nobody could hinder him from bringing Rum into the Nation and that the Rum I had stopped from him at Keowee would be no Loss to him." Demere could not believe a lawyer would venture such an

DEADLY MEDICINE

opinion. "I am sure that such a Lawyer did value more his Fee than the common Welfare and Tranquility of the Province," he declared. "I wish that Lawyer was here amongst these Indians when drunk."[101]

Traders' intransigence and the emergence of Indian liquor purveyors placed colonial officials in a peculiar bind; so did the continued demand for alcohol. With unlicensed traders always willing to travel into Indian country with rum, and with no enforcement procedure to regulate sales beyond the boundaries of established provinces, colonial officials, perhaps divided among themselves on the question, never agreed to a total ban on liquor. To do so would have violated one of the central purposes of the empire in North America: to expand the world of English-dominated commerce as far as possible.

In the eighteenth century Indians who sought to end the alcohol trade found their efforts fruitless; even after the Revolution temperance remained an elusive goal in many Indian communities.[102] Officials' decisions to allow the alcohol trade to continue demonstrated their belief that the fur trade was vital to the empire, regardless of its social costs for Indians. In their view the legislative acts to limit the trade were sufficient response to Indians' complaints.

The failure of those complaints seems particularly striking in comparison with responses to other efforts to battle alcohol in the British world. When drinking led to disorder in London in the early eighteenth century, government officials worked to end the problem and succeeded in reducing the consumption of gin.[103] And colonists, though they drank heavily, similarly limited drunken disorder in their communities; colonists became intoxicated, but laws and customs prevented the types of widespread havoc that so often followed drinking bouts in Indian villages.[104]

Ultimately temperance-minded Indians failed for two reasons. First, they could never attract enough Indians to their cause; those who profited from the trade were only the most obvious opponents. Second, they encountered unrelenting pressure from traders. People who wanted to buy and sell liquor, Indians and colonists alike, served the economic interests of the empire. Rum, perhaps the most important product of the sugar plantations in the British West Indies, found its largest market in North America in the eighteenth century—a situation some Britons bemoaned after the American Revolution had cut off the lucrative trade.[105] Many Britons believed that this type of alcohol, praised at times for its medicinal properties, caused far fewer physiological problems than gin and brandy.[106] The interests of the empire and its ceaseless competition with the French thus fueled and legitimated the rum trade. And the profits available to individual traders from the sale of watered rum ensured an ample supply of colonists willing to do the work to sustain the commerce.

Once participation in the fur trade had opened the possibility of the expansion of the Atlantic market into the rural hinterland, and the liquor trade became an effective means of wedding Indians to that economic system, no revulsion of Indians against alcohol could prevent or end its inclusion in the trade. In pursuit of commercial gain for themselves and the empire, the people in control of the liquor trade proved indifferent to Indians' appeals because such appeals constituted a threat to their very purpose in North America.

But the ideology of the empire did not alone sustain the trade. The commerce survived because many Indians wanted liquor, and not only those who stood to profit from its distribution and sale. Whether they wanted alcohol for ritual purposes or to seek temporary escape from the catastrophes that continually befell them in an age of demographic collapse, loss of land, and threats to their culture, many Indians wanted to get drunk. When their demand met the fur traders' lust for profits, it must have been clear to temperance-minded Indians and their colonial allies that their cause could not prevail.

The story of the Indians' failure to stop the liquor trade during the colonial period demonstrates the deep divisions within Indian country engendered by colonial expansion. The brutality of the liquor trade must have seemed to Indian leaders all the more ubiquitous because the violence unleashed in drunken brawls was almost always directed at other Indians. But this apparently hopeless story also contains a lesson. Indians battled the liquor trade because they deemed it a threat to their lives, especially by the mid-eighteenth century. They did not meekly succumb to the threat; they firmly believed that this was a struggle they could win. To twentieth-century observers, the Indians' fight against the alcohol trade seems a Sisyphean quest. But it did not seem so to the Indians who continually worked to stop the flow of rum to their communities. For in the battle against alcohol, Indian temperance reformers were fighting to maintain their sense of cultural identity.

CHAPTER SIX
New Spain, New France

The health of the colony depends on it.
—René-Robert Cavelier de La Salle, on control of the brandy
trade in New France, 1678

In some ways, the continued difficulties of Indians in the British colonies resembled those of Indians in territory claimed by France and Spain. Alcohol disrupted those communities, too. So widespread were the social costs of the liquor trade that it is tempting to ascribe them to some transnational phenomenon—the immersion of Indians in a capitalist world economy, or perhaps a physiological or psychological response to liquor in particular. Yet such explanations obscure more than they reveal. The impact of alcohol on Indians varied substantially from region to region. When we scrutinize the liquor trade, then, we must keep an eye on cultural and demographic factors. Indians in the southwest, who were already familiar with alcohol, had less difficulty coping with the freshets of liquor loosed by Spanish colonists than Indians in French Canada, who had no more experience with liquor than those in the British colonies and were prey to the same problems.

In Mexico and the southwest, where Indians had been making alcoholic beverages long before they came into contact with Europeans, their drinking customs changed—they bought new forms of alcohol from colonizers, and they no longer confined drinking to religious occasions—but with one exception, the Indians of New Spain seldom fell into the pattern that became all too familiar in the north. The exception was Florida. Liquor was as unfamiliar to the Indians there as to those in British America, and its effects on them were much the same.

In French Canada, the liquor trade outwardly mirrored the business in the

British mainland colonies. Indians became involved in the liquor trade through the fur trade; they often experienced the same sorts of drink-related problems as Indians in British America, and some battled the trade as well. But the liquor trade in Canada differed from that in the British colonies, and the differences arose from the role of the fur trade in the plans the French devised for the colonization of the Western Hemisphere. By observing the history of Indians and alcohol in Canada we can better grasp what was peculiarly British about events to the south.

New Spain

Long before Columbus made his westward journey, Indians in North American territory that would become part of New Spain—modern-day Mexico and the southwest of the United States—drank alcohol in carefully regulated ceremonies; they were quick to limit drinking that violated social customs. During the colonial period, which brought previously unimaginable horror to Indians in New Spain through both epidemics and warfare,[1] drinking patterns changed abruptly in two ways: more Indians drank more often, and they incorporated distilled beverages into their diets. Each of these changes had wide-ranging implications. Sumptuary restrictions fell into abeyance; Indians produced more pulque for sale (instead of local consumption) and taverns and inns turned drinking into a casual pastime as never before. The brandy and wine imported from Spain desacralized drinking even further. Indians continued to imbibe alcohol for religious reasons, and drank to excess to fulfill their spiritual commands properly, but drinking became increasingly secularized. Though these people never entirely divorced liquor from its socioreligious function—Christianized Indians still incorporate liquor in their civic-religious gatherings—the amount of alcohol they consumed grew dramatically during the colonial period, much to the chagrin of Spanish bureaucrats and clerics. Not all early observers condemned Indian drinking in territory claimed by the Spanish. One early commentator noted that when Indians "assemble at their festivals, the whole tribe bring eatables, and they sing and dance till they get drunk and are tired; and so they freely pass a happy time."[2] As would become typical in eastern North America, some colonizers plied Indians with alcohol while others excoriated them for their drunkenness. Yet for all the problems that liquor brought, Mexico's demographic history ultimately prevented the trade from having the far-reaching effects it had on Indians in British America.

From the southwest of the present-day United States, where knowledge of alcohol production dated back to at least the fourth century, to South America, Indian groups had traditionally incorporated liquor into a variety of rituals. The Pimas and Papagos, who strove to produce crops in an unforgiving and generally dry climate, annually drank a juice taken from the saguaro cactus which was mildly intoxicating. They drank to drunkenness, believing that the more they drank, the more abundant would be the rainfall that season. In what is now northern Mexico some Indians, notably the Tarahumaras and Tepehuanes, produced a corn liquor for feasts. *Tesvino*, the alcohol they fermented from corn, played a vital role in rites of passage, such as the feast marking the transition from boyhood to manhood. Like other Indians, the Tarahumaras and Tepehuanes believed that alcohol had sacred properties; before drinking, in modern times, they continued to offer some to divine beings, including Christ, in the belief that the gods liked to drink. Other Indians, notably the Navajos and Apaches, used alcohol on social occasions to cement bonds between community members, while still other Indians, such as the Yumas, drank to reinforce alliances with other Indians or in their preparations for war.[3] Well into South America, Indians also fitted alcohol into agricultural ceremonies.[4]

Records from the Conquest and the colonial period reveal much about precontact drinking beliefs in Mexico, especially among the Aztecs. Before the Spanish arrived, Indians drank pulque, the fermented juice of the maguey, a century plant. They believed that pulque had been created by gods, and was properly used in rituals of obeisance to divine powers. Class distinctions shaped consumption patterns, so that the nobility was able to indulge more often than commoners. Nearly all adults drank on ceremonial occasions, but some also drank on the sly.

The conquistadors believed the Aztecs drank to excess, but they failed to understand the specific role alcohol played in Indian society. Drunkenness, so the Aztecs believed, allowed one to come into contact with the sacred. Ceremonies dictated proper drinking practices; the *Florentine Codex*, the collected writings of Aztecs brought together under the direction of the Franciscan Bernardino de Sahagún in the mid–sixteenth century and perhaps the richest source of material relating to Indian practices, describes acceptable and unacceptable drinking. A specific ceremony instructed the producers and distributors of salt to drink pulque and become intoxicated on a particular feast day; another described the ritual undertaken for Ome Tochtzin, the god of pulque, involving a contest to determine who would drink the sacred alcohol. Properly used, pulque allowed the drinker to grasp the sacred. Yet the *Florentine Codex* also enumerated problems associated with its misuse: poverty, lack of control, sexual incontinence, violence, and accidents; drunkenness was one of the defining characteristics of the harlot, the evil woman whose vanity and use of her body brought ruin to herself and anyone with whom she came in contact. Hence the use of pulque had to be regulated, lest the entire society be endangered by the unwise actions of a besotted few. Only such a belief would justify the capital punishment meted out to men and women who flouted the law, though officials often chose to execute only a few of the accused at any given time.[5]

The Mayas, too, drank before the Conquest, though their practices differed in some ways from those of the Aztecs. For the Mayas, the consumption of *balche*, a liquor made from fermented honey and bark, was vital to public ceremonies. Public drunkenness during these occasions served two functions: it allowed the *macehuales* (commoners) to come into contact with the supernatural; at the same time, intoxication released pent-up hostilities in a socially controlled way. Spanish authorities feared the drunken revelry of Carnival time, especially the ritualistic warfare that often followed in the wake of drinking sessions, but these outbursts of ritualized violence posed no threat to the social order. On the contrary, they solidified the proper ordering of the society by giving a legitimate outlet to tensions that could otherwise threaten the control of the *principales* (the local nobility). Mayas continued to get drunk on important holidays well after the Spanish arrived and they still drank *balche* to honor the idols they made. The Spanish lost their battle against ritual drunkenness because the Mayas, like the Aztecs, had woven it into the very fabric of their lives.[6]

With colonization, traditional controls broke down and unauthorized drunkenness, once a minor problem, became widespread. The incidence of drunkenness varied from countryside to city, and court records reveal a connection between drinking and criminal behavior. Yet even late in the colonial period community controls survived; Indians' problems with alcohol, when they occurred, tended to represent violations of community norms that remained in place. Some European observers worried that alcohol threatened Indian communities; the English priest Thomas Gage informed the readers of *The English-American, . . . or, A New Survey of the West India's*, published in London in 1648, that the "Spaniards, knowing this inclination of the Indians to drunkenness, do much abuse and wrong them." But despite such reports, including official accounts that by their nature were less critical of the colonizers, there is no evidence of widespread abuse of alcohol among the Indians of Mexico. Previous experience with liquor enabled these people to control their drinking, though the establishment of distilleries for the production of *aguardiente* (burning water), a type of rum, certainly increased the amount of liquor available to them, at least in certain areas.[7]

Further, when colonial officials did try to limit consumption, as many did in Mexico City at the end of the eighteenth century, they failed. They lacked the resources to patrol the barrios of the poor Indians who accounted for almost nine-tenths of the city's population, and the economic advantages of the trade, especially for those involved in the production of pulque and the collection of taxes on it, tempered enthusiasm for the task. The trade ultimately survived because of the importance of alcohol in the social lives of the poor. Regardless of the potential costs associated with drinking, most of the Indians in the largest city in New Spain proved unwilling to abandon liquor.[8]

Although drinking patterns changed over the colonial period, the variation between groups, and within them as well, reveals the vital role that culture played in shaping consumption. The limits that Indians had earlier imposed on alcohol made sense in view of their belief that it had sacred qualities. That belief is hardly surprising; Europeans too believed that alcohol taken at communion either became or represented the blood of a god. As long as Indians confined the use of alcohol within traditional boundaries, liquor gave them few problems. It was only after their daily lives were severed from their customary moorings that liquor become a commodity. Once it did so, its impact led to higher incidences of social pathologies in Indian communities. Previous experience and long-held customs simply proved insufficient to prevent a transformation in the use and meaning of alcohol.

But in spite of changes in consumption patterns, alcohol proved less threatening in Mexico and the southwest than it did in British America. No fur or skin trade drove Spanish colonizers to pursue the alcohol trade; those who wanted to sell liquor to Indians did so as an end in itself, not as a means toward some more lucrative commerce. Further, though Indians in New Spain experienced a demographic catastrophe, the conquistadors and those who followed did not initially represent the same sort of threat as colonists from England and France. Spanish colonizers seized land for their settlements and fields for their livestock, and in places enslaved Indians and put them to work in their mines. But many Indian villages survived because the Spaniards did not seek land in large quantities. Instead, the encomienda system relied on tributes of Indians who resided in their villages, the *indios de pueblo*. Though many migrants were eager to replicate a familiar world, especially hidalgos (nobles) whose family fortunes were diminishing and other young men who sought economic opportunity, their migration was slight compared to the movement of Europeans to British America. Until at least 1600 men constituted the great majority of migrants from Spain, though over time more women and many families crossed the Atlantic, most of them eventually settling in the urban areas of New Spain.[9] Eventually growing numbers of Europeans, mestizos, and Africans gave Mexico a racially mixed population, but Indians constituted the vast majority of its people well into the seventeenth century.[10]

Alcohol consumption grew within the confines of a traditional village world where indigenous social controls continued to limit excessive drinking. In these circumstances, one would expect *indios de pueblo* to suffer less from alcohol-related problems than Indians who lived in Mexico City, where the forces of colonization were most intense. And this is precisely what the documentary record reveals.[11]

In Florida, however, the pattern of Indian drinking came to resemble the one to the north. Here, where the Spaniards' colonization efforts were less intense, missionaries tried to teach Indians how to behave like good Catholics, but found their efforts frustrated by the Indians' fondness for strong drink. Archaeological evidence confirms reports of seventeenth-century Spanish observers that some Indians already liked wine.[12] By the mid–eighteenth century, when rum was more widely available there, some missionaries believed that they needed military assistance to maintain the peace. Alcohol abuse was apparently widespread among the Calusas of south Florida, a once populous group that had encountered Ponce de León but who had suffered greatly from epidemic diseases by the mid–eighteenth century.[13] "There have been daily [complaints] over our not having brought them any" rum, two Jesuits reported in 1743. "They have advanced a thousand arguments [for having it] that the Devil suggests to them. They have gone so far as to throw up to us the matter of the wine for the Holy Mass. And, to sum it up, they have told us clearly that, without the rum, they neither can be or wish to be Christians." But when the Indians got liquor, they got drunk, and then "there is no hope for moderation from them." Once inebriated, the Indians attacked anyone in the area; their wives, apparently familiar with their husbands' ways, "fled into the woods."[14]

Missionaries and colonial officials in Florida, like their counterparts in Mexico, wanted to stop the trade but could not. As one observer noted, "it will be difficult to contain the avarice of a poor fisherman who knows that without rum the Indian is not going to help him with the fishing and the [greed] of anyone else at all, to whom the Indian is accustomed to give the equivalent of a hundred pesos for a flask of rum, at the sight of which he [the boatman] would fear nothing, as is clear to us from many individual cases." Colonial officials could not control the problem. "[T]here are bound to be drunks in the village," the missionaries concluded, arguing that they needed soldiers there "for punishment to prevent its most pernicious effects and so that vice does not triumph with impunity."[15]

The similarity between Florida and the eastern woodlands reveals the limits of colonial officials' power to enforce imperial dictates. Of course, the true test of such a proposition is evident not in Florida but in other territory where a Catholic European nation tried to control drinking by Indians: Canada.

New France

In much of Spanish America, the liquor commerce elicited little attention other than periodic complaints; in New France, the trade became crucial to the definition of the colonial venture. There were, to be sure, similarities between the Spanish and French expansion efforts. The Catholic Church played a major role in each, and neither attracted so many immigrants as British America. But one thing that made Canada different was the fact that French colonizers—missionaries and imperial bureaucrats and fur traders— recognized the importance of the liquor trade. For in Canada, the debate over the alcohol trade became just that: an actual debate, argued explicitly in 1678. Its outcome revealed the central role that liquor played in France's vision of its colonial enterprise in North America. That debate represented a clash of the two dominant French ideologies in Canada, the churchmen's mission to spread the faith and the merchants' plans to increase trade. Though the debate ostensibly made only minor changes in the liquor trade, colonists recognized that that commerce served a different function in New France than it did elsewhere in the Western Hemisphere.[16]

To understand the liquor trade in Canada it is necessary to look well beyond the limited and often self-serving arguments of clerics and merchants to other developments. Issues that seem unrelated, especially the demographic history of New France, are particularly revealing. The brandy trade in early Canada became important because commerce between natives and newcomers played a crucial role in France's North American venture. Though habitants made agriculture the basis of their economy in many settlements, especially in the St. Lawrence Valley, the French, particularly women, were unwilling to migrate to Canada in substantial numbers. Even most of those who went there as *engagés* refused to remain after they had fulfilled the terms of their contracts. Under such demographic circumstances, the fur trade took on greater significance than it might otherwise have had or than it had, by comparison, in British America.[17]

In the absence of large numbers of colonists, who might have neglected the fur trade to pursue an agricultural life, the business became a central feature of the economy of New France. The commerce brought together representatives of the three dominant groups that sought to influence trade in Canada: Christian clerics and Indians (notably converts) who shared their abstemious vision; secular royal officials and merchants, who found common cause on this point; and Indians engaged in the fur trade. Each group had its own reasons for promoting or attacking brandy. During the initial development of the liquor trade, up to 1660 or so, clerics attacked the commerce, seeing in it a threat to their plans to convert Canada's Indians to Christianity. At the same time, Indians who lived near colonial settlements in the St. Lawrence Valley and eastern Canada were incorporating alcohol into their cultures in very public ways, and their demand shaped the debate over brandy. The demand for liquor in these communities must have pleased European fur traders, for Indians who wanted it would continue to bring pelts to exchange. But the problems liquor brought to Indian communities so enraged clerics that they mounted a sustained attack on the trade. Their campaign triggered a debate on the trade, a royal proclamation, and the articulation of a new political economy of the brandy trade. But clerics did not concede defeat; instead they promulgated nothing less than a divinely sanctioned crusade against the commerce. Yet however powerful their arguments, eighteenth-century trade figures make it abundantly clear that the clerics could not stop the spread of the commerce westward and northward and down the Mississippi Valley as well.

"Lovers of Brandy"

No one could have predicted the ultimate importance of brandy to the fur trade in Canada. Unfortunately, the documentary record does not reveal exactly when Indians began to trade furs for liquor. Lacking any experience with alcohol, Canadian Indians may have encountered it first when Jacques Cartier gave wine to the chief Donnacona in 1535. Regrettably, Cartier did not record what the chief and his companions thought about it, noting only in passing that they were "much pleased" after consuming wine and bread.[18] Donnacona's receptivity to alcohol was not widely shared in the sixteenth century. When the Indians first saw Frenchmen "covered with their cuirasses, eating biscuits, and drinking wine," according to the Montagnais Pierre Pastedechouan, who in 1633 told Jesuit missionaries stories from his grandmother's time, they thought they "were dressed in iron, ate bones, and drank blood."[19]

However revolting wine may have been to some Indians, by the early seventeenth century the trade was already well under way. The missionary Pierre Biard informed readers in 1616 that his Indian charges suffered from "gorging themselves excessively" during the summer, when French ships arrived, and they got "drunk, not only on wine but on brandy"; such behavior contributed, he asserted, to the rising mortality among the Indians. At this point, with Canada's demographic future still uncertain and the importance of the trade not yet fully recognized, secular officials agreed with clerics that liquor sales to Indians needed to be halted. As early as 1619 a prominent Paris newspaper carried news that the liquor trade would not be permitted in New France. The *Mercure François* noted that "our Savages— not only men, but women and girls—are such lovers of brandy that they get swinishly intoxicated"; liquor caused them to fight each other and sometimes murder colonists. Lt. Gov. Samuel de Champlain, "considering this, and realizing the misfortunes that would arise therefrom, deems it expedient to issue a stringent prohibition of traffic, in any manner whatsoever, in brandy,—under penalty of corporal punishment, and loss of his wages, for any one caught in selling brandy and wine."[20]

But the ban had little actual effect on the trade, or so temperance-minded Jesuits believed. Time and again they reported drunken debauches and Indians beserk after drinking binges. The 1640s and 1650s apparently brought particular devastations. The *Jesuit Relation* for 1640–1641 reported the murder of Makheabichtichiou by an Abnaki. According to Indians present, "this deed was done in drunkenness," and as a result two other Abnakis were in search of the victim's family in order "to give satisfaction."[21]

Although Jesuits occasionally encountered Indians who apparently could control their thirst for liquor, most missionaries had already come to the conclusion that such abstemious ways were not common.[22] Writing to her son in August 1644, the Ursuline Marie de L'Incarnation ably summarized clerical views when she noted that the "French having let [the Indians] taste brandy and wine, they find these much to their taste, but they need only drink of them once to become almost mad and raging." Liquor "ruins their health," but Governor Charles Hualt de Montmagny's efforts to stop the commerce generally failed. "[W]hen the vessels arrive," she concluded, "it is not possible to prevent the sailors from trafficking in it with them secretly." By the early 1660s she had joined other missionaries in their efforts to end a trade that had led to innumerable social conflicts, including so many "murders, violations, and monstrous and unheard-of crimes" that even some Indians wanted the trade stopped.[23]

By that time other missionaries had become even more insistent. One Jesuit informed his congregants that it was "a mortal sin to sell brandy to the Indians because they ask for it only in order to become intoxicated." Another wrote that liquor was "a demon that robs [Indians] of their reason, and so inflames their passion that, after returning from the chase richly laden with beaver-skins, instead of furnishing their families with provisions, clothing, and other necessary supplies, they drink away the entire proceeds in one day and are forced to pass the winter in nakedness, famine, and all sorts of deprivation." Some Indians, he claimed, even sold their own children to purchase alcohol, and the social consequences of drinking included intoxicated children who beat their parents, young men who "corrupt[ed] the girls after making them drunk," and countless nights of violence, often fatal. Such conditions, he complained, prevented Indians from receiving necessary instructions from missionaries.[24]

Since the Bible repeatedly warned against drunkenness, missionaries were understandably sensitive to any sign of it. Perhaps that sensitivity led some of them to exaggerate the consequences of the brandy trade. But we cannot avoid the evidence here, especially since many clerics were keen observers and their ethnographic observations provide perhaps the most detailed evidence available for the Indian communities during colonial times. Of course not every colonist in Canada agreed with their assessments.

"The Liberty Is Necessary to Commerce"

Most missionaries steadfastly believed that brandy brought evil to Indian communities, and that only clerics could stop this demonic destruction. No cleric fought the trade more consistently than François Xavier de Laval de Montigny, bishop of Quebec. By 1660 he had had enough. In his opinion, the brandy trade threatened the entire colonization effort. Using what he believed was his greatest power, he ordered the excommunication of any French trader who sold liquor to Indians, and then promptly excommunicated two offenders and threatened to excommunicate others.[25] He pushed the clerical view so far into the open that merchants responded with a stinging rebuke. From that point on, the brandy trade became the central item in a fight between priests and traders over the future course of French colonization efforts in Canada.

One Jesuit claimed immediate results for the bishop's efforts: the order to excommunicate "all the French who should give intoxicating liquors to the Savages, suppressed all these disorders, and they have not broken out again since the excommunication, so richly has it received Heaven's blessing." Temperance-minded Indians were especially pleased; "they could not sufficiently admire the power of [Laval's] word, which had accomplished in a moment what had been so long attempted in vain."[26]

But Laval's accomplishment was short-lived. Civil authorities demanded that the excommunication order of 1660, as well as another of 1662, be lifted. Not surprisingly, Laval did not easily concede. It did not matter whether the church could excommunicate them or not, he declared in 1668; brandy vendors were still committing a mortal sin.[27] Laval's tireless efforts took a toll, or so Marie de L'Incarnation believed: his campaign almost killed him, she told her son.[28] His defeat did not diminish the praise he received from some like-minded associates. Across the Atlantic the professors of theology at the Sorbonne issued a declaration in support of his efforts in March 1675.[29]

In the wake of the failed excommunication order, the liquor trade progressed, as dismayed clerics throughout Canada came to realize. Even flogging of people caught selling liquor to Indians failed to have any measurable impact on the business.[30] As the Jesuit Pierre François Xavier de Charlevoix succinctly noted, "the evil continued its rapid progress" in the early 1660s, and the Indians, "who are not able to refrain from it when offered, and in whom the least effect of this drink is the suspension of their reason, plunged into scandals which cost many tears to those who had at such cost begotten them to Christ."[31] And violence associated with drunkenness seemingly increased as well, some clerics reported by the end of the decade.[32] François Dollier de Casson, the superior of the Sulpicians in Montreal, noted that some Hurons "whom God preserves in a manner almost miraculous" escaped the ravages associated with drunkenness, but the Algonquins and Iroquois were "so greedy for liquor, that they can only leave it alone when they are drunk and can take no more. In fine, it is a commodity of which, morally speaking, they make the same use as the madman makes of his sword."[33] But in spite of clerical appeals, liquor remained widely available to Indians who lived in or near French settlements. If local French traders did not sell it, Indians were willing to travel southward to find other Europeans, notably the Dutch in New Netherland, who did.[34] By the early 1670s the trade was actually expanding as coureurs de bois transported brandy ever farther into New France.[35]

Some Indians, too, complained about the liquor trade, but Charlevoix believed that their appeals "could produce no impression on a man [the governor general] who believed, in his prejudice, that they were exaggerating the evil."[36] An Algonquin convert who encountered Marie de L'Incarnation apparently agreed. He noted that Onontio, the term Algonquian Indians used for the French governor, was " 'killing us by permitting people to give us liquors.' " When clerics suggested that he tell the governor, his answer revealed a sense of powerlessness. " 'I have already told him twice,' he answered, 'and yet he does nothing. You beg him to forbid it. Perhaps he will obey you.' "[37]

Still, Indians of various communities proved themselves quite able to refuse liquor. Missionaries particularly singled out converts, including some women, who resisted the entreaties of drinkers and remained sober.[38] A few particularly devout communities, such as those at La Prairie de la Magdelain and Lorette, gained reputations for the sobriety of their inhabitants, and Caughnawaga attracted Mohawks into the 1690s in part because they were seeking a community they believed would be free from drunken binges.[39] Residents of La Prairie de la Magdelain, where newcomers had to promise to give up "the idolatry of dreams, the changing of wives, and drunkenness," were especially proud of their community's success. A Jesuit there in 1679 touted the hundred Iroquois who left "their own country, in which the excesses which drink Causes are horrible," and had remained sober since they arrived in the village. And one thirty-year-old Oneida, only a year after his baptism, received special praise from a Jesuit when, during a drinking party at the house of a French colonist,

he purposely made a false step, but so cleverly that his foot struck the kettle as if by accident, and upset all the liquor contained in it. This accident gave rise to much mirth among the Savages; but I think it gave incomparably more pleasure to their good angels who saw it. And so well did God bless the ingenuity of his servant that, after having had a good laugh, they thought only of going to bed, as the night was already advanced,—a very rare thing among Savages, when once they have begun drinking. This was the conduct of a Savage who had been a Christian four months, who is already zealous for God's glory, and who knows how to temper zeal with prudence.[40]

But for every Indian who avoided liquor, countless others continued to drink, and to do so publicly. They expressed their desire for alcohol in the most tangible way possible: by continuing to buy it with pelts whenever it was available. Their repeated purchases gave traders all the incentive they needed to make sure the trade continued. And when Frontenac convened a meeting on the brandy trade at Quebec in 1678, the economics of the trade dominated the discussions.

Indians were not invited to the meeting, but their views were much in evidence all the same. The Iroquois in particular, who had been trading with French and Dutch traders before the 1660s and with French and English traders after the British gained control of New York, had the economic sophistication to seek out whichever group of Europeans offered the most desirable goods. Since the French crown depended on the fur trade to provide revenue needed in the colony, any threat to the trade presumably caused great alarm.[41] Indians who wanted to buy alcohol, then, did not have to go to Quebec to voice their concerns, for their demands had already dictated the merchants' response to the issue.

The meeting quickly became a forum for the articulation of the political economy of the brandy trade. Participants claimed that profits alone did not always dictate their responses. Two seigneurs, Alexandre Berthier and Pierre de Sorel, noted that if French traders did not supply the Iroquois with liquor, they would only go to the Dutch for it. Others mentioned that the English were also a threat, and Sidrac Dugué added that Indians who visited any Protestant colony would "fall into heresy" or retain "their superstitions" and thus never convert to Catholicism. He also claimed that when some traders had been unable to sell brandy, three hundred Iroquois had taken their furs elsewhere. Still others elaborated on these points, claiming that drunken excesses rarely caused serious problems and noting that such occurrences could be limited if the trade were properly managed. Chorel de St-Romain even argued that Indians needed to learn how to drink if they were to be fully converted to European ways; since many deals were closed "by drinking together," if Indians were denied "the freedom to live as we do, they will never become Christians." Besides, the cas réservé relating to brandy sales, which allowed only the bishop or the pope to absolve those who committed the mortal sin of selling liquor to Indians, prevented priests from alleviating the despair of the dying who had sold brandy to Indians.[42]

La Salle provided statistics and rhetoric to support these arguments. He noted that the French annually received 60,000 to 80,000 beaver skins and that liquor went to perhaps 20,000 Indians; eliminating the trade would reduce the number of skins brought in. He also minimized the potential danger of alcohol for Indians, claiming that over 800 Indians at La Prairie de la Magdelaine and Lorette did not drink. Besides, two or three fairs in Brittany occasioned greater disorder than drunken Indians managed to do in five or six years. Ending the trade could make the Iroquois so angry that they might start a war against the French; the danger of stopping the commerce far outweighed the purported benefits. In case anyone doubted his analysis, La Salle sounded a rousing defense of the brandy trade: "this liberty is necessary to commerce because the usage is not all criminal," and besides, "the health of the colony depends on it."[43]

La Salle's argument presumably received wide support in Quebec, but several dissenters still argued that if the trade could not be eliminated, it should at least be limited. Like those who supported the commerce, the opponents based their case on economic grounds, and sprinkled their statements with references to religious issues as well. Nicolas Duplessis-Gatineau argued that the Indians became so indebted to traders that their behavior threatened the fur trade. Jacques Le Ber, who agreed with Louis Jolliet that the trade should be permitted if it was confined to French settlements, argued that Indians had to bring their pelts to habitants whether they could get brandy in exchange or not. Jean Bourdon de Dombourg made perhaps the most significant argument when he noted that limiting the trade in brandy would limit the fur trade, and that French colonists would then turn their energies to agriculture, which would lead the colony to success.[44]

In the end, the king determined that the trade should continue. In 1679 he issued a proclamation declaring that the trade could remain open so long as no liquor was carried into Indian communities. The ruling displeased both Laval and Frontenac, but widespread evasion of the limits certainly reveal that the governor's views ultimately triumphed over the bishop's.[45] The proclamation, following the dominant logic of the Quebec meeting, represented the emergence of a new political economy of the brandy trade. By allowing the business to continue, the king and his advisers made a specific economic point: New France needed the fur trade to survive, and brandy lubricated the fur trade. In the absence of migrants willing to transform Bourdon de Dombourg's argument about agriculture into reality, the logic of the proclamation fitted the quotidian realities of early Canada. It also, not surprisingly, reinvigorated the clerics' assault on the liquor trade.

NEW SPAIN, NEW FRANCE

"The Poison of the Liquor Traffic"

After 1679, when virtually everyone in Canada believed that traders would ignore the few restrictions on the business, missionaries launched a series of new offensives in what became a more wide-ranging cultural war against brandy. Now that the trade was officially permitted, Indians did not have to travel so far for liquor, and some Indians, notably the Iroquois, were drinking themselves to "continual suffering," as the missionary Claude Chauchetière wrote in 1682, noting that the "french are the cause of its giving us much trouble here; for, in order to strip the Savages to their Very Shirts, they follow them everywhere, to make them drink and become intoxicated." Though some Indians tried to battle the trade in their villages by breaking bottles and spilling liquor—some apparently were even willing to risk death for their cause—they could not hope for success without assistance. Brandy sellers carted their wares anywhere beyond the control of missionaries, as one noted in 1686 when he wrote that the commerce could not be prevented at Tadoussak or Chegoutimy. Well into the 1690s missionaries feared for their own safety, as well as that of their charges, and continued to lament the fact that brandy prevented conversion.[46] Although the quantities of brandy sold in Montreal were limited, the settlement was still ravaged by the trade, a seeming vortex of violence and despair, or so Dollier de Casson believed in the early 1690s. He wished the king could "see the truth of the matter, how happy we should be, for the rectitude of his intentions would no longer be perverted by so many emissaries of Satan who spread the belief that without liquor we should have neither savages nor furs, most true though it is that we should be the favourites of all the native tribes if the sweetness of Christianity were not so destroyed here by the poison of the liquor traffic."[47] The liquor trade was an assault on everything the clerics had been trying to achieve in Canada since the early decades of the century. And who better to assist the allegedly beleaguered Indians, the clerics seemingly asked themselves, than those who best knew the stakes in this cultural war (figure 14)?

Clerics took a variety of routes in their efforts to battle the trade. Clerical historians who had spent time in Canada, such as Charlevoix and Chrestian Le Clercq, no doubt drawing on the reports that had circulated in the *Jesuit Relations*, condemned the trade for their audiences. Charlevoix, ever careful to support the efforts of other clerics to convert the Indians, shared the missionaries' view that brandy undermined any program of cultural conversion.

14. This drawing by the missionary Claude Chauchetière (1645–1709) was intended to accompany one of his annual reports about the activities of the Christian Indian community at Sault-Saint-Louis. As Chauchetière and other missionaries realized, Indian converts often played active roles in securing a ban on the liquor trade in their villages. Courtesy Archives Départementales de la Gironde, Bordeaux.

When he saw some Indians drinking, he wrote, "one would have thought that a gang of devils had broke loose from hell." Like other observers, Charlevoix knew that alcohol caused violence in Indian villages; Europeans' liquors "have not a little contributed to the depopulation of all the Indian nations, who are at present reduced to less than the twentieth part of what they were one hundred and fifty years ago." But Charlevoix recognized that ending the trade would be difficult, especially when Hurons and Potawatomis warned him that any attempts by the French to halt the sale of brandy would send Indians to the English to purchase rum. In the end he believed that the only places Indians could escape the trade were missionary communities such as those at Sillery and Cap de la Magdelaine.[48] Le Clercq, a Recollet missionary who worked in New France from 1675 to 1686, wholeheartedly endorsed the missionaries' critique of Indian drinking and their condemnation of traders. He too recognized that the central feature of Indian drinking was an effort to become intoxicated. "These barbarians," he wrote, "who formerly mistook wine for blood, and brandy for poison, and who fled with horror from the French who would give them these liquors, are to-day so enamoured with these kinds of drinks that they make it a principle of honour to gorge themselves therewith like beasts; and they only drink, properly speaking, in order to get drunk." But his emphasis was on traders, who got their clients "drunk quite on purpose, in order to deprive these poor barbarians of the use of reason, so that the traders can deceive them more easily, and obtain almost for nothing furs that they would sell only for a just and reasonable price if they were in their right minds." The traders were committing fraud twice over, for they watered their brandy. Indians, from this perspective, lacked the responsibility necessary to control themselves.[49]

The most elaborate clerical effort to redefine the brandy trade appeared in François Vachon de Belmont's *Histoire de l'eau-de-vie en Canada.* Presumably written in the early eighteenth century, the manuscript remained unpublished until 1840. But though it never reached its intended audience, it tells us the precise ways in which clerics understood the liquor trade.

Belmont's depiction of Indian drinking patterns (described in chapter 3) is one of the most systematic clinical analyses of alcohol consumption among Indians. And he went beyond the drinking to describe the cultural conflict it aroused in Canada. Belmont listed the people killed by intoxicated Indians at the mission on Lake Ontario. But the catastrophes transcended the level of individual violence. According to Belmont, when drunken Indians sacked the mission at Lachine, they called down divine retribution on their heads. "The participants were about eighty canoes of Ottawas and Hurons who came down in 1690, and indulged in drinking in a frightening manner," he wrote. "That year, the harvest was the best in the world. On the morrow of the drinking bout, the grain was found rusted and shrivelled from a [frost]. From that time, corn has cost upwards of ten and twelve francs the minot.

One would have to be blind," Belmont concluded, "not to attribute other misfortunes which have befallen the country to the disorders of brandy." Clearly the brandy trade hindered, not helped, the colonization of Canada because it cheated the king out of revenues that would otherwise have come in trade and brought about "the malediction and vengeance of God on the colony." The French who sold liquor to Indians were "scoundrels" and they would "be damned."[50]

The logic that Belmont applied to the liquor trade perfectly fitted the temperance plans of missionaries, especially Jacques Bigot, the resident Jesuit in the mission community of Sillery in the mid-1680s. Bigot, like other Jesuits, believed that the liquor trade was destroying the Indians of Canada, and he devised an elaborate plan for battling drunkenness among his charges.

By 1685, Bigot already thought he had evidence that Indian drinkers, under the proper guidance, could resist brandy. Since many Indians drank "merely out of human respect," and since they lacked "any great craving for liquor," he wrote to a colleague in 1682, it should not be too difficult to break drunkards of their habits. Besides, he had proof that some Indians at Quebec had been "cured" of their intemperate ways under the guidance of a local priest.[51] Sillery, though, presented a more serious problem. To battle Indian drinking there, Bigot created social mechanisms for ensuring sobriety through a series of punishments. He too borrowed economic logic to make his point, though his program proved a drastic contrast to the economic visions of liquor vendors. Chief among his initiatives was what he termed "Holy pillage"—"le Saint pillage"—a ritualistic plundering of the goods of drunkards; he also believed that drunken Indians should be imprisoned in Quebec. Bigot claimed that "for the better observance of [the governor's] orders, he Desired that I should, with a Holy audacity, take away from every Savage whom I found intoxicated some petty effects belonging to his Cabin, in order that the effects so taken might Serve to pay the Archers who would come to put that drunken Savage in prison." Indians, Bigot asserted, came to accept the legitimacy of his tactics, even when he furthered his goals through deception: at times he pretended to plunder goods before Indians got drunk in a farce of his own ritual, and he claimed to speak for the governor and attributed to the governor speeches that he never made.

But plunder was only one aspect of his campaign; Christian repentance joined le Saint Pillage as a goad to sobriety. Local Indians, Bigot reported, proved more than willing to join the cause; they flocked to the local church during a novena to the mission's patron, St. Francis de Sales. "The communion took place on All Saints' Day," Bigot wrote, "in order to obtain, through the intercession of all the blessed, a general pardon for all the sins that had been committed in the mission for many years during drunken excesses; and to ask God to grant to all the christians of our mission a firm resolution never again to fall into that sin." So many Indians turned out for the services that Bigot "left the church open throughout the night, to satisfy the devotion of those who might wish to pray longer." Though Bigot took responsibility for the mission's success—"I have prevented probably Seven or eight hundred mortal sins during the few days while I have worked to suppress the evil of intemperance," he claimed—he knew he could succeed only if French traders stopped selling brandy to Indians. The "strict prohibition of drunkenness," he noted, would "not make the savages averse to the french," as some traders were claiming; on the contrary, "it is the most effective means for winning them to us, and of making them happy with us."[52]

Bigot was wrong, of course; the cause of abstinence did not win many converts to Christianity. But by pressing his case in unabashedly religious terms, he, like Belmont and other clerics, made a point that must have been inescapable to their contemporaries: the liquor trade was an affront to God, and God's emissaries needed to battle it. Better to steal from Indians in the name of God than to allow them to thwart God's desire for their conversion. By relegating liquor vendors to damnation and seeking ritualistic cures for Indian drinkers, the clerics demonstrated that the king's proclamation of 1679 was fatally misguided. To them the political economy of the brandy trade violated the infinitely more precious plans of the Lord. Some Recollets proved susceptible to the logic of secular leaders and merchants on the need for the trade,[53] but the vast majority of clerics never gave in on this point. To do so would have been to repudiate their mission and abandon their vision of Canada's future. Their failure to stem the flow of liquor into New France thus suggests a failure not of will but of power. The brandy trade survived because the clerics could not stop the merchants from selling liquor or the Indians from buying it.

"The Only Commodity That Encourages Your Trade of Small Furs"

By the beginning of the eighteenth century, the brandy trade had become indispensable to traders, Indian and colonist alike, and their activities dominated the economy of Canada. Indians who participated in the trade were not innocent dupes but ever more sophisticated consumers of an increasing range of European commodities.[54] What they wanted was liquor, Baron La Hontan wrote in 1703. In an "Inventory of the Goods" that he felt were "proper for the Savages," he noted that "Brandy goes off incomparably well." His list included such goods as awls, "Caps of blew Serge," Brazil tobacco, and "Venice beads," but liquor was the only item to which he appended a comment.[55]

Missionaries, for their part, did not meekly give in to the forces of commerce. Three anonymous reports written in 1693 provide harrowing details of the psychic turmoil that brandy brought to Indian communities. Observers claimed that alcohol contributed to family violence, sexual licence, theft, and murder. Pregnant women killed their babies or aborted them. And the economic consequences remained: Indians involved in the brandy trade became poor and lazy, thereby reducing the number of pelts that could be sent back to France. Further, the liquor trade impeded French colonization of Canada because drunken Indians attacked colonists and made life unbearable. Finally, colonists who sold brandy to Indians were away from home so long that they could not tend to their farming. "Such are the tragic results of the sale of eau-de-vie," one noted, "which lessens trade, weakens and ravages the colony, and ruins the bodies and souls of the infortunate Savages of New France. . . ."[56]

The unknown authors of the 1693 reports were not alone. In 1718 the missionary François Joseph Lafitau noted that liquor destroyed Indian communities by leading to violence, marital strife, impoverishment, and debt; that the trade threatened the "well-being of the habitants, who, attracted by the hope held out by the profits of that trade, abandon their farms and their families to go, sometimes without permission, among the savage nations" and then "give themselves up to debauchery" and a "dissolute life"; that it threatened the interests of French merchants by making Indians less reliable trade partners; and that the continued sale of liquor to Indians was "calculated to alienate the Savages from us" and send them straight into the arms of the English. Liquor was "almost the sole obstacle to the labors of the missionaries," and he thus joined others in calling for renewed government efforts to stop the trade.[57] For their part, the bishops of Quebec hotly contested claims about the importance of this commerce and never wavered from their desire to stop the liquor trade.[58]

Lafitau's petition, representing as it did what had become the standard clerical attack on brandy, did not succeed in reestablishing a total ban on the trade. Though members of the council agreed "as to the evils of the trade in brandy," they believed "at the same time, that it is necessary." The governor added that "it was indispensable to give two or 3 pots of brandy per man to the savages from the upper country who come into the colony, and even to allow the traffic to be carried on with moderation at Fort Frontenac." His logic persuaded the council to allow the transport of "moderate quantities" to the places he suggested.[59] Contrary to the Jesuits' desire, civic officials continued to believe that Indians had come to expect presents of brandy during formal meetings; since the giving of presents had long been an accepted practice in intercultural affairs (and accepted by the French more readily than it ever was by the British), the importance of continuing the practice was clear.[60]

For much of the eighteenth century, French traders were apparently supplying a demand. Royal officials allowed increased sales of brandy to Algonquians in the Great Lakes region because the Indians there wanted alcohol; the French supported the commerce because they were in the process of doing all they could to maintain that region's commerce and the political alliances trade seemingly assured.[61] However repugnant, the brandy trade kept Indians away from the English. As Count de Pontchartrain, writing from Versailles, informed Governor de Vaudreuil in June 1706, the king understood that the governor provided the chief of the Outaoucas "with a little Brandy in order to restrain him, when that alone will effectually prevent them resorting to the English for purposes of trade." The governor could continue to allow limited allocations to the Indians, "provided moderation and propriety be observed."[62] Later French officials made an even stronger case. One official, ignoring the horrors of the brandy trade, noted in 1720 that the Indians would "become more tractable, and more submissive to the French," when they could get liquor; if they got it, they "will devote themselves to procuring good furs, and will listen to the advice of the Commandants. This Conversion can not be brought about without threats on their part of going to the English to get brandy, for the drunkards will not easily be cured of the desire for drink."[63]

The trade thrived in the west and even in the extreme southerly reaches of New France, where by the early 1730s some Indians even refused to hunt without first getting alcohol.[64] Jesuits in the lower Mississippi Valley complained, as their northern counterparts had been doing for decades, that when Indians there got alcohol, their drinking led to chaos.[65] By the mid–eighteenth century French officials in Louisiana also regretted the expansion of the trade, but found themselves powerless to stop it; they could not even reign in the entrepreneurial spirit of some French soldiers, who violated military rules by selling their own rations of wine and liquor to Indians.[66]

Efforts to halt the trade here were no more successful than those of the missionaries to the north.[67]

Further, habitants and officials in Canada had no ability to control the trading efforts of the English liquor purveyors in the Illinois country and the Great Lakes region, or of the Hudson's Bay Company, whose sales of brandy increased dramatically during the first half of the eighteenth century and remained strong until the end of the colonial period.[68] But British territory in the north had little bearing on the liquor commerce in the St. Lawrence Valley, where the French managed to keep the business thriving on their own. Well into the eighteenth century, the logic of the trade remained: intoxicated Indians, so traders believed, sold their skins more cheaply than sober Indians. No matter how far west the trade extended, this central element of fraud always lingered near its heart. After arriving with a group of Indians at a French trading post in the west of Canada, Anthony Hendry (Henday) noted in his journal that the "Natives received from the Master [of the post at Fort La Corne] ten Gallons of Brandy half adulterated with water; and when intoxicated they traded Cased Cats, Martens, & good parchment Beaver skins, refusing Wolves & dressed Beaver." The trader, according to Hendry, profited well by the exchange. "In short, he received from the Natives nothing but were prime Winter furs." Five days later and 200 miles downriver, at the French trading post at Fort Poskoyac (or Pasquia), "they gave the Natives 10 Gallons of Brandy adulterated, and they are now drunk." The hunters apparently remained inebriated the next day. "The Indians drank so much I could not get them away, nor was I capable to prevent them from trading their prime furs." Though the Indians Hendry traveled with rarely had liquor during his journey between the Blackfeet country and York Factory from June 1754 to June 1755, brandy was certainly available when they brought their furs west for trade.[69]

To complicate matters, in the eighteenth century more Indians themselves became involved in the sale of liquor. La Salle had argued that cutting off the trade in Indian villages would have little effect because Indians were in the habit of buying brandy at French settlements and taking it home with them to sell.[70] Decades later, his comment was still apt. The Assiniboines in particular became the vital link between European traders, British and French alike, and Indians farther west who chose not to make the long and often perilous journey to colonial posts. Montreal-based merchants used brandy to solidify their alliance with the Asssiniboines and the Indians with whom they traded. In spite of occasional proclamations to the contrary, then, merchants in Canada actually promoted the trade in an effort to maintain their share of the market.[71] Though some Indians such as the Chipewyans refused rum well into the century, by the early nineteenth century the alcohol trade was steadily and seemingly inexorably expanding.[72]

By the time the English defeated the French and gained control of Canada, the liquor trade had become inextricable from the fur trade. In spite of virtually relentless missionary efforts and occasional official limits on the trade, brandy continued to be available and Indians continued to desire it. In all likelihood the physiological problems often associated with alcoholism, such as cirrhosis, were not widespread, but observers recorded in great detail the social pathologies brought by drinking.[73] The persistence of the trade indicated that many Indians in New France, like their counterparts in New Spain, ignored the missionaries' teachings about abstinence. The liquor trade survived wherever traders sought to obtain pelts from Indians, and it remained alive until the end of the colonial period.[74] Further, it could be argued that since the fur trade was so vital to the imperial interests of the French, the alcohol trade proved even more important in Canada than elsewhere in North America.[75]

For all of its similarities to the trade in British America, the liquor trade in Canada followed its own distinctive course. By the beginning of the eighteenth century or so, the liquor trade had become marginal to the economic interests of most British colonists; it thrived where colonists were few, and where those few depended principally on the fur and skin trade. The unwillingness of many French families to become permanent residents of Canada made trade with Indians the necessary path to whatever success New France was to enjoy. Greed, not patriotism, certainly motivated the merchants who supported the trade. But the debate of 1678 also reflected the fact that the colony would prosper only if traders took Indians the goods they wanted. Commerce prevailed because there was no other viable means to establish relations with the majority of native peoples; only a minority of Indians subscribed to the missionaries' vision of a brandy-free society.

Under such circumstances, Indians in territory controlled by the French found themselves confronting what must have seemed an enormous paradox. On the one hand, the alcohol trade seemed to have the sanction of the state. On the other hand, the missionaries never abandoned the temperance cause. Whereas Indians in British America had requested and received statutory protection (however ineffective) from liquor traders and many of them could live out their lives without ever seeing a missionary, the simmering hostility between missionaries and governors in New France sent ambiguous messages to drinkers and nondrinkers alike.

After 1763, from New England to West Florida and from the Atlantic to the Mississippi, Indians in the eastern woodlands found no such ambivalence. Whatever their wishes, they then inhabited territory claimed by the British. And they recognized that the liquor trade fitted perfectly into the workings of the British Empire.

CHAPTER SEVEN
The British Imperial Moment, 1763–1775

As [the] saying is in an Ancient Book where the Carcass is,
there will the Eagles be gathered together.
—James Sterling to James Lyme, June 1762

After the Seven Years' War, the English realized that they had won the battle for control of North America. They had vanquished the French, their traditional foe, and for the time being felt little hostility toward Spanish colonizers to their south. Not since Elizabethan times had they had an opportunity to define what their relations with Indians should be without regard for the programs of other European colonizers. The end of hostilities offered colonists an opportunity to do what many claimed they had wanted to do much earlier: quit the liquor trade altogether. Rather than do so, however, many traders actually expanded their business, or so the available record suggests.

In that moment of imperial victory, British political economists mapped out what they thought would be a bright future based on the expansion of commerce through the Atlantic basin. "[T]he spirit of *commerce* will become that predominant power, which will form the general policy, and rule the powers of Europe," Thomas Pownall, a one-time governor of Massachusetts, wrote in 1765, "and hence a grand commercial interest, the basis of a great commercial dominion, under the present scite and circumstances of the world, will be formed and arise."[1] British colonists and policy makers ensured that the liquor trade remained a fixture of the empire. The commerce, once termed an "abominable filthyness" by the Rhode Island legislature, had become inseparable from the workings of the empire.

DEADLY MEDICINE

"Their Liberty of Trade"

By the early eighteenth century, agriculture dominated the economy of the colonies, especially the more densely settled regions near the coast. But despite the decline in the influence of the fur and skin trade in the colonies, it was still important to imperial officials. Although many colonists had perhaps lost interest in commerce with Indians, colonial bureaucrats seized the new opportunities of the postwar period to create plans for the future of Indian-colonist relations.

With war against France concluded, many colonists and British officials believed they had entered a new era of peace and prosperity. When colonists moved inland in search of new land, they quickly sought to replicate the settled, agricultural economy of the coastal regions. Many of these inland migrants were either the children of farm families that could not provide sufficient land for them or recent migrants whose reason for crossing the ocean was their overwhelming desire to own land. These people, by and large, wanted as little to do with Indians as possible, although they traded with them on occasion. Yet their presence came to define the limits of the Indian trade. Wherever settlers chose to remain, their growing numbers made the survival of nearby Indian communities precarious. Even in areas where Indians and colonists had often treated each other amicably, colonists' ever-increasing need for land tended to sour relations.[2]

Still, trade with Indians remained profitable, and colonial officials still argued that commerce had cultural benefits as well. Trade, that is, could advance the cause of civilizing Indians. The idea was not new, but it became more compelling after mid-century. Perhaps few made that idea so plain as Governor Arthur Dobbs of North Carolina. In a speech to that province's assembly in 1754, Dobbs urged the legislators to regulate the skin trade and "to promote an Intimacy of Friendship and living in Harmony with our Indian Neighbours and Allies that we may be enabled to Civilize and make them Industrious and to Incorporate with them by carrying on an Equitable Trade with them and treating them with Christian Benevolence. . . ." Such efforts would not only lead to an expansion of the skin trade and the profits resulting from it; they would also encourage Indians to become allied with the English and "form an Impregnable Barrier against our ever active Enemies the French." Dobbs was certainly not alone in his beliefs; the Lords of Trade in 1754 instructed him to maintain good relations with Indians in the region to preserve trade and peace, and to promote legislation to regulate the actions of traders.[3]

If trade was to have the desired effect, traders had to avoid angering their clients. Well before 1763, officials recognized that traders' actions could have political and military consequences. Any fur trader who angered Indians ran the risk of causing an Indian war or possibly driving Indians into the ever-welcoming hands of the French. It was just such fears that had led Pennsylvania officials in the mid-1740s to reinforce their efforts to suppress the illegal liquor trade, especially since a report from George Thomas noted that "the like Abuses of the Traders in *New-England* were the principal Causes of the *Indian* Wars there."[4] Given the potential danger, colonial officials sought ways to regulate trade even though most Indian groups dealt with individual traders.

The establishment of commissaries at British posts to regulate trade and the participation of leading civic officials in trade negotiations after mid-century suggest that commerce with Indians was too important to leave to the workings of the market alone. No one expressed the idea more clearly than Robert Hunter Morris. Trading houses, he wrote in 1756, "should be Erected in the Indian country, and the Price of all goods sold there should be settled by the government To regulate this trade so as to make it answer to the Publick purposes."[5] Not all colonists supported the effort. Writing to his mother in March 1763, John Dickinson noted that many Pennsylvanians woud oppose any act to regulate trade because they "are more desirous of the Trade being unrestrained—than they are afraid of the Indians." Still, he thought the renewal of the act would pass because the Indians had been promised that the provisions would remain, no doubt agreeing with him that the act "was calculated to preserve the Indians from the Impositions of the most infamous & extortionate Rascals who trade amongst them."[6] George Croghan, writing from Fort Pitt in 1767, summarized prevailing sentiment when he noted that "Confineing the Trade to the different Posts would Certainly be a means of making the Indian Nations Dependant on us & prevent many Irregularity's, in particular the Seal [sale] of spirituous Liquors which the Indians Complain much off," though he admitted that he did not know if such a plan could be installed.[7]

Regulation was especially necessary beyond the limits of colonial settlement, where the fur and skin trade remained vital to British plans and where colonial officials often had the least power.[8] British efforts to impose order on the liquor trade often foundered because unlicensed traders ignored regulations and repeatedly tried to make quick profits by defrauding Indians. Though their deceptions could have undermined the entire trade system, according to colonial officials, they nonetheless continued.[9]

Although some officials proposed strict regulation, others recognized that liquor should not be entirely forbidden. After all, imperial rivalries worried British officials, especially when newspaper reports noted that Indians who wanted liquor would go to the French or Spanish if the British did not supply it. This was the threat that the Creek Indian known as Duvall's Landlord made in 1760, and it was the reality in November 1761, when a group of Indians arrived in Charlestown with ten kegs of rum that they had gotten from the Spanish.[10] "The Savages should not be debarred spirituous Liquors," Colonel Bradstreet noted in the mid-1760s, "it is their darling passion; nay, they love it so much, they will sacrifice their all, at times, to obtain it. . . ." But the trade, which Bradstreet thought should be limited in quantity to prevent troubles, had more than economic significance. The Indians "will never live at peace with us without it."[11] Lieutenant Governor Elias Durnford of West Florida, fearing the consequences of an unrestrained rum trade, nonetheless informed Hillsborough in 1770 that a trader should be allowed to take "a small quantity or rum" into Indian nations "for his own private use," but Durnford must have known that the liquor would be sold to Indians. To prevent the "many abuses and irregularities" that so often accompanied the skin trade, he supported the appointment of commissaries to travel to Indian villages to carry on a proper trade; such a system, which presumably would lessen the amount of fraud perpetrated by traders, would also reduce the need for Indians to visit colonial settlements.[12] Here, then, was the system as colonial bureaucrats envisioned it: allow traders to carry only enough liquor to Indians to maintain political alliances and trade, and send government-appointed officials to treat with Indians, thus reducing the Indians' contact with other colonists.

The logic expressed by Bradstreet and Durnford fitted the concern of imperial officials in the late 1760s and early 1770s. Few made the connection between the fur trade and the interests of the empire as clearly as Major Robert Rogers, a one-time commander of the British post at Michilimackinac, between lakes Huron and Michigan. He wrote a lengthy report, apparently in the late 1760s, explaining the need for the British to supply the post, even though the venture could cost as much as £60,898 a year. The funds would provide for the maintenance of a trading house, at least one hundred canoes, and the supplies needed to keep the trade going. Like other trading operations, Rogers's post required a variety of goods, especially clothing, blankets, gunpowder, guns, and kettles; and he believed the post would need to distribute "Ten Keggs of British Brandy" each year. Since it is impossible to gauge the size of the post's clientele—Rogers estimated that there were

30,000 Indians in the region who could trade there, but it is unlikely that anywhere near that number actually traveled through regularly—it is difficult to determine the amount he thought would be consumed by individuals.

Whether the liquor available was enough to make many Indians drunk is not the issue. What was clear to this provincial official was that liquor was needed to draw Indians to the post, and thus to maintain not only the supply of pelts but also a market for goods produced abroad. Rogers demonstrated the breadth of his vision in his repeated concerns about French and Spanish encroachments on English territory, and the economic impact of the loss of the lucrative fur trade in the region. Losing the trade, which he estimated would cost approximately £40,500 a year, "is not the whole Loss that Great Britain must suffer by such a restriction," he wrote, "for whatever Lessens British Manufactures or puts a stop to Employments by which British Subjects may decently Subsist and increase their Substance may be Justly estimated a Public Injury or National Loss." Further, he added, decline in trade would hinder imports from London to Quebec and thus eliminate hundreds of jobs for colonists who would be involved in the transportation of British goods to the post. Since these people would not "increase their Substance and consequently add to the Riches of the Nation," the loss of the trade could be staggering.[13] Crown officials elsewhere apparently felt the same and at times participated directly in the distribution of alcohol to Indians.[14]

Colonial officials' toleration of the liquor trade demonstrated an enduring paradox: liquor lured Indians to the British, but drunken binges undermined Indian communities and made individual Indians less reliable hunters and allies. The apparent reluctance of British officials to prohibit the commerce after 1763 despite the many appeals suggests the power of inherited notions about colonial-Indian relations. In the first place, the imperial bureaucracy had never been very efficiently organized; even members of the Board of Trade, perhaps the most likely group of British officials to coordinate crown policy for the American colonies, complained at times that no single office was sufficiently informed about important events in the colonies.[15] This absence of effective organization signaled a second impediment to any attempt to create policy for the colonies: the belief held by most officials on both sides of the Atlantic that each colony had the authority to govern itself. The two men who served as superintendent of Indian affairs after the Seven Years' War, Sir William Johnson and John Stuart, did not have the authority to establish regulations that bound colonists to certain kinds of conduct.[16] To be sure, British officials recognized the dangers when colonists in the western reaches of the empire mistreated Indians, either by violating the terms of the

Proclamation of 1763 or by cheating them in trade.[17] But, in the opinion of prominent English officials, that was no reason for the superintendents to presume they had the powers to restrain colonists. Hillsborough declared the crown's position on the subject when he wrote to Governor William Tryon of North Carolina from Whitehall in April 1768. In response to a proposed plan to reorganize "the management of Indian Affairs," Hillsborough reported that "the Regulations of the Trade shall be left to the Colonies whose Legislatures must be the best judges of what their several situations and circumstances may require." The superintendents would remain, to be sure, "for such matters as are of immediate Negotiations between His Majesty and the Savages and cannot therefore be regulated by Provincial authorities," but their authority was subordinate to that of the individual colonies.[18]

Some colonial officials, to be sure, objected to the trade and wanted it stopped. Perhaps none so consistently battled against the liquor trade as Sir Jeffrey Amherst, who did all he could to prevent the commerce during the Seven Years' War. As he made clear in a series of letters to Johnson from late 1761 to mid-1763, he was moved less by humanitarian concern than by the conviction that the liquor trade endangered British interests. Extension of the wartime ban on the trade at British posts, he informed Johnson in December 1761, would have various benefits: it would force Indians to trade for goods that they really needed, thus making them less dependent on the crown's agents; the crown would save money by not having to provide alcohol, presumably in the form of gifts, to Indians who arrived at their posts; and the ban would reduce "their Committing outrages, for which they never fail to plead as an Excuse their being in Liquor." Johnson quickly agreed, though he informed Amherst that Indians needed to "be gradually weaned" from their expectations of receiving it in presents. Knowing that he had Johnson's support, Amherst pushed to maintain the ban, informing Johnson in June 1762 that he had encountered Indians who supported him and he told them the prohibition would continue "whilst I have the honor to Command in this Country." A year later he wrote that he was doing everything he could to keep the ban in force, and he regretted that he could not discipline a civilian "who is Chiefly Concerned in Debauching the Indians, as he is not Subject to the Military." When colonists continued to sell alcohol to Indians in spite of the ban, which could be enforced only at military posts, the situation evoked the concern not only of Amherst but of Johnson as well.[19]

In spite of reports that traders violated the ban during the war, it did prove effective in some areas. James Sterling, commissary of the post at Fort Detroit, was one colonist who agreed with the ban and recognized its usefulness. "[I]f all others are prohibited from bringing up Spirituous Liquors, we will gain considerably by it," he informed James Lyme in June 1762. "[I]t will help to engross the French Trade for as [the] saying is in an Ancient Book where the Carcass is, there will the Eagles be gathered together." Having referred to the French as vultures, he added that brandy was one of their "Tutelery Gods"; without them and their wares, the trade could only improve. Still, Sterling had little choice about the rum trade, especially during the war years. No matter how many times he asked for alcohol to sell to non-Indians around the fort, he could not get it. Even supporting letters from local military leaders to Amherst did no good. Sterling was not particularly concerned about the ban's effect on the trade if every post had to abide by it. But he feared that sales of alcohol elsewhere, such as Niagara, would greatly reduce the business at Detroit, because Indians would haul their furs to any market where they could buy liquor.[20]

But even when Amherst and any official who agreed with him got Johnson's attention and compliance, they could not banish liquor from the hinterland; once the war ended, so did any reasonable expectation of halting the commerce. Predictably, the impetus for maintaining the trade came from traders and merchants whose agenda conflicted with Amherst's plan. They were concerned with making a profit in the fur trade, and they justified their pursuit of it by using the language of free trade that had historically driven English policy in North America. In March 1764 a group of Albany merchants petitioned the Lords of Trade in London to prevent any ban on the sale of liquor to the Indians, despite the pleas of some Iroquois sachems; they argued that "other Tribes with whom your Petitioners carry on a far more considerable Trade, look upon such a Prohibition as the greatest Indignity, and as an encroachment on their liberty of trade." Any measure that prevented them from selling alcohol to the Indians had serious economic consequences. They found, they wrote, "a considerable decrease in the Trade which they can ascribe to no other reason than such a prohibition because when the Indians have nothing farther to provide for than bare necessaries, a very small quantity of Furs in Trade will abundantly supply that defect, Whereas when the Vent of Liquors is allow'd amongst them, it spurs them on to an unwaried application in hunting in order to supply the Trading Places with Furs and Skins in Exchange for Liquors."[21] In this view, the liquor trade did more than provide revenue for colonists; it also benefited Indians by making them more industrious and eager to participate in the market economy.

Responding to a plan issued by the Lords of Trade in October 1764, Johnson echoed the Albany merchants. Though he recognized the problems of Indian drunkenness, and indeed wanted the Indians to receive liquor only upon their departure from the posts, he believed that "the Trade will never be so extensive without" rum. The Indians would be "universally discontented without it." But the Indians' contentment was secondary to the economic interests at stake. Without the liquor trade, "the Indians can purchase their cloathing with half the quantity of Skins, which will make them indolent, and lessen the Fur Trade."[22]

Rather than limit the trade, Johnson wanted to raise revenue through it. "I have also recommended in a strong light the necessity of allowing the Sale of Rum," he informed Cadwallader Colden, lieutenant governor of New York, in 1764. "I was obliged to promise it to them . . . at Niagra, & without they will never be contented besides that they can supply themselves with other Articles on a much Smaller quantity of Peltry, & will gladly purchase that liquor at any rate, w[hic]h may enable us to encrease the Duty thereon, & the Ill consequences of that liquor will be guarded against by the Steps now to be taken." Though the duty would be high, the "Traders will think themselves happy that they have it to dispose of." Johnson held to his views through the 1760s. Fur traders not only continued to use rum in their dealings but, as Johnson informed Hillsborough in 1770, they carried little else with them to trade "because the profits upon it are so considerable." Though Johnson railed against liquor purveyors who undermined relations between Indians and the crown, especially during treaty negotiations, he must have considered the traders' strategy sound because at times he sent his own agents into Indian country supplied with little more than rum. By doing so, Johnson put into practice what he had known all along. As early as the 1730s, when he first proposed a trading post at Oquaga, on the banks of the Susquehanna, he recognized that liquor was the commodity that Indians wanted most.[23] No matter the ill effects on Indian communities or colonial government, the trade had to continue.

But the debate continued among imperial officials, not all of whom shared the views of Johnson and the Albany merchants. Even with the French threat diminished, some British leaders remained concerned about the business. General Thomas Gage repeatedly informed Hillsborough that the business continued unabated from the Great Lakes region to West Florida, and that it continued to upset relations between the British and the residents of Indian country. Once again, there seemed to be no way to stop the commerce. "The most general Complaint at present about the Trade is, of the vast Quantitys of Rum carried amongst the Indians," he wrote in February 1772. "It is possible that a Check might be given to it, but it's so easy for the Traders to smuggle it past the Posts, and the Temptation from the Gain upon that Article is so great, that I apprehend a great deal will always be carried up." His views of those involved in the commerce convinced him of the difficulty of any regulation. "[A]n Indian Trader, generaly a pretty Lawless Person, would not pay much Regard to Laws So many hundred Miles in the Desarts, where it is difficult to detect him, and will be much more so to convict him."[24] And Indian demand remained great as well, as Sterling realized in 1765 when he feared an attack at Detroit. "There is scarce any thing talk'd of here but War," he wrote to Ensign Magill Wallace, who was stationed at Michilimackinac. "[I]t is said that Genl Pontiac intends coming to this place w[it]h a large Army of the Nache's, but, I believe, the main Attack is design'd against the Rum Cags. . . ." If this was the case, he believed the troops would be able to protect the supply, for "I'll be hang'd if ever one of them offers to come past them 'till the last Drop is expended."[25]

Gage and Sterling lost the struggle to keep liquor away from Indians. In the end, Johnson's view prevailed, and the liquor trade expanded during the 1760s. After 1763, British traders quickly seized opportunities for the fur trade in Canada, and apparently decided to use alcohol quite extensively in their dealings. British merchants shipped large quantities of rum to Quebec, especially from 1768 through 1774. At least 200,000 gallons made their way to that port each year, and in 1774 merchants there imported 752,442 gallons. Given the continued importance of Quebec as a center of the fur trade— peltry dominated the exports to Great Britain during this same time period— it seems likely that a good part of the rum shipped to Canada was intended to supply fur traders and their Indian clients.[26]

Though existing records point to the continuation and apparent growth of the liquor trade in the 1760s, the amount of liquor used in the trade remained limited. After all, even if the estimates of Johnson and Stuart were correct, a total of 80,000 to 170,000 gallons of rum consumed by Indians annually, in addition to the Canadian trade, was ultimately a minor component of the distilled spirits trade in the Atlantic world.[27] Colonists, after all, imported or produced 8.6 million gallons of rum in 1770, and kept 7.5 million gallons for themselves.[28] Indians represented only a small fraction of the people who drank liquor in North America.

In the end, the traders' quest for profits and Indians' demand for rum maintained the trade despite the social chaos so evident in Indian villages. Under the banner of free trade, some traders even argued that Indians must not be deprived of the cultural opportunities attendant on commerce. There could never be a more effective wedding of the cultural and economic logic that had driven Britain's Indian policy since the Elizabethan period.

Jonathan Carver's Dream

Jonathan Carver had traveled among the Naudowessies, a group of Sioux, during the 1760s and learned their ways, and he wrote down what he learned about their world. He knew how important the fur trade was to the British Empire in the 1760s, having worked with Major Robert Rogers at Michilimackinac. Like any other good servant of the king, Carver wanted to make sure that pelts from America continued to fill ships crossing the Atlantic. He was not one to engage in idle hopes that the trade would prosper. Carver, or someone working for him, drew up a plan to promote the trade under the humble title "An Account of the situation, Trade and Number of Hunting Indians at Lake Pepin in the Mississippi, North America." Central to the plan was a single idea: If the British controlled the liquor trade in the area, they would monopolize the fur trade there.[29]

The plan began with a description of the strategic importance of Lake Pepin, in modern-day Minnesota. The lake "is about Twenty Miles in length, and five broad. Through Which the Mississippi runs, and is about two Thousand Miles by its Course from the entrence into the Gulph of Mexico, and nearly the same distance westerly from Quebec Boston and New York." The area around the lake was like paradise; it had "very Spacious Plains and Meadows open and fit for immediate Cultivation." Elk, deer, buffalo and "other Quadrupeds" abounded, "with Fowl and Fish in their Seasons, Likewise Beaver, Otter, Mink, Martins, Sable, and Must Rats." Large groves of sugar maples yielded the local Indians "great Quantities of Sugar." But most important, "the Country abounds with Graps of a Good sort sufficient for any Quantity of Brandy."

Sufficient natural resources for a contented life were not what the author had in mind; these goods should be put to work for profit, and for this enterprise Lake Pepin was ideally situated. "The Number of Hunting Indians who frequent Lake Pepin, at present are upwards of two Thousand, who at a Moderate Computation, will annually bring, not less than a Hundred weight of Beaver each or other Furrs to the same value, Besides Skins, Horns, and other articles, whi[ch] will easily raft Down the Mississippi to West Florida. . . ." When traders brought an "assortment of goods" there, presumably the numbers would increase.

The fur trade was not new in the region. "The French Carryed on something of a Trade at Lake Pepin before the English made a Conquest of this Country. But never attempted the very lucrative part, of making spiritious or Strong Drink, by reason of its being Contrary to the Doctrine of their Missionarys to sell such to the Indians." Still, "some [alcohol] has been carry['d] as far as this place, tho two thousand miles of Difficult Carriage, and Sold to good advan[tage.]" How much liquor was necessary to drive the trade? "It is Computed that upwards of two Thousand Gallons of Rum & Brandy can be made [on] the spot as Cheap as in the West Indies, of Consequence three Thousand Miles of the Carriage will according to a proper Estimate, make a Saving of near two Thousand pct. in that Comodity alone, besides the saving of Duty and the Certainty of having it on the spot at the most Convenient time for sale, together with the Probability of Drawing the whol trade of that vast Country into the Companys hands."

The economics of the fur trade was unmistakable, and liquor was ideally suited to maximize profit. "It is Judged that every Gallon of Spirits will fetch there in trade, what will produce ten pounds in the London Market. So that near twenty Thousand pounds annually can be made to the Company with very little more Expence then it would require to Carry on the Trade of English Goods alone." Still, care needed to be taken not to oversaturate the market. "[T]here is a great probability that much more Spirits can be Expended at the place to equal profit and not overstock the Market so as to Lower the price, which must be carefully managed by the Company."

After laying out the economics of the situation, and suggesting again that company members would be able to feed themselves with ease near the lake, the author offered a proposal: A stock of £4,000 would be needed to start the venture, and profits would start eighteen months or so later. The company would send furs to Montreal, where they would be shipped to London for the English market. And "heavy articles that may be acquird in the way of trade Such as Buffaeloe Skins Horns Elk and Bear Skins Deer Skins &c may be raft Down the Mississippi to pensacola or Mobile, with very little Expence, and from thence Shiped for the Colonies for Sale as the Company may think best."

The company, to comprise thirty-two men, would be supervised by Carver. His qualifications for the post were beyond reproach. He had recently been conducting surveys of the lake and so knew the area well. He was "adopted a Chief of the Naudowissis a Powerfull Nation to whom this Country belongs." Carver's "Genu[ine] Knowledge in Indian affairs and Extraordinary influence over the Nations in those parts will likely render the Situation of Trade more safe then any one Else." Peter Fowler would be second in command and in charge of the distillery; agents would conduct the company's business. The author did not note that Carver had received from the Sioux a grant of territory near the lake, nor did it mention that Carver (who knew the ritual importance of giving alcohol to Indians) was well aware that Indians in the region had long suffered from the liquor trade when the French were powerless to stop it.[30] The author also failed to note that Carver knew that the liquor trade had impoverished Indians near Winnebago Lake, and that some Indians, including many of the Naudowessie, refused to drink alcohol.[31]

No documentation survives to tell us whether the plan was ever put into effect. But whether Carver and his associates ever set up the distillery is not the point here; Indians in that region certainly had an ample supply of liquor available to them well into the nineteenth century.[32] The significance of the plan lies in Carver's assumption that the prosperity of the fur trade was linked to the expansion of the liquor trade. In his imperial fantasy, Carver betrayed the Indians who had adopted him and conferred a great honor upon him. Though he knew that alcohol disrupted their communities and brought suffering to individuals and families, he hoped to serve the king and to profit himself by bringing more liquor to them.

Although Indian drinking fitted into some colonial theorists' vision of the empire, few imperial bureaucrats ever wanted to transform America's natives into alcoholics. Since later British imperial planners did attempt to solidify their control over parts of Asia with opium,[33] the difference in the American situation is worth noting. There was no single British imperial view of the North American liquor trade, no order from the king demanding that his subjects maintain the commerce. British officials and colonists who had to deal with Indian affairs—the superintendents for the northern and southern colonies; provincial officials who had to treat with Indians in land deals and for trade relations; military leaders who struggled to maintain alliances with various Indian groups to prevent them from becoming allies of the French; and the negotiators who shuttled back and forth between colonial capitals and Indian country—never agreed on a single "British" view of the liquor trade. Nor did they agree on any other issue, with the exception of the need to keep Indians away from the French. The decentralized structure of the empire in British America was not conducive to a uniform strategy in Indian affairs. The overlapping levels of authority only exacerbated the differences of opinion among policy makers.

Jonathan Carver knew how the empire worked, and he dreamed of the profits that would be his if he could solidify his hold on his own niche in it. By asking for £4,000 to put his plan into action, he was only giving voice to the acquisitive desires that British colonists had demonstrated for almost 150 years in Indian country.

EPILOGUE
Legacies

They are by the constant use of spirituous Liquors become Effeminate and Debilitated.
—[Commandant Forbes?] to General Thomas Gage, [July?] 1768

You Rot Your grain in Tubs.
    —Catawba chief Hagler to North Carolina representatives,
    August 1754

At the end of the colonial period, Alexander Hewatt knew why Indians had
fared so miserably over the previous centuries. They had suffered, he wrote
in 1779, at the hands of settlers who captured them and sent them to the
West Indies as slaves. They lost the lands near the sea, which had supplied
them with food. They warred against other Indians in efforts to halt the
spread of European colonists. And they had succumbed to smallpox, which
had "proved exeedingly fatal" because it spread so rapidly and because their
water cure hastened their death. "But, of all other causes," Hewatt declared,
"the introduction of spirituous liquors among them, for which they discovered an amazing fondness, has proved the most destructive."[1]

Indians had been deceived by "unprincipled and avaricious traders" who
"first filled the savages drunk, and then took all manner of advantages of
them in the course of traffic." Awakening to their new poverty, Indians became filled with rage, breathing "vengeance and resentment." Excessive
drinking weakened Indians before the onslaught of other diseases. All of
these calamities were ultimately caused by colonists. "[T]hose Europeans
engaged in commercial business with them, generally speaking, have been
so far from reforming them, by examples of virtue and purity of manners,
that they rather served to corrupt their morals, and render them more treach-
erous, distrustful, base and debauched than they were before this intercourse
commenced." And the result of those indiscretions was demographic catastrophe. "In short," Hewatt concluded in language aimed to inflame the sen-

sibilities of Englightenment-era Europeans who had come to celebrate the primitive dignity of the American savages, "European avarice and ambition have not only debased the original nature and stern virtue of that savage race, so that those few Indians that now remain have lost in a great measure their primitive character; but European vice and European diseases, the consequences of vice, have exterminated this people insomuch that many nations formerly populous are totally extinct, and their names entirely forgotten."[2]

Had other colonists shared Hewatt's views, Indians might not have suffered so much from the liquor trade. But despite the often well-meaning efforts of colonial legislators and the appeals of temperance-minded Indians, the trade continued, and not just because of the avarice of liquor purveyors. The efforts to stop the commerce failed for two reasons: many Indians chose to drink and colonists were deeply divided over the liquor trade. Drunken Indians surely caused problems, thoughtful colonists acknowledged, but Indians needed to trade if they were to have any hope of completing the process of cultural evolution. And economic necessity—the desire for pelts and deerskins for the British market—as well as rivalry with France (at least until 1763) went hand in hand with any argument about the cultural progress that came with commerce. In the end, the interests of Indian drinkers and colonists who supported the trade coalesced to keep the outlawed commerce flourishing.

Liquor was not a minor component of the so-called Columbian exchange, the mingling of peoples, plants, animals, goods, and pathogens of the Americas with those of the Eurasian landmass.[3] The alcohol trade entailed more than an exchange of commodities. It became, especially in the last decades of the colonial period, crucial to the way colonists and Indians understood each other. Indians' responses to liquor reinforced colonists' notions about their cultural and racial inferiority; colonists' desire to maintain the trade despite its all too apparent costs reinforced Indians' notions about the deeply rooted problems of colonial culture. From such a perspective, the alcohol trade becomes a vehicle for exploring, at its most human level, the nature of colonization in North America.

The issues here cannot be easily quantified. We cannot assess the impact of the liquor trade by determining how many pelts traders obtained with rum. Few Indians traded for alcohol alone; they still wanted blankets, clothing, guns and gunpowder, and other manufactured goods. Hence the alcohol business needs to be viewed in a wider context. The liquor trade joined with the growing colonial population and recurring epidemics to destabilize Indian villages, and perhaps contributed to the decision of countless Indians to sell their lands to colonists and move westward, beyond colonial settlements.

The struggle for the control of British America ultimately came down to demographics. The colonists found North America a remarkably healthy place to live, and their numbers exploded as a result, doubling every twenty-seven years or so by the late colonial period, a fact of life recognized at the time and openly discussed by Benjamin Franklin and others.[4] Indians, their numbers sharply reduced by deadly diseases, could not hope to retain exclusive control of eastern North America.[5] Even if they were to join together in some pan-Indian movement—a highly unlikely development in view of the separate identities and often antagonistic relationships they had developed over centuries—they could never have stopped the westward movement of colonists. In the context of these diametrically opposed demographic histories, the alcohol trade is surely no more than a footnote. Its impact on Indian populations was trivial in comparison with the horrors of epidemic diseases.

Since we know that colonists eventually took control of eastern North America and continued westward in that mythic pageant we tend to think of as the inexorable progress of the American people, we presume that events took place as they did because they could not have done otherwise. Most of us no longer believe, as seventeenth-century Puritans and New England Indians did, that Providence or Manitou directs the course of human events, but we are still prisoners of our own untested and outdated assumptions about the inevitability of Western progress.

The horrors that alcohol brought to Indians in early America require us to think more closely about that sequence of historical events. The alcohol trade began as an outgrowth of a particular economic system. By the time of the American Revolution the trade had a new purpose. In England's great age of empire in North America, liquor became the primary commodity that brought Indians and colonists together and simultaneously drove them apart. Whatever its precise role in the decline of Indian communities or its specific contribution to the coffers of fur traders and merchants, the alcohol trade's greatest impact was cultural. The liquor trade became a crucible of culture in North America. Its persistence signaled a victory of British American values over those of Indian country.

But neither germs nor alcohol caused the hatred and racism that bedeviled

Indians and colonists alike. All were convinced that their own culture was better than the other, though Indians did not generally seek to impose their ways on colonists as colonists sought to impose theirs on Indians.[6]

The battle for North America became a clash of peoples promoting opposing cultures, and the colonizers left precious little room for Indian contributions.[7] In that clash, colonists and Indians constantly judged one another. They were, as Conrad Weiser's description of Andrew Montour's drinking suggests, more sensitive to idiosyncrasy than we tend to believe. Yet they were also, in their own ways, ethnographers: they made cultural determinations, often painted in broad strokes, about the nature of colonial or Indian culture. The animus that developed between them grew over time (and would continue to grow after the colonial period) and resulted from their differing interpretations of their common experiences.

The alcohol trade plagued relations between Indians and colonists precisely because each group interpreted its existence as a sign of the other's failings. At the end of the colonial period many colonists believed that Indians' inability to control their thirst for rum signaled deep-seated, permanent inferiority. Nothing else could explain their continued demand for a commodity that so palpably destroyed their communities. After all, since colonists themselves drank alcohol in prodigious quantities and did not suffer greatly from it, Indians' intemperance and its associated risks must have been proof of something forever alien about America's natives, a confirmation of their savagery. Even clergymen who ministered to Indians on the presumption that Indian souls could be saved believed at times that Indians could never convert to abstinence. As one minister recalled in the late eighteenth century, even Indians who were raised by Christians could not control their thirst for liquor once they had spent time around other Indians; "soon after they had the command of themselves and of their time, and had associated with those who were of the same complexion, [they] became *Indians* in the reproachful sense of the word, were idle, indolent, and intemperate. . . ."[8] Another offered a blunter epitaph to the decades of missionary efforts to stop Indians from drinking: "With respect to drinking spirits . . . they are generally, and we fear incurably, addicted to intemperance, whenever they have the means in their power. This is the character of all the savages of North America."[9] The stereotype of the intoxicated native was so firmly in place that one colonist who had extensive contact with drinking Indians in late colonial western Pennsylvania could describe an unpalatable group of whites as arriving "about Dusk like so many Drunken Indians."[10]

Even after extensive interactions with Indians, many colonists still feared

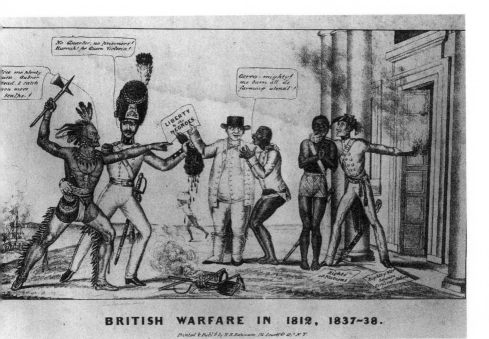

BRITISH   WARFARE   IN   1812, 1837-38.

Printed & Publ'd by H.R.Robinson, 52 Court'St. N.Y.

15. The original version of this cartoon, created during the War of 1812, showed British soldiers encouraging slaves to burn farm equipment. In the late 1830s, in the age of Removal, a later artist depicted a stereotypically savage Indian with an insatiable thirst for alcohol in alliance with the nation's enemies. Courtesy, American Antiquarian Society.

them (figure 15). Perhaps to some colonists the scalpings and tortures and murders that littered the pages of captivity narratives revealed Indians' fundamental inability to evolve beyond the status of *sauvages*, those mythic people whose lack of civilization rendered them morally deficient.[11]

Hence colonists' views of Indians and the alcohol trade contained an unspoken paradox: Indians could get liquor only from colonists, but by trading for it they further distanced themselves from the course of cultural progress. When provincial officials felt compelled to give alcohol to Indians in order to maintain political alliances, they only exacerbated the problem, or so one official wrote to General Thomas Gage from the Illinois country in 1768. "I have for some time observed that the more Presents they receive, the oftner they Return, and are less contented," the official wrote, noting that the Indians became more dependent

upon his Majesty's Bounty, than their own Industry; for while they are supplied with necessary's, and Provisions, they never move from their

Village, but beging and hanging upon the Inhabitants, which gives them such a habit of Idleness (particularly the four Tribes in this District) that they are by the constant use of Spirituous Liquors become Effeminate and Debilitated: so much that nothing can be apprehended, from such a Dastardly Race of Cowards, who impute, the Bounty they receive, proceeds from fear not of Love.[12]

Fears that Indians who did not trade would become "indolent," as Johnson declared, persisted over the centuries. Indians needed trade to become civilized, so the Elizabethan argument ran. By the late colonial period, after Indians had traded actively with English colonists for almost two centuries, Indians needed to trade lest they revert to their lazy ways; they needed to produce for the market if they were to become civilized and cast off the final vestiges of savagery. Though prominent colonists such as Benjamin Franklin drew opposite conclusions, their protests mattered little. Nor did the temperance appeals of Indians who wanted to stop the liquor trade. If Indians could not control themselves when they consumed colonists' goods, this was a further indication of their cultural depravity. The solution was not to stop the flow of rum to Indian communities but, presumably, to maintain the trade as (still) the surest way to "reduce" Indians to civilization. And Indians who wanted to stop the British trade were perhaps unconscious allies of the French. Since Indians would go wherever liquor was for sale, any efforts to stop the rum trade at British posts necessarily boosted the attraction of French trading houses where brandy could be had.

Indians, most notably the temperance reformers, would not have agreed with this assessment. They knew that the alcohol trade brought destruction to their communities, eroding the customary web of relations that bound the old to the young and women to men with a sense of reciprocity desperately needed for survival in a world often under siege. Those who battled the trade knew that they were doing all they could to preserve their villages. Colonists' promotion of the liquor trade rested, Indians realized all too well, on cupidity. Colonists' greed was no stranger to Indians, who had been engaged with them in a struggle for their own land, animals, and souls since the early seventeenth century. The liquor trade was a logical outgrowth of a system built on the desire to amass goods, an idea initially alien to most Indians in the eastern woodlands.[13]

When Johnson and others tolerated and even promoted the trade, they provided evidence to Indians that colonists had not yet learned to control their own insatiable appetites. To many Indians, such demands demonstrated the moral failings of colonists. When the Catawba chief Hagler informed North Carolina officials that "You Rot Your grain in Tubs," he was not simply alluding to the process of distilling alcohol; he was also giving voice to the contempt that Indian temperance reformers felt toward liquor purveyors. John Doubty, "an old Indian Man Born in Jerseys," told James Kenny that colonization had led to spiritual decline among Indians, for "after ye White people brot Rum & supply'd Indians with it, they forgot God & lost their former Devotion."[14] The Shawnee chief Gischenatsi in 1773 expressed the anger that many Indians then felt for colonists. "The white people," he declared, "always profess to have great wisdom and understanding from above, at the same time, they deceive us at will, for they regard us as fools and say, the Indians know and understand nothing and are poor people, which is partly true." Such authority gave colonists power, as Gischenatsi realized. "As the white people understand the weakness and incapacity of the Indians, they have a certain power over us, while pretending that with all their deception they mean well by the Indians. They come and bring rum into our Towns, offer it to the Indians and say, drink; this they will do until they become quite beside themselves and act as though they were out of their heads." Then "the white people stand, point at them with their fingers, laugh at them and say to one another, see what great fools the Shawanose are. But who," Gischenatsi asked, "makes them so foolish, who is at fault?"[15]

Hagler and Gischenatsi were not alone in the contempt for liquor purveyors. The Pequot writer William Apess consistently deplored the liquor trade during the early nineteenth century. Apess knew well the sufferings that alcohol abuse caused; he claimed that he was beaten by intoxicated relatives when he was a child, and at one point he became "addicted to drinking rum" himself. Yet though he recognized the personal failings of Indians who could not control their thirst for liquor, and though he became the president of a temperance society among the Mashpee Indians, Apess was unequivocal in his assessment of the problem. "My sufferings certainly were through the white man's measure," he wrote in 1833, "for they most certainly brought spirituous liquors first among my people, until the burning curse and demon of despair came among us: Surely it came through the hands of the whites. Surely the red man had never sought to destroy one another as this bane of hell would! And we little babes of the forest had much to suffer on its account. Oh white man! How can you account to God for this? Are you not afraid that the children of the forest will rise up in judgment and condemn you?"[16] The frontispiece in one of his books vividly captures his contempt for the liquor trade (figure 16). And what message must have spread among

MANNER OF INSTRUCTING THE INDIANS.

16. The Pequot William Apess became an outspoken critic of the liquor trade in Massachusetts in the early nineteenth century. "How much better would it be if the whites would act like a civilized people and, instead of giving my brethren of the woods 'rum!' in exchange for their furs, give them food and clothing for themselves and children," he wrote in his 1829 autobiography, *A Son of the Forest*. "If this course were pursued, I believe that God would bless both the whites and natives threefold." This image was the frontispiece of Apess's *Indian Nullification of the Unconstitutional Laws of Massachusetts Relative to the Marshpee Tribe; or, The Pretended Riot Explained* (Boston, 1835). Courtesy, American Antiquarian Society.

groups of Indians, such as the Passamaquoddys of Maine, who came to believe that alcohol came from the Devil? Such notions, voiced in a European vocabulary and brilliantly captured in a nineteenth-century image (figure 17), reveal the depth of alienation between Indians and colonists.

Indian temperance reformers found many sympathetic ears among whites. The minister Samuel Hopkins, striving to get colonists to treat Indians "in a just, kind and charitable manner," in 1753 asked his readers, "if we furnish them with large Quantities of Rum, make them Drunk, and then defraud them of what they have, do we not reduce them to a Necessity, either of living low and miserable with us, or of going from us, that they may fare

17. In this frontispiece for Eugene Ventromile's *Ahiamihewintuhangan: The Prayer Song* (New York, 1858), a collection of Gregorian chants translated from Latin into Eastern Abenaki (Penobscot) and Micmac, T. W. Strong captured the belief that alcohol was a tool of demonic forces. Courtesy, Boston Athenaeum.

better?"[17] The Quaker Anthony Benezet offered a more pointed critique. "That Indians may be tempted or provoked to the perpetration of great evils, by the intemperate love and use of strong liquors, is easily conceived," he wrote in 1784, "but whether they, who to gratify the cravings of sordid avarice, furnish them with the intoxicating potion, and then take advantage of them, and tempt them to evil, are not principally accountable, for the crimes they commit, and their consequences, is not a query worthy of their most awful consideration."[18] Gilbert Imlay offered perhaps the simplest statement of such views at the end of the eighteenth century when, in a description of the Catawbas, he noted that the "cause of civilization proving repugnant to their population, I think, may be sufficiently accounted for in the whites encouraging their thirst for intoxication."[19] The painter George Catlin's famous image "Pigeon's Egg Head (The Light) going to and returning from Washington" (figure 18) reinforced the idea that white society threatened Indians.[20] Colonists may have believed that Indians were incapable of mastering the fine points of civilization. But many Indians must have wondered what benefits they could expect from joining a society in which even prominent leaders were, in some sense, in league with evil.

For both colonists and Indians, alcohol was what the Sioux called *mni wakon*, sacred water. Some colonists hoped that the drink trade would allow them to

18. In "Pigeon's Egg Head (The Light) going to and returning from Washington"
George Catlin captured the sorry transformation of the Assiniboine Wi-jun-jon, who
"had in Washington exchanged his beautifully garnished and classic costume, for a
full dress 'en militaire,' " perhaps given to him by the president. From the pockets
of his military coat protrude bottles of whiskey. From Catlin's *Letters and Notes on
the Manners, Customs, and Conditions of North American Indians* (1876). Courtesy,
Library of the American Philosophical Society.

continue their divinely sanctioned efforts to civilize America's savages. Many
Indians, more wary of the destructive force of things sacred, tried to keep their
distance, and perhaps by doing so to demonstrate to colonists that there was
more to life than filling the holds of ships with beaver pelts. In such a context,

it is not surprising that the Iroquois Handsome Lake, the Delaware Prophet, the Shawnee Tenskatawna, and the Kickapoo prophet Kenekuk all made temperance a central part of their movements for cultural rebirth in the late eighteenth and early nineteenth centuries.[21]

Relations between Indians and colonists were eroded not only by the intense cultural conflict over liquor but by their mutual liking for strong drink. Conrad Weiser and the Indians he met at Logstown in September 1748 certainly knew this. Recognizing the need to limit the trade, Weiser told them that "you never agree about it; one will have, the others won't have it, (though very few of them) a third says he will have it cheaper." Weiser added that "this last we believe speaks out of your heart, (here they laughed.)"[22] In that moment of laughter, Weiser believed, the Indians who had complained to the colonial negotiator recognized the attractions of drinking. Alcohol may have been a tool of empire builders, and these Indians knew well its destructive powers. But they also knew that no one forced them to drink. They may have recognized their own failing, perhaps their own complicity in a trade that so manifestly endangered their world. We may never really understand why the Indians at Logstown laughed, but their laughter reminds us that they were not mere victims of an aggrandizing colonial power. Perhaps, for reasons inexplicable to modern observers, they thought the joke was on Weiser.

To us the trade was so horrific that we wonder how anyone, colonist or Indian, could put up with it. But its survival is not all that mysterious. By the age of George III, colonists were confident in their ability to seize control of eastern North America and increasingly cavalier in their dealings with Indians. If ever there was a time to abandon the liquor trade and seek to create better ties with Indians, it was after the Seven Years' War. But by then, so many colonists profited from the liquor trade that they could not let it vanish. Indians' demand for rum, traders' determination to provide it, and British officials' inability or unwillingness to stop the business proved too potent a mixture for even the most sympathetic colonial official or dogged Indian temperance reformer. The logic of traders and merchants appealed to some imperial bureaucrats, who agreed that Indians should be free to buy liquor if they wanted it. The consequences, as thoughtful observers knew, were disastrous. "Will not it be impossible for Indians and White people to live together?" the governor of Pennsylvania, Richard Peters, asked George Croghan in 1754. "Will not there be an eternal Intercourse of Rum and a perpetual Scene of quarrelling?"[23]

DEADLY MEDICINE

At the end of the colonial period, when other Americans were liberating themselves from the shackles of an old world, Indians could not escape the "bewitching Tyranny" of the liquor trade. Neither Indians nor colonists could sever the alcohol trade from the workings of the empire. The peculiar vice of Europeans had become a fixture in Indian country, deadly medicine that remained to poison relations between the peoples of North America.

Appendix I

Value of rum and of all goods traded to Indian groups in Illinois country by Baynton, Wharton & Morgan for the crown, 1767–1768

			Rum traded			
Indians				Value		Value of all
Tribal group[a]	Number present	Gallons	Amount	Rank	goods traded
Missouri	120	72	£10 16s	3	£90 4s 3d
Kaskakis	80	40	6	2	26 15s 2d
Illinois	13	48	7 4s	3	73 12s 6d
Pioras	209	64	9 12s	3	91 2s 8d
Tobacco	60	48	7 4s	2	59 10s 7d
Mitches	40	32	4 16s	2	22 14s 4d
Cuanpous	60	48	7 4s	3	63 8s 11d
Kaskaskis	–	64	9 12s	3	70 13s
Ouatona & Cocaupous	75	48	7 4s	2	68 12s 1d
Vermillion	40	40	6	1	29 3s 2d
Osages	30	32	4 16s	1	22 11s 5d
Missouris	50	32	4 16s	4	39 10s 5d
Kaskaskis	15	24	3 12s	1	18 11s
Illinois	45	48	7 4s	1	36 19s
Musketons	35	32	4 16s	2	26 11s 2d
Mitchigamie	35	24	3 12s	4	25 7s 1d
Kaskaskia	68	64	9 12s	1	37 7s 3d
Mitchigamie	–	20	3	2	17 11s
Piora	21	24	3 12s	1	27 4s 3d
Kuskuskia	56	48	7 4s	1	32 13s 3d
Missouri	44	32	4 16s	1	36 1s 6d

APPENDIX I

	Indians		Rum Traded			Value of all goods traded
				Value		
Tribal group[a]	Number present	Gallons	Amount	Rank	
Kaskaskia	47	24	3 12s	2	£17 8s 2d
Piorias	75	48	7 4s	1	40 2s
Kuskuskis	17	20	3	3	26 15s
Piorias	–	56	8 8s	2	49 4s 3d

[a]As listed in company records.
Source: BWM, reel 7, frames 477–490.

Appendix II

The Speech of a Creek-Indian, against the Immoderate Use of Spirituous Liquors

INTRODUCTION;
By the TRANSLATOR.

Of all the Vices which prevail in the World, none more degrades human Nature, and dishonours the glorious Image of the Deity, than immoderate *Drinking*; and there is none against which more has been said, both from the Press and Pulpit: Yet still this Vice rears its shameless Front, and reels from Street to Street in broad Day. Hence it was thought that the following Translation of the *Speech* of a *Creek-Indian* on this Subject, might, at least, be acceptable to the Curious; and should it have no good Effect, it will be but one Patriot-remonstrance more thrown away.

Charity bids us suppose, that our Laws, our Religion, and civil Accomplishments; elevate the People of this Country, far above the Enormities that gave rise to this Oration among a People we esteem *Barbarians*; yet so frail is the Texture both of public and private Virtue, and so mutable the State of human Affairs, that tho' we could think such a Remonstrance unnecessary at present, it may be preserved as a Beacon in Time to come. The Wise and Good it cannot displease; and if there is one that wears the human Form in these Christian Realms, a Slave to this enormous Vice, let him be roused

THE
SPEECH
OF A
CREEK-INDIAN,
AGAINST THE
IMMODERATE USE
OF
SPIRITUOUS LIQUORS.
DELIVERED

In a National Affembly of the *Creeks*, upon
the breaking out of the late WAR.

To which are added,

1. A LETTER from YARIZA, an *Indian*
Maid of the Royal Line of the *Mohawks*, to
the principal Ladies of *New York*. 2. INDIAN
Songs of Peace. 3. An AMERICAN *Fable*.

Together with

Some REMARKS upon the Characters and
Genius of the *Indians*, and upon their Cuftoms
and Ceremonies at making War and Peace.

Viri Ninivitæ, & REGINA *Auftri, exfurgent in judicio
cum viris hujus gentis, & condemnabunt eos.*
——*Nec longum tempus, et ingens
Exiit ad cœlum, ramis felicibus, arbos.*

LONDON:

Printed for R. GRIFFITHS, Bookfeller, in *St. Paul's
Church-Yard.* M.DCC.LIV.

19. Title page of the London edition of *The Speech of a Creek-Indian, Against the Immoderate Use of Spirituous Liquors* (1754). The pamphlet was allegedly first printed in New York, but no copy has been found. By permission of Houghton Library, Harvard University.

when he hears the Sentiments of a Heathen, and, trembling, reflect upon the Condemnation in the Motto inserted in the foregoing Title Page.

The *Creek-Indians* are settled between the Rivers *Halbana* and *Locushatche*, about 5 or 600 Miles Westward from *Charlestown* in *South-Carolina*. They are found to be a brave, polished, and wise People. Upon the Breaking out of the late War, the *English*, *French*, and *Spanish* made Application to them for their Alliance. They were then at War with some other *Indians*; and finding themselves in a very critical Situation, a national Council was assembled, in which the following Harangue was delivered.

If we are not mistaken, it will be found, on a critical Examination, to contain all the Parts of Members of the most perfect Oration. It is impossible to do it Justice by a literal Translation into our Language, which is very different from the *Indian Phraseology*. The *Indian* Orators have a certain Loftiness of Expression, Boldness of Figures, and Pomp of Imagery, which we want Abilities to naturalize. We have not, however, been wanting in our Endeavours to support the Spirit of the Original; and we hope the Matter, rather than the Form, will employ the Attention of the candid Reader.

APPENDIX II

A
SPEECH,
BY A
CREEK-INDIAN,
On The
Breaking out of the late WAR.

Fathers, Brethren and Countrymen,

In this solemn and important Council, rising up before the Wisdom and Experience of so many venerable *Sachems,* and having the Eyes of so many heroic Chieftains upon me, I feel myself struck with that awful Diffidence, which I believe would be felt by any one of my Years, who had not relinquished all the Modesty of Nature.

Nothing, O ye *Creeks*! could enable me to bear the fixed Attention of this illustrious Assembly, or give to my Youth the Power of an unembarassed Utterance, but the animating Conviction that there is not one Heart among us, that does not glow for the Dignity, the Glory, the Happiness of his Country. And in those Principles, how inferior soever my Abilities may otherwise be, I cannot, without violating my own Consciousness, yield to any one of the Superiority.

Fathers, Friends and Countrymen

We are to deliberate—upon what? Upon no less a Subject, *Than whether we shall, or shall not, be a People?* On the one Hand, we are at War with a Nation of our own Colour, brave, active, and sagacious. They bear us unquenchable Hatred, and threaten us with all that *Prudence* ought to fear, and *Valour* be excited to repel.—On the other Hand, we are surrounded and courted by three powerful Nations, of Colour, Laws, and Manners different from our own. Courted, I say, for though each is Rival to the other, yet it is to be feared none of them mean our Prosperity.

I do not stand up, O *Countrymen!* to propose the Plans of War, or to direct the sage Experience of this Assembly in the Regulation of our Alliances: Your Wisdom renders this unecessary for me.

My Intention is to open to your View a Subject not less worthy your deliberate Notice; and though equally glaring, though equally involving your Existence and Happiness, yet, from the bewitching Tyranny of Custom, and the Delusion of Self-love, if it has not escaped general Observation, it has eluded public Censure, and been screened from the Animadversions of our national Council.

I perceive the Eye of this *august Assembly* dwells upon me. Oh! may every Heart be unveiled from its Prejudices, and receive, with Patriot-candour, the disinterested, the pious, the filial Obedience I owe to my Country, when I step forth to be the Accuser of my Brethren,—not of Treachery, not of Cowardice, not of Deficiency in the noblest of all Passions, the *Love of the Public.* These, I glory in boasting, are incompatible with the Character of a *Creek!*

The Traitor, or rather the Tyrant, I arraign before you, O *Creeks!* is no Native of our Soil; but rather a *lurking Miscreant,* an *Emissary* of the evil *Principle* of Darkness. 'Tis that pernicious Liquor, which our pretended *white Friends* artfully introduced, and so plentifully pour in among us.

Oh Countrymen!

I will spare myself the ungrateful Task of repeating, and you the Pain of recollecting, those shameful Broils, those unmanly Riots, and those brutal Extravagances, which the unbounded Use of this Liquor has so frequently produced among us. I must, however, beg Leave to assert, and submit to your Impartiality my Arguments to support this Assertion, that our prevailing Love, our intemperate Use, of this Liquid, will be productive of Consequences the most destructive to the Welfare and Glory of the Public, and the Felicity of every individual Offender. It perverts the Ends of Society, and unfits us for all those distinguishing and exquisite *Feelings,* which are the Cordials of Life, and the noblest Privileges of *Humanity.*

I have already declined the Mortification which a Detail of Facts would raise in every Breast, when unpossessed by this *Demon.* Permit me then, in general, only to appeal to public Experience, for the many Violations of civil Order, the indecent, the irrational Perversions of Character, which these inflammatory Draughts have introduced amonst us. 'Tis true, these are past, and may they never be repeated.—But tremble, O ye *Creeks!* when I thunder in your Ears this *Denunciation;* that if the Cup of Perdition continues to rule among us with Sway so intemperate, *Ye will cease to be a Nation!* Ye will have neither *Heads* to direct, nor *Hands* to protect you.—

While this diabolical Juice undermines all the Powers of your Bodies and Minds, with offensive Zeal the *Warrior's* enfeebled Arm will draw the Bow, or launch the Spear in the Day of Battle. In the Day of Council, when national Safety stands suspended on the Lips of the hoary *Sachem,* he will shake his Head with uncollected Spirits, and drivel the Babblings of a second Childhood.

Think not, O ye *Creeks!* that I presume to amuse or affright you with an imaginary Picture. Is it not evident,—(alas, it is too fatally so!) that we find the Vigour of our Youth abating; our Numbers decreasing; our ripened Manhood a premature Victim to Disease, to Sickness, to Death; and our venerable *Sachems* a solitary scanty Number?

Does not that Desertion of all our reasonable Powers, which we feel when under the Dominion of that deformed Monster, that barbarian Madness, wherewith this Liquor inspires us, prove beyond Doubt that it impairs all our intellectual Faculties, pulls down Reason from her Throne, dissipates every Ray of the *Divinity* within us, and sinks us below the Brutes?

I hope I need not make a Question to any in this *Assembly*, whether he would prefer the intemperate Use of this Liquor, *to clear Perceptions, sound Judgement,* and a *Mind* exulting in its own *Reflections.* However great may be the Force of Habit, how insinuating soever the Influence of Example, and however unequal we may sometimes find ourselves to this insidious Enemy; I persuade myself, and I perceive by your Countenances, O *Creeks!* there is none before whom I stand, so shameless, so lost to the weakest Impulses of Humanity, and the very Whisperings of Reason, as not to acknowledge the Baseness of such a Choice.

Fathers and Brethren,

I must yet crave your Patience, while I suggest to you, that this Intoxication of ourselves disqualifies us from acting up to our proper Characters in social Life, and debars us from all the soothing, softening, endearing Joys of domestic Bliss.

There is not within the whole Compass of Nature, so prevailing, so lasting a Propensity, as that of associating and communicating our Sentiments to each other. And there is not a more incontestable Truth than this, that *Benignity* of *Heart*, the calm Possession of ourselves, and the undisturbed Exercise of our *thinking* Faculties, are absolutely necessary to constitute the eligible and worthy Companion. How opposite to these Characters Intoxication renders us, is so manifest to our own Experience, so obvious to the least Reflection, that it would be both Impertinence and Insolence to enlarge farther upon it, before the Candour and *Wisdom* of this *Assembly*.

And now, O ye *Creeks!* if the Cries of your Country, if the Pulse of Glory, if all that forms the *Hero*, and exalts the *Man*, has not swelled your Breasts with a Patriot Indignation against the immoderate Use of this Liquor;—if these Motives are insufficient to produce such Resolutions as may be effectual—there are yet other Ties of Humanity, tender, dear, and persuading. Think on what we owe to our Children, and to the gentler Sex.

With Regard to our Children, besides affecting their Health, enervating all their Powers, and endangering the very Existence of our Nation, by the unbounded Use of these pernicious Draughts, think how it must affect their Tenderness, to see the Man that gave them Being, thus sunk into the most brutal State, in Danger of being suffocated by his own Intemperance, and standing in Need of their infant Arm to support his staggering Steps, or raise his feeble Head, while he vomits forth the foul Debauch?

O Warriors! O Countrymen!

How despicable must such a Practice render us even in the Eyes of our own Children! Will it not gradually deprive us of all Authoriy in the Families which we ought to govern and protect? What a Waste of Time does it create, which might otherwise be spent round the blazing Hearth, in the most tender Offices? It perverts the great Designs of Nature, and murders all those precious Moments, in which the Warrior should recount, to his wondering Offspring, his own great Actions and those of his Ancestors. By these Means the tender Bosom has often caught the Patriot-flame, and an illustrious Succession of *Sachems* and Warriors were formed among us from Generation to Generation, before our Glory was eclipsed by the Introduction of this destructive Liquid.

O Creeks!

You all remember the great *Garangula*, who is now gone to our Fathers, and from whose Loins I immediately sprang. You know how often he has led forth our Warriors to Conquest, while his Name sounded like Thunder, and flashed Terror upon our Foes. You will then pardon the necessary Vanity, if I presume to remind you how piously he adhered to our original Simplicity of Life. Oft has he said, that if he did not fly from this Cup of Perdition, his Name would never be sounded from Hill to Hill by the Tongue of Posterity; and I can affirm that, if he had wasted his Time in such Practices, my Bosom would never have been fired to Glory by the oft-repeated Story of our Family-Virtues and Atchievments; nor should I have dared, on this Occasion, fondly to emulate them, by raising my unpracticed Voice, in the Cause of my Country, before such a venerable Assembly of Chiefs and Warriors.

But farther, besides what we owe to our Children, let us think on that delicate Regulation of Conduct, that Soul-enobling *Love*, which it is at once the Happiness and Honour of *Manhood* to manifest towards the gentler Sex. By the *Love* of this Sex I do not mean meer Desire of them. Those amiable Creatures are designed not only to gratify our Passions, but to excite and fix all the kind and sociable Affections. They were not meant to be the Slaves of our arbitrary Wills in our brutal Moments, but the sweet Companions of our must reasonable Hours, and exalted Enjoyments. Heaven has endowed them with that peculiar Warmth of Affection, that disinterested Friendship of Heart, that melting Sympathy of Soul, that entertaining Sprightliness of Imagination, joined with all the sentimental Abilities of Mind, that tend to humanize the rough Nature, open the reserved Heart, and polish the rugged Temper, which would otherwise make Men the Dread and Abhorrence of each other.

Thus were Women formed to allay the Fatigues of Life, and reward the Dangers we encounter for them. These are their Endowments; these their Charms. Hither, Nature, Reason, Virtue call—And shall they call in vain? Shall an unnatural, an unreasonable, a vicious Perversity of Taste be preferred to those heaven-born Joys of Life? Will you treat the *Sovereign Principle* of *Good* with a thankless Insensibility, and offer Libations to the Spirit of all Evil? Will any *Creek* henceforth dare to approach those lovely Creatures with unhallowed Lips, breathing the noisome Smell of this diabolical Juice, or roll into their downy Embrace in a State inferior to the Brutes, losing all *that rapturous Intercourse of Love and Friendship*, all those most exalted of human Pleasures, which *they, they* only are formed capable of communicating to us?

Oh no!—*Fathers, Warriors and Countrymen!*

Let me conjure you by all these softer Ties, and inexpressible Endearments; —let me conjure you too, as you yet hope to behold the TREE of PEACE raise its far-seen Top to the Sun, and spread its odorous Branches, watered by the Dew of Heaven, over all your Abodes, while you rejoice unmolested under its Shade; and as you yet wish to behold the Nations round about you, bound with the sacred CHAIN of CONCORD, every Hand maintaining a Link:—By all these Ties, by all these Hopes, I conjure you, O *Creeks!* henceforward let the Cup of Moderation be the Crown of your Festivities. Save your Country; maintain and elevate her Glory. Transmit to your Posterity *Health, Freedom,* and *Honour.* Break not the great Chain of Nature; but let an honest, rational, and delicate Intercourse of the Sexes be the Plan of Social

Joy. Let each domestic Bliss wreathe the Garland of connubial Life. Let Truth and Friendship sanctify the Lover's Wish, and secure to the brave, the wise, and the temperate Man, a Felicity worthy his Choice, and worthy his Protection.—

But, perhaps, my unpracticed Youth has gone too far. If so, O *Fathers* and *Brethren*, impute it to an honest Zeal and Love, for the Commonweal and Honour of the illustrious and ancient Nation of *Creeks*.

Onughkallydawwy Garangula Copac.

Notes

Prologue: History and Physiology

1. [Jean] Bossu, *Travels through that part of North America formerly called Louisiana*, trans. John Reinhold Forster, 2 vols. (London, 1771), 117–123.

2. Ibid., 119.

3. For the most thorough review of this issue see Herbert Fingarette, *Heavy Drinking: The Myth of Alcoholism as a Disease* (Berkeley, 1988), esp. 1–30. The disease concept of alcoholism derives from the work in particular of E. M. Jellinek; see Jean-Charles Sournia, *A History of Alcoholism*, trans. Nick Hindley and Gareth Stanton (Oxford, 1990), 149–154.

4. The genetic aspect of alcoholism is currently a topic of great interest among research scientists; see, for example, Constance Holden, "Probing the Complex Genetics of Alcoholism," *Science* 251 (1991), 163–164; Donald W. Goodwin, "The Gene for Alcoholism," *Journal of Studies on Alcohol* 50 (1989), 397–398; idem, "Genetic Influences in Alcoholism," *Advances in Internal Medicine* 32 (1987), 283–297; Eric J. Devor and C. Robert Cloninger, "Genetics of Alcoholism," *Annual Review of Genetics* 23 (1989), 19–36; John Searles, "The Role of Genetics in the Pathogenesis of Alcoholism," *Journal of Abnormal Psychology* 97 (1988), 153–167; Gilbert Omenn, "Genetic Investigations of Alcohol Metabolism and of Alcoholism," *American Journal of Human Genetics* 43 (1988), 579–581; J. G. Oakeshott and J. B. Gibson, "The Genetics of Human Alcoholism: A Review," *Australia–New Zealand Journal of Medicine* 11 (1981), 123–128. Many of the issues involved in the genetic aspects of alcoholism are reviewed in "Genetics and Alcoholism," ed. H. Warner Goedde and Dharam P. Agrawal, a special issue of *Progress in Clinical and Biological Research* 241 (1987); a recent exchange in *Archives of General Psychiatry* 46

(1989), 1151–1152; National Institute on Alcohol Abuse and Alcoholism, *Alcoholism: An Inherited Disease* (Rockville, Md., 1985); George E. Vaillant, *The Natural History of Alcoholism* (Cambridge, Mass., 1983), esp. 64–71; and Donald Goodwin, *Is Alcoholism Hereditary?* 2d ed. (New York, 1988).

5. For a collection of articles suggesting the varied approaches to understanding alcoholism, see Thomas F. Babor et al., eds. *Types of Alcoholics: Evidence from Clinical, Experimental, and Genetic Research*, Annals of the New York Academy of Sciences 708 (New York, 1994).

6. Kyoko M. Parrish et al., "Average Daily Alcohol Consumption during Adult Life among Decedents with and without Cirrhosis: The 1986 National Mortality Followback Survey," *JSA* 54 (1993), 450–456; Charles S. Lieber, *Medical Disorders of Alcoholism: Pathogenesis and Treatment* (Philadelphia, 1982). The effects of alcohol on the heart have become the focus of intensive interest in the aftermath of studies suggesting that consumption of alcohol may protect one from coronary heart disease. For the most important study to date, which notes that any purported protective benefit decreases if one has more than two drinks a day, see J. Michael Gaziano et al., "Moderate Alcohol Intake, Increased Levels of High-Density Lipoprotein and Its Subfractions, and Decreased Risk of Myocardial Infarction," *NEJM* 329 (1993), 1829–1834; see also Gary D. Friedman and Arthur L. Klatsky, "Is Alcohol Good for Your Health?" *NEJM* 329 (1993), 1882–1883.

7. Maurice Victor and Raymond Adams, "The Effect of Alcohol on the Nervous System," in *Metabolic and Toxic Diseases of the Nervous System* (Baltimore, 1953), 526–573; Maurice Victor et al., *The Wernicke-Korsakoff Syndrome* (Philadelphia, 1971) and "Deficiency Amblyopia in the Alcoholic Patient," *Archives of Ophthalmalogy* 64 (1960), 1–33; Elliott L. Mancall, "Some Unusual Neurologic Diseases Complicating Chronic Alcoholism," *American Journal of Clinical Nutrition* 9 (1961), 404–413.

8. In this respect, alcohol-related disease does not survive in the archaeological record even though there is abundant paleopathological evidence of other diseases that afflicted North American Indians. For descriptions of other diseases see John W. Verano and Douglas H. Ubelaker, eds., *Disease and Demography in the Americas* (Washington, D.C., 1992).

9. Roland J. Lamarine, "Alcohol Abuse among Native Americans," *Journal of Community Health* 13 (1988), 143–155. See also Patricia Silk-Walker et al., *Alcoholism, Alcohol Abuse, and Health in American Indians and Alaska Natives*, American Indian and Alaska Native Mental Health Research, monograph no. 1 (1988), 65–67.

10. Margaret M. Cortese et al., "High Incidence of Invasive Pneumococcal Disease in the White Mountain Apache Population," *Archives of Internal Medicine* 152 (1992), 2277–2282, esp. 2279, 2281.

11. L. P. Peterson et al., "Pregnancy Complications in Sioux Children," *Obstetrics and Gynecology* 64 (1984), 519–523; Albert DiNicola, "Might Excessive Maternal Alcohol Ingestion during Pregnancy Be a Risk Factor Associated with an Increased Likelihood of SIDS?" (letter), *Clinical Pediatrics* 24 (1985), 659. On the long-term impact of FAS see Ann P. Streissguth et al., "Fetal Alcohol Syndrome

in Adolescents and Adults," *JAMA* 265 (1991), 1961–1967. The impact of FAS on one Indian family is described at great length in Michael Dorris, *The Broken Cord* (New York, 1989) and *Paper Trail* (New York, 1994), 77–117. The specific problems associated with maternal drinking, especially binge drinking, are often horrific. Clinical reports note the sudden death of a two-year-old girl with profound brain abnormalities caused by first-trimester binge drinking and cases of congenital heart disease with the same etiology; see Cynthia L. Coulter et al., "Midline Cerebral Dysgenesis, Dysfunction of the Hypothalmic-Pituitary Axis, and Fetal Alcohol Effects," *Archives of Neurology* 50 (1993), 771–775; Joseph S. Alpert et al., "Heart Disease in Native Americans," *Cardiology* 78 (1991), 3–12, esp. 10. Despite widespread reports about the dangers of maternal drinking, some pregnant women in selected Indian communities still engage in binge drinking; see John C. Godel et al., "Smoking and Caffeine and Alcohol Intake during Pregnancy in a Northern Population: Effect on Fetal Growth," *Canadian Medical Association Journal* 147 (1992), 181–188, esp. 186–187.

12. Ronet Bachman, "The Social Causes of American Indian Homicide as Revealed by the Life Experiences of Thirty Offenders," *American Indian Quarterly* 15 (1991), 471, 484–487; Richard Goodman et al., "Alcohol and Fatal Injuries in Oklahoma," *JSA* 52 (1991), 156–161.

13. J. David Kinzie, "Psychiatric Epidemiology of an Indian Village: A 19-Year Replication Study," *Journal of Nervous and Mental Disease* 180 (1992), 33–39 (statistics on 37); Philip A. May, "Suicide and Self-Destruction among American Indian Youths," *American Indian and Alaska Native Mental Health Research* 1 (1987), 62.

14. Margaret M. Gallaher et al., "Pedestrian and Hypothermia Deaths among Native Americans in New Mexico," *JAMA* 267 (1992), 1345–1348.

15. Lawrence R. Berger and Judith Kitzes, "Injuries to Children in a Native American Community," *Pediatrics* 84 (1989), 152–156; Carol Lujan et al., "Profile of Abused and Neglected American Indian Children in the Southwest," *Child Abuse and Neglect* 13 (1989), 449–461.

16. Robert Blum et al., "American Indian–Alaska Native Youth Health," *JAMA* 267 (1992), 1637–1644, esp. 1642–1643; David Swanson et al., "Alcohol Abuse in a Population of Indian Children," *Diseases of the Nervous System* 32 (1971), 835–842; Duane Sherwin and Beverly Mead, "Delirium Tremens in a Nine-Year-Old Child," *American Journal of Psychiatry* 132 (1975), 1210–1212.

17. See, in particular, Jerrold E. Levy and Stephen J. Kunitz, *Indian Drinking: Navajo Practices and Anglo-American Theories* (New York, 1974), esp. 179–187; S. J. Kunitz, J. E. Levy, and M. Everett, "Alcoholic Cirrhosis among the Navajo," *QJSA* 30 (1969), 682. Kunitz and Levy have also suggested that professionals concerned with drinking in Indian communities have drawn distinctions between acceptable and unacceptable behavior, and have identified "alcoholics" among a population that had not experienced any measurable change in drinking styles or quantity; as they astutely point out, the redefinition thus reveals more about a growing concern about the problems of alcohol than an actual change in social behavior. See S. J. Kunitz and Jerrold E. Levy, "Changing Ideas of Alcohol Use

NOTES TO PAGES 7–8

among Navajo Indians," *QJSA* 35 (1974), esp. 257. For a different view, one that stresses "a universal tendency toward physiological relaxation and social disinhibition" but notes "culturally patterned variations," see John A. Price, "An Applied Analysis of North American Indian Drinking Patterns," *Human Organization* 34 (1975), 17–26, quotations at 24.

18. Ray Stratton, Arthur Zeiner, and Alfonso Paredes, "Tribal Affiliation and Prevalence of Alcohol Problems," *JSA* 39 (1978), 1166–1177.

19. See David Goldman et al., "DRD2 Dopamine Receptor Genotype, Linkage Disequilibrium, and Alcoholism in American Indians and Other Populations," *Alcoholism: Clinical and Experimental Research* 17 (1993), 199–204.

20. Lynn Bennion and Ting-Kai Li argue that no measurable differences exist; see "Alcohol Metabolism in American Indians and Whites: Lack of Racial Differences in Metabolic Rate and Liver Alcohol Dehydrogenase," *NEJM* 294 (1976), 9–13. Bernard Segal and Lawrence Duffy claim that Alaska Natives eliminate ethanol more rapidly than Caucasians in the United States and American Indians, though their study lacked sufficient data on body weight to allow them to comment more precisely on rates of metabolism; see Segal and Duffy, "Ethanol Elimination among Different Racial Groups," *Alcohol* 9 (1992), 213–217. See also Philip A. May, "The Epidemiology of Alcohol Abuse among American Indians: The Mythical and Real Properties," *American Indian Culture and Research Journal* 18:2 (1994), 124. These studies refute an earlier study that had found that Indians metabolize alcohol more slowly than whites: D. Fenna et al., "Ethanol Metabolism in Various Racial Groups," *Canadian Medical Association Journal* 105 (1971), 472–475.

21. Arthur W. K. Chan, "Racial Differences in Alcohol Sensitivity," *Alcohol and Alcoholism* 21 (1986), 93–104; Lillian E. Dyck, "Absence of the Atypical Mitochondrial Aldehyde Dehydrogenase (ALDH2) Isozyme in Sasketchewan Cree Indians," *Human Heredity* 43 (1993), 116–120; Shi-Han Chen et al., "Gene Frequencies of Alcohol Dehydrogenase$_2$ and Aldehyde Dehydrogenase$_2$ in Northwest Coast Amerindians," *Human Genetics* 89 (1992), 351–352.

22. Philip A. May and Matthew B. Smith, "Some Navajo Indian Opinions about Alcohol Abuse and Prohibition: A Survey and Recommendations for Policy," *JSA* 49 (1988), 324–334, esp. 328–329.

23. A modern study that is particularly applicable is Edward P. Dozier, "Problem Drinking among American Indians: The Role of Sociocultural Deprivation," *QJSA* 27 (1966), 72–87. On Indians taking "time out" see Craig MacAndrew and Robert B. Edgerton, *Drunken Comportment: A Social Explanation* (Chicago, 1969), 83–99.

24. See William J. Rorabaugh, *The Alcoholic Republic: An American Tradition* (New York, 1979), 123–146; Paul Johnson, *A Shopkeeper's Millennium: Society and Revivals in Rochester, New York, 1815–1837* (New York, 1978), 59–61, 79–84, 113–114, 128–135.

25. Sournia, *History of Alcoholism*, 3–13.

26. Dorothy George, *London Life in the Eighteenth Century*, 2d ed. (Chicago, 1984), 41–55; Roy Porter, *English Society in the Eighteenth Century* (Harmondsworth, 1982), 33–34. As Wolfgang Schivelbusch has noted, "gin held out the

promise to working-class people to help them forget their unbearable situation at least momentarily. It provided alcoholic stupefaction, not social intoxication." See his *Tastes of Paradise*, trans. David Jacobson (New York, 1992), 159.

27. Thomas Brennan, *Public Drinking and Popular Culture in Eighteenth-Century Paris* (Princeton, 1988), 76.

28. Vaillant, *Natural History of Alcoholism*, 99–100. Sournia traces the spread of heavy drinking from the ancient world to the modern, noting that by the end of the early modern period, and especially in the nineteenth century, public health campaigns aimed at battling perceived alcohol abuse had become widespread even though their rate of success was often limited; see his *History of Alcoholism*, 14–97.

1. Stereotypes

1. Benjamin Franklin, *The Autobiography of Benjamin Franklin*, ed. Leonard Labaree et al. (New Haven, 1964), 198–199.

2. Ibid., 108, 111, 120–122.

3. As Robert D. Arner has noted, Franklin's first writings on alcohol appeared in the "Silence Dogood" essays published in the *New England Courant* in 1722. His move from Boston to Philadelphia and his rise to ownership of the *Pennsylvania Gazette* gave Franklin a more prominent platform to air his views, including his criticisms of Philadelphia workers' drinking patterns; he chose not to dwell on the consuming patterns of elite drinkers in the city. See Arner, "Politics and Temperance in Boston and Philadelphia: Benjamin Franklin's Journalistic Writings on Drinking and Drunkenness," in *Reappraising Benjamin Franklin: A Bicentennial Perspective*, ed. J. A. Leo Lemay (Newark, Del., 1993), 52–77, esp. 53–59; see also Peter Thompson, " 'The Friendly Glass': Drink and Gentility in Colonial Philadelphia," *PMHB* 113 (1989), 549–573.

4. *Pennsylvania Gazette*, January 13, 1737; Harry G. Levine, "The Vocabulary of Drunkenness," *JSA* 42 (1981), 1038, 1046–1050. The "Dictionary" was reprinted on April 30, 1737, in the *South-Carolina Gazette* (Arner, "Politics and Temperance," 67).

5. See, for example, stories about drunken Indians who committed a murderous assault in New Jersey (August 7, 1736) and a drunken Indian who stabbed two men in Newwon, Conestoga County (March 14, 1738).

6. The *Gazette* ran articles describing a drunken Indian woman who confessed to an Indian plot to burn the houses of colonists in Martha's Vineyard (October 14, 1738), a drunken Indian captured in battle (October 18, 1744), and drunken Indians who allowed a colonist to escape captivity (August 4, 1757).

7. Franklin, *Treaties*, 11–13, 130, 134, 269.

8. "A Treaty held with the Ohio Indians at Carlisle, in October, 1753" (Philadelphia, 1753), ibid., 134.

9. Drinking figured prominently in the experiences of two colonists whose diaries reveal much about eighteenth-century life: William Byrd and Dr. Alexander Hamilton. See Louis B. Wright and Marion Tinling, eds., *The Secret Diary*

of William Byrd of Westover, 1709–1712 (Richmond, 1941), 11, 45, 53, 56, 75, 98, 174, 218, 233, 298, and 442; and Carl Bridenbaugh, ed., *Gentleman's Progress: The Itinerarium of Dr. Alexander Hamilton, 1744* (Chapel Hill, N.C., 1948), 6–7, 11, 17, 46–47, 88–89, 92–93, 165, 168, 179–180.

10. John J. McCusker, "The Rum Trade and the Balance of Payments of the Thirteen Continental Colonies" (Ph.D. diss., University of Pittsburgh, 1970), 468. Other estimates vary only slightly from this figure; see William J. Rorabaugh, *The Alcoholic Republic: An American Tradition* (New York, 1979), 7–8, 29, 32–34, and Mark Edward Lender and James Kirby Martin, *Drinking in America: A History* (New York, 1982), 14.

11. Israel Acrelius, "Drinks Used in North America," in his *Description of the Former and Present Condition of the Swedish Churches, in what was formerly called New Sweden* (1759), trans. William M. Reynolds (Philadelphia, 1874), 160–164.

12. James Boswell, *Life of Johnson* (1791), ed. R. W. Chapman (Oxford, 1980), 1022.

13. For alcohol's place in pre-modern European society see Wolfgang Schivelbusch, *Tastes of Paradise*, trans. David Jacobson (New York, 1992), 22–34; for one vivid example of a folk ballad that describes the consequences of excessive drinking see "The Wofull Lamentation of William Purcas," in *The Roxburge Ballads*, ed. W[illia]m Chappell (Hertford, 1880), 3:29–35.

14. See *A Description of the Province of South Carolina, drawn up at Charles Town, in September, 1731*, in Force, *Tracts*, 2:11; Richard Ligon, *A True & Exact History of the Island of Barbados* (London, 1673), 21; Hans Sloane, *A Voyage to the Islands Madera, Barbados, Nieves, S. Christophers and Jamaica . . .*, 2 vols. (London, 1707–1725), 1:cxliii–cxlv. Ligon drew attention to problems with rum, noting that "the people drink much of it, indeed too much; for it often layes them asleep on the ground, and that is accounted a very unwholsome lodging." But in spite of the dangers of excessive consumption, Ligon realized that colonists had to drink some alcohol because "the spirits being exhausted with much sweating, the inner parts are left cold and faint, and shall need comforting, and reviving." He also believed that liquor helped to preserve the health of slaves. See *True & Exact History*, 27, 32–33, 93. The combination of liquor and heat particularly concerned English writers, who had a fear of hot climates; but drinking in a cold climate, such as Canada, could have health benefits. For the benefits of brandy in cold regions see William Barr and Glyndwr Williams, eds., *Voyages in Search of a Northwest Passage, 1741–1747*, vol. 1, *The Voyage of Christopher Middleton, 1741–1742*, Works Issued by the Hakluyt Society, 2d ser., no. 177 (London, 1994), 80, 85. For English attitudes toward such climates see Karen Ordahl Kupperman, "Fear of Hot Climates in the Anglo-American Colonial Experience," *WMQ*, 3d ser., 41 (1984), 213–240.

15. See, for example, Esther 1:7–8.

16. Increase Mather, *Wo to Drunkards: Two Sermons Testifying against the Sin of Drunkenness* (Cambridge, 1673), 4–8, 10, 13, 26–27, 34; in these pages Mather particularly drew on Job 6:12 and 1 Cor. 6:11.

17. See [Cotton Mather], *Sober Considerations, on a growing Flood of Iniquity. Or an Essay, to Dry up a Fountain of Confusion and Every Evil Work; And to Warn People,*

Particularly of the Woful Consequences, which the Prevailing Abuse of Rum, will be attended withal (Boston, 1708), esp. 1–3, 7–8, 10, 12–19, 26–27, 34; Samuel Danforth, *Piety Encouraged: Brief Notes of a Discourse Delivered unto the People of Taunton* (Boston, 1705), 23–24; Benjamin Wadsworth, *An Essay to do Good, By a disswasive from Tavern-haunting, and Excessive Drinking* (Boston, 1710), esp. 2–8, 12–15, 17–22; and a co-authored work with contributions by ministers including Cotton Mather, Benjamin Wadsworth, John Danforth, and John Cotton: [Thomas Foxcroft], *A Serious Address to those who Unnecessarily Frequent the Tavern, And Often Spend the Evening in Publick Houses* (Boston, 1726), esp. 2–11, 14, 17, 23.

18. See Josiah Smith, *Solomon's Caution Against the Cup* (Boston, 1730).

19. See, for example, "Proceedings of the Virginia Assembly" for 1619 in *Narratives of Early Virginia, 1606–1625*, ed. Lyon G. Tyler (New York, 1907), 263.

20. Paton Yoder, "Tavern Regulation in Virginia: Rationale and Reality," *VMHB* 87 (1979), 259–278, 526; Edwin Powers, *Crime and Punishment in Early Massachusetts, 1620–1692* (Boston, 1966), 367–399; David W. Conroy, "Puritans in Taverns: Law and Popular Culture in Colonial Massachusetts, 1630–1720," in *Drinking: Behavior and Belief in Modern History*, ed. Susanna Barrows and Robin Room (Berkeley, 1991), 29–60; Thompson, "Friendly Glass." For court records see, for example, "Extracts from the Records of the Courts held in Germantown, from 1691 to 1707," *HSP Colls.* 1 (1853), 253, 256. Where drinking was concerned, even Harvard College students, typically sons of elite families, were no different from other colonists; records of the college from 1726 to 1740 include fourteen entries for drink-related problems, some involving multiple students. The references to Harvard students are scattered in the following volumes, all located in the Harvard University Archives: "Corporation, College Books," vols. 1–6: minutes and other records, 1636–1893; "Faculty Records," vols. 1–5 (1725–1780); and "Records of the Board of Overseers." I thank Thomas Siegel for these references, based on his extensive research in Harvard's archives.

21. *Pennsylvania Gazette*, July 29, 1731. The father, it should be noted, had given two of his older children rum before he left the house; the drinking of distilled spirits by minors, then, apparently was considered acceptable.

22. Alcohol, particularly beer, played a role in perhaps 7 percent of murders in the fourteenth century and drunken brawls accounted for approximately 4.3 percent of all rural homicides; see Barbara A. Hanawalt, *Crime and Conflict in English Communities, 1300–1348* (Cambridge, Mass., 1979), 144, 181.

23. Peter Clark, *The English Alehouse: A Social History, 1200–1800* (London, 1983), 2; Judith M. Bennett, *Women in the Medieval English Countryside: Gender and Household in Brigstock before the Plague* (New York, 1987), 120–128.

24. See, for example, Richard Brathwait, *Barnabae Itinerarium: Barnabees Journall* (1638; London, 1932), 43–45.

25. Harris G. Hudson, *A Study of Social Regulations in England under James I and Charles I: Drink and Tobacco* (Chicago, 1933), 4–5, 8–9; Keith Wrightson, "Alehouses, Order, and Reformation in Rural England, 1590–1660," in *Popular Culture and Class Conflict, 1590–1914: Explorations in the History of Labour and Leisure*, ed. Eileen Yeo and Stephen Yeo (Brighton, 1981), 2–11; Robert B. Shoemaker, *Prose-*

cution and Punishment: Petty Crime and the Law in London and Rural Middlesex, c. 1660–1725 (Cambridge, 1991), 36; Clark, *English Alehouse*, 166–194. For examples of attacks on alcohol see Thomas Nashe, *Pierce Penilesse, His Supplication to the Divell* (1592; London, 1924), 79–80, and Philip Stubbs, *Anatomy of the Abuses of England*, ed. Frederick J. Furnivall (1877–1879; Vaduz, 1965), 102–114, 150–152.

26. "A Speech in the Starre-Chamber," June 20, 1616, in *The Political Works of James I*, ed. Charles H. McIlwain (Cambridge, Mass., 1918), 342.

27. Peter Clark, "The 'Mother Gin' Controversy in the Early Eighteenth Century," *Transactions of the Royal Historical Society*, 5th ser., 38 (1988), 63–84; T. C. Curtis and W. A. Speck, "The Societies for the Reformation of Manners: A Case Study in the Theory and Practice of Moral Reform," *Literature and History* 3 (1976), 45–64, esp. 56–57; Lee Davison, "Experiments in the Social Regulation of Industry: Gin Legislation, 1729–1751," in *Stilling the Grumbling Hive: Responses to Social and Economic Problems in England, c. 1689–1750*, ed. Davison et al. (London, 1992), 25–48; T. G. Coffey, "Beer Street, Gin Lane: Some Views of 18th-Century Drinking," *QJSA* 27 (1966), 669–692; George Rudé, " 'Mother Gin' and the London Riots of 1736," *Guildhall Miscellany* 10 (1959), 53–63. For contemporary British temperance tracts see Philotheos Physiologus [Thomas Tryon], *The Way to Health, Long Life and Happiness, or, A Discourse on Temperance and the particular Nature of all things requisit for the Life of Man . . .* (London, 1683), esp. 48–52, and Josiah Woodward, *A Disswasive from the Sin of Drunkenness* (Lancaster, 1755).

28. On the origins of the concept of addiction to alcohol see Harry G. Levine, "The Discovery of Addiction: Changing Concepts of Habitual Drunkenness in America," *JSA* 39 (1978), 145–151.

29. This issue is treated in chapter 7, below.

30. On the entire cultural program of the English see James Axtell, "The Invasion Within: The Contest of Cultures in Colonial North America," in Axtell, *The European and the Indian: Essays in the Ethnohistory of Colonial North America* (New York, 1981), 39–86. On early observers' beliefs about the necessary preconditions for cultural conversion and the importance of eyewitness accounts see Kupperman, *Settling with the Indians: The Meeting of English and Indian Cultures in America, 1580–1640* (London, 1980), 47, 56–57, 62–63, 70, 108, 112–113, 106. The gender roles of Eastern woodlands Indians continued to baffle and exasperate would-be cultural converters, as the Quakers learned well after the Puritans in New England and the Catholics in New France had learned their lesson; see Carol F. Karlsen, "Property and Gender Relations among the Iroquois in the Late 18th and Early 19th Centuries," paper presented at the Center for Seventeenth- and Eighteenth-Century Studies at the University of California, Los Angeles, May 5, 1990. For Elizabethan views of the need for Indian cultural conversion see the introduction to Peter C. Mancall, ed., *Envisioning America: English Plans for the Colonization of North America, 1580–1640* (Boston, 1995).

31. *Americae Pars Quarta, sive Insignis & Admiranda Historia de reperta primum Occidentali India a Christophoro Columbus* (Frankfurt, 1594), x.

32. See, for example, the reports of David Ingram's experiences in the early 1580s and Sir Francis Drake's along the California coast in 1579 in *The Elizabethans' America*, ed. Louis B. Wright (Cambridge, Mass., 1966), 56, 100.

33. For New England see Neal Salisbury, *Manitou and Providence: Indians, Europeans, and the Making of New England, 1500–1643* (New York, 1982); for the Chesapeake see Edmund Morgan, *American Slavery, American Freedom: The Ordeal of Colonial Virginia* (New York, 1975), esp. chap. 4; for trading food after the hostilities of 1622 see Kupperman, *Settling with the Indians*, 182; for the origins of trade see James Axtell, "At the Water's Edge: Trading in the Sixteenth Century," in Axtell, *After Columbus: Essays in the Ethnohistory of Colonial North America* (New York, 1988), 144–181. For the Virginia Company regulation see [William Strachey], *For the Colony in Virginia Britannia: Lawes Diuine, Morall, and Martiall, &c* (1612; Boston, 1936), 7. For the importance of the fur trade in early New England see William Bradford, *Of Plymouth Plantation*, ed. Samuel Eliot Morison (New York, 1952), passim.

34. John J. McCusker and Russell R. Menard, summarizing the available literature, argue that trade with the periphery, while important, was no more profitable than other pursuits, and was not, as some historians have argued, largely responsible for economic development in the metropolis; see *The Economy of British America, 1607–1789* (Chapel Hill, N.C., 1985), esp. 43–45. Still, imports from overseas colonies in America and Asia accounted for 34.7 percent of all imports to London in 1700, a substantial change from 1621, when these imports amounted to only 6.4 percent of goods imported to the city. Further, shipments to America and Asia amounted to 14.8 percent (£661,000 out of £4,443,000) of total exports from England at the end of the seventeenth century. Though profits may not have been as great as the promoters had hoped, overseas trade had become vital to the growth of the empire. See Ralph Davis, *English Overseas Trade, 1500–1700* (London, 1973), 55–56. For the importance of overseas trade in New England see Bernard Bailyn, *The New England Merchants in the Seventeenth Century* (Cambridge, Mass., 1955), 86–91.

35. For English tactics in Ireland see Nicholas P. Canny, "The Ideology of English Colonization: From Ireland to America," *WMQ*, 3d ser., 30 (1973), 575–598; idem, *The Elizabethan Conquest of Ireland: A Pattern Established, 1565–76* (Hassocks, Sussex, 1976); idem, "The Marginal Kingdom: Ireland as a Problem in the First British Empire," in *Strangers within the Realm: Cultural Margins of the First British Empire*, ed. Bernard Bailyn and Philip D. Morgan (Chapel Hill, N.C., 1991), 48–53; Michael McCarthy Morrogh, "The English Presence in Early Seventeenth Century Munster," in *Natives and Newcomers: Essays on the Making of Irish Colonial Society, 1534–1641*, ed. Ciaran Brady and Raymond Gillespie (Bungay, 1986), 171–190; Liam de Paor, *The Peoples of Ireland* (London, 1986), 115–208; James Muldoon, "The Indian as Irishman," *Essex Institute Historical Collections* 111 (1975), 267–289. For a discussion of earlier Anglo-Norman expansionism see Marjorie Chibnall, *Anglo-Norman England, 1066–1166* (Oxford, 1986), and esp. R. R. Davies, *Domination and Conquest: The Experience of Ireland, Scotland and Wales, 1100–1300* (Cambridge, 1990); for a comprehensive treatment of English expansionism see Michael Hechter, *Internal Colonialism: The Celtic Fringe in British National Development, 1536–1966* (Berkeley, 1975), esp. pt. 2.

36. Elizabethan promoters were so concerned with what they would get from North America that they paid little attention to what they would have to give

NOTES TO PAGES 25–30

Indians in exchange; in this respect Richard Hakluyt the elder was typical. See his "Inducements to the Liking of the Voyage intended towards Virginia in 40. and 42. degrees" (1585), in *New American World*, ed. David B. Quinn and Alison Quinn, 5 vols. (London, 1979), 3:64–69.

37. Kathleen J. Bragdon, "Crime and Punishment among the Indians of Massachusetts, 1675–1750," *Ethnohistory* 28 (1981), 25.

38. These laws are examined in chapter 5, below.

39. William Nelson to the Earl of Hillsborough, February 5, 1771, in *Docs. Am. Rev.*, 3:37.

40. Peter Chester to the Earl of Dartmouth, June 4, 1774, in *Docs. Am. Rev.*, 8: 128.

41. Conrad Weiser to Richard Peters, September 13, 1754, in Manuscript Papers of the Indian and Military Affairs of the Province of Pennsylvania, 1737–1775, 197–200, APS. For an excellent analysis of Montour see James H. Merrell, " 'The Cast of His Countenance': Reading Andrew Montour," paper presented at the conference "Through A Glass Darkly: Defining Self in Early America," Williamsburg, 1993.

42. Teedyuscung appears intoxicated in many colonial records, but even when he was drinking he was still capable of negotiating, as the governor of Pennsylvania discovered in December 1759 when he suggested that a treaty be postponed until Teedyuscung sobered up. To the governor's surprise, Teedyuscung proceeded to make a speech, and the negotiations continued. See the minutes of a council held in Philadelphia, December 4, 1759, in Manuscript Papers of the Indian and Military Affairs of the Province of Pennsylvania, 1737–1775, 765–767, APS. For references to Teedyuscung's drinking see "James Kenny's 'Journal to Ye Westward,' 1758–59," ed. John W. Jordan, *PMHB* 37 (1913), 438, and "John Hays' Diary and Journal of 1760," ed. William A. Hunter, *Pennsylvania Archaeologist* 24 (1954), 63; for other references to his abstaining from liquor see "John Hays' Diary," 68, 70, 79.

2. Trade

1. Settlers, many of them presumably farmers who owned a still, continued to provide liquor to Indians after the colonial period. See, for example, Earl P. Olmstead, *Blackcoats among the Delawares: David Zeisberger on the Ohio Frontier* (Kent, Ohio, 1991), 131–132, 146; and the petition of Davit Secuter and [Davit?] Harry, Washington County, Rhode Island, March 2, 1787, and the subsequent act of the General Assembly, Narragansett Indian File, item 31, Rhode Island State Archives.

2. Though Indians throughout the eastern woodlands experienced a demographic crisis, that crisis varied substantially over time and from place to place. The Iroquois, for example, declined from perhaps 22,000 in 1630 to 5,260 in 1750 before beginning a partial recovery to 8,260 in 1770. Indians in the southeast fared better: the combined population of the Choctaws and Chickasaws was perhaps 35,000 in 1680; in 1760 it was 14,900. Over the same years the Illinois In-

dians, who numbered perhaps 10,500 in 1670, declined to 1,950 by 1760 and to 500 in 1800; Indians on Nantucket declined from 2,500 in 1640 to 358 in 1763 and to 22 in 1792. Given the disparity in Indian populations, it is perhaps not surprising that liquor peddlers spent so much of their time hauling alcohol to Iroquoia and the southeast. For Iroquois population figures see Dean R. Snow, "Disease and Population in the Northeast," in *Disease and Demography in the Americas*, ed. John W. Verano and Douglas H. Ubelaker (Washington, D.C., 1992), 184; for Choctaws/Chickasaws see Peter H. Wood, "Changing Population of the Colonial South," in *Powhatan's Mantle: Indians in the Colonial Southeast*, ed. Peter H. Wood et al. (Lincoln, Neb., 1989), 38–39; for Illinois Indians see Russell Thornton, *American Indian Holocaust and Survival* (Norman, Okla., 1987), 88; for Nantucket see Daniel Vickers, "First Whalemen of Nantucket," *WMQ*, 3d ser., 40 (1983), 577.

3. The quotation is from Charles Verlinden, *The Beginnings of Modern Colonization: Eleven Essays with an Introduction*, trans. Yvonne Freccero (Ithaca, 1970), 18. On the early modern use of sugar see, among other works, [Pierre?] Pomet, *A Compleat History of Druggs*, 2d ed. (London, 1725), 54, 57–58. The best history of the rise of sugar and its importance to Western Europe, particularly to Britain, is Sidney W. Mintz, *Sweetness and Power: The Place of Sugar in Modern History* (New York, 1985), esp. chaps. 2 and 3; see also Noel Deerr, *The History of Sugar*, 2 vols. (London, 1949–1950).

4. Alfred W. Crosby, *Ecological Imperialism: The Biological Expansion of Europe, 900–1900* (New York, 1986), 67, 77–78, 96.

5. Verlinden, *Beginnings of Modern Colonization*, 17–26, 135, 151; Stuart B. Schwartz, *Sugar Plantations in the Formation of Brazilian Society: Bahia, 1559–1835* (Cambridge, 1985), 193–194.

6. See, for example, the correspondence of Nathanial Butler, the British governor of Bermuda: Butler to the Earl of Warwick, October 9, 1620, and to Sir Nathaniel Rich, November 30, 1620, in *The Rich Papers: Letters from Bermuda, 1615–1646*, ed. Vernon A. Ives (Toronto, 1984), 186, 223.

7. Even before the English had made great profits from sugar, English writers in the Caribbean urged that early mortality of colonists should not put a stop to the establishment of colonies there. Thus Edmund Hickeringill, in his account of Jamaica, acknowledged that the island *"was* rather the Grave then [sic] Granary to the first *English* Colony" but went on to describe the climate and soil in terms that encouraged colonization: *Jamaica Viewed: With All the Ports, Harbours, and their several Soundings, Towns, and Settlements thereunto belonging . . .* (London, 1665), 1.

8. Richard Ligon, *A True & Exact History of the Island of Barbados* (London, 1673), 85–93, 108–118; quotation at 108–109; Gary A. Puckrein, *Little England: Plantation Society and Anglo-Barbadian Politics, 1627–1700* (New York, 1984), 60–61.

9. [Joshua Gee], *The Trade and Navigation of Great-Britain Considered* (London, 1729), 43–47.

10. Richard Sheridan, *Sugar and Slavery: An Economic History of the British West Indies, 1623–1775* (Baltimore, 1973), 20–25; Mintz, *Sweetness and Power*, 39, 73.

11. For an excellent description of the workings of a plantation see Michael Craton and James Walvin, *A Jamaican Plantation: The History of Worthy Park, 1670–1970* (London, 1970), esp. chap. 5.

12. Michael Craton, "Reluctant Creoles: The Planters' World in the British West Indies," in *Strangers within the Realm: Cultural Margins of the First British Empire*, ed. Bernard Bailyn and Philip D. Morgan (Chapel Hill, N.C., 1991), 314–362, and Richard S. Dunn, *Sugar and Slaves: The Rise of the Planter Class in the English West Indies, 1624–1713* (Chapel Hill, N.C., 1972; New York, 1973), 263–334.

13. J. Oldmixon, *The British Empire in America, Containing the History of the Discovery, Settlement, Progress and present State of all the British Colonies, on the Continent and Islands of America*, 2 vols. (London, 1708), 2:115.

14. Ligon, *True & Exact History*, 86, 94; Puckrein, *Little England*, 61–62.

15. According to Hans Sloane, a refinery for the production of fine sugar cost £6,000, a price so high that Jamaica had only two by the time he wrote his natural history of the West Indies in the early eighteenth century; see Sloane, *A Voyage to the Islands Madera, Barbados, Nieves, S. Christophers and Jamaica . . .* , 2 vols. (London, 1707–1725), 1:lx–lxi.

16. [Edward Littleton], *The Groans of the Plantations: or A True Account of their Grievous and Extreme Sufferings by the Heavy Impositions upon Sugar, and other Hardships* (London, 1689), 14–21. For the requirements of running a plantation see Mintz, *Sweetness and Power*, 44–50.

17. [Littleton], *Groans of the Plantations*, 26–30, 33–34.

18. Sloane, *Voyage to the Islands*, 1:lxi. For other contemporary descriptions see [Charles de Rochefort], *Histoire naturelle et morale des iles Antilles de l'Amérique . . .* , dernière ed. (Rotterdam, 1681), 333–335, and *The History of the Caribby-Islands . . .* , trans. John Davies (London, 1666), 194–196; Ligon, *True & Exact History*, 86–92; Griffith Hughes, *The Natural History of Barbados, in Ten Books* (London, 1750), 248–251; Pomet, *Compleat History of Druggs*, 54.

19. [Rochefort], *Histoire naturelle et morale*, facing 232; Guilielmi Pisonis, *Historia naturalis Brasiliae* (Leyden and Amsterdam, 1648), 50–51. Though it is impossible to know how many people saw such images, at least Sloane makes a direct reference to "the Figure whereof is to be seen in *Piso*, and several Authors"; *Voyage to the Islands*, 1:lxi. For an excellent series of drawings of machines without people, see Ligon, *True & Exact History*, following 84.

20. See, for example, Zucker-Mühle in [J. Schroeter], *Algemeine Geschichte der Länder und Volker von America*, 2 vols. (Halle, 1752), facing 2:806; Mulino da zucchero in *Il gazzettiere americano*, 3 vols. (Livorno, 1763), facing 2:113; Jean Baptiste Labat, *Nouveau Voyage aux Iles de l'Amérique*, 4 vols. (Paris, 1722), facing 3:222; and Pomet, *Compleat History of Druggs*, facing 54.

21. [Littleton], *Groans of Plantations*, 19–20; Richard Blome, *The Present State of His Majesties Isles and Territories in America* (London, 1687), 33–34; Pomet, *Compleat History of Druggs*, 54. For accidents relating to newly produced rum see Ligon, *True & Exact History*, 92–93.

22. Hughes, *Natural History of Barbados*, 251–252.

23. [Littleton], *Groans of the Plantations*, 19.

24. Richard Blome, *A Description of the Island of Jamaica; with the other Isles and Territories in America, to which the English are Related* (London, 1678), 36–39. Blome noted that diets were somewhat better in Jamaica, but otherwise conditions were "much the same, the *Island* producing the same *Commodities*" (40). Concern about the treatment of slaves did not dissipate; for a later appeal to alter the harsh conditions see *No Rum!—No Sugar! or, The Voice of Blood* (London, 1792).

25. On Nevis, for example, any slave who struck a colonist had his hand cut off; a slave who drew blood could be executed. The Reverend William Smith, after describing the punishments meted out to slaves who struck colonists, wrote: "You will say, that these Proceedings are very despotick: But if you consider, that we have ten Blacks to one White Person, you must owe them to be absolutely necessary": *A Natural History of Nevis, and the rest of the English Leeward Charibee Islands in America* (Cambridge, 1745), 233.

26. Richard Sheridan, *Doctors and Slaves: A Medical and Demographic History of Slavery in the British West Indies, 1680–1834* (Cambridge, 1985), 132.

27. Dunn, *Sugar and Slaves*, 323, 314. Plantations in Barbados and Jamaica, the two most important sugar islands in the British Empire, as Sidney Mintz noted, "consumed" slaves over the course of the eighteenth century; Barbados received 252,500 slaves and Jamaica 662,400 by the end of the nineteenth century. See *Sweetness and Power*, 43, 53. Mortality rates for slaves on sugar plantations in Brazil were similar, and at times higher; see Schwartz, *Sugar Plantations*, 364–378.

28. Craton and Walvin, *A Jamaican Plantation*, 130, 140.

29. For the Chesapeake see Russell R. Menard, "From Servant to Freeholder: Status Mobility and Property Accumulation in Seventeenth-Century Maryland," *WMQ*, 3d ser., 30 (1973), 37–64; for Carolina see Peter H. Wood, *Black Majority: Negroes in Colonial South Carolina from 1670 through the Stono Rebellion* (New York, 1974); for the middle colonies see John J. McCusker and Russell R. Menard, *The Economy of British America, 1607–1789* (Chapel Hill, N.C., 1985), 199; for New England see Bernard Bailyn, *The New England Merchants in the Seventeenth Century* (Cambridge, Mass., 1955), and Paul Boyer and Stephen Nissenbaum, *Salem Possessed: The Social Origins of Witchcraft* (Cambridge, Mass., 1974).

30. Dunn, *Sugar and Slaves*, 59, 67. For one view of the vegetation of Barbados before the rise of sugar plantations see "The Voyage of Sir Henry Colt," in *Colonising Expeditions to the West Indies and Guiana, 1623–1667*, ed. V. T. Barlow, Works published by the Hakluyt Society, 2d ser., 56 (London, 1925), 67.

31. McCusker and Menard, *Economy of British America*, 289–293. Sugar planters elsewhere in the Americas were less willing to reduce rum production; in the Bahia region of northeast Brazil rum (*aguardiente*), as well as molasses, was vital because exports of sugar alone did not bring sufficient income. See Schwartz, *Sugar Plantations*, 162–163, 213–214.

32. See the records of the port of Quebec in *Calendar of Haldiman Collection*, vol. 3, *Statistics of the Trade of Quebec, 1768–1783*, ed. Douglas Brymner, Report on Canadian Archives (Ottawa, 1889), 5–6.

33. *N.Y. Col. Docs.*, 13:76–77.

34. Donald A. Rumrill, "An Interpretation and Analysis of the Seventeenth-

Century Mohawk Nation: Its Chronology and Movements," *Bulletin and Journal of Archaeology for New York State* 90 (1985), 6, 8, 27, 30, 36.

35. See Charles Wooley, *A Two Years Journal in New York, and Part of Its Territories in America* (1701), ed. E. B. O'Callaghan (New York, 1860), 31–32.

36. *Pa. Col. Recs.*, 2:603–604, 4:86–87; for similar problems at Easton see ibid., 8:172.

37. "The Journal of Christian Frederick Post, from Philadelphia to the Ohio . . . ," in *EWT*, 1:185.

38. Documentary references to Indians' production of alcohol for themselves are rare. Arthur Barlowe, visiting a group of Carolina Algonquians in the mid-1580s, noted that "their drinke is commonly water, but while the grape lasteth, they drinke wine, and for want of casks to keepe it all the yeere after, they drink water, but it is sodden with Ginger in it, and blacke Sinamon, and sometimes Sassaphras, and divers other wholesome, and medicinable hearbes and trees": See [Barlowe], "The first voyage made to the coasts of America, . . ." [1584], in Richard Hakluyt, *The Principall Navigations, Voiages, and Discoveries of the English Nation* (1589; Cambridge, 1965), 729. Daniel Gookin noted in the late seventeenth century that some Indians fermented cider, but most Indians apparently purchased liquor from traders. As Gookin noted, "the Indians are great lovers of strong drink, as aqua vitae, rum, brandy, or the like, and are very greedy to buy it of the English": "Historical Collections of the Indians in New England," *MHS Colls.*, 1 (1792), 151.

39. Thomas Norton, *The Fur Trade in Colonial New York, 1686–1776* (Madison, Wis., 1974), 69, 113; *CRSC Journals*, 101; Demere to Lyttleton, January 31, 1757, *CRSC Indian Affairs, 1754–1765*, 328–329.

40. J. Russell Snapp, *John Stuart and the Issue of Empire on the Southern Colonial Frontier* (Baton Rouge, forthcoming).

41. "Review of Trade and Affairs in the Northern District of America [September 22, 1767]," in *Trade and Politics, 1767–1769*, ed. Clarence Alvord and Clarence Carter, *Ill. Colls.* 16 (1921), 29.

42. Berthold Fernow, ed., *Records of New Amsterdam, 1653–1674*, 7 vols. (New York, 1897), 6:76, 87. It should be noted that colonists on occasion did give beer to Indians, but the rum trade was more common and elicited greater concern; for references to beer given by provincial officials to Indians at treaties see Franklin, *Treaties*, 269, 311.

43. [Barlowe], "First voyage made," 730; *Henry Hudson the Navigator: The Original Documents*, ed. G. M. Asher, Publications of the Hakluyt Society (London, 1860), 85–86.

44. *A Relation of Iornall of the Beginning and Proceedings of the English Plantation settled at Plimoth in New England (Mourt's Relation)* (1622), ed. Henry M. Dexter (Boston, 1895), 92–93.

45. In Albert C. Meyers, ed., *Narratives of Early Pennsylvania, West New Jersey, and Delaware, 1630–1707* (New York, 1912), 29.

46. John Smith, *The Generall Historie of Virginia, New-England, and the Summer Isles . . .* , (1624), in *The Complete Works of Captain John Smith*, ed. Philip L. Barbour, 3 vols. (Chapel Hill, N.C., 1986), 2:211.

47. See the session of December 13, 1649, in *Minutes of the Court of Rensselaerswyck, 1648–1652*, ed. A. J. F. Van Laer (Albany, 1922), 97.

48. For fines only see the cases against Jacob Symonsz (July 1653), Egbertjen Egberts and Dirckie Harmense (both in October 1656), and Susanna Janssen (August 1657) in *Minutes of the Court of Fort Orange and Beverwyck, 1652–1660*, ed. A. J. F. Van Laer, 2 vols. (Albany, 1920–1923), 1:73–74, 286–287, 289–290; 2:71–72; the cases against George Keaser and Alister Mackmaly (March 1670), Thomas Johnson (April 1671), and Mary Bound (June 1671) in *Records and Files of the Quarterly Courts of Essex County, Massachusetts, 1656–1683*, 8 vols. (Salem, 1912–1921), 2:243–244; 4:214, 370–371; 8:435–436; the case against William Ffurbish (June 1675) in *N.H. Prov. P.*, 40:322; the case against William Trowbridge (August 1660), in *Ancient Town Records, New Haven Town Records, 1649–1662*, ed. F. B. Dexter, 2 vols. (New Haven, 1917–1919), 1:459–460, 503; *Records of the Particular Court of Connecticut, 1639–1663* (Hartford, 1928), 128, 129, 204. For fines and banishment see the cases against Willem Hoffmeyr (October 1656), Hans Vos (April 1657), Jan Teunissen (January 1658), and Poulos Janssen (July 1658) in Van Laer, *Minutes of the Court of Fort Orange and Beverwyck*, 1:288–289; 2:32–33, 92–93, 95–96, 135–137.

49. See the punishment of Charles Sheepey in the case against Abraham Seniors, May 8, 1691, in *The Burlington Court Book: A Record of Quaker Jurisprudence in West New Jersey, 1680–1709*, ed. H. Clay Reed and George J. Miller (Washington, D.C., 1944), 125.

50. For women tavernkeepers see the cases against Egbertjen Egberts and Dirckie Harmense in October 1656, in Van Laer, *Minutes of the Court of Fort Orange and Beverwyck*, 1:286–287, 289–290; for a woman who claimed she had sold less beer than was alleged in 1660 see the case against William Trowbridge in Dexter, *New Haven Town Records*, 1:459–460; for a brewer charged with selling beer to Indians see the case against Harme Rutgers in April 1678 in *The Andros Papers, 1674–1680*, ed. Peter Christoph et al. 3 vols. to date (1989–), 2:297–315; for Indians' bringing their own containers see the case against Marten Hendricksen, August 1, 1657, in Van Laer, *Minutes of the Court of Fort Orange and Beverwyck*, 1:67; and the case against Walter Reeves, "8th 6th Month 1685," in Reed and Miller, *Burlington Court Book*, 45. For sale by neighbors see Samuel Hopkins, *Historical Memoirs Relating to the Housatunnuk Indians* (Boston, 1753), 59, 80–81; for the Charleston case see Daniel H. Usner, Jr., "Rebeckah Lee's Plea on 'Fetching of Drink for an Indian Squaw,' " *South Carolina Historical Magazine* 85 (1984), 317–318.

51. See Peter Greeley's deposition, April 25, 1734, in *N.H. Prov. P.*, 18:54.

52. *N.Y. Col. Docs.* 12:156 (for a case in 1657), 290–291 (for a case in 1660); *N.H. Prov. P.*, 40:322 (for a case in 1675). In one revealing document, relating to a murder trial in Bethlehem, Pennsylvania, in 1763, a tavernkeeper and others noted that two Indians accused of the crime could not have done it because they had spent the night without incident at a local tavern; the fact that the depositions relating to the case did not even hint that the Indians acted improperly, and that those who testified did so on behalf of the Indians, suggests that their presence at the tavern was not particularly unusual. The documents can be found among

the records of the Indian Renatus Murder Trial, 1763–1764, box 124, folder 6, RMM.

53. See the case against Mattys, servant of Johannes Withart, in 1658 in Van Laer, *Minutes of the Court of Fort Orange and Beverwyck*, 2:170–171, and the complaints of Indians in Pennsylvania against the servants of Jasper Farmer in 1685 in *Pa. Col. Recs.*, 1:147–148.

54. *Conn. Pub. Recs.*, 3:228.

55. The statutes are discussed in chapter 5, below.

56. Hopkins, *Historical Memoirs*, 81.

57. The attack took place in the aftermath of a *cantica*, a ritual dance, at which the colonist was present; he was not only known to his assailants but quite familiar with them at the time. See William Markham to William Penn, August 22, 1686, in *The Papers of William Penn*, ed. Richard Dunn and Mary Maples Dunn, 5 vols. (Philadelphia, 1981–1986), 3:106–107.

58. Stuart to Hillsborough, January 3, 1769, in *N.C. Col. Recs.*, 8:1.

59. Jaspar Danckaerts, "Journal of a Voyage to New York in 1679–1680," in *Memoirs of the Long Island Historical Society* 1 (1867), 273–274.

60. Francis Daniel Pastorius, "Circumstantial Geographical Description of Pennsylvania" (1700), in Meyers, *Narratives of Early Pennsylvania*, 419.

61. *N.Y. Col. Docs.*, 12:318.

62. See the minutes of the Provincial Council meeting and the order issued by Logan, October 9, 1736, in *Pa. Col. Recs.*, 4:86–87.

63. *Ga. Col. Recs.*, 18:223.

64. See, for example, the petition of the residents of Crewcorne, near the Delaware River, in 1680 and the reference to complaints by residents of Lancaster in 1745 in *N.Y. Col. Docs.*, 12:658–659, and *Pa. Col. Recs.*, 4:759–761.

65. *N.Y. Col. Docs.*, 12:339–341.

66. *Doc. Hist. N.Y.*, 2:91–92.

67. *N.Y. Col. Docs.*, 5:795–798, 865–867.

68. See, for example, minutes of a council in Virginia in November 1752 in *Va. Exec. J.*, 5:414; "Journal of Conrad Weiser at the Albany Treaty of 1745," in Franklin, *Treaties*, 311. And Pastorius noted in 1700 that he gave brandy to Indians in Pennsylvania, refusing payment for it even though others in the colony had already been trading liquor for furs; see his "Circumstantial Geographical Description," 382, 400.

69. Delaware chiefs to Governor Gordon, August 8, 1732, in Society Miscellaneous Collections, box 11c, folder 2, HSP.

70. See the list of provisions given to one group in 1741 in *Pa. Col. Recs.*, 4:502; Franklin, *Treaties*, 12 (1736), 26 and 39 (1742), 44, 69–70, 73, 78–79 (1744), 133 (1753), 243 (1758), 269 (1763).

71. *Ga. Col. Recs.*, 27:173; Harmon Verelst to Thomas Carston, August 11, 1737, ibid., 29:211.

72. Arthur Dobbs to Board [of Trade?], August 24, 1755, *N.C. Col. Recs.*, 5:360.

73. George Croghan to an unnamed person, May 14, 1760, in George Croghan Papers, Correspondence, 1761, HSP.

74. See the inventory of goods dated March 28, 1749, in the papers of Hockley,

Trent, & Gordon, Cadwallader Collection, George Croghan Section, 6:18 (under Hockley, Trent & Croghan), HSP; and the transactions for April 1765 in the account between Croghan and Devereux Smith, ibid., 1:28, box 1: Accounts, 1744–1765. Croghan had offered rum to Indians in Pennsylvania while conducting business for the province; see Croghan to Richard Peters, November 28, 1747, *Md. Arch.*, 46: 7. Still, he recognized the problems associated with Indians' drinking; at one point he tried to stop any sales of spirits to Indians and claimed that he did not keep any in his own house. See Croghan to Governor James Hamilton, August 30, 1754, George Croghan Letters, Miscellaneous Manuscript Collections, LC.

75. *N.Y. Col. Docs.*, 7:691.

76. *Johnson Papers*, 3:721–722.

77. *Ga. Col. Recs.*, 10:302–303.

78. Carolyn Gilman, ed., "Journal of a Voyage, 1766–67, by James Stanley Goddard," in *The Journals of Jonathan Carver and Related Documents, 1766–1770*, ed. John Parker (Minneapolis, 1976), 182, 187, 188.

79. In addition to the references already cited, see *CRSC Journals* 152, 153, 235, 287; *CRSC Indian Affairs, 1750–1754*, 12, 88, 268, 313; *CRSC Indian Affairs, 1754–1765*, 104, 147, 173, 329, 402, 438, 456, 457; *Collections of the Maine Historical Society: Documentary History of the State of Maine*, 6:266.

80. Though liquor appeared early in the fur trade in Pemaquid, the trading post disappeared by the end of the century and subsequent exchange, for liquor and other goods, was less extensive than in other regions. See Neill De Paoli, "Beaver, Blankets, Liquor, and Politics: Pemaquid's Fur Trade, 1614–1760," *Maine Historical Society Quarterly* 33 (1993–1994), 166–201; for references to alcohol see 180–181, 190, 192.

81. Thomas Glover, *An Account of Virginia, its Scituation, Temperature, Productions, Inhabitants and their manner of planting and ordering Tobacco & c.* (1676; Oxford, 1904), 25. During the Revolution, similar logic encouraged British officials to provide gifts of alcohol to Indians in order to preserve their alliances; British officials often provided large quantities of rum then as well, even though they realized that if Indians "Continue to be Supplied with Rum—no Dependance can be put in any thing they say—for what they resolve this Day they will break thro' Tomorrow": Charles Stuart to John Stuart, April 8, 1777, CO5/78, PRO Trans., reel 7.

82. William P. Cumment, ed., *The Discoveries of John Lederer* (Charlottesville, Va., 1958), 42.

83. *N.Y. Col. Docs.*, 5:663.

84. Arthur J. Ray and Donald B. Freeman, *"Give Us Good Measure": An Economic Analysis of Relations between the Indians and the Hudson's Bay Company before 1763* (Toronto, 1978), 132–134. The alcohol trade continued there into the nineteenth century; see J. C. Yerbury, *The Subarctic Indians and the Fur Trade, 1680–1860* (Vancouver, 1986), 69.

85. Honoré de La Rouvillière Michel to Antoine Rouillé, July 20, 1751, in *Mississippi Provincial Archives: French Dominion*, ed. Dunbar Rowland and Albert G. Sanders, rev. Patricia K. Galloway, 5 vols. (Baton Rouge, 1984), 5:100–101.

86. *Pa. Col. Recs.*, 2:33.

87. John Long, *John Long's Voyages and Travels in the Years 1768–1788*, ed. Milo M. Quaife (Chicago, 1922), 143, 168.

88. "Copy of a Journal of the proceedings of Conrad Weiser, in his journey to Ohio . . . ," *HSP Colls.* 1 (1853), 25–27.

89. *Pa. Col. Recs.*, 2:141; 4:502, 758.

90. [Joseph Powell], "Shamokin (Sunbury) Pa. Diary, 1748," in box 121, folder 4, RMM, entry for April 3.

91. *Pa. Arch.*, 8th ser., 6:4938–4939.

92. David Jones, *A Journal of Two Visits Made to Some Nations of Indians on the West Side of the River Ohio, in the Years 1772 and 1773* (1784; New York, 1865), 88.

93. John Lawson, *A New Voyage to Carolina*, ed. Hugh T. Lefler (Chapel Hill, N.C., 1967), 63, 64, 224; David Taitt to John Stuart, June 5, 1777, CO5/78, PRO Trans., reel 7.

94. "Croghan's Journal, 1765," in *EWT*, 1:158.

95. *Johnson Papers*, 3:962–963; see also 942–943 and 976.

96. See the complaints of the Oswego traders in June 1754, *Doc. Hist. N.Y.*, 2: 561–562.

97. *N.Y. Col. Docs.*, 5:569.

98. See the invoices for Philadelphia dated January 1763 and for Fort Augusta dated May 6, 1763, Indian Commissioners Papers, Accounts, 1758–1766, HSP.

99. Indian Commissioners Papers, Pittsburgh Store Journal, June 23, 1760, to August 21, 1761 (microfilm), HSP, entries for November 20, December 20, and December 30, 1760, and February 5, February 19, and March 15, 1761.

100. "Goods wanted for Pittsburgh Tradg. House," January 28 (no year given); invoice dated November 15, 1763; and a price schedule dated April 13, 1763, in Indian Commissioners Papers, Accounts, 1758–1766, HSP.

101. For examples see the records of the firm's accounts from August 1769 to June 1770 in reel 9, frames 94, 103, 111, 119, 125, and 134, BWM.

102. The accounts start on July 7 and run to August 22, 1766, reel 7, frames 384–387, BWM. This rum was distinct from the liquor Croghan received for his personal use from June 5 to August 12, 1766; see ibid., frame 388. See also his account with John Jennings, September 17, 1766, ibid., reel 8, frame 302.

103. Ibid., reel 7, frames 388–389.

104. Ibid., frame 422.

105. George Morgan letter book, 1767–1788, p. 35, HSP. The letterbook is reprinted in Alvord and Carter, *Trade and Politics*; see 138 (for the list of alcohol) and 360 (explaining why he still had liquor on hand). See also "Account of Baynton, Wharton & Morgan, September 25, 1766: Goods sent to Edward Cole, Commissary for Indian Affairs of the Illinois &c," in *Johnson Papers*, 13:400–404; and "Baynton, Wharton & Morgan against the Crown, June 12, 1766," *Johnson Papers*, 5:248, 256.

106. BWM, reel 7, frame 527. As these references suggest, Baynton, Wharton & Morgan sold alcohol throughout the year. This does not mean that all liquor traders had alcohol available every time Indians showed up to trade. As Jack O. Waddell has pointed out in an analysis of an early nineteenth-century trader's accounts, Chippewa purchasing patterns revealed a distinct seasonality, with

peak sales during the early autumn, few sales during the hardest parts of winter, and then moderate sales during the spring and summer. See Waddell, "Malhiot's Journal: An Ethnohistoric Assessment of Chippewa Alcohol Behavior in the Early Nineteenth Century," *Ethnohistory* 32 (1985), 253–254.

107. "Report of Indian Trade," in *Johnson Papers*, 12:396–400.

108. "A Scheme for Meeting the Expenses of Trade," October 8, 1774, in *Johnson Papers*, 4:559; Stuart to Lord George Germain, October 26, 1776, in *Docs. Am. Rev.*, 12:241. This information, from the late colonial period, suggests that John McCusker, who noted that traders were carrying no more than 30,000 gallons westward each year by 1770, underestimated the extent of the liquor trade with Indians; see McCusker, "The Rum Trade and the Balance of Payments of the Thirteen Continental Colonies, 1650–1775" (Ph.D. diss., University of Pittsburgh, 1970), 502–504. The estimates provided by Johnson and Stuart provide evidence needed for judging per capita consumption by Indians. If the Indian population of territory east of the Mississippi River was approximately 150,000 at the end of the colonial period, and if we combine the estimates of Johnson and Stuart for a total volume of rum per year at 80,000 gallons, then per capita consumption across the region was approximately 0.53 gallons. Since Stuart's estimate was for three months only, Indians in the south may have consumed 10,000 gallons a month, or 120,000 gallons a year. If so, then the full extent of the trade each year would have been 170,000 gallons, or a per capita estimate of 1.13 gallons. If these figures constitute the lowest and highest estimates, and a total per capita range of 0.53 to 1.13, it is useful to recall that consumption was not uniform across Indian country. Men drank more than women and children, and young men drank more than older men. If we presume, then, that no more than one-quarter of the Indian population drank *most* of the available liquor, the actual per capita consumption by active drinkers would have been between 2.13 gallons and 4.53 gallons. Was this in fact the case? The available evidence does not provide firm answers, but the records of trading houses do suggest the enormous demand for alcohol among Indians. Liquor made up 13 percent of the goods Indians received at Detroit in 1732 and 19 percent in 1739; 5 percent of the goods at Green Bay in 1740 and 4 percent in 1747. Those low figures are in striking contrast to late eighteenth- and early nineteenth-century consumption by Ojibways. According to surviving records, traders obtained 60 to 88 percent of their furs with alcohol alone. The records of Baynton, Wharton & Morgan from the 1760s suggest that liquor sales constituted from 10 to 20 percent of the value of their sales. The lack of reliable estimates for individual southern traders makes it risky to validate the claims of Stuart and Johnson, but given the large populations of Indians in the southeast and the apparent demand for alcohol there, it is conceivable that Indians there spent many of their deerskins on rum. While no claim is made here for the accuracy of these per capita estimates, the range seems reasonable in view of what can be reconstructed from the records of trading houses. For the population of Indians see James H. Merrell, " 'The Customes of Our Countrey': Indians and Colonists in Early America," in *Strangers within the Realm: Cultural Margins of the First British Empire*, ed. Bernard Bailyn and Philip D. Morgan (Chapel Hill, N.C., 1991), 124; for trading records for Detroit and Green Bay see

Richard White, *The Middle Ground: Indians, Empires, and Republics in the Great Lakes Region, 1650–1815* (New York, 1991), 138; for the Ojibways see Bruce M. White, "A Skilled Game of Exchange: Ojibway Fur Trade Protocol," *Minnesota History* 50 (1987), 235; for Baynton, Wharton & Morgan see Appendix 1.

109. Ray and Freeman, *"Give Us Good Measure,"* 132–142. See also Daniel Francis and Toby Morantz, *Partners in Furs: A History of the Fur Trade in Eastern James Bay, 1600–1870* (Kingston and Montreal, 1983), 38–40, 62.

110. Toby Morantz, "The Fur Trade and the Cree of James Bay," in *Old Trails and New Directions: Papers of the Third North American Fur Trade Conference,* ed. Carol M. Judd and Arthur J. Ray (Toronto, 1980), 44.

111. General letter of Anthony Beale, August 2, 1714, in *Letters from Hudson Bay, 1703–40,* ed. K. G. Davies, Publications of the Hudson's Bay Record Society 25 (London, 1965), 29–30.

112. General letter from Thomas McCliesh, July 16, 1716, in Davies, *Letters from Hudson Bay,* 43.

113. General letter from Thomas McCliesh and others, August 24, 1735, in Davies, *Letters from Hudson Bay,* 209. See the general letter from Joseph Adams and others from Fort Albany, August 12, 1734, ibid., 195; for the sale of an Indian boy in exchange for one pound of Brazil tobacco, one and one–half yards of blue broadcloth, and one gallon of brandy see ibid., 273n. For later use of alcohol in the Indian trade see Francis and Morantz, *Partners in Furs,* 127–128. For the amount of brandy available, in comparison with other goods, at one post see the list of commodities available at Fort Albany in 1706 in *Hudson's Bay Miscellany, 1670–1870,* ed. Glyndwr Williams, Publications of the Hudson's Bay Record Society 30 (Winnipeg, 1975), 66–67.

114. Glyndwr Williams, ed., *Andrew Graham's Observations on Hudson's Bay, 1767–1791,* Publications of the Hudson's Bay Record Society 27 (London, 1969), 152; Sylvester Stevens, Donald Kent, and Emma Woods, eds., *Travels in New France by J.C.B.* (Harrisburg, 1941), 89.

115. Emily J. Blasingham, "The Depopulation of the Illinois Indians," pt. 2 *Ethnohistory* 3 (1956), 388–390.

116. "Account of the Crown directed to Baynton, Wharton and Morgan for goods by order of Edward Cole, Comm. for Indian Affairs at the Illinois, February 16, 1768," in BWM, folder 9.

117. BWM, reel 7, frames 539, 546–547.

118. *Pa. Arch.,* 1st ser., 1:265–266, 551; Archer B. Hulbert and William N. Schwarze, eds., "The Diaries of Zeisberger Relating to the First Missions in the Ohio Basin," *Ohio Archaeological and Historical Quarterly* 21 (1912), 68; see also 73.

119. Lawson, *New Voyage to Carolina,* 232–233.

120. *CRSC Indian Affairs, 1750–1754,* 297; *CRSC Indian Affairs, 1754–1765,* 354.

121. "Journal of James Kenny, 1761–1763," ed. John W. Jordan, *PMHB* 37 (1913), 14, 16, 17.

122. *CRSC Indian Affairs, 1750–1754,* 368, and *CRSC Indian Affairs, 1754–1765,* 147. The carrying of rum back to Indian communities at times was reported in newspapers; the *Pennsyvania Gazette* reported on April 24, 1760, that the Twin's Son had recently returned to the Creeks with three kegs he had purchased.

123. "Journal of David Taitt's Travels from Pensacola, West Florida, to and through the Country of the Upper and the Lower Creeks, 1772," in *Travels in the American Colonies*, ed. Newton D. Mereness (New York, 1916), 555, 560.

124. Jones, *Journal of Two Visits*, 59.

125. "Diary of Schonbrunn, on the Muskingum, September 1774 to September 1775," in RMM, box 141, folder 15, entry for July 16, 1775.

126. "Journal . . . of Conrad Weiser," 31.

127. Peter Bard to Governor Denny, July 1, 1758, in Manuscript Papers of the Indian and Military Affairs of the Province of Pennsylvania, 1737–1775, 593–594, APS.

128. "Diary of David Zeisberger and Gottlieb Sensemann's Journey to Goschgoschink on the Ohio, . . . May 8, 1768, to February 20, 1769," in RMM, box 135, folder 7, entry for October 23, 1768.

129. Archer B. Hulbert and William N. Schwarze, eds., "David Zeisberger's History of the Northern American Indians," *Ohio Archaeological and Historical Quarterly* 19 (1910), 90.

130. Usner, "Rebeckah Lee's Plea," 317–318.

131. Patrick Frazier, *The Mohicans of Stockbridge* (Lincoln, Neb., 1992), 50.

132. [Powell], "Shamokin (Sunbury) Pa. Diary, 1748," in box 121, folder 4, RMM, entry for March 24.

133. Squadook to governor of Massachusetts, September 12, 1751, in *Dawnland Encounters: Indians and Europeans in Northern New England*, ed. Colin Calloway (Hanover, N.H., 1991), 202.

134. "Journal of Beatty's Trip to the Ohio Country in 1766," in *Journals of Charles Beatty, 1762–1769*, ed. Guy S. Klett (University Park, Pa., 1962), 67. On these and other sexual relations in the region see White, *Middle Ground*, 60–75, 214–215, 334.

135. See the case for October 1656 in Van Laer, *Minutes of the Court of Fort Orange and Beverwyck*, 1:288–289.

3. Consumption

1. Charles Woodmason, *The Carolina Backcountry on the Eve of the Revolution: The Journal and Other Writings of Charles Woodmason, Anglican Itinerant*, ed. Richard J. Hooker (Chapel Hill, N.C., 1953), 83.

2. William Bradford, *Of Plymouth Plantation*, ed. Samuel Eliot Morison (New York, 1952), 205–206; John Clayton, "Another 'Account of Virginia' by the Reverend John Clayton," ed. Edmund Berkeley and Dorothy S. Berkeley, VMHB 76 (1968), 436.

3. Nicolas Denys, *The Description and Natural History of the Coasts of North America* (1672), trans. William F. Ganong (Toronto, 1908), 448. It remains, of course, impossible to grasp with any certainty the psychological inner world of early American Indians, especially when the surviving documents were written by colonists. But by reading documents with care, historians have sought ways

to "penetrate the silence," to use James Merrell's phrase (*The Indians' New World: Catawbas and Their Neighbors from European Contact through the Era of Removal* [Chapel Hill, N.C., 1989], xi).

4. As the anthropologist A. Irving Hallowell recognized years ago, early texts provide us with our best evidence for pre–contact Indian cultural norms and beliefs; though no doubt the seventeenth- and eighteenth-century Indians described by travelers, traders, and missionaries already bore the scars of colonization, they show fewer signs of acculturation than Indians in the twentieth century. See his "Some Psychological Characteristics of the Northeastern Indians" (1946), in *Culture and Experience* ([Philadelphia], 1955), 126–127. On the utility of these early texts for understanding Indian drinking see Christian F. Feest, "Notes on Native American Alcohol Use," in *North American Indian Studies: European Contributions*, ed. Pieter Hovens (Göttingen, 1981), 202.

5. Words for "alcohol" and "drunkenness" appeared across the continent by the early nineteenth century, and much earlier among Indians who had extensive contact with Europeans during the colonial period. See the Onondaga and Delaware terminology in *Zeisberger's Indian Dictionary* (1887; New York, n.d.), 28, (brandy), 61 (to drink, drunk) 62 (drunkard), 114 (liquor), 162 (rum); Sebastian Rasle, *A Dictionary of the Abnaki Language, in North America* (Cambridge, Mass., 1833), 437 (eau de vie), 473 (drinking, drunkenness), 542 (vin); Peter S. Du Ponceau, "Indian Vocabularies," microfilm no. 1284, APS, 16 (whisky in Osage); 58 (rum in Shawanese), 71 (spirits in Nottaway), 84 (whiskey in Omaha), 105 (vin or eau de vie in Omaha), 195 (drunkard in Algonkin and Delaware, 214 (drunken in Cree), 218 (drunken in Tacully or Carrier); Henry B. Kelso, "Indian Dictionary, Green Bay" (1822), APS, 1 (cider, whiskey, rum, brandy, wine); Carl Masthay, ed., *Schmick's Mahican Dictionary*, Memoirs of the APS 197 (Philadelphia, 1991), s.v. "brandy," "gin"; Fr. Jean Baptiste Le Boulanger, "French and Miami-Illinois Dictionary and Texts" (c. 1720?), APS, s.v. "ivre," and "ivresse"; Emma Gardiner, "Vocabulary of the Penobscot Indians" (1821), APS, 19 ("I am thirsty for wine"; "Will you give me a drink?"); John K. Townsend, "Vocabularies of the Languages of Indians Inhabiting N.W. America, collected . . . 1834, 35 & 36" (1838), APS, 58 ("He is drunk" and "He feigns to be drunk" in Okonchgon), 66 (similar phrases in Shoughap or Altnaha). Not surprisingly, an early seventeenth–century dictionary of the Huron language contained no words for drunkenness or any kind of liquor; see Gabriel Sagard, "Dictionnaire de la Langue Huronne" (1632), APS.

6. "The Indians, who had not developed the technique of making their own liquor and hence had established no rules about drinking, came to enjoy not only drinking but getting drunk": Yasuhide Kawashima, *Puritan Justice and the Indian: White Man's Law in Massachusetts, 1630–1763* (Middletown, Conn., 1986), 216. For a similar assessment see Kathryn E. Holland Braund, *Deerskins and Duffels: Creek Indian Trade with Anglo–America, 1685–1815* (Lincoln, Neb., 1993), 125–126. As the anthropologist Sidney Mintz has pointed out, we need to understand why people use substances in the ways they do to understand the meaning that consumption of certain goods had for them; see his *Sweetness and Power: The Place of Sugar in Modern History* (New York, 1985), xxix.

7. See Charles M. Hudson, ed., *Black Drink: A Native American Tea* (Athens, Ga., 1979), esp. Charles H. Fairbanks, "The Function of Black Drink among the Creeks," 120–141. For an eighteenth–century reference see M. Le Page Du Pratz, *The History of Louisiana* (1774), ed. Joseph Tregle, Jr. (Baton Rouge, 1975), 245.

8. For a Spaniard's description of the ceremony among the Guale Indians in 1595 see Lewis H. Larson, Jr., "Historic Guale Indians of the Georgia Coast and the Impact of the Spanish Mission Effort," in *Tacachale: Essays on the Indians of Florida and Southeastern Georgia during the Historic Period*, ed. Jerald Milanich and Samuel Proctor (Gainesville, Fla., 1978), 128–130.

9. John Smith, *General Historie of Virginia, New-England, and the Summer Isles* ... (1624), in *The Complete Writings of Captain John Smith*, ed. Philip Barbour, 3 vols. (Chapel Hill, N.C., 1986), 2:121.

10. Women's patterns for drinking differ in the modern world as well; see Frances K. Del Broca, "Sex, Gender, and Alcoholic Typologies," in *Types of Alcoholics: Evidence from Clinical, Experimental, and Genetic Research*, ed. Thomas F. Babor et al., Annals of the New York Academy of Sciences 708 (1994), 34–48.

11. See Mary Douglass, ed., *Constructive Drinking: Perspectives on Drinking from Anthropology* (Cambridge, 1987).

12. For the desire for alcohol at weddings see Thomas Butler to Sir William Johnson, January 6, 1757, in *Johnson Papers*, 2:664; for dances see *R. I. Col. Recs.*, 4:425–426. For the use of alcohol to stop pain see *Pennsylvania Gazette*, February 17, 1730, which tells of a trader who was allowed to give liquor to an Indian to dull his senses while he was being ritually tortured. The incident is noteworthy because descriptions of ritual tortures throughout the eastern woodlands virtually never reveal such concern by torturers for the pain of the victim.

13. *Jes. Rel.*, 6:251. Le Jeune knew that problems with liquor continued; see ibid., 9:201–207.

14. Ibid., 6:253, 9:205. Hugh Jones observed the same phenomenon later in Virginia; see his *Present State of Virginia*, ed. Richard C. Morton (Chapel Hill, N.C., 1956), 56.

15. For a discussion of the alleged impact of Europeans on Indian drinking styles and a suggested reason for the ways Indians drank, see Craig MacAndrew and Robert Edgerton, *Drunken Comportment: A Social Explanation* (Chicago, 1969), 100–164.

16. *Jes. Rel.*, 52:193.

17. [François Vachon de Belmont], "Belmont's History of Brandy," ed. Joseph Donnelly, *Mid-America* 34 (1952), 45.

18. Ibid., 47–49; elsewhere (53–57) Belmont noted that virtually every member of an Indian community became inebriated on occasion.

19. John Clayton, "The Aborigines of the Country," in *The Reverend John Clayton: A Parson with a Scientific Mind: His Scientific Writings and Other Related Papers*, ed. Edward Berkeley and Dorothy Smith Berkeley (Charlottesville, Va., 1965), 37–38; see also his "Another 'Account of Virginia,'" 436.

20. Daniel Denton, *A Brief Description of New-York, formerly called New-*

Netherlands, (1670, in *Historic Chronicles of New Amsterdam, Colonial New York and Early Long Island*, ed. Cornell Jaray, Empire State Historical Publications Series 36 (Port Washington, N.Y., n.d.), 7. See also Pierre François Xavier de Charlevoix, *Journal of a Voyage to North America*, trans. and ed. Louise P. Kellogg, 2 vols. (Chicago, 1923), 2:98.

21. Samuel Hopkins, *Historical Memoirs Relating to the Housatunnuk Indians* (Boston, 1753), 168; *Adair's History of the American Indians*, ed. Samuel C. Williams (Johnson City, Tenn., 1930), 6, 326.

22. Francis Daniel Pastorius, "Circumstantial Geographical Description of Pennylvania" (1700), in *Narratives of Early Pennsylvania, West New Jersey, and Delaware*, ed. Albert C. Meyers (New York, 1912), 433; Cadwallader Colden, *The History of the Five Indian Nations Depending on the Province of New-York in America* (1727; Ithaca, 1958), 60. Linguistic evidence reinforces this early desire for intoxication; the Passamaquoddys' language included *sputsuwin* to describe a person on a binge and *kotuhsomuin* to refer to a person who was regularly inebriated, but until recently lacked a term for moderate drinking. See Susan M. Stevens, "Alcohol and World View: A Study of Passamaquoddy Alcohol Use," in *Cultural Factors in Alcohol Research and Treatment of Drinking Problems*, ed. Dwight B. Heath, Jack O. Waddell, and Martin Topper, *JSA*, (1981), 122–142.

23. "Review of the Trade and Affairs in the Northern District of America [September 22, 1767]," in *Trade and Politics, 1767–1769*, ed. Clarence Alvord and Clarence Carter, *Ill. Colls.* 16 (1921), 36. According to Anthony F. C. Wallace, "all observers [of the Delawares] agreed that liquor dissolved the inhibitions against aggression": "Some Psychological Characteristics of the Delaware Indians during the 17th and 18th Centuries," *Pennsylvania Archaeologist* 20 (1950), 38. As Gregory Dowd has pointed out, "power lay at the center of all concerns" for eastern woodlands Indians during the eighteenth century, and the desire to "secure power and to gain the favor of powerful beings" led Indians to celebrate specific rituals. In such a psychological universe, perhaps the desire to drink to the point of intoxication became, for some Indians, a new form of ritual; once intoxicated, many certainly acted out as if they possessed powers they did not have when they were sober. For an excellent discussion of eastern woodlands Indians' notions of power see Dowd, *A Spirited Resistance: The North American Indian Struggle for Unity, 1745–1815* (Baltimore, 1992), 1–22; quotations on p. 3.

24. Denys, *Description and Natural History*, 448–450.

25. Bernard Romans, *A Concise Natural History of East and West Florida* (1775; New Orleans, 1961), 55.

26. Alexander Henry, *Travels and Adventures in Canada and the Indian Territories between the Years 1760 and 1776* (1809; New York, 1976), 243–244. For Ojibways' uses of alcohol during the late eighteenth and early nineteenth centuries see Bruce M. White, " 'Give Us a Little Milk': The Social and Cultural Significance of Gift Giving in the Lake Superior Fur Trade," *Minnesota History* 48 (1982), 66–71, and "A Skilled Game of Exchange: Ojibway Fur Trade Protocol," *Minnesota History* 50 (1987), 232–236.

27. John Lawson, *A New Voyage to Carolina*, ed. Hugh T. Lefler (Chapel Hill, N.C., 1967), 190.

28. Ibid., 212.

29. Ralph Hamor, *A True Discourse of the Present Estate of Virginia, and the Successe of the Affaires there till the 18 of June, 1614* (1615), ed. A. L. Rowse (Richmond, 1957), 43; Carl Bridenbaugh, ed., *Gentleman's Progress: The Itinerarium of Dr. Alexander Hamilton* (Chapel Hill, N.C., 1948), 98. Another early colonist, Christopher Levett, noted that a "reputed Queene" in Maine, the daughter of a sagamore, offered him a drink and toasted his associates, as well as her husband, but he did not reveal whether the drink was alcoholic; see "Christopher Levett, 1624, York and Portland," in *Sailors' Narratives of Voyages along the New England Coast, 1524–1624*, ed. George P. Winship (1905; New York, n.d.), 273–274.

30. Richard White, *The Middle Ground: Indians, Empires, and Republics in the Great Lakes Region, 1650–1815* (New York, 1991), 205.

31. "Croghan's Journal, 1765," in *EWT*, 1:165–166.

32. *Pennsylvania Gazette*, July 5, 1733; "Journal of the Proceedings of Conrad Weiser, in his Journey to Ohio . . . ," *HSP Colls.* 1 (1853), 25–26; "Croghan's Journal, 1765," 161, 166; Franklin, *Treaties*, 37, 39, 69–70.

33. "The Treaty held with the Indians of the Six Nations, at Philadelphia, in July 1742," in Franklin, *Treaties*, 25. See also Conrad Weiser to Richard Peters, September 28, 1752, and "Proceedings of a Conference Held at Pittsburgh, July 1759," in Manuscript Papers Relating to Indian and Military Affairs in Pennsylvania, APS, 128, 756.

34. "Extract of Conrad Weiser's Journal amongst the United Indians of the 6 Nations, copy, with notes thereupon," in Daniel Horsmanden Papers (microfilm), APS, entries for June 13 and June 14, 1745.

35. "Journal of Weiser, in his Journey to Ohio," 25. Governor James Glen sent alcohol to the Cherokee headman Canachaute in the hope that these Indians would also toast the king's health; see Glen to Canachaute, October 14, 1755, *CRSC Indian Affairs, 1754–1765*, 77. And Johnson gave a group of Indians in New York rum to toast the king's health; see *Pennsylvania Gazette*, July 5, 1764. Colonists on occasion also closed negotiations at the end of the day by drinking with Indians; see, for example, *Va. Exec. J.*, 5:414.

36. "The Journal of Christian Frederick Post, . . . to the Indians on the Ohio," in *EWT*, 1:243.

37. "Toasts," in George Croghan Papers, box 8, file 14, HSP; "Journal of James Kenny, 1761–1763," ed. John W. Jordan, *PMHB* 37 (1913), 192.

38. Clayton, "Another 'Account of Virginia,' " 436.

39. "A Treaty held at the Town of Lancaster . . . in June, 1744" in Franklin, *Treaties*, 73, 78–79.

40. There is no doubt that Indians were deeply concerned about the content of dreams and spent time deciphering their meaning; there is also ample documentation suggesting that Indians felt compelled to act on the suggestions they received during dreams. As visions were important to some colonial observers as well, notably Jesuit missionaries, much evidence on Indians' dreams and their interpretation of them has been preserved. For the importance of dreams to Indians see Samuel de Champlain, *Des sauvages, or Voyage de Samuel Champlain, de Brouge* (1603), vol. 1 of *The Works of Samuel de Champlain*, ed. H. P. Biggar, 6 vols.

(1922; Toronto, 1971), 118; *Jes. Rel.*, 22:227, 243 and 23:53. For modern scholars' links between drinking and dreaming see Edmund S. Carpenter, "Alcohol in the Iroquois Dream Quest," *American Journal of Psychiatry* 116 (1959), 148–151; R. C. Dailey, "The Role of Alcohol among North American Indian Tribes as Reported in the *Jesuit Relations*," *Anthropologica* 10 (1968), 48–50; and Calvin Martin, *Keepers of the Game: Indian-Animal Relations and the Fur Trade* (Berkeley, 1978), 119–121. For some vivid examples of missionaries and visions see the writings of St. Isaac Joques in *An Autobiography of Martyrdom: Spiritual Writings of the Jesuits in New France*, ed. François Roustang (St. Louis, 1964), 185–195. Indians were not alone in interpreting dreams long before Freud. Various medieval Europeans were also eager to interpret the messages they saw in dreams. See Lisa M. Bitel, " 'In Visu Noctis': Dreams in European Hagiography and Histories, 450–900," *History of Religions* 31 (1991), 39–59; Jacques LeGoff, "Dreams in the Culture and Collective Psychology of the Medieval West," in *Time, Work, and Culture in the Middle Ages* (Chicago, 1980), and "Christianity and Dreams, 2nd–7th Centuries," in *The Medieval Imagination* (Chicago, 1988), 193–231.

41. See Robert C. Turner et al., "Alcohol Withdrawal Syndromes: A Review of the Pathophysiology, Clinical Presentation, and Treatment," *Journal of General Internal Medicine* 4 (1989), 432–444, esp. 435. For a review of this particular issue see Maia T. Conrad, "Disorderly Drinking: Reconsidering Seventeenth-Century Iroquois Alcohol Use," paper presented at the annual meeting of the American Society for Ethnohistory, 1989.

42. *Jes. Rel.*, 22:227, 243; Carpenter, "Alcohol in the Iroquois Dream Quest"; Dailey, "Role of Alcohol," 48–50.

43. Mackintosh to Lyttleton, February 17, 1758, in *CRSC Indian Affairs, 1754–1765*, 448.

44. Louis Antoine de Bougainville, *Adventure in the Wilderness: The American Journals of Louis Antoine de Bougainville, 1756–1760*, ed. Edward P. Hamilton (Norman, Okla., 1964), 179.

45. See Bruce Trigger, *The Children of Aataensic: A History of the Huron People to 1660*, rev. ed. (Kingston and Montreal, 1987), 462.

46. Gerald Mohatt, "The Sacred Water: The Quest for Personal Power through Drinking among the Teton Sioux," in *The Drinking Man*, ed. David C. McClelland et al. (New York, 1972), 264–265; Joan Weibel–Orlando, "Indians, Ethnicity, and Alcohol: Contrasting Perceptions of the Ethnic Self and Alcohol Use," in *The American Experience with Alcohol: Contrasting Cultural Perspectives*, ed. Linda Bennett and Genevieve Ames (New York, 1985), 202.

47. Charlevoix, *Journal of a Voyage*, 2:77. Charlevoix's quotation struck a chord with nineteenth-century historians; two of them used it in their books. See John Halkett, *Historical Notes respecting the Indians of North America* (1825; Millwood, N.Y., 1976), 171, and Samuel Morewood, *A Philosophical and Statistical History of the Innovations and Customs of Ancient and Modern Nations in the Manufacture and Use of Inebriating Liquors* (Dublin, 1838), 349.

48. Bruce M. White, "A Skilled Game of Exchange: Ojibway Fur Trade Protocol," *Minnesota History* 50 (1987), 234; Stevens, "Alcohol and World View," 122–142.

49. For early descriptions of Indian burials see, for example, William Wood, *New England's Prospect* (1634), ed. Alden T. Vaughan (Amherst, Mass., 1977), 110–112; Thomas Harriot, *A Briefe and True Report of the New Found Land of Virginia* (1590; New York, 1972), 72–73. On eastern woodlands burial practices and how they changed over the course of the colonial period see James Axtell, "Last Rites: The Acculturation of Native Funerals in Colonial North America," in Axtell, *The European and the Indian: Essays in the Ethnohistory of Colonial North America* (New York, 1981), 110–128.

50. David Pietersz. de Vries, *Short Historical and Journal Notes of several voyages made in the four parts of the World, namely Europe, Africa, Asia, and America* (1655), in *Historic Chronicles of New Amsterdam, Colonial New York and Early Long Island*, ed. Cornell Jaray, Empire State Historical Publications Series 35 (Port Washington, N.Y., n.d.), 55–56.

51. Hopkins, *Historical Memoirs*, 37–38; "Rev. Gideon Hawley's Journey to Oghquago (Broome Co.), 1753," in *Doc. Hist. N.Y.*, 3:1043–1046.

52. "The Narrative of Peter Pond," in *Five Fur Traders of the Northwest*, ed. Charles M. Gates (St. Paul, 1933), 35–36. Though he did not describe any other drinking activities in such depth, Pond noted (41) that drinking, along with "Dancing, Smokeing, Matcheis, Gameing, Feasting," and "Playing the Slite of Hand," was a ritual associated with preparations for the winter hunt.

53. John Long, *John Long's Voyages and Travels in the Years 1768–1788*, ed. Milo M. Quaife (Chicago, 1922), 89. For an early nineteenth-century description of whiskey incorporated into a mourning ritual see Earl P. Olmstead, *Blackcoats among the Delaware: David Zeisberger on the Ohio Frontier* (Kent, Ohio, 1991), 144–145.

54. "Diary of David Zeisberger and Gottlieb Sensemann's Journey to Goschgoschink on the Ohio, May 8, 1768–February 20, 1769," box 135, folder 7, entry for October 21, 1768, RMM; the excerpt can also be found in "The Diaries of Zeisberger Relating to the First Missions in the Ohio Basin," ed. Archer B. Hulbert and William N. Schwarze, *Ohio Archaeological and Historical Quarterly* 21 (1912), 85.

55. See chapter 6, below.

56. Eastern woodlands Indians' conceptions of law differed substantially from those of English common law, but certain concepts related to revenge crossed tribal boundaries and constituted a loosely organized structure for maintaining order that resembled a legal system. At the heart of that system was a vital idea, as Yasuhide Kawashima has noted: "Retributive justice was the essence of Indian law." See Kawashima, *Puritan Justice and the Indian*, 5–7, quotation at 5.

57. *Jes. Rel.*, 51:123–125, 53:257; see also [François] Dollier de Casson and René de Bréhant de Galinée, *Exploration of the Great Lakes, 1669–1670*, ed. James H. Coyne, (1903; Millwood, N.Y., 1975), 29.

58. Gabriel Thomas, "An Historical and Geographical Account of Pensilvania and of West-New-Jersey" (1698), in Meyers, *Narratives of Early Pennsylvania*, 335.

59. Memorial of Louvigny to Council, October 15, 1720, *Wis. Colls.* 16:388–389.

60. *The Memoirs of Lieut. Henry Timberlake* (1765), ed. Samuel C. Williams (Johnson City, Tenn., 1927), 79.
61. Denonville to Seignelay, January 1690, *N.Y. Col. Docs.* 9:441.
62. *Jes. Rel.*, 61:173.
63. Casson and Galinée, *Exploration of the Great Lakes*, 29.
64. Merrell, *Indians' New World*, 39, 102.
65. *Pennsylvania Gazette*, November 8, 1733.
66. Bougainville, *Adventure in the Wilderness*, 225, 179.
67. [Conrad Weiser], "Description of the Indians: Iroquois and Delaware, in Communications to Christopher Saur, which appeared in the Years 1746–1749," comp. Abraham H. Cassell, trans. Helen Bell, manuscript copy (1873), 21, HSP.
68. In the western Arctic reaches of Canada, drinking was a way for community members, particularly hunters, to express their individualism well into the twentieth century. Liquor allowed the Vunta Kutchins of Old Crow in the Yukon and the Kwakiutls of British Columbia to overcome traditional inhibitions and communicate more freely. See John A. Price, "An Applied Analysis of North American Indian Drinking Patterns," *Human Organization* 34 (1975), 19–20.
69. See George Vaillant, *The Natural History of Alcoholism* (Cambridge, Mass., 1983), 99–101.
70. Twentieth-century studies provide ample support for such ideas. "Under the weight of these deprivations [discrimination, poverty, poor housing, and lack of education] it is not surprising that American Indians have sought relief in alcohol. Alcoholic beverages have been the easiest and quickest way to deaden the senses and to forget the feeling of inadequacy. Under the influence of liquor the real world becomes substituted by an unreal one where the Indian sees himself as an equal to others, and with the physical and psychological support provided by drinking companions, the world appears less hostile and even tolerable": Edward P. Dozier, "Problem Drinking among American Indians: The Role of Sociocultural Deprivation," *QJSA* 27 (1966), 77. See also Thomas W. Hill, "Ethnohistory and Alcohol Studies," in *Recent Developments in Alcoholism*, ed. Marc Galanter (New York, 1984), 2:317–318.
71. The benefits of drinking, especially the sense of empowerment that can come through communal intoxication, have been explored in an important essay by Nancy Lurie: "The World's Oldest On-Going Protest Demonstration: North American Indian Drinking Patterns," *Pacific Historical Review* 40 (1971), 311–332.
72. Clayton, "Aborigines of the Country," 37.
73. See, for example, Daniel K. Richter, "Cultural Brokers and Intercultural Politics: New York–Iroquois Relations, 1664–1701," *JAH* 75 (1988–89), 40–67; and Merrell, *Indians' New World*, esp. 134–166.

4. Costs

1. Colonial observations quite possibly reflected empirical reality in this instance; at least they correspond to contemporary reports that young men drink more than other members of Indian communities. See, for example, J. David

Kinzie et al., "Psychiatric Epidemiology of an Indian Village: A 19-Year Replication Study," *Journal of Nervous and Mental Disease* 180 (1992), 36–37.

2. *The Speech of a Creek-Indian, against the Immoderate Use of Spirituous Liquors* (London, 1754), 11.

3. White's pictures, subsequently engraved by Theodor de Bry, accompanied the 1590 edition of Thomas Harriot's *A Briefe and True Report of the New Found Land of Virginia*; for a modern copy of his rendering of Secota see the Dover reprint edition (New York, 1972), 69.

4. For references to drinking bouts that stretched over several days see Daniel Pepper to Governor Lyttleton, June 28, 1757, *CRSC Indian Affairs, 1754–1765*, 388; John Long, *John Long's Voyages and Travels in the Years 1768–1788*, ed. Milo M. Quaife (Chicago, 1922), 74, 132; George Croghan's Journal, 1754, in Manuscript Papers on the Indian and Military Affairs of the Province of Pennsylvania, 1737–1775, APS, 142; "Mémoire touchant l'yvrognerie des sauvages en Canada," AC, C 11, A, f. 384 (microfilm). For the "Raiging Divels" see "John Hays' Diary and Journal of 1760," ed. William A. Hunter, *Pennsylvania Archaeologist* 24 (1954), 75.

5. George Croghan's Journal, 1754, 142.

6. "Diary of G. Buttner, Shekomecko, New York, August 10–December 3, 1743," box 111, folder 2, entry for November 27, RMM.

7. Even a nonmissionary believed that drinking interfered with Indians' proper appreciation of God; see Samuel C. Williams, ed., *James Adair's History of the American Indians* (Johnson City, Tenn., 1930), 122–123.

8. See *Jes. Rel.*, 22:243 and 46:105; "Mémoire touchant l'yvrognerie des sauvages," f. 387; Proceedings in French Council of Marine, March 28, 1716, *Wis. Colls.*, 16:340; and James Axtell, *The Invasion Within: The Contest of Cultures in Colonial North America* (New York, 1985), 65–67. The views of missionaries on the brandy trade in Canada are treated at length in chapter 6, below.

9. Jonathan Edwards, *Memoirs of the Rev. David Brainerd, Missionary to the Indians* (1822; St. Clair Shores, Mich., 1970), 233, 239.

10. [Cotton Mather], *Sober Considerations, on a growing Flood of Iniquity* (Boston, 1708), 16.

11. "Mr. Occom's Address to His Indian Brethren," (1772). For more on Occom's views see chapter 5, below.

12. "A Québec des hommes et des femmes Sauvages ivres et nus se sont entrainés dans les rues où à vue et au grand scandale de tout le monde ils ont fait publiquement comme des bêtes brutes des choses honteuses et infâmes les uns avec les autres. . . .": "Mémoire touchant l'yvrognerie des sauvages," f. 388. The same author claimed that men got Indian women drunk so that the women would have sex with them, and that Indian women who thus became pregnant either had or sought abortions ("avortent ou se font avorter"), committed infanticide, or could not provide sufficient milk for their infants (f. 384–385). I have found no evidence to support these specific claims, and I suspect that they reflect this anonymous observer's concerns about morality rather than actual events.

13. Nicholas Denys, *The Description and Natural History of the Coasts of North America* (1672), trans. William F. Ganong (Toronto, 1908), 448–450; Bernard Ro-

mans, *A Concise Natural History of East and West Florida* (1775; New Orleans, 1961), 55.

14. William Bartram, *Travels through North and South Carolina, Georgia, East and West Florida, the Cherokee Country, the Extensive Territories of the Muscogulges, or Creek Confederacy, and the Country of the Chactaws* (1791; New York, 1988), 214–215.

15. Nathaniel B. Shurtleff, ed., *Records of the Governor and Company of the Massachusetts Bay in New England*, 5 vols. (Boston, 1855–1861), 1:406–407.

16. William Bradford, *Of Plymouth Plantation*, ed. Samuel Eliot Morison (New York, 1967), 205–206. On the threat Morton posed to the settlers of Plymouth and Massachusetts Bay see Michael Zuckerman, "Pilgrims in the Wilderness: Community, Modernity, and the Maypole at Merry Mount," *New England Quarterly* 50 (1977), 255–277.

17. "Colonel Chicken's Journal to the Cherokees," in *Travels in the American Colonies*, ed. Newton D. Mereness, (New York, 1916), 171.

18. *Md. Arch.*, 29:229.

19. "Un mari tuera sa femme, et les femmes que s'enivrent aussi bien que les hommes tuent leurs maris et leurs enfants à coups de couteau et les étouffent sans savoir ce qu'elles font": "Mémoire touchant les boissons enyvrant les sauvages du Canada," AC, C 11 A, f. 382.

20. See, for example, Timothy Horsfield to Governor James Hamilton, September 3, 1761, Horsfield Papers, 2:441–444, APS; James Sullivan, "History of the Penobscot Indians," *MHS Colls.* 9 (1804), 232.

21. "Journal of Beatty's Trip to the Ohio Country in 1766," in *Journals of Charles Beatty, 1762–1769*, ed. Guy S. Klett (University Park, Pa., 1962), 67. On this and other sexual relations in the region see Richard White, *The Middle Ground: Indians, Empires, and Republics in the Great Lakes Region, 1650–1815* (New York, 1991), 60–75, 214–215, 334. Other stories of familial breakdown related to drinking include a report of a Block Island Indian who purportedly sold his siblings into slavery for thirteen gallons of rum and four coats; see John A. Sainsbury, "Indian Labor in Early Rhode Island," *New England Quarterly* 48 (1975), 385. English observers were not alone in reporting such indiscretions; French observers also claimed that colonists gave Indian women liquor so that they could have sex with them, with resultant problems in Indian families; see "Mémoire touchant les boissons enyvrant les sauvages du Canada," f. 380–381, and "Mémoire touchant l'yvrogneries des sauvages," f. 384–385.

22. James Sterling to John Dunbar, January 10, 1762, in Sterling letter book, 23–24, Clem. Lib.

23. James Adair, *The History of the American Indians* (London, 1775), 286; see also "Journal of David Taitt's Travels from Pensacola, West Florida, to and through the Country of the Upper and Lower Creeks, 1772," in Mereness, *Travels in the American Colonies*, 544.

24. Dunbar Rowland, ed., *Mississippi Provincial Archives, 1763–1766: English Dominion* (Nashville, 1911), 1:219–220.

25. Sir William Johnson to James Abercromby, May 17, 1758, in *Johnson Papers*, 9:905–906.

26. "Journal of Indian Affairs," February 25, 1767, in *Johnson Papers*, 12:273–275.

27. Johnson to Lords of Trade, October 1764, in *N.Y. Col. Docs.*, 7: 665; and see White, *Middle Ground*, 335.

28. John Lawson, *A New Voyage to Carolina*, ed. Hugh T. Lefler (Chapel Hill, N.C., 1967), 18, 211–212, 232.

29. Samuel Danforth, *The Woful Effects of Drunkenness* (Boston, 1710), 10–11.

30. Adair, *History of the American Indians*, 224.

31. Louis B. Wright, ed., *The Prose Works of William Byrd of Westover* (Cambridge, Mass., 1966), 302–303.

32. As quoted in Helen C. Rountree, *Pocahontas's People: The Powhatan Indians of Virginia through Four Centuries* (Norman, Okla., 1990), 127.

33. "Extract of the Reverend Mr. Bolzius's Journal . . ." (1734), in Force, *Tracts*, 4, no. 5, 20.

34. Andrew Burnaby, *Travels through the Middle Settlements in North America, in the Years 1759 and 1760 . . .*, 3d ed. (1798; New York, 1904), 62.

35. Milton W. Hamilton, ed., "Guy Johnson's Opinions on the American Indian," *PMHB* 77 (1953), 325–326.

36. "Review of the Trade and Affairs in the Northern District of America [September 22, 1767]," in *Ill. Colls.* 16 (1921), 32. Phillip Pittman, reporting on settlements in the Mississippi Valley in 1770, similarly attributed the rapid demographic collapse of one group of Indians to "immoderate use of spirituous liquors": *The Present State of the European Settlements on the Mississippi* (1770; Memphis, 1977), 35.

37. John Stuart to Lord George Germain, June 14, 1777, CO5/78, PRO Trans., reel 7.

38. Benjamin Franklin, *The Autobiography of Benjamin Franklin*, ed. Leonard W. Labaree (New Haven, 1964), 199.

39. Peter Kalm, *Peter Kalm's Travels in North America* (1770), ed. Adolph B. Benson (New York, 1964), 258–259. Kalm, ever the natural historian, did not see all liquors as equal; he believed that rum was healthier than brandy (325). Two decades earlier he had reported the story of two Indians who went out in a canoe, drank brandy, fell asleep, and were awakened by the roar of Niagara Falls just in time to keep from being swept to their deaths. See Kalm's report in the *Pennsylvania Gazette*, September 20, 1750.

40. According to a late seventeenth-century French writer, Indians "will drink until they die and will not stop until the barrel is dry" ("ils boivent jusqu'à crever et ne cessent point de boire"); see "Mémoire touchant les boissons envirant les sauvages," f. 380. For an apparent case of alcohol poisoning see "Kingston (New York) Court Records, 1668–1675," in *New York Historical Manuscripts: Dutch: Kingston Papers*, ed. Peter Christopher et al. (Baltimore, 1976), 2:463. For the deaths of perhaps forty Indians apparently attributable to tainted rum they had gotten at Michilimackinac in the late 1760s see Thomas Gage to Lord Hillsborough, April 1, 1769, in *The Correspondence of General Thomas Gage, with Secretaries of State, 1763–1775*, ed. Clarence E. Carter (New Haven, 1931), 1:223. For suicide see "Mémoire touchant l'yvrognerie des sau-

vages," f. 384, and Thomas Morton, *New English Canaan* . . . (1632), in Force, *Tracts*, 1:38.

41. Lawson, *New Voyage to Carolina*, 18, 211; Long, *Voyages and Travels*, 74, 86, 109, 132; Samuel Sewall, *The Diary of Samuel Sewall, 1624–1729*, ed. M. Halsey Thomas, 2 vols. (New York, 1973), 1:90. Conrad Weiser in August 1748 "found a dead man on the road who had killed himself by drinking too much whiskey." Though he did not identify the man as either an Indian or a colonist, it seems likely that he was an Indian; see "Journal . . . of his Journey to Ohio," *HSP Colls*. 1 (1853), 23. One missionary reported the accidental death of an Indian in a ritual for the drink-related death of a Mohawk; see "Journal of Christian Frederick Post . . . to the Indians on the Ohio," in *EWT*, 1:284.

42. See, for example, Matthew Toole to James Glen, October 28, 1752; Ludowick Grant to Glen, February 8, 1753; and Glen to Lieutenant Governor Dinwiddie, June 1, 1754, in *CRSC Indian Affairs, 1750–1754*, 359, 367, 526.

43. See, for example, the case against "Henry Sparke and Cromwell ye Indian," in Portsmouth, New Hampshire, in September 1667, *N.H. Prov. P.*, 40:229.

44. For one notable case see the depositions relating to the death of Thomas Wright in a fight with drunken Indians initiated by the trader John Burt in *Pa. Col. Recs.*, 3:285–287; see also *Md. Arch.*, 17:177.

45. "Moses & Indians W. H. & G. recd by Mrs Hamond July 1, [16]77," in *Documentary History of the State of Maine*, ed. James P. Baxter, Collections of the Maine Historical Society, 2d ser. (Portland, 1900), 6:178–179.

46. "Minutes of Conferences held at Fort Pitt in April and May 1768, under the Direction of George Croghan, . . . with the Chiefs & Warriors of the Ohio, & other Western Indians," Peter Force Collection, ser. 8D, no. 29 (microfilm reel no. 35), LC. Virginia officials, presented with evidence that a colonist had set a drunken Saponi on fire (he later died of his burns), launched an effort to apprehend the perpetrator, but apparently even a £10 reward did not lead to his arrest; see *Va. Exec. J.*, 4:133, 453.

47. "A Treaty of Friendship held with the Chiefs of the Six Nations, . . . September and October, 1736," in Franklin, *Treaties*, 11–12.

48. See, for example, *Pa. Arch.*, 1st ser., 1:254–255.

49. Charles Stuart to John Stuart, April 8, 1777, CO5/78, PRO Trans., reel 7; Richard White, *The Roots of Dependency: Subsistence, Environment, and Social Change among the Choctaws, Pawnees, and Navajos* (Lincoln, Neb., 1983), 85–86. James Kenny would have agreed with this assessment; whenever liquor appeared in western Pennsylvania in the late 1750s and early 1760s, violence seemingly followed in its wake. See "James Kenny's 'Journal to Ye Westward,' 1758–59," ed. John W. Jordan, *PMHB* 37 (1913), 438, and "Journal of James Kenny, 1761–1763," ed. John W. Jordan, ibid., 16, 38.

50. "Journal of David Taitt's Travels," 513–515, 525n, 553n, 555–556, 560; see also John Stewart to John Pownall, August 24, 1765, in *N.C. Col. Recs.*, 7:110.

51. See Denys, *Description and Natural History*, 450; and James H. Merrell, *The Indians' New World: Catawbas and Their Neighbors from European Contact through the Era of Removal* (Chapel Hill, N.C., 1989), 39.

52. Thomas Bosworth to Mr. Elsinor, December 23, 1752, and Lachland Mc-Gillivray to Glen, April 14, 1754, in *CRSC Indian Affairs, 1750–1754*, 325, 502.

53. The Indians' actions and the subsequent charges against the liquor seller, who claimed the Indians had stolen rum from him, are documented in Baxter, *Documentary History of the State of Maine*, 6:413–420. Indians in Massachusetts, it should be noted, received harsh punishments if they were found inebriated; see Edwin Powers, *Crime and Punishment in Early Massachusetts, 1620–1692* (Boston, 1966), 379–380.

54. The story is documented in a series of complaints dated February 15, 1750, in the Conrad Weiser papers, Correspondence, 1:25, HSP.

55. *American Magazine*, January 1740–41, facs. (New York, 1937), 7; for the murder of a colonist in New Hampshire in 1688 see Colin Calloway, ed., *Dawnland Encounters: Indians and Europeans in Northern New England* (Hanover, N.H., 1991), 185–186.

56. Weequehela's life and death are analyzed in Robert S. Grumet, "The King of New Jersey," *Bulletin of the Archaeological Society of New Jersey* 48 (1993), 45–52.

57. See, for example, "Rev. Gideon Hawley's Journey to Oghquago (Broome Co.), 1753," in *Doc. Hist. N.Y.*, 3:1043–1046.

58. Helena Wall, *Fierce Communion: Family and Community in Early America* (Cambridge, Mass., 1990); David Jones, *A Journal of Two Visits Made to Some Nations on the West Side of the River Ohio, in the Years 1772 and 1773* (1774; New York, 1865), 23, 26; A. Irving Hallowell, "Some Psychological Characteristics of the Northeastern Indians" (1946), in his *Culture and Experience* (Philadelphia, 1955), 132–143, esp. 141–142. For the beliefs of one group of Indians about slander see *Jes. Rel.*, 6:247.

59. Thomas Budd, *Good Order Established in Pennsilvania & New-Jersey in America* ([Philadelphia], 1685), 29.

60. Some anthropologists agree. Craig MacAndrew and Robert B. Edgerton write that "in the course of socialization persons learn about drunkenness whatever their society presumes to be the case; and that, comporting themselves in consonance with what is thus imparted to them, they become the living confirmation of their society's presumptions." Or, in more economic language, "drunken comportment is an essentially *learned* affair." See their *Drunken Comportment: A Social Explanation* (Chicago, 1969), 138, 87–88. See also Michael Dorris, *The Broken Cord* (New York, 1989), 83–84.

61. [Jean] Bossu, *Travels through that part of North America formerly called Louisiana*, trans. John Reinhold Forster, 2 vols. (London, 1771), 1:119–120. Some Americans continued to blame traders. Hector St. John de Crèvecoeur argued that duplicitous traders got Indians drunk in order to defraud them, prompting the Indians to retaliate against all settlers. See his *Letters from an American Farmer* (1782; Gloucester, Mass., 1968), 60–61.

62. Jaspar Danckaerts, "Journal of a Voyage to New York in 1679–1680," *Memoirs of the Long Island Historical Society* 1 (1867), 149–150.

63. See the instructions of the commissioners of the Indian trade to traders for July 27, August 2, and August 3, 1711, in *CRSC Journals*, 11, 13–15.

64. Journal of Thomas Bosomworth, in *CRSC Indian Affairs, 1750–1754*, 298.

65. Paul J. Lindholdt, ed., *John Josselyn, Colonial Traveler: A Critical Edition of Two Voyages to New-England* (Hanover, N.H., 1988), 99.

66. *N.Y. Col. Docs.*, 5:663; Patrick Frazier, *The Mohicans of Stockbridge* (Lincoln, Neb., 1992), 173–174.

67. Wilbur R. Jacobs, ed., *The Appalachian Indian Frontier: The Edmund Atkin Report and Plan of 1755* (Lincoln, Neb., 1967), 35–36, 45, 59.

68. "Mémoire touchant l'yvrognerie des sauvages," f. 387.

69. Memorial of Louvigny to Council, October 15, 1720, *Wis. Colls.*, 16:388.

70. William Beauchamp, ed., *Moravian Journals Relating to Central New York, 1745–1766* (Syracuse, 1916), 199–200; Peter C. Mancall, *Valley of Opportunity: Economic Culture along the Upper Susquehanna, 1700–1800* (Ithaca, 1991), 61. The missionaries apparently accepted the Nanticokes' claim, even though planting was traditionally women's work in their communities. For the southeast see David Taitt to John Stuart, June 5, 1777, CO5/78, PRO Trans., reel 7.

71. John Parker, ed., *The Journals of Jonathan Carver and Related Documents, 1766–1770* (Minneapolis, 1976), 79; see 90 for his gift of rum to a group of Naudowessees.

72. See "The Opinions of George Croghan on the American Indian," *PMHB* 71 (1947), 159; Hamilton, "Guy Johnson's Opinions," 325.

73. "A Treaty held with the Ohio Indians at Carlisle, in October, 1753," in Franklin, *Treaties*, 130, and *Pa. Col. Recs.*, 5:676.

74. "Narrative of a journey, made in the year 1737, by Conrad Weiser, Indian Agent and Provincial Interpreter, from Tulpehocken in the Province of Pennsylvania to Onondaga," trans. H. H. Muhlenberg, *HSP Colls.* 1 (1853), 17; see also Mancall, *Valley of Opportunity*, 61–62; White, *Middle Ground*, 281; Gregory Dowd, *A Spirited Resistance: The North American Indian Struggle for Unity, 1745–1815* (Baltimore, 1992), 29.

75. See *Pa. Arch.*, 1st ser., 3:237, 437, 519; *Va. Exec. J.*, 3:592–593; [Charles Thomson], *An Enquiry into the Causes of the Alienation of the Delawares and Shawanese Indians from the British Interest and the Measures Taken for Recovering Their Friendship* (London, 1759), 11, 13, 24, 31–32, 74–76; *Speech of the Creek-Indian.*

76. ". . . qu'on ne peut mieux représenter l'enfer, que par la vue des Sauvages et Sauvagesses ivres qui sont alors capables de toutes sortes de brutalités, violences et meurtres . . .": AC, C 11 A, 12:2, f. 381.

77. *Pa. Arch.*, 1st ser., 1:262.

78. "Diary of David Zeisberger and Gottlieb Sensemann's Journey to Goschgoschink on the Ohio . . . May 8, 1768–Feb. 20, 1769," in RMM, Box 135, folder 7, entry for January 12, 1769.

79. Chester to Earl of Dartmouth, January 4, 1774, in *Docs. Am. Rev.*, 8:127; cf. Tom Hatley, *The Dividing Paths: Cherokees and South Carolinians through the Era of Revolution* (New York, 1993), 49. See also Taitt to Stuart, June 5, 1777, CO5/78, PRO Trans., reel 7.

80. For a single report detailing some of these problems, though with some exaggeration, see Daniel Claus to Sir William Johnson, July 8, 1772, in *Johnson Papers*, 12:971–972. Consumption of alcohol increased the risk of hypothermia;

see Margaret M. Gallaher et al., "Pedestrian and Hypothermia Deaths Among Native Americans in New Mexico," *JAMA* 267 (1992), 1346–1347.

5. Temperance

1. Most historians and anthropologists have paid little attention to the battles of historic Indian communities against alcohol, but two works have treated the issue: Christian F. Feest, "Notes on Native American Alcohol Use," in *North American Indian Studies: European Contributions*, ed. Pieter Hovens (Göttingen, 1981), esp. 206, 210–211, 213, 215; and Richard White, *The Roots of Dependency: Subsistence, Environment, and Social Change among the Choctaws, Pawnees, and Navajos* (Lincoln, Neb., 1983), esp. 190–192.

2. For the histories of later movements see William J. Rorabaugh, *The Alcoholic Republic: An American Tradition* (New York, 1979), 187–222; and Mark Edward Lender and James Kirby Martin, *Drinking in America: A History* (New York, 1982), 41–168.

3. See James D. McCallum, ed., *The Letters of Eleazer Wheelock's Indians* (Hanover, N.H., 1932), 45–46, 61–62, 259–260.

4. Nancy O. Lurie argued that Indians in the twentieth century drank as a form of protest, finding in collective inebriation a way to demonstrate their hostility toward Euroamericans. Perhaps similar motivations led some Indians to drink to excess in early America as well, though I argue here that Indians protested their situation by standing up to the liquor trade. See Lurie, "The World's Oldest Ongoing Protest Demonstration: North American Indian Drinking Patterns," *Pacific Historical Review* 40 (1971), 311–330.

5. Bernard Romans, *A Concise Natural History of East and West Florida* (1775; New Orleans, 1961), 163.

6. E. B. O'Callaghan, ed., *Laws and Ordinances of New Netherland, 1638–1674* (Albany, 1868), 34–35, 52, 95, 100, 182–183, 260, 446–447, 451.

7. Nathanial Shurtleff, ed., *Records of the Governor and Company of the Massachusetts Bay in New England*, 5 vols. (Boston, 1853–1854), 1:106, 323; 2:84–85, 258; 3:369; Yasuhide Kawashima, *Puritan Justice and the Indian: White Man's Law in Massachusetts, 1630–1763* (Middletown, Conn., 1986), 79–80.

8. On generational change and the religious tensions evident at this time see Edmund Morgan, *Visible Saints: The History of a Puritan Idea* (Ithaca, 1965), 130–138.

9. Shurtleff, *Records of Massachusetts Bay*, 3:425; 4, pt. 2:297.

10. Kawashima, *Puritan Justice*, 86–88; Kathleen J. Bragdon, "Crime and Punishment among the Indians of Massachusetts, 1675–1750," *Ethnohistory* 28 (1981), 25–26.

11. *Pennsylvania Gazette*, December 11, 1735.

12. Albert S. Bachellor, ed., *Laws of New Hampshire, Including Public and Private Acts and Resolves and the Royal Commissions and Instructions, with Historical and Descriptive Notes* (Manchester, N.H., 1904), 1:739–740, 117; *Acts and Laws of His Majesty's Province of New Hampshire, in New England* (Portsmouth, N.H., 1761), 220.

NOTES TO PAGES 105–107

13. Nathanial Shurtleff, ed., *Records of the Colony of New Plymouth in New England: Judicial Acts, 1636–1692* (Boston, 1857), 242–243, 247–248.
14. *R.I. Col. Recs.*, 1:279, 307–308, 413–414.
15. *Conn. Pub. Recs.*, 1:254–255, 263, 338.
16. Ibid., 2:119; 3:94; 5:5.
17. *R.I. Col. Recs.*, 2:487, 500–501.
18. Bragdon, "Crime and Punishment," 25–26.
19. *R.I. Col. Recs.*, 4:425–426.
20. *Conn. Pub. Recs.*, 6:31–32; 7:472–473.
21. *Doc. Hist. N.Y.*, 2:91–92; Colonel Dongan to M. de Denonville, December 1, 1686, ibid., 1:227.
22. *Colonial Laws of New York from the Year 1664 to the Revolution*, 5 vols. (1894–1896), 1:657–658, 685–686, 740–741, 751, 755; 3:1096–1098; 4:93.
23. *Pa. Col. Recs.*, 2:42–43. Public pressure could also prove effective in the late seventeenth century; Quaker opposition to one colonist's sales of alcohol to Indians in 1687 prompted him to stop such sales. See Miles White, Jr., "William Biles," *PMHB* 26 (1902), 194. Still, not all complied, as a disturbance of Indians seeking to purchase rum from a colonist who had earlier sold it to them demonstrated in 1686; see ibid., 1:140, and Gary Nash, "The First Decade in Pennsylvania: Letters of William Markham and Thomas Holme to William Penn," *PMHB* 90 (1966), 332–334. See also Thomas J. Sugrue, "The Peopling and Depeopling of Early Pennsylvania: Indians and Colonists, 1680–1720," *PMHB* 106 (1992), 24–26. For references to the earliest laws see *Pa. Arch.*, 8th ser., 1:12, 34, 50, as well as 57 and 119 on failed efforts to push similar legislation.
24. "Journal of James Kenny, 1761–1763," ed. John W. Jordan, *PMHB* 37 (1913), 44. See J. T. Mitchell and Henry Flanders, eds., *Statutes at Large of Pennsylvania from 1682 to 1801* (Harrisburg, 1896–1908), 2:168–170, 3:250, 310–313, 5:320–330; 6:283–293; Proclamation by Lt. Gov. James Hamilton, August 11, 1749 (broadside), Ab [1749]-2, HSP; *Pennsylvania Gazette*, August 21, 1731; March 1, 1748; May 4, 1758; and February 19, 1761. For an official carrying such news westward see "Instructions to Conrad Weiser, October 14, 1754," in Manuscript Papers Relating to Indian and Military Affairs in Pennsylvania, 195, APS. In addition to the proclamations, the *Gazette* published articles describing the proprietary government's fears of the rum trade and its efforts to stop the commerce; see the issues of May 26 and September 8, 1748.
25. For a local effort see H. Clay Reed and George J. Miller, eds., *The Burlington Court Book: A Record of Quaker Jurisprudence in West New Jersey, 1680–1709* (Washington, D.C., 1944), 2, 3; for the minor status of the trade in late colonial New Jersey see *N.J. Col. Recs.*, 10:222–223.
26. For three notable incidents see the case against John Wetherill in New Jersey in January 1716/17 in *N.J. Col. Recs.*, 4:276–285; the case against George (Ury) Klock in New York in *Johnson Papers*, 3:312, 314, 338–341, 619–629; 4:53–56, 112–115; and the case against the Susquehannah Company and its agent John Lydius in Pennsylvania in *Johnson Papers*, 3:714–717; Julian Boyd and Robert Taylor, eds., *The Susquehannah Company Papers*, 11 vols. (Wilkes-Barre and Ithaca,

[228]

1930–1971), 2:88–92, 93–94, 190–191; Peter C. Mancall, *Valley of Opportunity: Economic Culture along the Upper Susquehanna, 1700–1800* (Ithaca, 1991), 77–78.

27. *Md. Arch.*, 5:260, 557; 8:327–328; 15:260; 17:178; 22:511; 26:348; 38:15–16, 147–148.

28. William Hening, ed., *The Statutes at Large: Being a Collection of All the Laws of Virginia*, 13 vols. (New York, Richmond, and Philadelphia, 1810–1823), 3:468; 5:273; 7:117; 8:116; *Va. Exec. J.*, 3:81, 110–111, 312–313, 593.

29. Thomas Cooper and David J. McCord, eds., *Statutes at Large of South Carolina*, 10 vols. (Columbia, 1836–1841), 2:67, 309.

30. See *CRSC Journals*, 4, 18, 59, 298–299; *CRSC Indian Affairs, 1750–1754*, 57, 150, 325; *CRSC Indian Affairs, 1754–1765*, 43–44, 105, 160, 171, 354.

31. *Ga. Col. Recs.*, 18:223–224; Robert B. Rea and Milo B. Howard, Jr., eds., *The Minutes, Journals, and Acts of the General Assembly of British West Florida* (University, Ala., 1979), 347 (legislation later disallowed), 381, 390. North Carolina sought to control the liquor trade but never explicitly banned it; see *N.C. Col. Recs.*, 1:231; 4:507; 5:583, 902, 1141–1142; 6:616–617; 23:2.

32. Samuel C. Williams, ed., *Adair's History of the American Indians* (Johnson City, Tenn., 1930), 315; the passage does not indicate how the trader was punished.

33. *Pennsylvania Gazette*, August 2, 1744.

34. James Oglethorpe, for example, claimed in 1733 that he had "weaned those near me a good deal from [rum]"; see *Pennsylvania Gazette*, November 8, 1733.

35. James H. Merrell, "The Indians' New World: The Catawba Experience," *WMQ*, 3d ser., 41 (1984), 537–565, and *The Indians' New World: Catawbas and Their Neighbors from European Contact through the Era of Removal* (Chapel Hill, N.C., 1989).

36. See *Jes. Rel.*, 22:241 and 43:259–261; James Axtell, *The Invasion Within: The Contest of Cultures in Colonial North America* (New York, 1985), 65–67. Missionaries in British colonies similarly noted that Indians did not always remain sober; see Samuel Hopkins, *Historical Memoirs Relating to the Housatunnuk Indians* (Boston, 1753), 59.

37. *Jes. Rel.*, 58:81–83, 251–253; 60:81, 89, 145–147; 61:239–241; Bruce G. Trigger, *Natives and Newcomers: Canada's "Heroic Age" Reconsidered* (Kingston and Montreal, 1985), 293, 295.

38. Father Gabriel Druillettes's "relation" of 1647 in *Dawnland Encounters: Indians and Europeans in Northern New England*, ed. Colin Calloway (Hanover, N.H., 1991), 62.

39. *Md. Arch.*, 8:327–328, 15:260.

40. Penn to the Earl of Sunderland, July 28, 1683, in *The Papers of William Penn*, ed. Richard S. Dunn and Mary Maples Dunn, 5 vols. (Philadelphia, 1981–1987), 2:417–418.

41. John Parker, ed., *The Journals of Jonathan Carver and Related Documents, 1766–1770* (Minneapolis, 1976), 116.

42. Romans, *Concise Natural History*, 52.

43. "Diary of David Zeisberger and Gottlieb Sensemann's Journey to Gosch-

goschink on the Ohio, May 8, 1768–February 20, 1769," in RMM, box 135, folder 7, entry for October 23, 1768.

44. Jonathan Edwards, *Memoirs of the Rev. David Brainerd, Missionary to the Indians* (1822; St. Clair Shores, Mich., 1970), 218–219.

45. Hopkins, *Historical Memoirs*, 54, 81.

46. Earl P. Olmstead, *Blackcoats among the Delaware: David Zeisberger on the Ohio Frontier* (Kent, Ohio, 1991), 246.

47. "Diary of Welhik Tuppek and Gnadenhutten, on Muskingum, from Oct. 19th, 1772, to March 22, 1773," in RMM, box 141, folder 13, entry for March 8, 1773.

48. *Mr. Occom's Address to His Indian Brethren* (n.p., 1772).

49. Samson Occom, *A Sermon Preached at the Execution of Moses Paul*, 3d ed. (New London, 1772), esp. 21–23.

50. See McCallum, *Letters of Eleazar Wheelock's Indians*, 45–46, 61–62, 259–260. For Occom's own drinking history see W. DeLoss Love, *Samson Occom and the Christian Indians of New England* (Boston, 1899), 162–168 (outdated but still somewhat useful in its presentation of documentary evidence). Occom's sensitivity to his own drinking and to gossip about it indicates the stigma he associated with drunkenness; see David Murray, *Forked Tongues: Speech, Writing and Representation in North American Indian Texts* (London, 1991), 53–54.

51. [Jean] Bossu, *Travels through that part of North America formerly called Louisiana*, trans. John Reinhold Forster, 2 vols. (London, 1771), 1:197; see also "Rev. Gideon Hawley's Journey to Oghquago (Broome Co.), 1753," in *Doc. Hist. N.Y.*, 3:1043–1046.

52. *Pa. Arch.*, 1st ser., 1:549–551.

53. William Beauchamp, ed., *Moravian Journals Relating to Central New York, 1745–1766* (Syracuse, 1916), 193.

54. *Doc. Hist. N.Y.*, 2:591–592; *Pennsylvania Gazette*, September 5, 1754. For a similar incident, see "Relation by Frederick Post of Conversation with Indians, 1760," *Pa. Arch.*, 1st ser., 3:743.

55. David Jones, *A Journal of Two Visits Made to Some Nations of Indians on the West Side of the River Ohio, in the Years 1772 and 1773* (1774; New York, 1865), 105.

56. Archer B. Hulbert and William N. Schwarze, eds., "The Diaries of Zeisberger Relating to the First Missions in the Ohio Basin," *Ohio Archaeological and Historical Quarterly* 21 (1912), 68, 73, and "David Zeisberger's History of the Northern American Indians," ibid. 19 (1910), 90. Zeisberger also noted that sellers of rum too moved away in order to carry out their business ("History," 90). Anthony Benezet also recognized a link between temperance-minded Indians and Moravians. In the 1780s he wrote that Indians at Wyalusing, on the Susquehanna, had rejected liquor in the 1750s, and had to move westward when colonial settlers migrated to the region and the rum traffic increased. They settled on the Muskingum River and lived with Moravian missionaries, who shared the Indians' desire to prevent drinking. See Benezet's *Some Observations of the Situation, Disposition, and Character of the Indian Natives of This Continent* (Philadelphia, 1784), 24–25.

57. George Croghan to Richard Peters, November 28, 1747, in *Md. Arch.*, 46:7.

58. John Heckewelder, *History, Manners, and Customs of the Indian Nations Who Once Inhabited Pennsylvania and the Neighbouring States*, ed. William C. Reichel (Philadelphia, 1881), 267.

59. Edwards, *Memoirs of Brainerd*, 237–238.

60. "Narrative of a journey, made in the year 1737, by Conrad Weiser, Indian Agent and Provincial Interpreter, from Tulpehocken in the Province of Pennsylvania to Onondaga," trans. H. H. Muhlenberg, in *HSP Colls.* 1:17; Richard White, *The Middle Ground: Indians, Empires, and Republics in the Great Lakes Region, 1650–1815* (New York, 1991), 281; Mancall, *Valley of Opportunity*, 61–62; Gregory Dowd, *A Spirited Resistance: The North American Indian Struggle for Unity, 1745–1815* (Baltimore, 1992), 29, 33–34; Heckewelder, *History, Manners, and Customs*, 293–294; "Journal of James Kenny," 171, 188.

61. See, among other works, James Axtell, "The English Colonial Impact on Indian Culture," in Axtell, *The European and the Indian: Essays in the Ethnohistory of Colonial North America* (New York, 1981), 253–256; William Cronon, *Changes In the Land: Indians, Colonists, and the Ecology of New England* (New York, 1983), 82–84, 92–97; Timothy Silver, *A New Face on the Countryside: Indians, Colonists, and Slaves in South Atlantic Forests, 1500–1800* (New York, 1990), 192–193; and Charles Hudson, "Why the Southeastern Indians Slaughtered Deer," in *Indians, Animals, and the Fur Trade: A Critique of Keepers of the Game*, ed. Shepard Krech III (Athens, Ga., 1981), 157–176.

62. *N.Y. Col. Docs.*, 5:662–663; Patrick Frazier, *The Mohicans of Stockbridge* (Lincoln, 1992), 6–7.

63. Sachems of Oquaga to Johnson, January 22, 1770, in *Johnson Papers*, 7:348–349. For earlier efforts in the region see Timothy Woodbridge to Johnson, June 26, 1753, in *Doc. Hist. N.Y.*, 2:627–628.

64. "Journal of Indian Affairs," December 9–12, 1758, in *Johnson Papers*, 10:69, 73; Miamis to Commander at Fort Detroit, May 1767, ibid., 5:557–558; "An Indian Conference, November 12, 1768," ibid., 12:635.

65. John Stuart to Lord George Germain, June 14, 1777, CO 5/78, PRO Trans., reel 7.

66. *N.C. Col. Recs.*, 5:143, 581; 6:902.

67. "Speech of the Shawnees," July 1771, in *Johnson Papers*, 12:914–915.

68. For contemporary evidence see Anthony J. Mariaro et al., "Drinking-Related Locus of Control and the Drinking Status of Urban Native Americans," *JSA* 50 (1989), 331–338, esp. 336. On the origins of the concept of addiction to alcohol see Harry G. Levine, "The Discovery of Addiction: Changing Concepts of Habitual Drunkenness in America," *JSA* 39 (1978), 145–151. For the regulation of behavior within villages see Bruce Graham Trigger, "Order and Freedom in Huron Society," *Anthropologica* 5 (1963), 151–168; and Daniel Richter, *The Ordeal of the Longhouse: The Peoples of the Iroquois League in the Era of European Colonization* (Chapel Hill, N.C., 1992), esp. 44–47.

69. Report of the Proceedings of the Honble. Charles Stuart . . . on his late Tour thro the Choctaw Nation . . . , July 1, 1778, CO 5/79, PRO Trans., reel 7; White, *Roots of Dependency*, 84; Frazier, *Mohicans of Stockbridge*, 199, 208.

70. *Doc. Hist. N.Y.*, 2:592.

71. "Minutes of an Indian conference at Pittsburgh," October 9, 1773, in *Johnson Papers*, 12:1035.

72. "Journal of Indian Affairs," February 25, 1767, in *Johnson Papers*, 12:273, 275. At least here Johnson offered some serious help. A decade earlier he had told a group of Iroquois that their request to stop the "Sale of Rum . . . appears to me very whimsical as you well know that a Noise was made about stopping it before by some of every nation, nay several Sachems now present told me unless it was allowed to be sold again they were in Danger of their Lives. What an Opinion must the Govr. of New York, his Council & assembly (before whom & by whom only such Laws can be passed) have of the Six Nations? Why first they must think them divided amongst themselves as the Request comes only from some of the Nations. [I]n the next place they must imagine them very fickle to say no worse, being but 2 years ago since they passt such a Law at the 6 Nations earnest Request, tho against the Interest of the Subject. [T]he Year After at their desire the Law was repealed, now to desire the same Law to be renewed, must certainly appear to everybody extremly odd." Only when the Indians had all agreed on a ban should they ask for it again; if they did so, Johnson promised he would assist them. See ibid., 10:73 (December 9–12, 1758).

73. Lender and Martin, *Drinking in America*, 17; Paton Yoder, "Tavern Regulation in Virginia: Rationale and Reality," *VMHB* 87 (1979), 259–278; Edwin Powers, *Crime and Punishment in Early Massachusetts, 1620–1692* (Boston, 1966), 367–399. Ministers and legislators did not seek to prevent drinking (a task that would have been impossible), though New England ministers, including many of the most prominent Puritans, inveighed against public drunkenness. For their ideas see Increase Mather, *Wo to Drunkards* (Cambridge, Mass., 1673); [Cotton Mather], *Sober Considerations on a Growing Flood of Iniquity* (Boston, 1708); Samuel Danforth, *The Woful Effects of Drunkenness* (Boston, 1710); Benjamin Wadsworth, *An Essay to do Good, By a Disswasive from Tavern-haunting, and Excessive Drinking* (Boston, 1710), and [Thomas Foxcroft et al.], *A Serious Address to Those Who Unnecessarily Frequent the Tavern* (Boston, 1726). In spite of the rhetorical power of these sermons, Puritans still drank; see David W. Conroy, "Puritans in Taverns: Law and Popular Culture in Colonial Massachusetts, 1630–1720," in *Drinking: Behavior and Belief in Modern History*, ed. Susanna Barrows and Robin Room (Berkeley, 1991), 29–60.

74. For correspondence between colonial officials and policy makers in London see, for example, Johnson to the Earl of Hillsborough, August 14, 1770, in *Docs. Am. Rev.*, 2:165–166; Gage to Hillsborough, May 14 and September 8, 1770, and October 1, 1771, ibid., 2:95, 178, and 3:202; William Nelson to Hillsborough, February 5, 1771, ibid., 3:37; Peter Chester to Hillsborough, June 23, 1771, in ibid., 179–180; John Stuart to Lord George Germain, October 26, 1776, ibid., 12:240–241; Chester to Earl of Dartmouth, June 4, 1774, ibid., 8:127–128.

75. [Charles Thomson], *An Enquiry into the Causes of the Alienation of the Delawares and Shawanese Indians from the British Interest, and the Measures Taken for Recovering Their Friendship* (London, 1759), 11, 13, 24, 31–32, 74–76. For Tawenna's speech see *Pa. Col. Recs.*, 3:363.

76 *Pa. Col. Recs.*, 3:274–276, 4:759–761, 5:397–398, 8:172.

77. Ludovick Grant to Governor Glen, March 4, 1752, in *CRSC Indian Affairs, 1750–1754*, 222.

78. Bosomworth to Elsinor, December 23, 1752, and McGillivray to Glen, April 14, 1754, in *CRSC Indian Affairs, 1750–1754*, 325, 502.

79. *Pa. Col. Recs.*, 2:604.

80. James Logan to Colonel Keith on his report to the Board of Trade, April 8, 1719, in Miscellaneous Collections, box 11c, HSP.

81. *Pa. Col. Recs.*, 3:275.

82. "A Treaty of Friendship held with the Chiefs of the Six Nations, at Philadelphia in September and October, 1736," in Franklin, *Treaties*, 11.

83. See Craig MacAndrew and Robert B. Edgerton, *Drunken Comportment: A Social Explanation* (Chicago, 1969), 142–149; Samuel Hopkins, *Historical Memoirs Relating to the Housatunnuk Indians* (Boston, 1753), 81.

84. Robert Hunter Morris to an unnamed person, 1756, in Gratz Papers, case 15, box 18 (folder labeled "Morris, Robert Hunter, 1756"), HSP.

85. "Review of the Trade and Affairs in the Northern District of America [September 22, 1767]," in *Ill. Colls.* 16 (1921), 37.

86. William Nelson to Lord Hillsborough, February 5, 1771, in *Docs. Am. Rev.*, 3:37.

87. *N.Y. Col. Docs.*, 5:795–798. Other Indians also complained about duplicitous traders; see ibid., 663.

88. Ibid., 863–864; an alternative description of this meeting appears in Peter Wraxall, *An Abridgement of the Indian Affairs . . . in the Colony of New York, from the Year 1678 to the Year 1751*, ed. Charles McIlwain (Cambridge, Mass, 1915), 173–175.

89. *N.Y. Col. Docs.*, 5:865–867.

90. Colonists agreed with the Indians and on August 20 issued a proclamation banning the sale of liquor to Indians "in the Woods"; see *Pa. Col. Recs.*, 3:404–412.

91. *Doc. Hist. N.Y.*, 2:591; "A Treaty held with the Ohio Indians at Carlisle, in October, 1753" (Philadelphia, 1753), in Franklin, *Treaties*, 130; also in *Pa. Col. Recs.*, 5:676.

92. The message is included in Demere to Governor Lyttleton, January 31, 1757, in *CRSC Indian Affairs, 1754–1765*, 328–329; see also 326 for a request for rum by Old Hop.

93. "James Kenny's 'Journal to Ye Westward,' 1758–59," ed. John W. Jordan, *PMHB* 37 (1913), 429.

94. "Croghan's Journal, 1765," in *EWT*, 1:158–159. During the Revolution, Stockbridge Indians continued to recognize the dangers of alcohol, but nonetheless requested that British officials provide them with at least moderate amounts of rum; see Frazier, *Mohicans of Stockbridge*, 199.

95. *CRSC Journals*, 49–50, 102, 110.

96. Ibid., 152, 153, 235, 287.

97. George Cadagan to Glen, March 21, 1751, in *CRSC Indian Affairs, 1750–1754*, 12.

98. George Galphin to Glen, January 28, 1752/53, in *CRSC Indian Affairs, 1750–1754*, 268; Lachlan McGillivray to Glen and Council, February 12, 1756, in *CRSC Indian Affairs, 1754–1765*, 104.

99. *CRSC Indian Affairs, 1754–1765*, 146–147, 173, 328–329, 401–402, 438, 456–457; Glen to Canachaute, October 14, 1756, ibid., 77.

100. "A Scheme for Regulating the Indian Trade," in *CRSC Indian Affairs, 1750–1754*, 88.

101. Raymond Demere to Governor Lyttelton, March 26, 1757, in *CRSC Indian Affairs, 1754–1765*, 348–349.

102. For the postrevolutionary efforts see Anthony F. C. Wallace, *The Death and Rebirth of the Seneca* (New York, 1970), chap. 10; William L. McLoughlin, *Cherokee Renascence in the New Republic* (Princeton, 1986), 56, 334–335; Dowd, *Spirited Resistance*, 31–33, 126; White, *Middle Ground*, 506.

103. Peter Clark, "The 'Mother Gin' Controversy in the Early Eighteenth Century," *Transactions of the Royal Historical Society*, 5th ser., 38 (1988), 63–84; Lee Davison, "Experiments in the Social Regulation of Industry: Gin Legislation, 1729–1751," in *Stilling the Grumbling Hive: Responses to Social and Economic Problems in England, c. 1689–1750*, ed. Davison et al. (London, 1992), 25–48; T. G. Coffey, "Beer Street: Gin Lane: Some Views of Eighteenth-Century Drinking," *QJSA* 27 (1966), 669–692; George Rudé, "'Mother Gin' and the London Riots of 1736," *Guildhall Miscellany* 10 (1959), 53–63.

104. Conroy, "Puritans in Taverns"; Peter Thompson, "'The Friendly Glass': Drink and Gentility in Colonial Philadelphia," *PMHB* 112 (1989), 549–573; Rorabaugh, *Alcoholic Republic*, chap. 1.

105. Bryan Edwards, *The History, Civil and Commercial, of the British Colonies in the West Indies*, 2 vols. (London, 1793), 2:396–397.

106. See Robert Dossie, *An Essay on Spirituous Liquors, with regard to the Effects on Health* (London, [1770]), and *Doc. Hist. N.Y.*, 1:227.

6. New Spain, New France

1. On the devastations of the colonial period see J. H. Parry, *The Spanish Seaborne Empire* (New York, 1966), 213–228, and, for a contemporary account, Miguel Leon-Portillo, ed., *The Broken Spears: The Aztec Account of the Conquest of Mexico* (Boston, 1962). The Indian population of central Mexico declined from 25.2 million in 1518 to 1.075 million in 1605, a loss of approximately 95 percent in less than a century; see Sherburne F. Cook and Woodrow Borah, "Royal Revenues and Indian Population in New Spain, ca. 1620–1646," in their *Essays in Population History: Mexico and California*, 3 vols. (Berkeley, 1974–1979), 3:1.

2. Girolamo Benzoni, *History of the New World* (1572), trans. and ed. W. H. Smyth, Works Issued by the Hakluyt Society, 1st ser., 21 (1857; New York, n.d.), 83.

3. Jack O. Waddell, "The Use of Intoxicating Beverages among the Native Peoples of the Aboriginal Greater Southwest," in *Drinking Behavior among Southwestern Indians: An Anthropological Perspective*, ed. Jack O. Waddell and Michael

W. Everett (Tucson, 1980), 1–32. Knowledge of production did not necessarily lead to ritual or any other use of liquor; there is no evidence of precontact drinking among the Hopis, some Navajos, and Rio Grande Pueblos. See Jerrold E. Levy and Stephen J. Kunitz, *Indian Drinking: Navajo Practices and Anglo-American Theories* (New York, 1974), 62, and Christian F. Feest, "Notes on Native American Alcohol Use," in *North American Indian Studies: European Contributions*, ed. Pieter Hovens (Göttingen, 1981), 206.

4. Steve Stern, *Peru's Indian Peoples and the Challenge of Spanish Conquest: Huamanga to 1640* (Madison, Wis., 1982), 19.

5. William Taylor, *Drinking, Homicide, and Rebellion in Colonial Mexican Villages* (Stanford, 1979), 28–34; Inga Clendinnen, *Aztecs: An Interpretation* (Cambridge, 1991), 48–51, 117–118, 198; Bernardino de Sahagún, *Florentine Codex: General History of the Things of New Spain*, trans. Arthur J. O. Anderson and Charles Dibble, 13 bks. in 12 vols. (Santa Fe, 1950–1982), bk. 2: 95, 207; bk. 4: 11–17; bk. 10: 55–56. On the *Florentine Codex* see Clendinnen, *Aztecs*, 8–9.

6. Nancy M. Farriss, *Maya Society under Colonial Rule: The Collective Enterprise of Survival* (Princeton, 1984), 195, 190, 313, 322, 343.

7. Taylor, *Drinking, Homicide, and Rebellion*, 34–45, 57–72; *Thomas Gage's Travels in the New World*, ed. Eric S. Thompson (Norman, Okla., 1958), 225; Farris, *Maya Society under Colonial Rule*, 196–198.

8. Michael C. Scardaville, "Alcohol Abuse and Tavern Reform in Late Colonial Mexico City," *Hispanic American Historical Review* 60 (1980), 643–671.

9. On motivations for moving see Ida Altman, "Emigrants and Society: An Approach to the Background of Colonial Spanish America," *Comparative Studies in Society and History* 30 (1988), 170–190; for sex ratios of the migrants see Peter Boyd–Bowman, "Patterns of Spanish Emigration to the Indies until 1600," *Hispanic American Historical Review* 56 (1976), 582–587, 596–601, and "Spanish Emigrants to the Indies, 1595–1598: A Profile," in *First Images of America: The Impact of the New World on the Old*, ed. Fredi Chiapelli, 2 vols. (Berkeley, 1976), 2:729–732.

10. Sherburne F. Cook and Woodrow Borah, "The Population of Yucatan, 1517–1960," and "Racial Groups in the Mexican Population since 1519," in their *Essays in Population History*, 2:75–83, 197–202. By the mid–seventeenth century approximately 437,000 Spaniards had crossed the Atlantic, and from 1561 to 1650 approximately 3,900 moved each year; see Magnus Morner, "Spanish Migration to the New World prior to 1810: A Report on the State of Research," in Chiapelli, *First Images of America*, 2:767.

11. See Taylor, *Drinking, Homicide, and Rebellion*, esp. 69–70.

12. Hale G. Smith and Mark Gottlob, "Spanish–Indian Relationships: Synoptic History and Archaeological Evidence, 1500–1763," in *Tacachale: Essays on the Indians of Florida and Southeastern Georgia during the Historic Period*, ed. Jerald Milanich and Samuel Proctor (Gainesville, Fla., 1978), 16; Clifford M. Lewis, "The Calusa," ibid., 44.

13. Jerald T. Milanich and Charles Hudson, *Hernando de Soto and the Indians of Florida* (Gainesville, Fla., 1993), 117–120.

14. "Report on the Indians of South Florida and Its Keys by Joseph María

NOTES TO PAGES 136–141

Mónaco and Joseph Javier Alana, Presented to Governor Juan Francisco de Guemes y Horcasitas, 1760," in *Missions to the Calusa*, ed. and trans. John H. Hahn (Gainesville, Fla., 1991), 425–426. The report, originally issued in 1743, was reissued in 1760; Hahn's translation is of the 1760 report, with notes describing the differences from the earlier report. For a copy, untranslated, of the 1743 report see William C. Sturtevant, "The Last of the South Florida Aborigines," in Milanich and Proctor, *Tacachale*, 154–161.

15. "Report on the Indians of South Florida," 427. Demand for rum among the Seminoles continued well into the nineteenth century; see Charles H. Fairbanks, "The Ethno–Archaeology of the Florida Seminole," in Milanich and Proctor, *Tacachale*, 167–168, 172–173. In the mid–eighteenth century one Cuban trader sold liquor along with French guns to Apalachee Indians in exchange for furs, but a plan devised by Bernardo de Gálvez, viceroy of New Spain in 1786, to provide alcohol to Indians in an effort to create "for them a new necessity which will oblige them to recognize their dependence" on the Spanish "more directly" was not put into operation. See David J. Weber, *The Spanish Frontier in North America* (New Haven, 1992), 178, 229–230.

16. For the most substantial studies of the brandy trade see Alfred G. Bailey, *The Conflict of European and Eastern Algonkian Cultures, 1504–1700: A Study in Canadian Civilization*, 2d ed. (Toronto, 1969), 66–71; André Vachon, "L'Eau-de-vie dans la société indienne," Report of the Canadian Historical Association (Ottawa, 1960), 22–32; George F. G. Stanley, "The Indians and the Brandy Trade during the Ancien Régime," *Revue d'Histoire de l'Amérique Française* 6 (1953), 489–505; and Jean Delanglez, *Frontenac and the Jesuits* (Chicago, 1939), 69–129.

17. For French migration patterns see Peter Moogk, "Reluctant Exiles: Emigrants from France in Canada before 1760," WMQ, 3d ser., 46 (1989), 463–505; Leslie Choquette, "Recruitment of French Emigrants to Canada, 1600–1760," in *"To Make America": European Emigration in the Early Modern Period*, ed. Ida Altman and James Horn (Berkeley, 1991), 137, 158–161; Louise Dechêne, *Habitants et marchands de Montréal au XVIIᵉ siècle* (Montreal, 1988), 77–80, 121. On the relationship between the fur trade and French imperial interests in North America see W. J. Eccles, "The Fur Trade and Eighteenth–Century Imperialism," WMQ, 3d ser., 40 (1983), 341–362.

18. H. P. Biggar, ed., *The Voyages of Jacques Cartier* (Ottawa, 1924), 122.

19. *Jes. Rel.*, 5:119–121.

20. Ibid., 3:107; 6:328–329.

21. Ibid., 21:67–69. The missionary Paul Le Jeune was particularly struck by Indians' drunken behavior; see ibid., 6:251 and 9:205.

22. See, for example, ibid., 21:97–99.

23. Marie de L'Incarnation to her son, August 26, 1644, and August 10, 1662, *Word from New France: The Selected Letters of Marie de L'Incarnation*, ed. Joyce Marshall (Toronto, 1967), 132, 273.

24. *Jes. Rel.*, 44:99, 46:103–105.

25. *Mandements, lettres pastorales et circulaires des éveques de Québec*, 4 vols. (Quebec, 1887–1888), 1:14–15, 30–32, 42–43.

26. *Jes. Rel.*, 46:105.

27. *Mandements . . . des évêques*, 1:72–73; Delanglez, *Frontenac and the Jesuits*, 96–97n.

28. Marie de L'Incarnation to her son, August 10, 1662, in *Word from New France*, 274.

29. *Mandements . . . des évêques*, 1:91–94.

30. For the flogging of one liquor trader in October 1661 see *Jes. Rel.*, 46:187.

31. Pierre François Xavier de Charlevoix, *History and General Description of New France*, trans. John G. Shea, 6 vols. (New York, 1900), 3:54–55.

32. *Jes. Rel.*, 53:247, 251, 257.

33. [François] Dollier de Casson, *A History of Montreal, 1640–1672*, trans. and ed. Ralph Flenley (New York, 1928), 339–341.

34. For references to the Dutch trade see *Jes. Rel.*, 51:123; 53:241; 55:85; 57:81; [François] Dollier de Casson and De Brehant de Galinée, *Exploration of the Great Lakes, 1669–1670*, ed. James H. Coyne (1907; Millwood, N.Y., 1975), 29, 35, 47.

35. Delanglez, *Frontenac and the Jesuits*, 102.

36. Charlevoix, *History and General Description of New France*, 3:55.

37. Marie de L'Incarnation to her son, August 10, 1662, in *Word from New France*, 274. On the significance of the term "Onontio" and its uses see Richard White, *The Middle Ground: Indians, Empires, and Republics in the Great Lakes Region, 1650–1815* (New York, 1991), xi and ff. The Iroquois too adopted this term in the late seventeenth century; see Daniel Richter, *The Ordeal of the Longhouse: The Peoples of the Iroquois League in the Era of European Colonization* (Chapel Hill, N.C., 1992), 131–132.

38. *Jes. Rel.*, 53:191–193; 55:85; 58:77, 193.

39. Ibid., 58:81–83, 251–253; 60:81, 89, 145–147; Bruce G. Trigger, *Natives and Newcomers: Canada's "Heroic Age" Reconsidered* (Kingston and Montreal, 1985), 293. Apparently these Mohawks did not find what they were seeking; Trigger notes (295) that Indians in Caughnawaga also drank alcohol.

40. *Jes. Rel.*, 58:77; 61:239–241, 59–61.

41. White, *Middle Ground*, 115.

42. "Délibération sur le cas réservé du commerce de l'eau-de-vie avec les sauvages, 1678," in *Découvertes et établissements des français dans l'ouest et dans le sud de l'Amérique septentrionale (1614–1754): Mémoires et documents originaux*, ed. Pierre Margry, 4 vols. (Paris, 1875–1886), 1:407–409, 412; G. B. Munro, "The Brandy Parliament of 1678," *Canadian Historical Review* 2 (1921), 174–175.

43. "Délibération sur le cas réservé," 1:413, 415–416; Munro, "Brandy Parliament," 177–178.

44. "Délibérations sur le cas réservé," 1:418–419; Munro, "Brandy Parliament," 178–179.

45. Delanglez, *Frontenac and the Jesuits*, 122–124; Stanley, "Indians and the Brandy Trade," 498–499; W. J. Eccles, *Frontenac: The Courtier Governor* (Toronto, 1959), 61–68. Eccles noted (66) that Frontenac did support a limited ban on the trade; he forbade residents of Batiscan, Champlain, and Trois Rivières to sell brandy to Indians.

46. *Jes. Rel.*, 62:183; see also 65–67; 63:259–261; 64:81–85, 89, 129–131, 145–147.

47. Dollier de Casson, *History of Montreal*, 375; Louise Dechêne, *Habitants and*

Merchants in Seventeenth-Century Montreal (1974), trans. Liana Vardi (Montreal, 1992), 82.

48. See Charlevoix, *History and General Description of New France*, 2:242–243; 3:53–55, 195–196; and Pierre François Xavier de Charlevoix, *Journal of a Voyage to North America*, trans. and ed. Louise P. Kellogg, 2 vols. (Chicago, 1923), 2:98–99, 72–73, 11.

49. Chrestian Le Clercq, *New Relation of Gaspesia, with the Customs and Religion of the Gaspesian Indians* (1691), ed. William F. Ganong (Toronto, 1910), 253–254.

50. François Vachon de Belmont, "Belmont's History of Brandy," ed. Joseph Donnelly, *Mid-America* 34 (1952), 53–55, 57–58, 63.

51. *Jes. Rel.*, 62:127–131.

52. Rev. Fr. Jacques Bigot to Rev. Fr. La Chaise, November 8, 1685, *Jes. Rel.*, 63:101–137, esp. 103–105, 115, 119–121, 125–127, 129. News of Bigot's success at Sillery made its way to France; see Fr. Thierry Beschefer, superior of the Jesuit missions in Canada to the Rev. Fr. Provincial of France, October 21, 1683, ibid., 62:259–265. But Indians at Sillery did not embrace Bigot's program as readily as he claimed; see James P. Ronda, "The Sillery Experiment: A Jesuit-Indian Village in New France, 1637–1663," *American Indian Culture and Research Journal* 3 (1979), 1–18.

53. Delanglez, *Frontenac and the Jesuits*, 104–105.

54. On Indians' purchasing practices see Arthur J. Ray, "Indians as Consumers in the Eighteenth Century," in *Old Trails and New Directions: Papers of the Third North American Fur Trade Conference*, ed. Carol M. Judd and Arthur J. Ray (Toronto, 1980), 255–271.

55. Baron de La Hontan, *New Voyages to North–America* (1703), ed. Reuben G. Thwaites, 2 vols. (Chicago, 1905), 1:466–467.

56. "Ce sont là les funestes effects de la vente de l'eau-de-vie quie diminue le commerce, qui affaiblit et désole la colonie, qui ruine les corps et les âmes des pauvres Sauvages en la nouvelle France. . . .": "Mémoire touchant l'yvrognerie des sauvages en Canada," AC, C 11, 12–2, f. 387. For the other reports see "Mémoire touchant les boissons enyvrant les sauvages de Canada," ibid., ff. 380–383.

57. "Memorial by Father Lafitau: On the Sale of Liquor to the Savages," in *Jes. Rel.*, 67:39–45.

58. *Mandements . . . des éveques*, 535–537.

59. *Jes. Rel.*, 67:45.

60. On presents see Cornelius J. Jaenen, "The Role of Presents in French-Amerindian Trade," in *Explorations of Canadian Economic History: Essays in Honor of Irene M. Spry*, ed. Duncan Cameron (Ottowa, 1985), 231–250 (brandy noted on 235, 239); Trigger, *Natives and Newcomers*, 292. Willingness to present gifts to Indians enabled the French to improve their relations with some Indian groups at the expense of the British, who were generally more reluctant to participate in gift exchange; see White, *Middle Ground*, 182–183, 257, 310.

61. White, *Middle Ground*, 127.

62. Count de Pontchartrain to Governor de Vaudreuil, June 9, 1706, *Wis. Colls.* 16:230.

63. Memorial of Louvigny to Council, October 15, 1720, *Wis. Colls.* 16:389.

64. Stanley, "Indians and the Brandy Trade," 500–505.

65. Daniel H. Usner, Jr., *Indians, Settlers, and Slaves in a Frontier Exchange Economy: The Lower Mississippi Valley before 1783* (Chapel Hill, N.C., 1992), 98.

66. Vandreuil to Rouillé, June 24, 1750; "Memoir on Indians by Kerlérec," December 12, 1758; and Michel to Rouillé, July 20, 1751, all in *Mississippi Provincial Archives: French Dominion*, vol. 5, *1749–1763*, ed. Patricia Kay Galloway and Dunbar Rowland (Baton Rouge, 1983), 47, 223, 100–101.

67. "Speeches of the Ouyatanons, Petikokias, Kikapoux, and Maskoutins to Monsieur the Marquis de Beauharnois, Governor-General of New france," July 8, 1742, *Wis. Colls.* 6:381, 384; "Summary of an Inspection of the Posts of Detroit and Michilimackinac, by D'Aigremont," ibid., 16:259; ——— to Claude de Ramezay, January 10, 1723, ibid., 422–427. Some colonial officials wanted to limit the commerce to western posts; see Sieur d'Aigremont to Count de Pontchartrain, November 18, 1710, ibid., 265.

68. British traders and officials reported extensive quantities of liquor at trading posts by the 1760s; see in particular George Morgan letterbook, 1767–1768, HSP, 35; "Account of Goods of Baynton, Wharton & Morgan, September 25, 1766: Goods sent to Edward Cole, Commissary for Indian Affairs of the Illinois &c.," in *Johnson Papers*, 13:400–404; "Baynton, Wharton & Morgan against the Crown, June 12, 1766," ibid., 5:248, 256; and "Report of the Indian Trade," ibid., 12:396–400. The Hudson's Bay Company is discussed in chapter 2.

69. Lawrence J. Burpee, ed., "York Factory to the Blackfeet Country: The Journal of Anthony Hendry, 1754–1755," *Proceedings and Transactions of the Royal Society of Canada*, 3d ser., 1 (1907), 352, 354.

70. Munro, "Brandy Parliament," 177.

71. Thomas F. Schilz, "Brandy and Beaver Pelts: Assiniboine-European Trading Patterns, 1695–1805," *Saskatchewan History* 37 (1984), 95–102.

72. W. A. Sloan, "The Native Response to the Extension of the European Traders into the Athabasca and Mackenzie Basin, 1770–1814," *Canadian Historical Review* 60 (1979), 291, 298. Variations in tribal responses to the liquor trade reflected, in all likelihood, a combination of traditional values and particular historical circumstances; for one discussion of these issues in respect to Indians living elsewhere see Ray Stratton, Arthur Zeiner, and Alfonso Paredes, "Tribal Affiliation and Prevalence of Alcohol Problems," *JSA* 39 (1978), 1166–1177.

73. Although the supply of brandy was probably insufficient to lead to cirrhosis or other somatic maladies associated with long-term drinking, enough alcohol was available to lead to short-term, often catastrophic health problems. Expansion of the trade could have led to more frequent episodes of alcohol-induced hypoglycemia or exposure, for example; see Jill R. Schumann, "The Diffusion of Alcohol: Through Membrane into Culture," in *Papers of the Thirteenth Algonquian Conference*, ed. William Cowan (Ottawa, 1982), 40–41; and Margaret M. Gallaher et al., "Pedestrian and Hypothermia Deaths among Native Americans in New Mexico," *JAMA* 267 (1992), 1345–1348. Alcohol continues to debilitate Canada's Indians, with often fatal consequences; see George K. Jarvis and Menno Boldt, "Death Styles among Canada's Indians," *Social Science Medicine* 16

(1982), 1345–1352; and Yang Mao et al., "Mortality on Canadian Indian Reserves, 1977–1982," *Canadian Journal of Public Health* 77 (1986), esp. 267.

74. For the continuance of the trade in the French territory south of the Great Lakes into the 1760s see *Jes. Rel.*, 70:255–257.

75. Liquor was vital to the trade even in places where it constituted a small percentage of the goods that merchants traded to Indians. As Louise Dechêne has noted, brandy "amounted to no more than 4 to 5 per cent of the value of shipments" of one merchant in Montreal, yet alcohol nonetheless played an important role in the trade because it facilitated exchange between Indians and colonists: *Habitants and Merchants*, 82; see also Denys Delâge, *Bitter Feast: Amerindians and Europeans in Northeastern North America, 1600–1664* (1985), trans. Jane Brierly (Vancouver, 1993), 136–140.

7. The British Imperial Moment, 1763–1775

1. Thomas Pownall, *The Administration of the Colonies*, 2d ed. (London, 1765), 4. For an excellent discussion of the British political economy in this period see Nancy F. Koehn, *The Power of Commerce: Economy and Governance in the First British Empire* (Ithaca, 1994).

2. See, for example, James H. Merrell, *The Indians' New World: Catawbas and Their Neighbors from European Contact through the Era of Removal* (Chapel Hill, N.C., 1989), 167–191; and Peter C. Mancall, *Valley of Opportunity: Economic Culture along the Upper Susquehanna, 1700–1800* (Ithaca, 1991), 124–126.

3. *N.C. Col. Recs.*, 5:235, 1141–1142. It should be noted that Dobbs's efforts did not represent the first attempts of Carolina officials to regulate trade with Indians. See ibid., 1:231, 4:507, 23:2.

4. *Pa. Arch.*, 8th ser., 4:2937–2938, 2943; see also 3178.

5. Draft of a plan dated 1756 in Gratz Collection, case 15, box 18, folder labeled "Morris, Robert Hunter, 1756," HSP.

6. John Dickinson to his mother, March 7, 1763, in Maria Dickinson Logan Family Papers, folder 1, HSP.

7. George Croghan to Sir William Johnson, October 18, 1767, in *Ill. Colls.* 16: 90.

8. The expansion of trade into the Ohio Valley spurred Pennsylvania officials to try to figure out ways to curb abuses in the region; see *Pa. Arch.*, 8th ser., 6:4938–4940.

9. "Review of the Trade," in *Ill. Colls.*, 16:37, 44.

10. *Pennsylvania Gazette*, August 7, 1760, and November 26, 1761. The Spanish, it should be noted, did not always provide the alcohol the Indians wanted; see ibid., August 26, 1762.

11. *N.Y. Col. Docs.*, 7:691.

12. Elias Durnford to Lord Hillsborough, February 17, 1770, in *Docs. Am. Rev.*, 2:45.

13. "Plan & Estimate of the Fur and Peltry Trade in the Back Country by Major Rogers," included in ? to Earl of Dartmouth, [1767?], APS.

14. A mid-1760s account describes allotments of rum to Indians totaling approximately 124 gallons from June 12, 1765, to March 29, 1766; transactions range from one quart, worth 3s in Pennsylvania currency, to two kegs containing 17½ gallons, worth £10 10s. See "An account of liquor given to the Indians by order of Capt Murray and Mr McKee from Sejt Major Cambell," Charles Swift Riche Papers, Am 6093, p. 2, HSP.

15. W. A. Speck, "The International and Imperial Context," in *Colonial British America: Essays in the New History of the Early Modern Era*, ed. Jack P. Greene and J. R. Pole (Baltimore, 1984), 396. As John Brewer has remarked in reference to Britain's difficulties in raising revenue in North America after the Seven Years' War, "State power declined at the periphery." Without effective power to control affairs abroad, crown officials could never hope to organize imperial affairs with any real success. See Brewer, *The Sinews of Power: War, Money, and the English State, 1688–1783* (New York, 1988), 176.

16. Stuart, for example, complained to the Board of Trade in 1766 that superintendents lacked the authority necessary to subordinate traders to the interest of the empire; see Stuart to Board of Trade, July 10, 1766, in *N.C. Col. Recs.*, 7:233–234.

17. See the circular letter from the Earl of Shelburne to all governors in America, September 13, 1766, in *N.J. Col. Recs.*, 9:569–570.

18. Hillsborough to Tryon, April 15, 1768, in *N.C. Col. Recs.*, 7:707–708.

19. Amherst to Johnson, December 30, 1761, in *Johnson Papers*, 3:597–598; Johnson to Amherst, January 7, 1762, ibid., 601; Amherst to Johnson, June 21, 1762, and August 20, 1763, ibid., 3:792, 4:192–193; Johnson to Amherst, August 1, 1762, ibid., 10:477–478; Amherst to Johnson, August 22 and August 28, 1762, ibid., 489, 496. See also Richard White, *The Middle Ground: Indians, Empires, and Republics in the Great Lakes Region, 1650–1815* (New York, 1991), 265–266.

20. See Sterling's letter to an unnamed correspondent, August 25, 1761; to James Lyme, May 31 and June 8, 1762; to Rutherford and Livingston, April 14, 1762, and January 25, 1763; and to Robert Holms, July 6, 1762, all in James Sterling letter book, 25, 37–38, 46–47, 40–41, 96, 56, Clem. Lib.

21. Petition of Merchants of Albany to Lords of Trade, March 1764, *N.Y. Col. Docs.*, 7:613–615.

22. Johnson to Lords of Trade, October 1764, *N.Y. Col. Docs.*, 7:665.

23. Johnson to Colden, October 9, 1764, in *The Letters and Papers of Cadwallader Colden*, vol. 6, *Collections of the New-York Historical Society for the Year 1922* (New York, 1923), 365–366; Johnson to Hillsborough, August 14, 1770, in *Doc. Hist. N.Y.*, 2:976; Johnson to Peter Warren, May 10, 1739, in *Johnson Papers*, 1:6–7.

24. Gage to Hillsborough, February 5, 1772, in *The Correspondence of General Thomas Gage with the Secretaries of State, 1763–1775*, ed. Clarence E. Carter (New Haven, 1931), 1:316–317; see also his earlier letters to Hillsborough of April 1, 1769, and May 14 and September 8, 1770, ibid., 223, 258, 268–269.

25. Sterling to Magill Wallace, May 29, 1765, in Sterling letter book, 141.

26. "A List of the Ships and Vessels which have arrived at Quebec, together with their Cargoes and the Duties arising to the Crown since the establishment of the American Board . . . to the 1st of January, 1780," in *Calendar of the Haldi-*

mand Collection, Volume III: Statistics of the Trade of Quebec, 1768–1783, in *Report on Canadian Archives*, ed. Douglas Brymner (Ottawa, 1889), 5–6, 12–13.

27. See chapter 2, note 108.

28. John J. McCusker, Jr., "The Rum Trade and the Balance of Payments of the Thirteen Continental Colonies, 1650–1775" (Ph.D. diss., University of Pittsburgh, 1970), 468, 476.

29. The plan bears no signature, but the role it gives Carver in the proposed settlement suggests that he either was the author or supervised its creation. The undated plan is in the Jonathan Carver Papers, Clem. Lib. For Carver's relationship with Rogers, which included Carver's search for the Northwest Passage, see *Jonathan Carver's Travels through America, 1766–1768: An Eighteenth-Century Explorer's Account of Uncharted America*, ed. Norman Gelb (New York, 1993), 13–28. Carver's account of his travels has been published many times; for its publishing history see "A Bibliography of Jonathan Carver's Travels," in *The Journals of Jonathan Carver and Related Documents, 1766–1770*, ed. John Parker (St. Paul, 1976), 222–231.

30. *Jonathan Carver's Travels*, 66, 170. For a reputed copy of the deed, now apparently lost, see p. 48.

31. *Journals of Jonathan Carver*, 79, 116.

32. The extensive records of a trader working in the region, François Victor Maillot, contain numerous references to the sale of liquor to Indians; see "A Wisconsin Fur-Trader's Journal, 1804–1805," *Wis. Colls.* 19 (1910), 216–233, esp. the unpaginated table headed "Statement of the Goods Given to the Savages for Nothing." See also "Ainsées Expedition to Wisconsin and Minnesota" (1787), ibid., 12 (1892), 88; and "M'Call's Journal," ibid., 190.

33. Wolfgang Schivelbusch, *Tastes of Paradise: A Social History of Spices, Stimulants, and Intoxicants*, trans. David Jacobson (New York, 1992), 215–223; Carl A. Trocki, *Opium and Empire: Chinese Society in Colonial Singapore, 1800–1910* (Ithaca, 1991), esp. 50–81.

Epilogue: Legacies

1. Alexander Hewatt, *An Historical Account of the Rise and Progress of the Colonies of South Carolina and Georgia*, 2 vols. (London, 1779), 1:78; 2:277–279.

2. Ibid., 1:24; 2:279. Nineteenth-century temperance reformers picked up on such suggestions, blaming alcohol for the peculiar intensity of the decline of America's native peoples. "More than any other single cause," wrote one of them, "drunkenness has extirpated them": Daniel Dorchester, *The Liquor Problem in All Ages* (New York, 1884), 117.

3. Alfred Crosby, Jr., *The Columbian Exchange: Biological and Cultural Consequences of 1492* (Westport, Conn., 1972).

4. J. Potter, "The Growth of Population in America, 1700–1800," in D.V. Glass and D.E.C. Eversley, eds., *Population in History: Essays in Historical Demography* (Chicago, 1965), 638–639; Benjamin Franklin, *The Papers of Benjamin Franklin*, ed. Leonard Labaree et al. (New Haven, 1959–), 3:438–441, 5:182–183; see also James

Cassedy, *Demography in Early America: Beginnings of the Statistical Mind, 1600–1800* (Cambridge, Mass., 1969), chap. 7.

5. For the most comprehensive assessment of overall Indian population trends see Russell Thornton, *American Indian Holocaust and Survival: A Population History since 1492* (Norman, Okla., 1987).

6. The only places where Indians could even hope to impose their values on colonists were their own villages, and with the notable exception of captives (some of whom apparently proved more than willing to shed the cultural baggage they brought with them), only traders and missionaries ever spent much time in those communities. Traders often adopted Indian ways, but there is little evidence that they encouraged other colonists to do so; and missionaries were perhaps the least likely of all colonists to adopt native ways. On the cultural conversion of captives see James Axtell, "The White Indians of Colonial America," *WMQ*, 3d ser., 32 (1975), 55–88; for the experiences of a trader who continued to serve his colonial governors after he married a Creek woman and settled in Creek territory, see Edward J. Cashin, *Lachlan McGillivray, Indian Trader: The Shaping of the Southern Colonial Frontier* (Athens, Ga., 1992); for a perceptive analysis of the experiences of a mission community in Canada see James P. Ronda, "The Sillery Experiment: A Jesuit-Indian Village in New France, 1637–1663," *American Indian Culture and Research Journal* 3:1 (1979), 1–18. Perhaps the most elaborate description of any captive's life is John Demos, *The Unredeemed Captive: A Family Story from Early America* (New York, 1994).

7. Indian contributions to colonial culture tended to be on the level of material culture, though James Axtell has traced other influences as well; see Axtell, "The Indian Impact on English Colonial Culture," in *The European and the Indian: Essays in the Ethnohistory of Colonial North America* (New York, 1981), 272–315.

8. "Historical and Characteristic Traits of the American Indians in General, and Those of Natick in Particular; in a Letter from the Rev. Stephen Badger, of Natick, to the Corresponding Secretary" (1797), *MHS Colls.*, 5 (1835), 41–42.

9. "The Report of a Committee of the Board of Correspondents of the Scots Society for Propagating Christian Knowledge, who visited the Oneida and Mohekenuh Indians in 1796," *MHS Colls.*, 5 (1835), 20. This observer went on to note that efforts by Oneida leaders ("chiefs") to stop drinking in their community failed because they lacked any authority over this aspect of village life; the community's proximity to white settlements where Indians could get alcohol also threatened any efforts to stop drinking among them.

10. "Journal of James Kenny, 1761–1763," ed. John W. Jordan, *PMHB* 37 (1913), 17.

11. On ideas about Indians and savagery see Olive P. Dickason, *The Myth of the Savage and the Beginnings of French Colonialism in the Americas* (Edmonton, 1984), 61–84; and Roy H. Pearce, *The Savages of America: A Study of the Indian and the Idea of Civilization*, rev. ed. (Baltimore, 1965), 3–49.

12. [Commandant Forbes?] to Gage, [July?] 1768, *Ill. Colls.*, 16:340.

13. As William Cronon, among others, has pointed out, amassing possessions made no sense for Indians who moved each year; see his *Changes in the Land: Indians, Colonists, and the Ecology of New England* (New York, 1983), 61–62. Yet

apparently some Indians who lived among colonists were quite able to become wealthy and acquire substantial goods; for one example see Robert S. Grumet, "The King of New Jersey," *Bulletin of the Archaeological Society of New Jersey* 48 (1993), 45–52.

14. "Journal of James Kenny," 165–166.

15. "Diary of Schonbrunn on the Ohio from the Month of June to Oct. 18, 1773," 17–18, in RMM, box 141, folder 13.

16. William Apess, *On Our Own Ground: The Complete Writings of William Apess, a Pequot*, ed. Barry O'Connell (Amherst, Mass., 1992), 5–7, 203–204, 121.

17. Samuel Hopkins, *Historical Memoirs Relating to the Housatunnuk Indians* (Boston, 1753), 164, 171–172.

18. [Anthony Benezet], *Some Observations of the Situation, Disposition, and Character of the Indian Nations of This Continent* (Philadelphia, 1784), 42–43.

19. Gilbert Imlay, *A Topographical Description of the Western Territory of North America* (London, 1797), 52–53.

20. George Catlin's description of Pigeon Egg's Head reveals the entire tragedy of this Indian, who eventually was murdered by fellow Assiniboines who did not believe the stories he told about his visit to Washington; fear and mistrust surrounded Pigeon Egg's Head, even though, it should be noted, he shared his alcohol with other Indians when he returned. See Catlin's *Letters and Notes on the Manners, Customs, and Conditions of North American Indians*, 2 vols. (1844; New York, 1973), 1:55–57, 2:194–200.

21. See chapter 5, note 102; and Joseph B. Herring, *Kenekuk: The Kickapoo Prophet* (Lawrence, Kans., 1988), 30–31, 64–66. For a later attempt to harness a religious movement to the temperance cause see Thomas W. Hill, "Peyotism and the Control of Heavy Drinking: The Nebraska Winnebago in the Early 1900s," *Human Organization* 49 (1990), 255–265.

22. "Copy of a Journal of the proceedings of Conrad Weiser, in his journey to Ohio . . . ," *HSP Colls.* 1 (1853), 31.

23. Richard Peters to George Croghan, December 10, 1754, in *Pa. Arch.*, 1st ser., 2:214; James H. Merrell, " 'The Cast of His Countenance': Reading Andrew Montour," paper presented at the conference "Through a Glass Darkly: Defining Self in Early America," Williamsburg, 1983.

A Note on Sources

Since the seventeenth century, observers have speculated about the effects of alcohol on American Indians. In this book I have drawn extensively on the documentary evidence relating to Indian drinking, and I have used clinical and anthropological reports to gain perspective. What follows here are some remarks on the most important sources that I used. Readers interested in particular points of the argument should consult the endnotes as well.

Works Written before 1800

Virtually all of the earliest descriptions of Indian drinking are contained in documents left by non-Indian observers. The most thorough of these witnesses were missionaries, particularly Jesuits, who observed Indian drinking in the northeastern portions of British America as well as New France. *The Jesuit Relations and Allied Documents*, ed. Reuben G. Thwaites, 73 vols. (Cleveland, 1896–1901), includes numerous accounts. "Délibération sur le cas réservé du commerce de l'eau-de-vie avec les sauvages, 1678," in *Découvertes et établissements des français dans l'ouest et dans le sud de l'Amérique septentrionale (1614–1754): Mémoires et documents originaux*, ed. Pierre Margry, 4 vols. (Paris, 1875–1886), 1:403–420, contains the minutes of a 1678 meeting on the brandy trade; the document is reprinted and described in G. B. Munro, "The Brandy Parliament of 1678," *Canadian Historical Review* 2 (1921), 172–189. Three anonymous manuscript reports, all apparently from 1693, contain extensive observations of brandy's effects on Indians in Canada: "Canada Mémoires," "Mémoire touchant les boissons enyvrant les sauvages de Canada," and "Mémoire touchant l'yvorognerie des sauvages en Canada," all in AC, C II, 12–2, ff. 380–388, Archives Nationale, Paris.

A NOTE ON SOURCES

A thorough account from a single missionary can be found in [François Vachon de Belmont], "Belmont's History of Brandy," ed. Joseph Donnelly, *Mid-America* 34 (1952), 42–63. [Jean] Bossu, *Travels through that part of North America formerly called Louisiana*, trans. John Reinhold Forster, 2 vols. (London, 1771), contains the description of the Indian drinker featured in the Prologue, as well as observations on alcohol use among Indians in the Illinois country in the late colonial period.

Sources for British America are in many ways less complete than those for New France, although the wide range of sources makes up for their brevity. Colonial observers and Indians described Indian drinking throughout eastern North America. The records for New York, Pennsylvania, and the Carolinas contain many references to the trade, testifying to the extent of the commerce and its effects on Indian villages throughout the eastern woodlands. *The Speech of a Creek-Indian, against the Immoderate Use of Spirituous Liquors* (London, 1754), though quite possibly the work of a non-Indian temperance reformer, summarizes mid-eighteenth-century views on the costs of drinking in the southeast; its focus on the damage to Indian families is especially powerful, and thus resembles in some ways twentieth-century reports describing the familial costs of drunkenness. Sansom Occom's "Address to His Indian Brethren" (n.p., 1772) and *A Sermon Preached at the Execution of Moses Paul*, 3d ed. (New London, 1772), provide the views of one of the most articulate Indian converts in early America. Other reports from Indians are contained in diverse collections of primary sources from the colonial period. Of particular use are the speeches of Indians contained in *The Papers of Sir William Johnson*, ed. James Sullivan et al., 14 vols. (Albany, 1921–1965), and in *Colonial Affairs of South Carolina: Documents Relating to the Indian Affairs*, ed. William L. McDowell, 2 vols. (Columbia, 1958–1970); each focuses on the later colonial period, when the liquor trade was extensive. The issues facing a colonial official living in Indian country are revealed in the James Sterling letter book at the William L. Clements Library, University of Michigan; many of the letters mention the liquor trade and Sterling's desire to keep alcohol away from Indians yet have it available for soldiers and colonists. The most extensive surviving records of any trading firm are in the Baynton, Wharton & Morgan Papers, available on microfilm from the Pennsylvania Historical and Museum Commission, Harrisburg; the records of their trading posts in the Illinois country, particularly at Kaskaskia, contain numerous references to their liquor sales to Indians and other residents of the area, especially soldiers. The records of the Moravian Mission among the Indians of North America, available on microfilm from the Archives of the Moravian Church, Bethlehem, Pennsylvania, include numerous references to the use of liquor in Indian communities in western Pennsylvania and the Ohio country. The papers of intermediaries, notably George Croghan (in the Historical Society of Pennsylvania and the Library of Congress) and Conrad Weiser (at the HSP), contain frequent mention of Indian drinking. So does the *Pennsylvania Gazette*, perhaps the most important newspaper in the colonies; under Benjamin Franklin's direction, the paper printed diverse articles from the entire Atlantic world, enabling his readers to learn about (among other things) Indian drinking throughout the east.

Excellent contemporary descriptions of the West Indies and the rum trade are available. See in particular E[dmund] H[ickeringill], *Jamaica Viewed: With All the Ports, Harbours, and their several Soundings, Towns, and Settlements thereunto belonging*... (London, 1665); [Charles de Rochefort], *The History of the Caribby-Islands*, trans. John Davies (London, 1666); Richard Ligon, *A True & Exact History of the Island of Barbadoes* (London, 1673); Richard Blome, *A Description of the Island of Jamaica; with the other Isles and Territories in America, to which the English are Related* (London, 1678) and *The Present State of His Majesties Isles and Territories in America* (London, 1687); [Charles de Rochefort], *Histoire naturelle et morale des îles Antilles de l'Amérique*... , dernière édition (Rotterdam, 1681); [Edward Littleton], *The Groans of the Plantations; or A true Account of their Grievous and Extreme Sufferings by the Heavy Impositions upon Sugar, and other Hardships* (London, 1689); Hans Sloane, *A Voyage to the Islands Madera, Barbados, Nieves, S. Christophers and Jamaica*... , 2 vols. (London, 1707–1725); and Griffith Hughes, *The Natural History of Barbados, in Ten Books* (London, 1750). On the importance of the sugar and rum trade see [Joshua Gee], *The Trade and Navigation of Great-Britain Considered* (London, 1729); and Robert Dossie, *An Essay on Spirituous Liquors, with Regard to their Effects on Health*... (London, [1770]), a work that weds clinical observations to national politics. [Pierre?] Pomet, *A Compleat History of Druggs*, 2d ed. (London, 1725), suggests some of the uses of sugar in the eighteenth century.

For works on drinking in the colonies and in Britain see Increase Mather, *Wo to Drunkards: Two Sermons Testifying against the Sin of Drunkenness* (Cambridge, 1673); [Cotton Mather], *Sober Considerations, on a growing Flood of Iniquity. Or an Essay, to Dry up a Fountain of Confusion and Every Evil Work; And to Warn People, Particularly of the Woful Consequences, which the Prevailing Abuse of Rum, will be attended withal* (Boston, 1708); Samuel Danforth, *Piety Encouraged: Brief Notes of a Discourse Delivered unto the People of Taunton* (Boston, 1705); Benjamin Wadsworth, *An Essay to do Good, By a disswasive from Tavern-haunting, and Excessive Drinking* (Boston, 1710); Cotton Mather et al., *A Serious Address to those who Unnecessarily Frequent the Tavern, And Often Spend the Evening in Publick Houses* (Boston, 1726); Josiah Smith, *Solomon's Caution Against the Cup* (Boston, 1730); and Israel Acrelius, *A History of New Sweden; or, The Settlements on the River Delaware* (1759), trans. William M. Reynolds (Philadelphia, 1874), 160–164. For English writings see Thomas Nashe, *Pierce Penilesse, His Supplication to the Divell* (1592; London, 1924); Philip Stubbs, *Anatomy of the Abuses of England*, ed. Frederick J. Furnivall (1877–1879; Vaduz, 1965); Philotheos Physiologus [Thomas Tryon], *The Way to Health, Long Life and Happiness; or, A Discourse on Temperance and the particular Nature of all things requisit for the Life of Man*... (London, 1683); and Josiah Woodward, *A Disswasive from the Sin of Drunkenness* (Lancaster, 1755).

Historical Works Written since 1800

Before assessing the specialized monographs dealing with particular aspects of Indians and alcohol, readers may want to consult works that provide necessary historical background. Of particular use are Jean-Charles Sournia, *A History of Alcoholism*, trans. Nick Hindley and Gareth Stanton (Oxford, 1990); and Su-

A NOTE ON SOURCES

sanna Barrows and Robin Room, eds., *Drinking: Behavior and Belief in Modern Times* (Berkeley, 1991). Thomas Brennan, *Public Drinking and Popular Culture in Eighteenth-Century Paris* (Princeton, 1988), examines the role of alcohol in early modern France. William B. Taylor, *Drinking, Homicide, and Rebellion in Colonial Mexican Villages* (Stanford, 1979), especially chapter 2, is an excellent analysis of alcohol use in Spanish-American society; Michael C. Scardaville, "Alcohol Abuse and Tavern Reform in Late Colonial Mexico City," *Hispanic American Historical Review* 60 (1980), 643–671, focuses on the problems caused by liquor in the largest city in Spanish America. Wolfgang Schivelbusch, *Tastes of Paradise: A Social History of Spices, Stimulants, and Intoxicants*, trans. David Jacobson (New York, 1992), provides one of the most stimulating discussions of the place of alcoholic beverages in modern society; see especially chapters 5–7. Readers interested in cross-cultural comparisons may find much of use in Jonathan Crush and Charles Ambler, eds., *Liquor and Labor in Southern Africa* (Athens, Ohio, 1992), though most of the essays deal with the twentieth century; and in David Christian, *'Living Water': Vodka and Russian Society on the Eve of Emancipation* (Oxford, 1990), especially 1–96. Marcia Langton, "Rum, Seduction, and death: 'Aboriginality' and Alcohol," *Oceania* 63 (1993), 195–206, explores the origins of drinking among Australia's native peoples and the creation of the stereotype of the "drunken aborigine" in a different English colonial setting. Gregory A. Austin, *Alcohol in Western Society from Antiquity to 1800: A Chronological History* (Santa Barbara, Calif., 1985), provides an overview of major developments, especially changes in laws involving the sale or use of alcohol, throughout the Western world.

For drinking practices in British America see William Rorabaugh, *The Alcoholic Republic: An American Tradition* (New York, 1979); Paton Yoder, "Tavern Regulation in Virginia: Rationale and Reality," *VMHB* 87 (1979), 259–278; Mark Edward Lender and James Kirby Martin, *Drinking in America: A History* (New York, 1982); Richard P. Gildrie, "Taverns and Popular Culture in Essex County, Massachusetts, 1678–1686," *Essex Institute Historical Collections* 124 (1988), 158–185; Peter Thompson, " 'The Friendly Glass': Drink and Gentility in Colonial Philadelphia," *PMHB* 113 (1989), 549–573; David W. Conroy, "Puritans in Taverns: Law and Popular Culture in Colonial Massachusetts, 1630–1720," in Barrows and Room, *Drinking*, 29–60; Jessica Kross, "The Sociology of Drinking in the Middle Colonies," paper presented to the Organization of American Historians, Chicago, 1992; and Robert D. Arner, "Politics and Temperance in Boston and Philadelphia: Benjamin Franklin's Journalistic Writings on Drinking and Drunkenness," in *Reappraising Benjamin Franklin: A Bicentennial Perspective*, ed. J. A. Leo Lemay (Newark, Del., 1993), 52–77. Allan M. Winkler, "Drinking on the American Frontier," *QJSA* 29 (1968), 413–445, surveys drinking in the nineteenth-century west. Harry G. Levine, in "The Discovery of Addiction: Changing Conceptions of Habitual Drunkenness in America," *JSA* 39 (1978), 143–174, and in "The Vocabulary of Drunkenness," *JSA* 42 (1981), 1038–1051, provides excellent treatment of the shifting understanding of abusive drinking in America. Rebecca H. Warner and Henry L. Rosett, "The Effects of Drinking on Offspring: An Historical Survey of the American and British Literature," *JSA* 36 (1975), 1395–1420, is a thorough review of the evolution in understanding of the generational effects of alcohol abuse. Joel Bernard, "The Transit of 'Small, Merry' Anglo-American Culture: Sir John Barley-Corne and Sir Richard Rum (and Captain Whiskey)," *Proceedings of the American Antiquarian Society* 100 (1990), 81–136, traces the English influences on a satirical pamphlet titled *The Indictment and Tryal of Sr. Richard Rum*, 3d. ed. (Boston, 1724); as Bernard notes, the pamphlet "was a rationalistic parody of Puritan attitudes toward drinking that mocked strict morality in the name of economic prosperity" (p. 84).

Historians have ably described the role of alcohol in early modern England. The most logical starting point is Peter Clark, *The Alehouse: A Social History* (London, 1983). John M. Bowers, " 'Dronkenesse Is Ful of Stryvyng': Alcoholism and Ritual Violence in Chaucer's *Pardoner's Tale*," *ELH* 57 (1990), 757–784, explores the representation of inebriation in an important fourteenth-century text. For the seventeenth century see Harris G. Hudson, *A Study of Social Regulations in England under James I and Charles I: Drink and Tobacco* (Chicago, 1933); and Keith Wrightson, "Alehouses, Order and Reformation in Rural England, 1590–1660," in *Popular Culture and Class Conflict, 1590–1914: Explorations in the History of Labour and Leisure*, ed. Eileen Yeo and Stephen Yeo (Brighton, 1981), 2–11. For the crises engendered by the rise of the gin industry in the eighteenth century see George Rudé, " 'Mother Gin' and the London Riots of 1736," *Guildhall Miscellany* 10 (1959), 53–63; T. G. Coffey, "Beer Street, Gin Lane: Some Views of Eighteenth-Century Drinking," *QJSA* 27 (1966), 669–692; Hans Medick, "Plebeian Culture in the Transition to Capitalism," in *Culture, Ideology and Politics: Essays for Eric Hobsbawm*, ed. Raphael Samuel and Gareth Stedman Jones (London, 1982), 84–113; Peter Clark, "The 'Mother Gin' Controversy in the Early Eighteenth Century," *Transactions of the Royal Historical Society*, 5th ser., 38 (1988), 63–84; Thomas B. Gilmore, "James Boswell's Drinking," *Eighteenth-Century Studies* 24 (1991), 337–357; and Lee Davison, "Experiments in the Social Regulation of Industry: Gin Legislation, 1729–1751," in *Stilling the Grumbling Hive: Responses to Social and Economic Problems in England, c. 1689–1750*, ed. Davison et al. (London, 1992), 25–48. For regulation of drinking in England see Sidney Webb and Beatrice Webb, *The History of Liquor Licensing, Principally from 1700 to 1800* (1903; Hamden, Conn., 1963).

Several studies focus on Indians and alcohol in Canada (New France). George F. G. Stanley, "The Indians and the Brandy Trade during the Ancien Régime," *Révue d'Histoire de l'Amérique Française* 6 (1953), 489–505, and André Vachon, "L'Eau-de-vie dans la société indienne," *Report of the Canadian Historical Association* (1960), 22–32, focus on the liquor trade, though each must be read with caution. Edmund S. Carpenter, "Alcohol in the Iroquois Dream Quest," *American Journal of Psychiatry* 116 (1959), 148–151, contains excellent references to materials gathered from Canadian sources, mostly the *Jesuit Relations*, but its conclusions about Iroquois dream quests do not fit the evidence as closely as Carpenter suggested. R. C. Dailey, "The Role of Alcohol among North American Indian Tribes as Reported in the *Jesuit Relations*," *Anthropologica* 10 (1968), 45–59, suggests the

A NOTE ON SOURCES

range of materials that can be drawn from those documents. Jean Delanglez, *Frontenac and the Jesuits* (Chicago, 1939), 69–129, provides the most thorough account of the clerical battle against the liquor trade. Jill R. Schumann, "The Diffusion of Alcohol: Through Membrane into Culture," in *Papers of the Thirteenth Algonquian Conference*, ed. William Cowan (Ottawa, 1982), 37–45, draws on clinical reports in an analysis of Indian drinking in eastern Canada in the seventeenth and eighteenth centuries. Alfred G. Bailey, *The Conflict of European and Eastern Algonkian Cultures, 1504–1700: A Study in Canadian Civilization*, 2d ed. (Toronto, 1969), 66–71; Cornelius Jaenen, *Friend and Foe* (New York, 1976), 110–116; and Denys Delâge, *Bitter Feast: Amerindians and Europeans in Northeastern North America, 1600–1664* (Vancouver, 1993), 136–140, describe the liquor trade in the context of their analyses of colonization and its consequences for Canada's native peoples. Thomas F. Schilz, "Brandy and Beaver Pelts: Assiniboine-European Trading Patterns, 1695–1805," *Saskatchewan History* 37 (1984), 95–102, explores commerce, including the liquor trade, in respect to a particular Indian group. Arthur J. Ray, *Indians in the Fur Trade: Their Role as Trappers, Hunters, and Middlemen in the Lands Southwest of Hudson Bay, 1660–1870* (Toronto, 1974), and Arthur J. Ray and Donald B. Freeman, *"Give Us Good Measure": An Economic Analysis of Relations between the Indians and the Hudson's Bay Company before 1763* (Toronto, 1978), provide careful analyses of the brandy trade in Canada.

Several fine historical works focus on West Indies plantation society, sugar production, and the rum trade. See in particular Richard S. Dunn, *Sugar and Slaves: The Rise of the Planter Class in the English West Indies, 1624–1713* (Chapel Hill, N.C., 1972); Richard Sheridan, *Sugar and Slavery: An Economic History of the British West Indies, 1623–1775* (Baltimore, 1973) and *Doctors and Slaves: A Medical and Demographic History of Slavery in the British West Indies, 1680–1834* (Cambridge, 1985); Michael Craton and James Walvin, *A Jamaican Plantation: The History of Worthy Park, 1670–1970* (London, 1970); and Michael Craton, "Reluctant Creoles: The Planters' World in the British West Indies," in *Strangers within The Realm: The Cultural Margins of the First British Empire*, ed. Bernard Bailyn and Philip D. Morgan (Chapel Hill, N.C., 1991), 314–362. The most important work on the sugar trade is Sidney W. Mintz, *Sweetness and Power: The Place of Sugar in Modern History* (New York, 1985). Noel Deerr, *The History of Sugar*, 2 vols. (London, 1949–1950), provides an enormous amount of data on the sugar business in the early modern period; so does John J. McCusker, "The Rum Trade and the Balance of Payments of the Thirteen Continental Colonies in 1770" (Ph.D. diss., University of Pittsburgh, 1970).

Of all the secondary sources, none are more suggestive than the ever-growing body of works that describe the eastern woodlands in the early modern period. Many of these works are cited in the notes. Excellent reviews of the literature and descriptions of the major issues confronting all historians of early American Indians can be found in James H. Merrell, "Some Thoughts on Colonial Historians and American Indians," *WMQ*, 3d ser., 46 (1989), 94–119; and Daniel Richter, "Whose Indian History?" *WMQ*, 3d ser., 50 (1993), 379–393. Readers interested in all aspects of the changes in eastern North America may want to

A NOTE ON SOURCES

start with the following, virtually all of them published since the early 1980s: James Axtell, *The Invasion Within: The Contest of Cultures in Eastern North America* (New York, 1985); Kathryn E. Holland Braund, *Deerskins & Duffels: Creek Indian Trade with Anglo-America, 1685–1815* (Lincoln, Neb., 1993); Colin Calloway, *The Western Abenakis of Vermont, 1600–1800: War, Migration, and the Survival of an Indian People* (Norman, Okla., 1990); William Cronon, *Changes in the Land: Indians, Colonists, and the Ecology of New England* (New York, 1983); Matthew Dennis, *Cultivating a Landscape of Peace: Iroquois-European Encounters in Seventeenth-Century America* (Ithaca, 1993); Gregory E. Dowd, *A Spirited Resistance: The North American Indian Struggle for Unity, 1745–1815* (Baltimore, 1992); Tom Hatley, *The Dividing Paths: Cherokees and South Carolinians through the Era of Revolution* (New York, 1993); Karen Ordahl Kupperman, *Settling with the Indians: The Meeting of English and Indian Cultures in America, 1580–1640* (London, 1980); Peter C. Mancall, *Valley of Opportunity: Economic Culture Along the Upper Susquehanna, 1700–1800* (Ithaca, 1991); Calvin Martin, *Keepers of the Game: Indian–Animal Relationships and the Fur Trade* (Berkeley, 1978); James H. Merrell, *The Indians' New World: Catawbas and Their Neighbors from European Contact through the Era of Removal* (Chapel Hill, N.C., 1989); Kenneth M. Morrison, *The Embattled Northeast: The Elusive Ideal of Alliance in Abenaki-Euramerican Relations* (Berkeley, 1984); Daniel K. Richter, *The Ordeal of the Longhouse: The Peoples of the Iroquois League in the Era of European Colonization* (Chapel Hill, N.C., 1992); Neal Salisbury, *Manitou and Providence: Indians, Europeans, and the Making of New England, 1500–1643* (New York, 1982); J. Russell Snapp, *John Stuart and the Issue of Empire on the Southern Colonial Frontier* (Baton Rouge, forthcoming); Bruce Trigger, *The Children of Aaetatensic*, 2 vols. (Montreal, 1976); Daniel H. Usner, Jr., *Indians, Settlers, and Slaves in a Frontier Exchange Economy: The Lower Mississippi Valley before 1783* (Chapel Hill, N.C., 1992); Richard White, *The Middle Ground: Indians, Empires, and Republics in the Great Lakes Region, 1650–1815* (Cambridge, 1991); idem, *The Roots of Dependency: Subsistence, Environment, and Social Change among the Choctaws, Pawnees, and Navajos* (Lincoln, Neb., 1983); and Peter Wood et al., eds., *Powhatan's Mantle: Indians in the Colonial Southeast* (Lincoln, Neb., 1989). John W. Verano and Douglas H. Ubelaker, eds., *Disease and Demography in the Americas* (Washington, D.C., 1992), contains an excellent group of articles on the demography of the eastern woodlands; and Russell Thornton, *American Indian Holocaust and Survival: A Population History since 1492* (Norman, Okla., 1987), provides the most comprehensive analysis for the period. John Halkett, *Historical Notes Respecting the Indians of North America; with Remarks on the Attempts Made to Convert and Civilize Them* (1825; Millwood, N.Y., 1976), devotes two chapters (pp. 164–205) to Indian drinking and represents an early effort to place Indian drinking in a historical context. In addition to these published works, useful references to Indian drinking may be found in Debra R. Boender, "Our Fires Have Nearly Gone Out: A History of Indian-White Relations on the Colonial Maryland Frontier, 1633–1776" (Ph.D. diss., University of New Mexico, 1988), and Eric Hinderaker, "The Creation of the American Frontier: Europeans and Indians in the Ohio River Valley, 1673–1800" (Ph.D. diss., Harvard University, 1991).

A NOTE ON SOURCES

Anthropological Evidence

Anthropologists have taken a very different approach to the study of alcohol and its use by American Indians. Seemingly eschewing historians' predilection for consumption figures and temperance movements, anthropologists have instead sought to describe why specific groups of people drink as they do in certain situations. By doing so, they have explored the crucial questions of motivations for drinking. Perhaps the best starting place for this literature is Mary Douglas, ed., *Constructive Drinking: Perspectives on Drink from Anthropology* (Cambridge, 1987). As Douglas points out in her introductory essay, anthropologists "do not necessarily treat [alcohol] as a problem." Anthropologists "dispute that drunken behavior exemplifies a relaxation of cultural constraints before the levelling effects of nature: Drunkenness also expresses culture in so far as it always takes the form of a highly patterned, learned comportment which varies from one culture to another: pink elephants in one region, green snakes in another" (pp. 3–4). These are the core ideas that lie at the heart of most anthropological assessments of alcohol use. Drawing on anthropological studies of drinking habits, historians can reconstruct drinking patterns that are often only barely evident in the documentary record. Such anthropological studies, especially in the hands of scholars sensitive to changes in consumption patterns over time, suggest many ways to understand the use of alcohol in the past. Ron Roizen, "The World Health Organization Study of Community Responses to Alcohol-Related Problems: A Review of Cross-Cultural Findings," a report intended as an annex to the *Final Report of Phase I of the WHO Project on Community Response to Alcohol-Related Problems* (July 1981), is a thorough and thoughtful cross-cultural study of drinking in disparate modern cultures; Roizen's attention to issues relating to gender are particularly important.

Many anthropologists have paid attention to drinking among American Indians. A. Irving Hallowell, in his 1946 essay "Some Psychological Characteristics of the Northeastern Indians," reprinted in his *Culture and Experience* (Philadelphia, 1955), recognized the important role that alcohol played among some Indian groups during the colonial period (see 141–143). The boom in this particular subfield began during the 1960s. Edward P. Dozier, "Problem Drinking among American Indians: The Role of Sociocultural Deprivation," *QJSA* 27 (1966), 72–87, remains a vital work and one that fits much of the historical evidence. Three years later the most important book on Indian drinking to that point appeared in the pioneering work of Craig MacAndrew and Robert B. Edgerton: *Drunken Comportment: A Social Explanation* (Chicago, 1969). *Drunken Comportment* argued that Indian drinking patterns are social artifacts. "Rather than viewing drunken comportment as a function of toxically disinhibited brains operating in impulse-driven bodies," they concluded, "we have recommended that what is fundamentally at issue are the learned relations that exist among men living together in a society. More specifically, we have contended that the way people comport themselves when they are drunk is determined not by alcohol's toxic assault upon the seat of moral judgement, conscience, or the like, but by what their

A NOTE ON SOURCES

society makes of and imparts to them concerning the state of drunkenness" (p. 165). The position seems obvious to many people now, though its validity is brought into question by accounts suggesting the power of genetics to determine human behavior and action. In the wake of *Drunken Comportment* anthropologists and other observers using anthropological techniques followed up MacAndrew and Edgerton's analysis by trying to decipher the specific causes of Indian drinking in disparate communities. Nancy Ostreich Lurie, in an important article that quickly followed *Drunken Comportment*, argued that sub-Arctic Indians drink as they do as a form of protest against centuries of colonization and conquest ("The World's Oldest Ongoing Protest Demonstration: North American Indian Drinking Patterns," *Pacific Historical Review* 40 [1971], 311–332).

In this book I have not accepted every point made by these important works. In particular, I do not agree with MacAndrew and Edgerton that early American Indians learned how to drink from traders and adopted the traders' alleged intemperate ways. Liquor traders, after all, may have caroused with Indians, but the documentary record does not suggest that they left trading sessions impoverished, as their Indian trading partners did. On the contrary, traders may have been duplicitous in their dealings, and many certainly broke existing laws that prohibited the trade, but their use of alcohol rarely interfered with their economic goals. Further, to suggest that Indians used alcohol in the ways traders used alcohol does not fit a historical record that reveals that Indians adapted colonial goods in ways that made sense in Indian villages. If they were not bound by colonists' views on how to use such goods as pots, there is no reason to presume that they intended to mimic colonists' drinking patterns either. As various scholars have demonstrated, Indians wanted colonial goods but they used them in their own ways. On this point see, among other works, Bruce M. White, "Encounters with Spirits: Ojibwa and Dakota Theories about the French and Their Merchandise," *Ethnohistory* 41 (1994), 369–405; Christopher Miller and George R. Hammell, "A New Perspective on Indian-White Contact: Cultural Symbols and Colonial Trade," *Journal of American History* 73 (1986), 311–328; Calvin Martin, "The Four Lives of a Micmac Copper Pot," *Ethnohistory* 22 (1975), 111–133; James Axtell, "At the Water's Edge: Trading in the Sixteenth Century," in his *After Columbus: Essays in the Ethnohistory of Colonial North America* (New York, 1988), 144–181, and "The First Consumer Revolution," in his *Beyond 1492: Encounters in Colonial North America* (New York, 1992), 125–151. And Lurie's essay, though persuasive in many respects, does not correspond to what I believe was the most important way in which early American Indians protested the alcohol trade: by creating and sustaining a movement to end the commerce.

Other anthropological and ethnological studies are also vital to an understanding of Indian drinking. Perhaps the best introduction to the issues in this field are presented in two excellent essays by Dwight B. Heath: "American Indians and Alcohol: Epidemiological and Sociocultural Relevance," in *Alcohol Use among U.S. Ethnic Minorities*, ed. Danielle L. Spiegler et al., National Institute on Alcohol Abuse and Alcoholism, Research Monograph no. 18 (Rockville, Md., 1989), 207–222, and "Alcohol Use among North American Indians: A Cross-Cultural Survey of Patterns and Problems," in *Research Advances in Alcohol and Drug Problems*, ed.

A NOTE ON SOURCES

Reginald G. Smart et al., vol. 7 (New York, 1983), 343–396. Jerrold E. Levy and Stephen J. Kunitz, *Indian Drinking: Navajo Practices and Anglo-American Theories* (New York, 1974), remains the most important sustained analysis of a particular Indian group's alcohol consumption. Other important and suggestive studies treat alcohol use among various groups of Indians. See especially John A. Price, "An Applied Analysis of North American Indian Drinking Patterns," *Human Organization* 34 (1975), 17–26; Ray Stratton, Arthur Zeiner, and Alfonso Paredes, "Tribal Affiliation and Prevalence of Alcohol Problems," *JSA* 39 (1978), 1166–1177; Christian F. Feest, "Notes on Native American Alcohol Use," in *North American Indian Studies: European Contributions*, ed. Pieter Hovens (Göttingen, 1981), 201–222; and Andrew J. Gordon, "Alcohol Use in the Perspective of Cultural Ecology," and Thomas W. Hill, "Ethnohistory and Alcohol Studies," both in *Recent Developments in Alcoholism*, ed. Marc Galanter (New York, 1984), 2:355–373, 313–337; Hill's study contains an excellent bibliography. There is an extensive bibliography in Patricia D. Mail and David R. McDonald, comps., *Tulapai to Tokay: A Bibliography of Alcohol Use and Abuse among Native Americans of North America* (New Haven, 1981). Mac Marshall, ed., *Beliefs, Behaviors, and Alcoholic Beverages: A Cross-Cultural Survey* (Ann Arbor, 1979); Michael W. Everett, Jack O. Waddell, and Dwight Heath, eds., *Cross-Cultural Approaches to the Study of Alcohol: An Interdisciplinary Perspective* (The Hague, 1976); Dwight B. Heath, Jack O. Waddell, and Martin Topper, eds., *Cultural Factors in Alcohol Research and Treatment of Drinking Problems*, supplement no. 9 of *JSA* (1981); and Edith L. Gomberg et al., eds., *Alcohol, Science, and Society Revisited* (Ann Arbor, 1982), include important articles on Indian drinking as well as anthropological accounts of the drinking practices of other peoples. Dwight Heath's "Anthropological Perspectives on Alcohol: An Historical Review," in Everett et al., *Cross-Cultural Perspectives*, 41–118, and "A Decade of Development in the Anthropological Study of Alcohol Use, 1970–1980," in Douglas, *Constructive Drinking*, 16–69, are excellent analyses of the development of the field. Edwin M. Lemert, "Drinking among American Indians," in Gomberg et al., *Alcohol, Science, and Society*, 80–95, is a very suggestive overview of the literature on Indian drinking. John Hamer and Jack Steinbring, eds., *Alcohol and Native Peoples of the North* (Lanham, Md., 1980), and Jack O. Waddell and Michael Everett, eds., *Drinking Behavior among Southwestern Indians: An Anthropological Perspective* (Tucson, 1980), contain thoughtful and stimulating essays about North American Indian drinking practices. Joy Leland has written a series of important works on Indians and alcohol; see especially *Firewater Myths: North American Indian Drinking and Alcohol Addiction*, Monographs of the Rutgers Center of Alcohol Studies no. 11 (New Brunswick, 1976); "Native American Alcohol Use: A Review of the Literature," in Mail and McDonald, *Tulapai to Tokay*, 1–49; and "Women and Alcohol in an Indian Settlement," *Medical Anthropology* 2 (1978), 85–119.

For studies of alcohol use and abuse within particular groups see Wesley R. Hurt and Richard M. Brown, "Social Drinking Patterns of the Yankton Sioux," *Human Organization* 24 (1965), 222–230; John H. Hamer, "Acculturation Stress and the Functions of Alcohol among the Forest Potawatomi," *QJSA* 26 (1965), 285–302; Richard T. Curley, "Drinking Patterns of the Mescalero Apache," *QJSA*

A NOTE ON SOURCES

28 (1976), 116–131; Gerald Mohatt, "The Sacred Water: The Quest for Personal Power through Drinking among the Teton Sioux," in *The Drinking Man*, ed. David McClelland et al. (New York, 1972), 261–275; Jack O. Waddell, "For Individual Power and Social Credit: The Use of Alcohol among Tucson Papagos," *Human Organization* 34 (1975), 9–15, and "Malhiot's Journal: An Ethnohistoric Assessment of Chippewa Alcohol Behavior in the Early Nineteenth Century," *Ethnohistory* 32 (1985), 246–268; Stephen J. Kunitz and Jerrold E. Levy, "Changing Ideas of Alcohol Use among Navajo Indians," *QJSA* 35 (1974), 243–259; Martin D. Topper, "Navajo 'Alcoholism': Drinking, Alcohol Abuse, and Treatment in a Changing Cultural Environment," in *The American Experience with Alcohol: Contrasting Cultural Perspectives*, ed. Linda A. Bennett and Genevieve M. Ames (New York, 1985), 227–251; Philip A. May and Matthew B. Smith, "Some Navajo Indian Opinions about Alcohol Abuse and Prohibition: A Survey and Recommendations for Policy," *JSA* 49 (1988), 324–334; and Susan Stevens, "Alcohol and World View: A Study of Passamaquoddy Alcohol Use," in Heath et al., *Cultural Factors in Alcohol Research*, 122–142. Thomas W. Hill, "Drunken Comportment of Urban Indians: 'Time-Out' Behavior?" *Journal of Anthropological Research* 34 (1978), 442–465, based on an analysis of Indian drinking in Sioux City, Iowa, questions one of the central notions of *Drunken Comportment* though it does not seek to undermine the basic findings of MacAndrew and Edgerton. Hill's "Peyotism and the Control of Heavy Drinking: The Nebraska Winnebago in the Early 1900s," *Human Organization* 49 (1990), 255–265, shows how a religious movement limited consumption of alcohol long after the colonial period.

Various anthropological and legal studies of the effectiveness of prohibition among Indian groups suggest the difficulties that attend any temperance efforts. Many of the basic issues are debated in vol. 4, no. 3, of *American Indian and Alaska Native Mental Health Research* (1992); that collection contains a compelling essay by Philip A. May, "Alcohol Policy Considerations for Indian Reservations and Bordertown Communities," and twelve responses. William D. Back, "The Ineffectiveness of Alcohol Prohibition on the Navajo Indian Reservation," *Arizona State Law Journal* (1981), 925–943, and Jon E. Doak, "Liquor Regulation in Indian Country: The Modern Picture in an Antique Frame," *Arizona Law Review* 23 (1981), 825–859, review the legal issues involved in prohibition, though each emphasizes developments in the twentieth century rather than the colonial period.

Among the most suggestive and disheartening studies are those that include testimony of Indians who witness abusive drinking and its consequences or are abusive drinkers themselves. Anyone interested in Indian drinking should read Michael Dorris, *The Broken Cord* (New York, 1989). The book's testimony on the costs of fetal alcohol syndrome is nothing less than astonishing, and Dorris tells the harrowing tale in unsparing prose. Dorris has followed up *The Broken Cord* with *Paper Trail* (New York, 1994); the section "Everybody's Children" (73–117) contains his more recent thoughts on the issue. Brian Maracle, *Crazywater: Native Voices on Addiction and Recovery* (New York, 1993), includes interviews with Indians trying to overcome abusive drinking. Anastasia M. Shkilnyk, *A Poison Stronger than Love: The Destruction of an Ojibwa Community* (New Haven, 1985), which contains moving excerpts from local Indians, is a devastating portrait of

A NOTE ON SOURCES

a community in which alcohol abuse is one of the most desperate and widespread problems. John Trudell, "Alcohol and the Native Peoples," *Akwesane Notes* 7:4 (1975), 38–39, and Douglas J. Cardinal, "Indian Alternative to Alcoholism," in *Fifth Annual Alberta Alcohol and Drug Research Symposium*, ed. R. W. Nutter and B. K. Sinha (Alberta, 1973), reinforce the testimony on the costs of liquor to Indian communities and stress the need for Indians to recapture traditional beliefs to eliminate the scourge of alcohol abuse.

Clinical Reports

The clinical evidence on which I have drawn falls into two categories: reports on the effects of alcohol on particular populations, and the genetic aspects of alcoholism. Each is important and necessary for interpreting the historical record. The best starting place is George E. Vaillant, *The Natural History of Alcoholism: Causes, Patterns, and Paths to Recovery* (Cambridge, Mass., 1983), a work that focuses on a wide range of issues involving alcohol abuse, including the etiology of alcoholism as well as its history. For briefer descriptions see Secretary of Health and Human Services, *Fifth Special Report to the U.S. Congress on Alcohol and Health* (Washington, D.C., 1983), and American Medical Association, *Manual on Alcoholism* (n.p., 1968). Charles S. Lieber, *Medical Disorders of Alcoholism: Pathogenesis and Treatment* (Philadelphia, 1982), is an excellent overview of the physiological consequences of alcohol abuse; and Elliott L. Mancall, "Prognosis in Diseases Due to Alcohol," in *Prognosis of Neurological Disorders*, ed. R. W. Evans et al. (New York, 1992), 577–588, is the most complete analysis of the neurological consequences of alcohol abuse. Herbert Fingarette, *Heavy Drinking: The Myth of Alcoholism as a Disease* (Berkeley, 1988), is a cogent assault on the so-called disease concept of alcoholism. In Thomas F. Babor, ed., *Alcohol and Culture: Comparative Perspectives from Europe and America*, Annals of the New York Academy of Sciences 472 (New York, 1986), various authors pay particular attention to cultural factors in the etiology of alcohol abuse; of particular interest are the contributions by Roberta L. Hall, "Alcohol Treatment in American Indian Populations: An Indigenous Treatment Modality Compared with Traditional Approaches" (168–178), and Joseph Westermeyer and John Neider, "Cultural Affiliation among American Indian Alcoholics: Correlations and Change over a Ten-Year Period" (179–188). Thomas Babor et al., eds., *Types of Alcoholics: Evidence from Clinical, Experimental, and Genetic Research*, Annals of the New York Academy of Sciences 708 (New York, 1994), is an excellent if often technical collection of articles summarizing current alcohol research. Peter D. Nathan, "Integration of Biological and Psychosocial Research on Alcoholism," *Alcoholism: Clinical and Experimental Research* 14 (1990), 368–374, treats the intersection of clinical work with insights from other disciplines.

Most clinical studies of drinking patterns focus on men. For an excellent review of the issues relating to women's drinking see France K. Del Boca, "Sex, Gender, and Alcoholic Typologies," in Babor et al., *Types of Alcoholics*, 34–48. Other material on women and alcohol can be found in Cristen C. Eddy and John L. Ford,

A NOTE ON SOURCES

eds., *Alcoholism in Women* (Dubuque, Iowa, 1980); Marian Sandmaier, *The Invisible Alcohlics: Women and Alcohol Abuse in America* (New York, 1980); and Louise Nadeau, Céline Mercier, and Lise Bourgeois, *Les Femmes et l'alcool en Amérique du Nord et au Québec* (Québec, 1984).

Many studies have been published on the causes and consequences of drinking in Indian communities. Among the most useful are Stephen J. Kunitz, Jerrold E. Levy, and Michael Everett, "Alcoholic Cirrhosis among the Navajo," *QJSA* 30 (1969), 672–685; Deborah Jones-Saumty et al., "Psychological Factors of Familial Alcoholism in American Indians and Caucasians," *Journal of Clinical Psychology* 39 (1983), 783–790; Roland J. Lamarine, "Alcohol Abuse among Native Americans," *Journal of Community Health* 13 (1988), 143–155; Patricia Silk-Walker et al., "Alcoholism, Alcohol Abuse, and Health in American Indians and Alaska Natives," *American Indian and Alaska Native Mental Health Research*, monograph no. 1 (1988), 65–93; Anthony J. Mariano et al., "Drinking-Related Locus of Control and the Drinking Status of Urban Native Americans," *JSA* 50 (1989), 331–338; Richard Goodman et al., "Alcohol and Fatal Injuries in Oklahoma," *JSA* 52 (1991), 156–161; J. David Kinzie, "Psychiatric Epidemiology of an Indian Village: A 19-Year Replication Study," *Journal of Nervous and Mental Disease* 180 (1992), 33–39; Margaret M. Gallaher et al., "Pedestrian and Hypothermia Deaths among Native Americans in New Mexico," *JAMA* 267 (1992), 1345–1348; Fred Beauvais, "The Consequences of Drug and Alcohol Use for Indian Youth," *American Indian and Alaska Native Mental Health Research* 5:1 (1992), 32–37; and Paul Kettl and Edward O. Bixler, "Alcohol and Suicide in Alaska Natives," *American Indian and Alaska Native Mental Health Research* 5:3 (1993), 34–45. The often deadly effects of alcohol on Indians in Canada is noted in George K. Jarvis and Menno Boldt, "Death Styles among Canada's Indians," *Social Science Medicine* 16 (1982), 1345–1352, and Yang Mao et al., "Mortality on Canadian Indian Reserves, 1977–1982," *Canadian Journal of Public Health* 77 (1986), 263–268. Patricia D. Mail and Saundra Johnson, "Boozing, Sniffing, and Toking: An Overview of the Past, Present, and Future of Substance Abuse by American Indians," *American Indian and Alaska Native Mental Health Research* 5:3 (1993), 1–33, seeks to explain long-term trends among American Indians, though the authors present little evidence from the colonial period and fail to support their connection that the colonial trade "may represent early chemical warfare to gain European advantage over an 'enemy' " (1). For an excellent summary of the recent literature see Philip A. May, "The Epidemiology of Alcohol Abuse among American Indians: The Mythical and Real Properties," *American Indian Culture and Research Journal* 18:2 (1994), 121–143.

The impact of drinking on children in Indian communities is described in Lawrence R. Berger and Judith Kitzes, "Injuries to Children in a Native American Community," *Pediatrics* 84 (1989), 152–156; Carol Lujan et al., "Profile of Abused and Neglected American Indian Children in the Southwest," *Child Abuse and Neglect* 13 (1989), 449–461; Robert Blum et al., "American Indian–Alaska Native Youth Health," *JAMA* 267 (1992), 1637–1644; and David Swanson et al., "Alcohol Abuse in a Population of Indian Children," *Diseases of the Nervous System* 32 (1971), 835–842. There are few more distressing accounts than Duane Sherwin and Beverly Mead, "Delirium Tremens in a Nine-Year-Old Child," *American Jour-

nal of Psychiatry 132 (1975), 1210–1212. Changes in attitudes toward alcohol's effects on children are traced in Rebecca H. Warner and Henry L. Rosett, "The Effects of Drinking on Offspring: An Historical Survey of the American and British Literature," *JSA* 36 (1975), 1395–1420. Materials on fetal alcohol syndrome are cited in note 11 to the Prologue.

The clinical studies enumerated here and others cited in the notes are based on analyses of specific populations. The proliferation of such reports suggests the importance of these studies to an understanding of alcohol use and abuse. But the study of alcohol behavior has not been limited to analyses of individuals and groups; genetic analyses of alcohol use have proliferated as well. Here perhaps the most logical place to start is Donald W. Goodwin, *Is Alcoholism Hereditary?*, 2d ed. (New York, 1988); Constance Holden, "Probing the Complex Genetics of Alcoholism," *Science* 251 (1991), 163–164; and National Institute on Alcohol Abuse and Alcoholism, *Alcoholism: An Inherited Disease* (Rockville, Md., 1985). An excellent collection of articles can be found in H. Warner Goedde and Dharam P. Agrawal, eds., "Genetics and Alcoholism," a special issue of *Progress in Clinical and Biological Research* 241 (1987). Reviews of the literature on the subject can be found in John S. Searles, "The Role of Genetics in the Pathogenesis of Alcoholism," *Journal of Abnormal Psychology* 97:2 (1988), 153–167; Gilbert S. Omenn, "Genetic Investigations of Alcohol Metabolism and of Alcoholism," *American Journal of Human Genetics* 43 (1988), 579–581; Eric J. Devor and C. Robert Cloninger, "Genetics of Alcoholism," *Annual Review of Genetics* 23 (1989), 19–36; and Jane Marshall and Robin M. Murray, "The Familial Transmission of Alcoholism," *British Medical Journal* 303 (1991), 72–73. Other references to the genetics of alcoholism are cited in note 4 to the Prologue.

The question whether Indians are genetically predisposed to abuse alcohol has received a great deal of attention. The topic is contentious, and needs to be addressed in any study of Indian drinking. I have not argued here that genetic predisposition to alcohol abuse shaped Indian drinking patterns in early America, but the literature is certainly suggestive. As Dwight Heath has pointed out, "One need not deny the possibility of physiological differences when emphasizing the importance of sociocultural differences, and the spirit of scientific enquiry is not enhanced by those who would suppress studies with which they disagree, regardless of how 'liberal' their basis for disagreement may be." ("Alcohol Use among North American Indians," 353).

Inquiries into the genetic aspects of Indian drinking have now been going on for a generation. One of the early studies in this field, D. Fenna et al., "Ethanol Metabolism in Various Racial Groups," *Canadian Medical Association Journal* 105 (1971), 472–475, argued that Indians metabolize alcohol more slowly than non-Indians. But subsequent, more plausible analyses, have refuted this thesis. I found the most useful studies to be the following: Lynn Bennion and Ting-Kai Li, "Alcohol Metabolism in American Indians and Whites: Lack of Racial Differences in Metabolic Rate and Liver Alcohol Dehydrogenase," *NEJM* 294 (1976), 9–13; Bernard Segal and Lawrence Duffy, "Ethanol Elimination among Different Racial Groups," *Alcohol* 9 (1992), 213–217; Lillian E. Dyck, "Absence of the Atypical Mitochondrial Aldehyde Dehydrogenase (ALDH2) Isozyme in Saskatchewan

A NOTE ON SOURCES

Cree Indians," *Human Heredity* 43 (1993), 116–120; and Shi-Han Chen et al., "Gene Frequencies of Alcohol Dehydrogenase$_2$ and Aldehyde Dehydrogenase$_2$ in Northwest Coast Amerindians," *Human Genetics* 89 (1992), 351–352. In "Alcohol and Acetaldehyde Metabolism in Caucasians, Chinese, and Amerinds," *Canadian Medical Association Journal* 115 (1976), 851–855, T. Edward Reed and his colleagues point out the importance of recognizing the disparities between groups of Indians, and note that the relation between metabolism rates and alcoholism remains unclear. A series of letters in *Canadian Medical Association Journal* 116 (1977), 476, indicates the difficulties of calculating metabolism rates among racial groups. John A. Ewing et al., "Alcohol Sensitivity and Ethnic Background," *American Journal of Psychiatry* 131 (1974), 206–210; Joel M. Hanna, "Ethnic Groups, Human Variation, and Alcohol Use," in Everett et al., *Cross-Cultural Approaches to the Study of Alcohol*, 235–242; and James J. Schaefer, "Firewater Myths Revisited: Review of Findings and Some New Directions," in Heath et al., *Cultural Factors in Alcohol Research*, 99–117, all provide insights into these issues. Arthur W. K. Chan, "Racial Differences in Alcohol Sensitivity," *Alcohol and Alcoholism* 21 (1986), 93–104, reviews various studies, including those involving Indian drinking, and is an ideal starting point for anyone interested in the genetic aspects of alcohol use.

Index

INDEX

beer, 14, 44, 48
Belmont, François Vachon de, 69, 147–148
Benewisco, 117
Benezet, Anthony, 177, 230n56
Berthier, Alexandre de, 143
Bethlehem, Pa., 207–208n52
Biard, Pierre, 139
Bigot, Jacques, 148–149
binge drinking, 59, 87–88, 119, 139
black drink, 66, 67
Black Prince, 73
Blackfeet, 152
Blome, Richard, 36–38
Board of Trade, 159
Bosomworth, Thomas, 97
Bossu, Jean, 1–4, 8–9, 114
Boston, Mass., 41–42
Boswell, James, 16
Bosworth, Thomas, 94
Bougainville, Louis Antoine de, 75, 81
Bourdon de Dombourg, Jean, 144
Bradford, William, 63, 89
Bradstreet, Colonel, 158
Brainerd, David, 87, 111, 115–116
brandy, 54, 68, 70, 132, 143–144, 149–150
Brazil, 32
Bristol, Avon, 32
Bruyas, Jacques, 79–80
Burnaby, Rev. Andrew, 92
Burnet, William, 50, 124
Byrd, William, 92

Cadagan, George, 127
calumet, 77
Calusas, 136
Canachaute, 127
Canada, 50, 68, 87, 131–132, 144, 152. See also New France
Canasatego, 74
Cap de la Magdelaine, 147
Captain Houma, 119
Caribbean area, 16, 39, 41
Carlisle, Pa., 11–12
Carolina, 16, 41, 43, 58, 81, 92. See also North Carolina; South Carolina
Carston, Thomas, 48
Cartier, Jacques, 138
Carver, Jonathan, 98, 111, 164–167
cas réservé, 143
Catawbas, 92, 73, 101, 117–118, 177. See also Hagler

Catholic Church, 137
Catlin, George, 177–178
Caughnawaga, 110, 142
Cayugas, 69, 117, 126
Central America, 79
Champlain, Samuel de, 139
Charleston, 42, 44, 60, 158
Charlevoix, Pierre François Xavier de, 75, 141–142, 145–147
Chauchetière, Claude, 145, 146
Chegoutimy, 145
Cherokees, 48, 73, 80, 122. See also Canachaute
Chesapeake region, 30, 41, 49, 67, 72, 92, 109
Chester, Peter, 27, 100
Chickasaws, 57, 63, 89, 90, 98
children, 6, 85, 95, 189
Chipewyans, 153
Choctaws, 43, 63, 70–71, 90, 92–93, 101, 111, 117. See also Captain Houma
cider (hard), 14, 206n38
cirrhosis, 5, 6–7, 153
Clayton, Rev. John, 63, 69
Colden, Cadwalader, 70, 162
Cole, Edward, 53, 55–56
Collbeck, John, 90
colonists: defend liquor trade, 45, 161–162; demography of, 171; drinking among, 14–20; fear French competition, 49; and Indian temperance efforts, 122–123; and laws regulating drinking, 16, 120, 128; and sales of alcohol to Indians, 44–46
Columbian exchange, 170
Columbus, Christopher, 32
commissaries, 157
Commissioners of Indian Affairs (Pa.), 52
Conestoga Pa., 121
Conestogas, 51, 121
Connecticut, 44, 72, 105, 106
Conochquieson, 117
Conoys, 121
Cook, Moses, 112
Coweta Town, S.C., 59
credit, sale of liquor on, 97, 109
Creeks, 67, 86, 88, 97. See also Lower Creeks; Upper Creeks
Croghan, George, 51, 87, 114, 126, 179; as agent of Baynton, Wharton & Morgan,

INDEX

Croghan, George (*cont.*)
53; on gifts of alcohol to Indians, 48–49,
72–73; on regulating trade, 157
Crossweeksung, 111

Danckaerts, Jasper, 46, 96
Danforth, Samuel, 91–92
Dartmouth, Lord, 27
Death: as cause for drinking, 82; caused by
drinking, 91–93; seasonal variability in,
100
debt and poverty, linked to liquor, 55, 86,
96–99, 116, 117, 121, 140, 150
deerskins, 7, 14, 97–98. *See also* trade
Delaware Prophet (Neolin), 116, 179
Delaware River, 43–44
Delawares, 48, 51, 52, 58–60, 114; decline
in population of, 92; temperance efforts
of, 101, 114, 117. *See also* Sasoonan
Delaware Valley Indians, 96
Demere, Raymond, 29, 126–128
Denny, William, 73
Denton, Daniel, 70
Denys, Nicholas, 64, 70, 88
Detroit, 51, 53–54, 89, 117, 126, 163
de Vries, David, 43–44, 76
Dickinson, John, 157
distilleries, 41–42
Dobbs, Arthur, 48, 156
Dollier de Casson, François, 141, 145
Donnacona, 138
Doubty, John, 175
dreams, 74–75
drinking: and accidents, 91; and death, 91–
93; and destruction of civility, 86–91; to
gain power, 67, 70, 75–76; and
generational hostility, 99–100;
motivations for, 82–84; in mourning
ceremonies, 76–79; and murder, 91–92,
95; prosecutions for, 104; and sexual
relations, 70–71, 87, 89–90
—and violence, 67, 86, 93–96, 150;
domestic, 89, 150; sexual, 95
—rituals, 64–65, 68, 71–74; communion as,
135; in British America, 68, 76–79, 106,
127; in New Spain, 132–134. *See also*
hospitality; mourning ceremonies;
toasting
Drunken Comportment, 252–253
drunken Indian, stereotype of, 11–14, 26–
27, 172–173

drunkenness, 68–72
Dugué, Sidrac, 143
Duplessis-Gatineau, Nicolas, 144
Durnford, Elias, 158
Dutch, 44, 141, 143
Duvall's Landlord, 158

East Florida, 88
eau-de-vie, 147, 150
Eliot, John, 25
engagés, 137–138
English colonists, 35; and antiliquor
campaign, 121–128; and civilizing of
Indians, 106, 170, 174; drinking practices
of, 19–20, 26; vs. French, 74, 170; after
Seven Years' War, 155; in West Indies,
32–33
epidemic disease, 7
Europeans and alcohol, 8
excommunication for brandy vendors,
140

Fanseen, 81
fetal alcohol syndrome (FAS), 6
Florentine Codex, 133–134
Florida, 131, 136–137. *See also* West Florida
Fort Albany–Eastmain, 54
Fort Augusta. *See* Shamokin, Pa.
Fort Chartres, 3, 53
Fort Churchill, 54
Fort Duquesne, 54–55
Fort La Corne, 152
Fort Pitt. *See* Pittsburgh, Pa.
Fort Poskoyac (Pasquia), 152
Fowler, Peter, 166
Fox Indians, 77–78
Franklin, Benjamin, 39, 74, 197n3; on
colonists' population growth, 171;
"Drinker's Dictionary," 12; on drink-
related mortality of Indians, 93; on
drunken Indians, 11–12, 16, 26, 28
French colonists, 114; on alcohol-related
poverty, 98; attitudes of, toward Indians,
23–24, 70; and brandy trade, 143–144,
151; vs. Dutch and English, 143; and fur
trade, 144, 153–154; in West Indies, 32.
See also Jesuits; New France
Friedensstadt. *See* Languntoutenunk
Frontenac, Louis de Buade de, Count de,
75, 143–144
fur trade, 7, 14, 144, 153–154

[263]

INDEX

INDEX

INDEX

INDEX